W9-BVI-698

DANTEAN DIALOGUES

Engaging with the Legacy
of Amilcare Iannucci

Amilcare Iannuci, 1946–2007

Dantean Dialogues

Engaging with the Legacy of Amilcare Iannucci

EDITED BY MAGGIE KILGOUR
AND ELENA LOMBARDI

UNIVERSITY OF TORONTO PRESS
Toronto Buffalo London

Toronto Buffalo London
www.utppublishing.com

ISBN 978-1-4426-4561-5

Printed on acid-free, 100% post-consumer paper with vegetable-based inks.
Toronto Italian Studies

Library and Archives Canada Cataloguing in Publication

Dantean dialogues : engaging with the legacy of Amilcare Iannucci
edited by Maggie Kilgour and Elena Lombardi.

(Toronto Italian studies)
Includes bibliographical references.
ISBN 978-1-4426-4561-5 (bound)

1. Dante Alighieri, 1265–1321 – Criticism and interpretation.
I. Iannucci, Amilcare A., honouree II. Kilgour, Maggie, 1957–, editor of compilation III. Lombardi, Elena, 1969–, editor of compilation IV. Series: Toronto Italian studies

PQ4383.D36 2013 851'.1 C2013-903275-4

This book has been published with the help of a grant from the Canadian Federation for the Humanities and Social Sciences, through the Awards to Scholarly Publications Program, using funds provided by the Social Sciences and Humanities Research Council of Canada.

University of Toronto Press acknowledges the financial assistance to its publishing program of the Canada Council for the Arts and the Ontario Arts Council.

University of Toronto Press acknowledges the financial support for its publishing activities of the Government of Canada through the Book Publishing Industry Development Program (BPIDP).

Contents

Preface

This volume is both a commemoration of and conversation with the works of the late, great Dante scholar Amilcare Iannucci, who for us was a colleague, teacher, mentor, and, above all, dear friend. Since his tragically early death in winter 2007 after a heroic battle with leukemia (which he referred to as his personal trip to hell), we have missed Amilcare's generous and enthusiastic intervention. Dialogue, discussion, and debate were central parts of his pedagogy and his life, as well as the themes of some of his finest readings of Dante and other writers. For him, literature was a conversation; in a series of brilliant studies, he traced Dante's dialogues with past sources, his own works, and with the future. Through writing, the artist finds a way to overcome death, as Dante realized when his *Commedia* allowed him to enjoy the brief companionship of his beloved Virgil, from whom history had separated him, and of Beatrice, taken from him by an untimely death. This volume comes from a desire to have Amilcare speak with us once again, to have his presence beside us, as we read the texts he loved so well.

It is almost impossible to account for the depth, extension, and variety of Amilcare's scholarship on Dante and Italian studies, which he elegantly displayed in both the English and the Italian languages. Amilcare was a prolific writer; by his own admission he aimed at writing "at least three pages a day," which he usually did in the early morning, often after driving his son Matthew to rowing practice at the crack of dawn. Amilcare's favourite format was the long essay, which allowed him both to exhaust arguments and to preserve variety. At least ten long essays of Amilcare's have been extremely influential in Dante studies, generating further debate and scholarship. Through these essays and throughout his career he pursued three linked strands of research, which he continuously expanded, deepened, and rethought: the metaliterary aspect of the *Commedia*, the role of Limbo, and Dante's afterlife in the media.

The first strand, the metaliterary aspect of Dante's work (which is best represented by essays such as the "Dante's Theory of Genres and the *Divina Commedia*" and "Autoesegesi dantesca: la tecnica dell' 'episodio parallelo' nella *Commedia*") reflects on genre theory, self- exegesis, and the discourse of authority within the *Comedy*. Since the seventies, Amilcare's work has contributed to bringing to light Dante's critical and self-critical personality. This has mobilized Dante studies in two ways. On the one hand, it liberated Dante studies from any "totalitarian" assumption and led to the acknowledgment of Dante's constitutional syncretism and eclecticism in dealing with genre, sources, and his own philosophical, poetic, and linguistic beliefs. On the other hand, this kind of study has revealed that under the apparently dispersive face of Dante's syncretism lies a stern exegete and self-exegete, who continually reflects on, modifies, and updates his own thought.

The study of Limbo constitutes Amilcare's great "monography," articulated in a dozen essays, especially "Limbo: the Emptiness of Time" and "The *Gospel of Nicodemus* in Medieval Italian Literature." Amilcare explored with unmatched depth the history, theology, and poetics of the controversial first circle of hell, bringing to light all the nuances of this complex first episode of the *Commedia*, in which Dante violently challenged the standard theology on the topic in order to accommodate his beloved classics, yet at the same time underlining the magnitude of their damnation. Investigating in depth the medieval Christian theme of the harrowing of hell and showing how Dante displaces it from canto 4 to other episodes in upper hell, Iannucci linked the somewhat eccentric and self-standing first circle with Dante's own mandate through the harrowing of Beatrice (canto 2) and that of the celestial messenger (canto 9).

Midway through his career, Iannucci became interested in the afterlife that Dante has had in media, such as theatre, cinema, and television, and produced a large number of essays and edited volumes, including the volume *Dante, Cinema and Television*. In this field too his research was groundbreaking, providing both a solid historical context for modern reworkings of Dante as well as the most detailed survey of such adaptations and valuable reflections on the "adaptable" nature of Dante's text.

Amilcare's fascination with inter- and intratextuality in Dante (with respect to his own work, the scriptures, and the classics) and his interest in Dante's thinking on personal and salvation history are present throughout all of his scholarship and help to connect and interconnect the various strands of his research. Moreover, he shed light on single episodes of the *Commedia*, especially *Inferno* 5, *Inferno* 15, *Purgatorio* 2, and *Paradiso* 31.

Amilcare's scholarship always coexisted with a wonderfully selfless dedication to his work as a teacher and to the academic and cultural community around him. This took place after he was finished writing, in the "other" hours of the day (Amilcare's day always seemed to have more hours than the average person's). A brilliant and inspiring lecturer, he was always a model of generosity, kindness, and true humanism to students. He was equally generous to his colleagues, university, and the academic community as a whole. Amilcare could boast an impressive, almost uninterrupted grant record. He sacrificed part of his time to the often dull process of writing grants in order to encourage research in Italian studies and to support graduate and postdoctoral students. Likewise, he fostered research and academic networking by serving on the boards of several learned societies, as the director of the Canadian Academic Centre in Rome, and as the founding head of the Humanities Centre at the University of Toronto. He also engaged in editorial activities through various journals in the United States, Canada, and Italy. It is not an exaggeration to say that Iannucci established the field of Italian studies in Canada, not only through his massive research and teaching record but also through the creation of the journal *Quaderni d'Italianistica*, which he cofounded in 1980, of the Italian Studies Series within University of Toronto Press, which he founded in 1984, and the Major Italian Authors Series within the same press, which he cofounded in 1991. These publications have since provided the academic community with outstanding work in Italian studies.

On top of all these other commitments, Amilcare was an indefatigable conference organizer, arranging two major conferences a year in his last years. Meetings such as the one on Marco Polo or on "Voicing Toronto," to name a couple, attracted world-class scholars to Canada and were an outstanding success not only for the scholarly world but also for the general public, enlivening and enlightening the cultural life of his beloved Toronto. The success and breadth of these conferences are even more impressive, as he organized them while recovering from harsh treatments for the disease that would ultimately defeat even his energy. His energy and willpower in all endeavours were inspirational to many.

The contributors to this volume all worked closely with Amilcare in one way or another, and their essays take up questions or episodes that he had influentially examined and reflect the variety of his interests. Appropriately, the essays have arranged themselves into pairs. The first two essays, by Zygmunt Barański and Teodolinda Barolini, look at Dante's early works, the *Vita nuova* and the *Rime*. Showing how later editorial and interpretive decisions have overdetermined the place of these works in Dante's development, they capture the exciting experimental nature of these works. For Barański, the young Dante was "intent on challenging and reconfiguring conventional distinctions between prose and verse, artistic text and commentary, narrative and lyric, in order to develop not just a new sort of macrotext but also a new idea of textuality" (10). Barolini's attention to *Lo doloroso amor* and *E' m'incresce di me*, poems, as she notes, often treated as marginal to Dante's development and less canonical in his work as a whole, allows us to see the young Dante on an ideological / poetic path that was first experimented with and then discarded, one that is surprisingly Cavalcantian even as it is recognizably Dantean. For both Barański and Barolini, moreover, the young Dante is already acutely self-conscious about how he will be read and aware of the importance of interpretation, which will be the theme of several of the other essays in this volume.

The next pair of essays, by Robert Hollander and Elena Lombardi, examine episodes in which Amilcare was particularly interested. As Hollander magisterially shows, the exhaustive commentary on the presence of Cato in *Purgatorio* only moves us further to admire the complexity of Dante's thinking, rather than leading us to an easy explanation. The wild and intricate intertextuality that surrounds the figure of Cato is a signal of Dante's awareness that he is tampering with established Christian dogma and of his desire to involve the reader in his ambitious and ambiguous violation. Hollander's conclusion to the essay on Cato, that there is no firm conclusion to Cato, shows the heavily pedagogic slant of Dante's relation to his readers and reminds us that the pleasure (and the lesson) of the text rests in interpretation and not in solution. Elena Lombardi's discussion of *Inferno* 5 is deeply indebted to Amilcare's important contribution to the meaning of this equally complex episode. In "Forbidden Love: Metaphor and History," Amilcare had identified within the canto a marked historical metaphor originating in the myth of Ares and Aphrodite and argued that Dante's moral conclusion in *Inferno* 5 is that passion leads to disorder, not only in the individual, but also in society. Taking the lead from this argument, Lombardi explores the relation between lust and law, reason and passion, within Dante's work, showing that the societal-historical aspect of canto 5 has profound ties to Dante's political discourse in the *Convivio*, the *Commedia*, and the *Monarchia*.

Much of Amilcare's work was focused on Dante's relation to the Bible and to the *bella scola* of classical poetry. The next two essays follow these interests to demonstrate what Barolini calls Dante's "intense writerliness" (47). Carolynn Lund-Mead's essay continues Amilcare's work on the interconnection between Dantesque episodes. As she notes, Dante's elaborate layering of encounters has a precedent in the Bible, which was shaped into a whole by the drawing of ultimately typological relations between what had originally been disparate works. Dante uses a similar method of creating patterns between his different episodes. Moreover, in these episodes, biblical models of exegesis become a way of representing character. Lund-Mead thus reads the relations among *Inferno* 15, *Purgatorio* 11–12, and *Paradiso* 15–17 (the encounters with Brunetto Latini, Oderisi da Gubbio, and Cacciaguida) as an illustration of Dante's spiritual development in terms of his growing understanding of how to read and adapt biblical sources. Maggie Kilgour's essay returns to the question of Dante's relation to the classics, especially Ovid, whose presence in the *Commedia* has been increasingly of great critical interest. While most critics have represented Dante's relation to his pagan source as one of correction, in which pagan metamorphosis is turned into Christian conversion, Kilgour argues that Dante's engagement with Ovid is more complex. While Lund-Mead shows Dante's sensitivity to the complexity of the network of biblical intratextuality, Kilgour argues that Dante paid equal attention to the themes that run through and unite Ovid's works, especially those related to questions of the nature of artistic creation.

The final two essays take up the question that principally occupied Amilcare at the end of his life: Dante's new life. As we noted earlier, Amilcare had already published a volume on Dante and cinema (*Dante and Cinema*), and his last, uncompleted project was an encyclopedic study of adaptations of Dante from the nineteenth century on. The essays by Massimo Ciavolella and Piero Boitani fill in some of the territory that Amilcare might have covered, focusing on perhaps less well-known areas in which Dante had an impact. Ciavolella explores a new and fascinating episode in Dante's "cultural afterlife": the esoteric interpretation of the *Comedy* in the nineteenth and twentieth centuries.

In addition to exploring an unwritten page of the last two centuries' cultural history, this essay reflects on the protean and adaptable nature of Dante's text and brings to light the possibility of a very radical and unidirectional reading of the *Commedia*. Ciavolella's insight into the esoteric reading of the *Commedia* leaves the reader to wonder at the extent of Dante's unspoken or uncontrolled textuality. Boitani takes on the wild and largely uncharted territory of Dante in Ireland. Noting first of all the imaginative power Dante has exerted on Irish writers, he traces the very different roles the poet played in the imaginations of Yeats, Joyce, Beckett, and finally Seamus Heaney. As he notes, Yeats's reading of Dante begins as similar to that of Rossetti, whose work influenced the reception of Dante at the end of the nineteenth century, but developed into something very different. The adaptations of Joyce, Beckett, and now Seamus Heaney make clear that Dante has had a particular meaning for writers in Ireland; for Heaney especially, as Boitani notes, Dante becomes a means not only of voicing northern Irish sectarianism but also for creating a genealogy of Irish poetry.

As these last essays show, Dante's works are highly adaptable and adaptive; they take new lives in new contexts and speak to different generations to whom they reveal different meanings. Scholarship, in contrast, too often seems to end with the individual scholar. This volume, however, is an attempt to recognize and be thankful for the contributions of a great Dantist who shaped so many other thinkers in Canada, the United States, Italy, and beyond. Amilcare's academic achievements were always tempered by his genuine humility and his belief that the forging of communities, both academic and otherwise, was an even more important accomplishment than research alone. It seems appropriate, therefore, that the scholarly community who loved him should dedicate a volume, which pays tribute to his critical legacy, to his even greater legacy in which he took such great pride: his children, Anna, Matthew, and Emily.

Acknowledgments

Parts of Piero Boitani's essay have appeared as "Irish Dante: Yeats, Joyce, Beckett," in *Metamorphosing Dante: Appropriations, Manipulations, and Rewritings in the Twentieth and Twenty-First Centuries*, ed. M. Gragnolati, F. Camilletti, and F. Lampart (Vienna-Berlin: Turia+Kant, 2011), 37–60.

Parts of Teodolinda Barolini's essay have appeared in Italian in her introduction to *Rime giovanili e della "Vita Nuova"* (Milan: Rizzoli, 2009).

Contributors

Zygmunt Barański, Serena Professor of Italian Emeritus in the University of Cambridge and Notre Dame Professor of Dante & Italian Studies in the University of Notre Dame, has published extensively on Dante, medieval poetics, fourteenth-century Italian literature, and modern Italian literature and culture. He is the former editor of the interdisciplinary journal *The Italianist* and current editor of *Le tre corone.*

Teodolinda Barolini, Lorenzo Da Ponte Professor, Columbia University, and past president of the Dante Society of America (1997–2003), is author of the award winning *Dante's Poets: Textuality and Truth in the "Comedy"* (1984); *The Undivine Comedy: Detheologizing Dante* (1992); *Dante and the Origins of Italian Literary Culture* (2006); and a commentary on Dante's lyrics, *Rime giovanili e della "Vita Nuova"* (2009).

Piero Boitani, FBA, is Professor of Comparative Literature at Sapienza, Rome. His numerous books include *The Shadow of Ulysses: Figures of a Myth* (1994); *The Bible and its Rewritings* (1999); *Winged Words: Flights in Poetry and History* (2007); *La prima lezione sulla letteratura* (2007); *Letteratura europea e Medioevo volgare* (2007); and *Il Vangelo secondo Shakespeare* (2009).

Massimo Ciavolella is Franklin D. Murphy Professor of Italian Renaissance Studies in the Departments of Comparative Literature and of Italian at UCLA. He is author and co-editer of many books, including *La malattia d'amore dall'antichità al Medioevo* (1976); *Saturn from Antiquity to the Renaissance* (1992); *Eros and Anteros: Medicine and the Literary Traditions of Love in the Renaissance* (1993); *Ariosto Today: Contemporary Perspectives* (2003); *Culture and Authority in the Baroque* (2005).

Robert Hollander, Professor Emeritus in European Literature, Princeton University, is the author of a dozen seminal books on Dante and Boccaccio, and some 100 articles on Dante and / or Boccaccio. He is the founding Director of the Dartmouth Dante Project and of the Princeton Dante Project. His many honours include the Charles T. Davis Award of the Dante Society of America (2005).

Maggie Kilgour: Maggie Kilgour's first university class was one on Dante, taught by Amilcare Iannucci. Molson Professor of English Language and Literature, McGill University, she is the author of *From Communion to Cannibalism: An Anatomy of Metaphors of Incorporation* (1990); *The Rise of the Gothic Novel* (1995); *Milton and the Metamorphosis of Ovid* (2012); and essays on topics ranging from classical literature to contemporary film.

Elena Lombardi is the Paget Toynbee Lecturer in Italian Studies, University of Oxford, and fellow of Balliol College. She is the author of *The Syntax of Desire: Language and Love in Augustine, the Modistae and Dante* (2007); *The Wings of the Doves: Love and Desire in Dante and Medieval Culture* (2012); and essays on early Italian poetry (the Sicilian school and Guido Cavalcanti, Petrarch).

Carolynn Lund-Mead, independent scholar, is an author of essays on Dante and co-author (with Amilcare Iannucci) of *Dante and the Vulgate Bible* (2012), a catalogue of the biblical references in the *Commedia* and a record of the history of their recognition.

Bibliography of Works by Amilcare Iannucci

Books

1. *Marco Polo and the Encounter of East and West*. Edited by Suzanne Conklin Akbari and Amilcare Iannucci, assoc. John Tulk. Toronto: University of Toronto Press, 2008.
2. *The Semiotics of Writing*. Edited by Marcel Danesi and Amilcare A. Iannucci. Madison, WI: Atwood Press, 2005.
3. *Dante, Cinema and Television*. Edited by Amilcare A. Iannucci. Toronto: University of Toronto Press, 2004.
4. *Dante: Contemporary Perspectives*. Edited by Amilcare A. Iannucci. Toronto: University of Toronto Press, 1997.
5. *Italian Studies in North America*. Edited by Massimo Ciavolella and Amilcare A. Iannucci. Ottawa: Dovehouse Editions, 1994.
6. *Dante e la "bella scola" della poesia: Autorità e sfida poetica*. Edited by Amilcare A. Iannucci. Ravenna: Longo Editore, 1993.
7. *Saturn from Antiquity to the Renaissance*. Edited by Massimo Ciavolella and Amilcare A. Iannucci. Ottawa: Dovehouse Press, 1992.
8. *Petrarch's Triumphs: Allegory and Spectacle*. Edited by Konrad Eisenbichler and Amilcare A. Iannucci. Foreword by Amilcare A. Iannucci. Ottawa: Dovehouse Press, 1990.
9. *Dante Today*. Edited by Amilcare A. Iannucci. Special Dante issue of *Quaderni d'italianistica*. Vol. 10, nos. 1–2. Toronto: University of Toronto Press, 1989.
10. *McLuhan e la metamorfosi dell'uomo*. Edited by Derrick de Kerckhove and Amilcare A. Iannucci. Rome: Bulzoni, 1984.
11. *Forma ed evento nella Divina Commedia*. Rome: Bulzoni, 1984.

Articles

1. "Dante's Limbo: At the Margins of Orthodoxy." In *Dante and the Unorthodox: The Aesthetics of Transgression*, edited by James Miller, 110–36. Waterloo, ON: Wilfrid Laurier Press, 2005.
2. "La discesa 'erittonica' di Virgilio e la crisi dell'intertestualità." In *La lotta con Proteo: Metamorfosi del testo e testualità della critica*. Proceedings of the Sixteenth AISLLI Conference, edited by Luigi Ballerini, Gay Bardin, and Massimo Ciavolella, 39–51. Florence: Edizioni Cadmo, 2000.
3. "Dante and Hollywood." In *Dante, Cinema and Television*, edited by Amilcare A. Iannucci, 3–20. Toronto: University of Toronto Press, 2004.
4. "Francesca da Rimini: The Movie." *Dante* 1 (2004): 67–79.
5. "*La Ciociara*: due uomini." In *La Ciociaria fra scrittori e cineasti*, edited by F. Zangrilli, 240–60. Pesaro: Metauro Edizioni, 2004.
6. "Dante, padre del cinema italiano." In *Incontro con il cinema italiano*, edited by Antonio Vitti, 25–44. Caltanissetta-Rome: Sciascia, 2003.
7. "Already and Not Yet: Dante's Existential Eschatology." In *Dante for the New Millennium*, edited by T. Barolini and H.W. Storey, 334–48. New York: Fordham University Press, 2003.
8. "Made in Italy: L'immagine dell' Italia e della cultura italiana all'estero dal secondo dopoguerra a oggi." Ch. 4, Sec. 5, Vol. 12 in *La storia della letteratura italiana*. Rome: Salerno Editrice, 2003.
9. "The Americanization of Francesca: Dante on Broadway in the Nineteenth Century." *Dante Studies* 120 (2002): 53–82.
10. "San Tommaso e il canone teologico di Dante." In *La Ciociaria tra letteratura e cinema*, edited by Franco Zangrilli, 317–26. Pesaro: Metauro Edizioni, 2002.
11. "Firenze, città infernale." In *Dante da Firenze all'aldilà*. Atti del terzo seminario dantesco internazionale, Firenze, 9–11 giugno 2000, edited by Michelangelo Picone, 217–32. Florence: Franco Cesati Editore, 2001.
12. "Dante, poeta o profeta?" In *"Per correr miglior acque …": Bilanci e prospettive degli studi danteschi alle soglie del nuovo millenio*. Atti del convegno di Verona-Ravenna, 25–9 ottobre 1999, edited by Enrico Malato, 93–114. Rome: Salerno Editrice, 2000.
13. "The Classical Canon"; "Dante and Film"; "Dante and Television"; "Dramatic Arts"; "The Harrowing of Hell"; "Limbo"; "Philosophy"; "The Noble Castle"; "The Virtuous Heathen"; "Theology." In *Dante Encyclopedia*, edited by Richard Lansing, 175–6; 246–50;

283–6; 319–24; 470–1; 565–9; 650–2; 692–6; 811–15; 871–3. New York: Garland Publishing, 2000.

14. "The Italian Canon Abroad." Special issue on the canon, *Quaderns d'Italià* 4–5 (1999–2000): 47–65.
15. "Dante's Theological Canon in the *Commedia*." Special issue in honour of Vittore Branca, *Italian Quarterly* 37, nos. 143–6 (Winter 2000): 51–6.
16. "Virgil's Erichthean Descent and the Crisis of Intertextuality." *Forum Italicum* 33, no. 1 (Spring 1999): 13–26.
17. "Il limbo dei bambini." In *Sotto il segno di Dante: Scritti in onore di Francesco Mazzoni*, edited by Leonella Coglievina and Domenico De Robertis, 153–64. Florence: Casa Editrice Le Lettere, 1998.
18. "From Dante's *Inferno* to *Dante's Peak*: The Influence of Dante on Film." *Forum Italicum* 32, no. 1 (Spring 1998): 5–35.
19. "Dante's Intertextual and Intratextual Strategies in the *Commedia*." In *Studies for Dante: Essays in Honor of Dante Della Terza*, edited by Franco Fido, Pamela Stewart, and Rena A. Syska-Lamparska, 61–87. Florence: Edizioni Cadmo, 1998.
20. "Canto IX: The Harrowing of Dante from Upper Hell." In *Inferno*, edited by Allen Mandelbaum, Anthony Oldcorn, and Charles Ross, 123–35. Berkeley: The University of California Press, 1998.
21. "Dante's Philosophical Canon (*Inferno* 4.130–44)." *Quaderni d'italianistica* 18, no. 2 (1997): 251–60.
22. "The Mountainquake of *Purgatorio* and Virgil's Story." *Lectura Dantis* 20–1 (Spring 1997): 48–58.
23. "Dante e l'autobiografia." In *Scrivere la propria vita: L'autobiografia come problema critico e teorico*, edited by Rino Caputo and Matteo Monaco, 83–103. Rome: Bulzoni Editore, 1997.
24. "Le similitudini musicali nell'episodio di Mastro Adamo." In *Letteratura italiana e musica*. Atti del XIV Congresso AISLLI, edited by Jørn Moestrup, Palle Spore, and Conni-Kay Jørgensen, vol. 1, 434–8. Odense: Odense University Press, 1997.
25. "The *Gospel of Nicodemus* in Medieval Italian Literature: A Preliminary Assessment." In *The Gospel of Nicodemus in Medieval Europe: Some Vernacular Perspectives*, edited by Zbigniew Izydorczyk, 65–105. Tempe, AZ: Medieval and Renaissance Texts and Studies, 1997.
26. "The Transcodification of the Text: Italian Literature in the Global Village." *McLuhan Studies* 2, no. 1 (1996). (http://www.mcluhan studies.com).

27. "Alighieri, Dante." In *An Encyclopedia of the History of Classical Archaeology*, edited by Nancy Thomson de Grummond, 349–50. Westport, CT: Greenwood, 1996.
28. "*Paradiso* XXXI." In *Lectura Dantis Virginiana*, III. *Dante's Paradiso: Introductory Readings*, edited by Tibor Wlassics, supplement, *Lectura Dantis* 16–17 (Spring–Fall 1995): 470–85.
29. "Dante's *Inferno*, Canto IV." In *Dante's Inferno: The Indiana Critical Edition*. Translated and edited by Mark Musa, 299–309. Bloomington and Indianapolis: Indiana University Press, 1995.
30. "Musical Imagery in the Mastro Adamo Episode." In *Da una riva e dall'altra: Studi in onore di Antonio D'Andrea*, edited by Dante Della Terza, 103–18. Firenze: Edizioni Cadmo, 1995.
31. "Dante autore televisivo." *Le forme e la storia*, n.s., 6, no. 1–2 (1994): 107–24.
32. "The Presence of Italian Literature (Old and New) Abroad in the Twentieth Century." In *Italian Studies in North America*, edited by M. Ciavolella and A.A. Iannucci, 17–54. Ottawa: Dovehouse Editions, 1994.
33. "L'insegnamento dell'italiano in Canada." Co-authored with M. Ciavolella. *Lettera dall'Italia* 36 (October–December 1994): 68.
34. "The *Gospel of Nicodemus* in Medieval Italian Literature." *Quaderni d'italianistica* 14, no. 2 (1993): 192–220.
35. "Dante Produces Television." *Lectura Dantis* 13 (Fall 1993): 32–46.
36. "La ricezione della letteratura italiana antica e moderna nel XX secolo." In *L'Italia e la civiltà europea: Letteratura e vita intellettuale*, edited by Francesco Bruni, 211–41; 372–3. Turin: UTET, 1993.
37. "Dante e la 'bella scola' della poesia (*Inferno* 4.64–105)." In *Dante e la "bella scola" della poesia: Autorità e sfida poetica*, edited by A.A. Iannucci, 18–40. Ravenna: Longo, 1993.
38. "The Figure of Saturn in Dante." In *Saturn from Antiquity to the Renaissance*, edited by Massimo Ciavolella and Amilcare A. Iannucci, 151–68. Ottawa: Dovehouse Press, 1992.
39. "Forbidden Love: Metaphor and History." *Annali della Facoltà di lettere e filosofia dell'Università di Siena* 11 (1990): 341–58. Reprinted as "Forbidden Love: Metaphor and History (*Inferno* 5)." In *Dante: Contemporary Perspectives*, edited by A.A. Iannucci, 94–112. Toronto: University of Toronto Press, 1997.
40. "Petrarch's Intertextual Strategies in the *Triumphs*." In *Petrarch's Triumphs: Allegory and Spectacle*, edited by Konrad Eisenbichler and Amilcare A. Iannucci, 3–10. Foreword by Amilcare A. Iannucci. Ottawa: Dovehouse Press, 1990.

41. "*Inferno* IV." In *Lectura Dantis Virginiana*, 1. *Inferno*, edited by Tibor Wlassics, supplement, *Lectura Dantis* 6 (Spring 1990): 42–53.
42. "Casella's Song and the Tuning of the Soul." *Thought* 65, no. 256 (1990): 27–46.
43. "Dante, from Illumination to Television." In *Italian Literature in North America: Pedagogical Strategies*, edited by John Picchione and Laura Pietropaolo, 242–61. Biblioteca di Quaderni d'italianistica 9. Ottawa: Canadian Society for Italian Studies, 1990.
44. "Musica e ordine nella *Divina Commedia*." In *Studi americani su Dante*, edited by Gian Carlo Alessio and Robert Hollander, 87–111. Milan: Angeli, 1989.
45. "Dante, Television, and Education." In *Dante Today*. Special issue of *Quaderni d'italianistica* 10, no.1–2 (1989): 1–33.
46. "Didattica dell'italiano e computer: tendenze attuali e prospettive per il futuro." Co-authored with M. Danesi. *Il Forneri* n.s., 3, no. 1 (1989): 30–9.
47. "Dottrina e allegoria in *Inferno* VIII, 67–IX, 105." In *Dante e le forme dell'allegoresi*, edited by Michelangelo Picone, 99–124. Ravenna: Longo, 1987.
48. "The Undergraduate Curriculum in Italian: Coping with Linguistic Diversity at the University of Toronto." Co-authored with M. Danesi. *Association of Departments of Foreign Languages Bulletin* 19, no. 1 (1987): 16–17.
49. "Il Centro Accademico Canadese in Italia." Special issue, *Il Veltro*, 29, no. 3–4 (1985): 539–46.
50. "Vergil and the Tragedy of the Virtuous Pagans in Dante's *Commedia*." In *Vergilian Bimillenary Lectures, 1982*, edited by Edward L. Harrison and Alexander G. McKay, 145–78. *Vergilius*, supplement 2. College Park, MD: The Vergilian Society of America, 1984.
51. "Dante e il *Vangelo di Nicodemo*: la 'discesa di Beatrice agl'Inferi.'" In *Letture Classensi* 12, edited by Vittore Branca, 39–60. Ravenna: Longo Editore, 1983.
52. "L'esilio di Dante: 'per colpa di Tempo e di Fortuna.'" In *Miscellanea di studi in onore di Vittore Branca, 1: Dal Medioevo al Petrarca*, 215–32. Florence: Olschki, 1983.
53. "*Inferno* XV.95–96: Fortune's Wheel and the Villainy of Time." *Quaderni d'italianistica* 3, no. 1 (1982): 1–11.
54. "Ariosto umanista: l'educazione di Virginio." In *Il Rinascimento: Aspetti e problemi attuali*. Atti del X Congresso dell'Associazione internazionale per gli studi di lingua e letteratura italiana,

Belgrado, 17–21 aprile 1979, edited by Vittore Branca, Claudio Griggio, Marco and Elisanna Pecoraro, Gilberto Pizzamaglio, and Eros Sequi, 485–98. Florence: Olschki, 1982.

55. "Teaching Dante's *Divine Comedy* in Translation." In *Approaches to Teaching Dante's Divine Comedy*, edited by Carole Slade and Giovanni Cecchetti, 153–9. New York: MLA, 1982.
56. "Autoesegesi dantesca: la tecnica dell' 'episodio parallelo' nella *Commedia*." *Lettere Italiane* 33, no. 3 (1981): 305–28.
57. "Limbo: The Emptiness of Time." *Studi danteschi* 52 (1979–80): 69–128.
58. "Ariosto's Satire-Epistle to Bembo: Meditations on Humanism and the Value of a Humanistic Education." *Humanities Association Review* 30, no. 3 (1979): 147–60.
59. "Beatrice in Limbo: A Metaphoric Harrowing of Hell." *Dante Studies* 97 (1979): 23–45.
60. "The Nino Visconti Episode in *Purgatorio* VIII (vv. 43–84)." *La Fusta* 3, no. 2 (1978): 1–8.
61. "Brunetto Latini: 'come l'uom s'etterna.'" *NEMLA Italian Studies* 1 (1977): 17–28.
62. "*L'Elegia di Madonna Fiammetta* and the First Book of the *Asolani*: The Eloquence of Unrequited Love." *Forum Italicum* 10, no. 4 (1976): 345–59.
63. "Ulysses' 'folle vole': The Burden of History." *Medioevo Romanzo* 3, no. 3 (1976): 410–45.
64. "Dante's Theory of Genres and the *Divina Commedia*." *Dante Studies* 91 (1973): 1–6.

Academic Reviews

1. Review of *Dante's Fearful Art of Justice*, by Anthony K. Cassell. *Speculum* 62, no. 2 (1987): 397–9.
2. Review of *Dante's Paradiso and the Limitations of Modern Criticism*, by Robin Kirkpatrick. *Italica* 59, no. 1 (1982): 62–4.
3. Review of *L'ultima dea*, by Giorgio Petrocchi. *Canadian Journal of Italian Studies* 2, no. 3 (1979): 182–4.
4. "The Vertigo Mosaic." Review of *The Canadian Ethnic Mosaic: A Quest for Identity*, edited by Leo Driedger. *Books in Canada* 7, no. 10 (1978): 25.
5. "The Plot Thickens ..." A review-article of Canadian multicultural magazines. *Books in Canada* 7, no. 3 (1978): 9–10.

6. "The Italian Immigrant: Voyage of No Return." *The Canadian Forum* no. 1699 (March 1977): 12–15.

Popular Articles and Teaching Materials

1. "Dante and Cinema.". *Cinemathèque Ontario*, Spring 2001 Program Guide, 16 March–5 May, 11–14.
2. "*Il nome della rosa*: come si crea un classic." *Il Messaggero* (Rome), 23 December 1994.
3. "Forging New Links: The Department of Italian Studies, 1984–1988." In *A History of Italian Studies at the University of Toronto (1840–1990)*, by Maddalena Kuitunen and Julius A. Molinaro, appendix 13, 241–4. Toronto: University of Toronto, Dept. of Italian Studies, 1991.

Videotapes

1. "Vulcan's Net: Passion and Punishment (*Inferno* 5)." Media Centre, University of Toronto, 1987. Videocassette (VHS), 22 min.
2. "Dante's Ulysses and the Homeric Tradition (*Inferno* 26)." Media Centre, University of Toronto, 1985. Videocassette (VHS), 28 min.

Note on Editions and Translations

Dante's texts and translations are taken from the online Princeton Dante Project (http://etcweb.princeton.edu/dante), unless otherwise noted. Commentaries are accessed through the online Dartmouth Dante Project (http://dante.dartmouth.edu/; cited here as DDP), unless otherwise noted.

1 "Lascio cotale trattato ad altro chiosatore": Form, Literature, and Exegesis in Dante's *Vita nova*

ZYGMUNT G. BARAŃSKI

I: Dante, Amil, and poesia "critica"

It is now axiomatic to consider Dante as a writer in whose oeuvre "la riflessione tecnica" coexists intimately with "la poesia." The words I cite are Gianfranco Contini's, and are taken from his groundbreaking 1938 introduction to the poet's *Rime* – an essay which, it is safe to say, inaugurated the "modern" interpretation of Dante.[1] To this day, many of its revelatory insights continue fundamentally to inform our study of Western culture's most ambitious and successful literary innovator. The poet's unrelenting concern with the structures, history, and exegesis of literature is, of course, directly connected to his artistic experimentation. "Technical reflection" and "poetry" constitute the two seamlessly interlocking sides of Dante's staunch commitment to renew and redirect the world of letters. Contini's assertion permanently dismantled entrenched attitudes regarding the nature of Dante's relationship both to his own works and to medieval literary culture. Instead of glorifying the uniqueness of the poet and his art – the solitary genius "divinely" inspired to create unprecedented and timeless texts – Contini pointed to the fact that Dante's works were the product of a sophisticated, informed, and tireless reflection on every aspect of the institution of literature. To put it another way, the poet and his writings were exceptional precisely because of their complex engagement with medieval literary theory, thought, and practice. As I have already observed, these views lie unproblematically at the core of present-day Dante scholarship. Yet, as is often the case with ideas that genuinely challenge cherished opinion, their acceptance was not straightforward. Despite Contini's magisterial standing, the undoubted validity, "obviousness" even, of his proposals, and the rapid success of his edition of the poet's lyric verse, which soon became a classic in its own right, and despite the fact that his claim regarding the self-conscious character of the poet's writing could find authoritative and long-standing support in Benvenuto da Imola's remarkable *comentum* to the *Commedia*, Dantists were initially slow, not to say reluctant, to acknowledge and appreciate the radically transformative consequences of the idea of Dante as both poet and (self-)critic. Indeed, it was probably not until the 1960s – it is enough to think of Domenico De Robertis's *Il libro della "Vita Nuova"*[2] at the beginning of the decade and Bob Hollander's *Allegory in Dante's "Commedia"*[3] at the end – that a small number of critics, fortunately of outstanding calibre, began seriously to develop and test the potential of the poet's literary self-reflectiveness as a vital key to understanding his artistic and intellectual achievements. During the course of the 1970s, they were joined in their endeavours by several younger scholars; and it is to Amil's lasting credit, a precious mark of his critical acumen and sensitivity, that he can be counted among this perspicacious group, which, among others, included Michelangelo Picone, who, tragically, managed to outlive Amil by only a matter of months. To lose one friend is difficult enough. To lose two leaves a murky void of sadness, which no amount of scholarly commemoration can ever start to fill or illumine.

Yet, as I reread their publications, I still hear their voices. Amil's reaches me with particular clarity and freshness as I leaf through his two seminal studies of the 1970s, which have as their point of departure the fact that "Dante non considera il compito del poeta ... terminato finché egli non abbia spiegato ... il significato del proprio scritto" (Dante does not consider the job of the poet to be over until he has explained the meaning of his own text).[4] In his articles "Dante's Theory of Genres and the *Divina Commedia*" and "Brunetto Latini: 'come l'uom s'etterna,'"[5] Amil illustrates the forceful impact of the medieval theory of the *stili* and of the methods of biblical exegesis on Dante's oeuvre. Indeed, while others, most notably Charles Singleton in North America, had already begun to establish the importance of scriptural forms of reading for a proper appreciation of the structure of the *Vita nova* and of the *Commedia*, in 1973 Amil was something of a pioneer when it came to the sustained study of the poet's thinking on genre. Furthermore, as far as the *dantismo* of the 1970s is concerned, what is striking about Amil's two papers is the fact that their focus is firmly on the *Commedia*. Given that the poem's ties to medieval literary theory and criticism are not immediately obvious, even those eager to follow in Contini's footsteps had tended to bypass the *Commedia*, concentrating instead on the *Vita nova* and the *Convivio*. In light of the prosimetrical works' unambiguous dependence on the structures of the commentary tradition and their direct discussion of matters literary alongside their refined lyricism, such a state of affairs is understandable. Amil, however, was shrewd enough to recognize the limitations of any overarching reading of Dante that marginalized the *Commedia*. He thus insisted that

> sebbene la *Commedia* sia composta esclusivamente di versi in essa troviamo quell'atteggiamento riflessivo, critico che abbiamo già notato nella *Vita Nuova* e nel *Convivio*, e Dante continua ad essere estremamente conscio di se stesso come poeta e critico. ... L'atteggiamento critico della *Commedia* è espresso in maniera molto più sottile e calibrata: qui è totalmente integrato nella struttura poetica dell'opera. La poesia della *Commedia* è poesia "critica" in quanto si ripiega continuamente sul proprio significato.[6]
>
> (Even though the *Commedia* is composed exclusively in verse, we find in it that reflective critical attitude that we have noted in the *Vita Nuova* and the *Convivio*, and Dante continues to be extremely self-aware of his own status as poet and critic. The *Commedia*'s critical attitude is expressed in a more subtle and calculated manner: it is entirely integrated into the work's poetic structure. The poetry of the *Commedia* is "critical" poetry insofar as it constantly folds back on to its own meaning.)

In the years since Amil penned these thoughts, a vast and authoritative body of scholarship, exploring every facet of the *Commedia*'s metaliterary dimension, has helped confirm the pertinence of his intuition.

Ironically, such has been the allure of the *sacrato poema* that, despite an excellent start, research on the critical character of the *prosimetra* during the last thirty or so years has lagged far behind the work done on the poem. The *Vita nova* in particular has fared relatively badly. Despite some notable contributions, scholars have not infrequently failed to examine its reflections on literature in a systematic manner.[7] Thus, no study exists of the extent to which Dante's references to literature and his deployment of the language and procedures of medieval literary theory and criticism should be read as constituting a coherent, organic, and evolving structure, which might cast light not just on the poet's thinking about literature in the early 1290s, but also on the interpretation and status of the *Vita nova* itself. Thus, it is not unlikely that Dantists have often underestimated the novelty and experimental character of the *libello* precisely because they have failed to appreciate the complexity and unity of its metaliterary discourse, which Dante largely developed to legitimate and illuminate his work's innovations. Finally, and at a more general level, limited attention has been paid to the possible interrelationship between the poet's literary, linguistic, cultural, and ideological concerns in the *Vita nova*. The aim of my present research on the *Vita nova* is to begin to reconsider the metaliterary dimension of Dante's youthful masterpiece by focusing on the organized interplay between, on the one hand, the poet's painstaking efforts to develop exegetical structures fit to elucidate the *libello* and, on the other, his distinctive treatment both of literary history – as well as of individual genres, writers, and texts – and of the conventions of literary criticism.[8] Although Amil's interest in the *Vita nova* was relatively circumscribed, I believe that the example he set regarding the study of "Dante critico" can serve to guide my reassessment of the *prosimetrum*. Just as Amil, somewhat *controcorrente*, drew our attention to the *Commedia*'s recourse to and reworking of traditional critical routines, so my hope is to demonstrate that there is still much that needs to be understood about the *Vita nova*'s engagement with such hermeneutic forms and about the ways in which Dante, in the *prosimetrum*, sought to develop new modes of criticism. What is certain is that, despite what is normally maintained, the poet's practice in the *libello* goes well beyond a passive imitation of the conventions of commentary, and that, even when Dante drew directly on these, he adapted them in original and unexpected ways. Indeed, several of the strategies he elaborated look forward noticeably to the *Commedia*'s self-reflective techniques.[9] However much, in constructing the *Vita nova*, Dante may have relied on easily identifiable independent critical structures, such as the *divisio textus*, his aim, as in the poem, was not to maintain their autonomy but to integrate these into a new, unified, and coherent form.

II: "Questo dubbio io lo intendo solvere e dichiarare"

It is very much to be hoped that today no one still persists in the view, widely held from the nineteenth century until at least the 1960s, that the *Vita nova*, because of its lyricism, its heart-on-the-sleeve autobiographicism, and the transparent linearity of its narrative development, is a straightforwardly accessible work. The toughness and range of its prose[10] and the complexity of its cultural referencing at once belie this misleadingly reductive perception. Indeed, just the fact that the poems require interpretation is an immediate signal that we are faced with texts of some complexity. It is extremely rare for Dante to announce, as he does in the case of "Lasso, per forza di molti sospiri," that "questo sonetto non divido, però che assai lo manifesta la sua ragione" (39.7 [28.7]; "Alas, on account of the many sighs," I do not divide this sonnet, because its prose explanation makes it clear enough).[11] Even in this instance, however, when the poet deems division unnecessary, the sonnet requires "la sua ragione," its clarificatory prose accompaniment – "ragione" here is the Italian equivalent of the Occitan *razon* – in order to be made "manifest." The *Vita nova*, namely the work in its entirety, what Domenico De Robertis famously termed, calquing Dante, "il libro della *Vita Nuova*,"[12] or what modern scholarship would term the *Vita nova* as macrotext, deals with difficult texts and presents its protagonist as having to resolve existential, artistic, and intellectual problems: "Allora, pensando a le sue parole, mi parea che [the 'Segnore de la nobiltade'] m'avesse parlato molto oscuramente; sì ch'io mi sforzava di parlare" (12.5 [5.12]; So, thinking about his words, it seemed to me that [the Lord of nobility] had spoken to me very obscurely; so that I made myself speak). In truth, the most difficult text of all is the *Vita nova* itself. The personal status of the "libro de la mia memoria" (1.1 [1.1]) underscores the need for appropriate guidance in what, at first sight, looks like a private realm.[13] Moreover, from the very start of the *libello*, Dante emphasizes that he is not simply passively transcribing his memories but is interpreting them: "le parole le quali è mio intendimento d'assemplare in questo libello; e se non tutte, almeno la loro sentenzia" (1.1 [1.1]; the words that I intend to copy in this little book; and if not all of them, at least their meaning).[14] The poet is acutely aware that his writing is a source of "doubts" and thus needs clarification:

> Potrebbe già l'uomo opporre contra me e dicere che non sapesse a cui fosse lo mio parlare in seconda persona, però che la ballata non è altro che queste parole ched io parlo: e però dico che questo dubbio io lo intendo solvere e dichiarare in questo libello ancora in parte più dubbiosa; e allora intenda qui chi qui dubita, o chi qui volesse opporre in questo modo. (12.17 [5.24]; and compare 25.1 [16.1])
>
> (Someone might object and say that he did know to whom I was speaking in the second person, given that the ballad is nothing other than the words that I speak: and thus I say that I intend to resolve and explain this doubt in this little book in an even more problematic part; and so may he understand there who doubts here and who here would wish to object in this way.)

It is thus quite exceptional for Dante to declare that interpretation is unnecessary or impossible, though, ironically, when he stated as much, he was in practice offering a gloss on his writerly choices:

> Vero è che tra le parole dove si manifesta la cagione di questo sonetto ["Con le altre donne mia vista gabbate"], si scrivono dubbiose parole, cioè quando dico che Amore uccide tutti li miei spiriti, e li visivi rimangono in vita, salvo che fuori de li strumenti loro. E questo dubbio è impossibile a solvere a chi non fosse in simile grado fedele d'Amore; e a coloro che vi sono è manifesto ciò che solverebbe le dubitose parole: e però non è bene a me di dichiarare cotale dubitazione, acciò che lo mio parlare dichiarando sarebbe indarno, o vero di soperchio. (14.14 [7.14])
>
> (It is true that among the words where the reason for this sonnet ["With the other women you mock my appearance"] is made clear, obscure words are written, namely when I say that Love kills all my spirits, and the visual ones remain alive, except outside their organs. And it is impossible to explain this obscurity to anyone who was not to the same extent one of Love's faithful; and to those who are what would explain the obscure words is clear; and thus it is not appropriate for me to clarify such an obscurity, since clarifying my speech would be pointless, or in truth redundant.)

The uniqueness of this passage, never mind its paradoxical inflections, brightly casts light on the key role that exegesis plays in the *Vita nova*, a role which is the direct result of the quite considerable demands the *libello* makes on its readers. The *Vita nova* is a perplexing text. Thus, it is a work of *subtilitas*: "ma più sottilmente pensando, e secondo la infallibile veritade .... Forse ancora per più sottile persona si vederebbe in ciò più sottile ragione" (29.3–4 [19.7]; and compare 33.2 [22.2]; 41.9 [30.9]; but thinking more subtly, and according to the infallible truth. ... Perhaps a still subtler person would see in this a more subtle explanation); this subtlety, paradoxically, is nevertheless accessible to "li più semplici" (3.15 [2.2]; to the most simple).[15] And this is just one among many such large-scale conundrums that go to the very core of the *Vita nova*'s textual status and ideological and formal integrity. It is a text that appears to stand at a bewildering and innovative cultural crossroad. One merely needs to think about the acute tensions that arise from the coexistence in the *libello* of Latin and the vernacular, of prose and poetry, of Christian and pagan imperatives, and of sacred and secular elements; and we are faced with all this before having to decide what the "book of memory" might actually include or what its precise relationship to the *Vita nova* might be. And then there is the matter of the status of the book's author-protagonist ...[16] Dante is keenly aware of his responsibilities in coming to his readers' aid and in "rimuov*ere* alcuna dubitazione" (37.4 [26.4]). However, the manner in which he does this, the ways in which he interprets and guides our interpretation, despite the *prosimetrum*'s seemingly close reliance on the established norms of medieval literary exegesis, is itself, at least initially,[17] a source of disquiet. Rather than offer clear-cut, comfortable, and conventional explanations using standard procedures, Dante involves us in a complex, potentially destabilizing, and hugely original exegetical exercise. The more problems he poses, the more the need to interpret is highlighted. Even more significantly, the fundamental standing of the *Vita nova* as a text that is both a work of interpretation and is itself interpretable is affirmed. In fact, Dante goes a step further and appears to suggest that the *libello,* at least as far as the poems are concerned, provides the correct, namely the rationally sanctioned, elucidation of their meaning: "acciò che la mia donna fue immediata cagione di certe parole che ne lo sonetto sono, sì come appare a chi lo intende" (7.2 [2.13]; given that my lady was the immediate cause of certain words, which are in the sonnet, as is apparent to who understands it) and "di ciò toccai alcuna cosa ne l'ultima parte de le parole che io ne dissi [lines 19-20 of "Morte villana"], sì come appare manifestamente a chi lo intende" (8.3 [3.3]; I touched on an aspect of this in the last part of the words that I composed of it [lines 19–20 of "Loutish Death"], as is clearly apparent to who understands it). In this regard, it is not difficult to agree with Justin Steinberg that one of the reasons for the *Vita nova*'s composition is to be sought in Dante's dissatisfaction with his reception in the late 1280s and early 1290s and, especially, in his anxiety regarding the misreading of his verses.[18]

III: "Le parole le quali è mio intendimento d'assemplare in questo libello"

Yet, on account of its difficulties and formal innovations, for all the poet's efforts at exercising a controlling authority over his text, the *libello* is a work very much prey to misreading. Its manuscript transmission offers sharp and uncomfortable evidence of this. The *Vita nova* creates doubts in the minds not just of its readers but also of its copyists. Thus, if one compares the extant fourteenth-century manuscripts of the "little book,"[19] the differences in the ways in which they present Dante's *prosimetrum* are striking.[20] It soon becomes apparent that there is limited consistency in their paragraphing, in their use of initial capitalization, and in their textual layout (this last affects the relationship on the page not just between verse and prose but also between Latin and vernacular). Indeed, on occasion, the divergences are substantial. It is enough to think of Boccaccio's notorious decision to separate and "marginalize" the *divisiones* in his autograph manuscript of the *Vita nova* now preserved in the Capitular of Toledo,[21] a decision that, of course, marks a startling failure to appreciate the fundamental coherence of the "libro della *Vita Nuova*," and, at one level, can simply be deemed as the most obvious example of the broad contemporary unease regarding the *libello*'s textual identity. Another area of scribal doubt concerns the treatment of the poetry, and hence its relationship to the prose. Thus, the Strozzi codex visibly sets the sonnets apart from the prose by means of paragraphing, spacing, and initial capitals, and, more specifically, by employing the established scribal format of two verses per line to copy them. Conversely, the Chigiano L. VIII. 305, the oldest extant manuscript of the *Vita nova*, the one that, according to Carrai, is "il più fededegno,"[22] treats the verse as if it were prose. However, even if not always consistently, it does introduce line markers, something that, when copying the canzoni, the scribe of the renowned early codex Martelli (produced between 1330 and 1350) omits. At the same time, the Martelli manuscript transcribes the sonnets by copying each verse on a new line and further emphasizes the poems' autonomy by using capitals at the start of quatrains[23] and tercets. Boccaccio's autograph Chigiano L. V. 176, on the other hand, treats "[l]e rime a mo' di prosa,"[24] as also occurs in the Toledano.[25] Even if, as is well known, the layout of prose and of poetry in medieval manuscripts could, though in no way needed to be "identical,"[26] on account of the "osmosi fra l'universo poetico e quello prosastico,"[27] it is also very much the case that, logically, given the mutual exclusivity of the scribal solutions, not all (or perhaps any?) of the fourteenth-century manuscripts of the *Vita nova* can be said to reflect Dante's original layout for his *prosimetrum*. To try to establish how the poet might have wanted his exceptional *libello* to look is a matter of some import. This is not just for reasons of philological precision. As will become better apparent below (see subsections 4–6), in the *Vita nova*, Dante strove to fashion a new relationship between prose and poetry, one that raised fundamental questions about the distinctiveness and functions of the two forms. In this respect, it is suggestive that, despite their individual solutions and eccentricities, if taken together, the fourteenth-century manuscripts of the *libello* do, in fact, conceivably reveal something about Dante's intentions as regards the *Vita nova*'s appearance. With one exception, all the codices in their design and arrangement diminish the differences between prose and verse[28] – a solution that was anything but usual in the scribal treatment of texts that, in one way or another, brought together the two forms.[29] This is, of course, self-apparent in those manuscripts that present the poetry as if it were prose. However, even the Martelli, by being written in two columns, whose width tidily matches the span of a hendecasyllable, and by using capitalizations at the beginning both of poems and of distinct sections of the prose,[30] standardizes the appearance of the text. It thus seems reasonable to hypothesize that those manuscripts which transcribe the poetry as if it were prose, especially in light of the Martelli's harmonizing tendencies, were not simply following scribal convention, but were attempting to replicate a feature originally sanctioned by the poet himself. This possibility is supported by another trait that Dante introduced into the *Vita nova* and that Wayne Storey has valuably highlighted: "Before each poem Dante always notes in the prose the poetic genre of the composition that will follow and either its partial or complete first verse. In the prose which immediately follows the poem, Dante reiterates the genre … . This essentially scribal system of reiteration establishes both linkage and framing devices for the physical act of copying the poems."[31]

It is hard to imagine that, unless the poet intended to present the prose and verse in a very similar, possibly identical, manner, such careful marking of the boundaries between the two forms would have been necessary.[32] That Dante should have wanted to diminish, possibly elide, the difference between verse and prose conforms well both with his re-evaluation of the role and standing of the two forms and with his aim to fashion the *Vita nova* as a new composite, syncretic "book," in which poetry and prose came together to fashion a new type of fused literary language.

In truth, the manuscripts also disclose another key aspect of the visual form that Dante had probably chosen for the *Vita nova*. The evidence of their quirks and discrepancies strongly points to the fact that the layout of the *Vita nova* on the page was peculiar (thereby bolstering what I suggested earlier regarding the unusual homogenized appearance of the prose and poetry). The *prosimetrum*'s atypical characteristics engendered what Storey has correctly termed scribal "uncertainty,"[33] which, in its turn, inevitably led to different solutions when the *scriptores* began the practical task of transcription. The problem, I suspect, was that copyists found it difficult to establish their scribal bearings when faced with Dante's *prosimetrum*, since, as I shall explore below (see subsection 6), it was a work that lacked an obvious precedent. Thus, given the predominance of prose in the *libello*, vernacular lyric collections offered little guidance on how the *Vita nova* might best be reproduced. Equally, when judged against its most obvious Latin textual models, the *libello* was neither a prosimetrical work in the manner of the *Consolation of Philosophy* nor a standard commentary to a corpus of lyrical texts, both of which had developed well-established and recognizable traits as regards their format on the page – traits to which, in both cases, the *Vita nova* did not evidently conform. In particular, it is normal for medieval manuscripts of Boethius's *Consolatio Philosophiae* to distinguish visibly between the prose and the poetry by means of decorated initials and paragraphing, which separates the two forms.[34] As a result, the metrical characteristics of the poems are carefully respected, and each line of verse is plainly distinguished; in addition, the *metra* are at times written in two columns. Finally, marginal, interlinear, and other modes of commentary are clearly distinguished from Boethius's text by their collocation and by the size of their script, as occurs too in glossed lyric collections,[35] such as the Ovidian erotic corpus.[36] The problem with the *Vita nova*, as far as its scribes were concerned, was that Dante had not respected such traditional types of textual organization and distinction.[37]

Instead, the poet was intent on challenging and reconfiguring conventional distinctions between prose and verse, artistic text and commentary, narrative and lyric, in order to develop not just a new sort of macrotext but also a new idea of textuality. To put it simply, and with all due caution, it is not unreasonable to assume that one of Dante's aims when composing the *Vita nova* was to fashion a new type of textual appearance that might grant his *libello* a distinct identity, not to say canonicity, which straightaway would distinguish it from the established forms not only of Latin textuality but also of vernacular writing.[38] In addition, the *Vita nova*'s original look would prefigure some of its primary concerns, most notably its committed engagement with *novitas*, which finds its principal literary expression, as with the *libello*'s outward form, through its dialectical relationship to the tradition. Dante's homogenizing synthesis of prose and verse unambiguously alters not just the conventional manuscript layout in which the two forms were presented together, but also the ways in which such hybrid texts were read. The poet's identical treatment of the prose and the poetry eliminated any sort of hierarchical relationship between the two, thereby countermanding the standard ranked rapport between canonical poetic text and subordinate prose commentary. Dante thus developed the traditional graded interdependence between verse and prose, which worked entirely in favour of the authoritative poetic text, since the status, though not the integrity, of the former was guaranteed by the presence of the latter, into a new system of mutual reliance, whereby the integrity of each form was absolutely predicated on the presence of the other within the macrotext, to whose overarching integrity both made an equal contribution. Differently from a conventional glossed poetic manuscript of an *auctor*, in which "the page was organized to present text and commentary simultaneously,"[39] the *Vita nova*'s poems and their accompanying prose could not be read "simultaneously," but had to be read consecutively, namely sequentially, as part of a logically developing, chronologically determined, narrative and argument, which assured the coherence of the "libro della *Vita Nuova*."[40] Thus, when Dante first arranged the manuscript of the *Vita nova*, in all likelihood he attempted to structure his page in a manner that would guarantee that his "little book" would be read correctly. Indeed, I cannot but wonder whether one reason for the various exordial references to the "libro," its layout, and its copying is to draw attention to the novelty of its appearance.[41] To tamper with Dante's design, as Boccaccio chose to do when he removed the *divisiones*, meant destroying the *libello*'s rigorous coherence and negating its newness.

The far-reaching *novitas* of Dante's operation is emblematically captured in the failure of the *libello*'s scribes to appreciate adequately the poet's structural experimentation and resystematization. Indeed, both Wayne Storey and Marco Pacioni proffer strong arguments for Dante having introduced elements into the *Vita nova* that were meant to help guide its copyists.[42] To resolve the doubts of his readers was a responsibility that the poet accepted unflinchingly. Indeed, there seems to be little question that, as we shall see more fully in the next subsection, Dante was bent on illuminating and regulating every aspect of the interpretation and dissemination of the *Vita nova*. An intense preoccupation with form, tradition, and exegesis, inseparable from an equally profound sense of his work's novelty and of its moral purpose, lies at the heart of the *libello*. Moving beyond the *Vita nova*'s telling external solutions, it is on the internal ramifications of Dante's heartfelt ethical and literary commitment that, in line with my stated aims, I must now concentrate.[43]

IV: "Dicer di lei quello che mai non fue detto d'alcuna"

I should like to begin my "reading" of the *Vita nova* where no medieval *lector* would have thought of starting a *comentum*, namely, the text's ending. The Middle Age's privileged critical textual space par excellence was, of course, the *incipit* and not the *explicit*. The former was deemed to offer the key introductory point of entry into a text's formal and ideological concerns; and it goes without saying that I shall have something to say about the "proemio che precede questo libello" (28.2 [19.2]; prologue that precedes this little book).[44] My opening focus might appear eccentric for two other reasons. First, the *Vita nova* is a work obsessed with "beginnings" – "e dissi allora questo sonetto, lo quale comincia: *Era venuta*; lo quale ha due cominciamenti, e però lo dividerò secondo l'uno e secondo l'altro" (34.3 [23.3]; and so I composed this sonnet, which begins: *She came*; which has two beginnings, and thus I will divide it according to the one and according to the other) – and with who and what is "first": "quelli cui io chiamo primo de li miei amici" (3.14 [2.1]; he whom I call the first of my friends). As I intend to discuss in the companion piece to this study, one way to consider the *Vita nova* is as a book of *incipit*s, which, as a consequence, is also seriously preoccupied with matters of origin, and hence of history. Second, the closing chapter seems to be looking firmly to the future (Dante starting a new superior work after a long period of study; Dante's soul contemplating Beatrice in eternity) and so seems to have turned its back on the *Vita nova*, whose "insufficiency" it peremptorily declares. The poet acknowledges the inadequacy of his present literary endeavour as an effective means for relating the marvellous divine experiences that have touched his life: "Apparve a me una mirabile visione, ne la quale io vidi cose che mi fecero proporre di non dire più di questa benedetta infino a tanto che io potesse più degnamente trattare di lei" (42.1 [31.1]; A marvellous vision appeared to me, in which I saw things that made me decide to say nothing more about this blessed one until such time as I might be able to treat of her more worthily). At the same time, precisely because Beatrice is a miracle, he is aware that, with hard work and God's help, he can seriously hope to write something quite exceptional about her: "Io spero di dicer di lei quello che mai non fue detto d'alcuna" (42.2 [31.2]; I hope to say of her that which has never been said of any woman). This phrase, more than any other in the *explicit*, has been commonly treated as a proleptic announcement of the *Commedia*. However, the powerful forward thrust of the chapter has largely prevented critics from appreciating its yet more powerful retrospective force.[45] What has not been appreciated is its importance for and effect on our interpretation of the *prosimetrum*. To be told that the *Vita nova* is somehow not up to scratch comes as a shock and creates confusion at precisely the point in the *libello* where resolution is expected. Indeed, it is Dante's declaration that he hopes to "treat" Beatrice in a unique manner, namely compose a text without precedent, that is especially disconcerting. As any reasonably literate contemporary reader would have been aware, and long before he had arrived at the *Vita nova*'s close, the book he was reading was exactly one which was "saying of a woman that which had never been said of any other" (I shall return to the question of the *libello*'s innovativeness shortly). Chapter 42 [31] is not really an admission of artistic failure; rather it is the final climactic and crowning declaration of the *prosimetrum*'s *novitas*. What it announces about the future is little more than pious hope. On the other hand, by equating Beatrice with literary innovation, it draws attention to the *Vita nova*'s remarkable inventiveness. As was to have been expected, Dante concludes the "booklet" asserting, for one last time, its originality.

He does this, however, in a challenging, allusive, and personal manner, which requires readers to engage with the text and to exercise their exegetical skills – a tactic that is a hallmark of Dante's metaliterary practice. To put it somewhat differently: although the poet presents us with a text whose "newness" is immediately made evident in its title and through its form, and which, furthermore, is relentlessly run through with critical language and critical activity, he actually appears – and I stress, appears – to leave it to us to assess the nature and extent of the *Vita nova*'s novelty, as well as to evaluate the full range of his work's functions and remit. As occurs in the *explicit*, Dante provides both the necessary data and the appropriate prods to promote interpretation; after that, the responsibility to interpret is ours. Much of this study, as I announced earlier, is dedicated specifically to understanding the character, logic, and workings of the *Vita nova*'s metaliterary system and its strategies. Dante expects "active" readers, not only to ensure that the *libello*'s moral and salvific message is heeded but also to create an audience attuned to his art and its new demands.[46] As scholars have increasingly noted, the poet was (and continues to be) highly adept at preparing and controlling his reception. Indeed, the key feature of Dante's construction and manipulation of his reading public is the subtle manner in which he seems to grant us exegetical freedom while constantly constraining our ability to interpret freely[47] and ineluctably granting primacy to himself and his works. Self-authorization is never far from Dante's purpose.[48]

There is, nonetheless, a glaring yet vital paradox, tension even, at the heart of the *Vita nova*'s metaliterary structure. At first sight, in the *libello*, Dante seems anything but the kind of author who encourages and expects his readers to exercise their critical skills. Thus, the *prosimetrum* seems effectively constrained and determined by the forms of the *comentum* tradition: the opening sentences recall an *accessus*;[49] large swathes of the prose are given over to the scholastic expository technique of the *divisio textus*, while other sections (the exegesis of the number nine or the discussion of different types of pilgrims and their different designations) are also typical of the information presented in poetic commentaries. It would appear, therefore, that Dante is actually intent on delimiting, denying even, independent interpretation by rigorously controlling textual meaning. However, the immediate impression created by the poet's large-scale recourse to the typical conventions of medieval hermeneutics is almost certainly partial, if not actually misleading. It is significant that these critical structures are overwhelmingly applied just to the poems in the *Vita nova* and are employed to analyze and define individual poems as self-sufficient textual entities. The *Vita nova*, with the possible exception of its first two *accessus*-like sentences, does not benefit from a similarly traditional commentary. Of course, one obvious reason for this is that much of the *libello* is already a kind of *commentarium*, so that piling commentary onto commentary would have led to redundancy. In particular, it would have implied that the *Vita nova* had the same status and thus could be read in the same conservative manner as the individual poems, which constitute just one aspect of its innovative stratified make-up. Furthermore, to overburden the *Vita nova* with commentary ran the risk of recreating the traditional hierarchical distinction between verse and prose, which would have irreparably damaged the organic character of the *Vita nova*, whose fundamental unity the poet established from the outset. The *prosimetrum* is the adapted reproduction of a visibly distinct, multifaceted, and coherent part of the "libro de la mia memoria." It is a text in its own right, as evidenced by the fact that, like any self-standing medieval work, it is prefaced by a "rubrica": "Sotto la quale rubrica io trovo scritte le parole le quali è mio intendimento d'assemplare in questo libello: e se non tutte, almeno la loro sentenzia" (1.1 [1.1]; Under this heading I find written the words that I intend to copy in this little book; and if not all of them, at least their meaning).

That the *Vita nova* should be introduced as a *compilatio* made up of copied "words" and exegesis was not in itself unusual. This was, in fact, the basic defining characteristic of many medieval manuscripts in which selected texts were accompanied by critical glosses. The *libello* takes a decidedly strange turn, however, with the entry of "A ciascun'alma presa." It now becomes clear that the copyist, who is equally the *compilator* and the *commentator*, is also the *auctor* of the "parole." The *libello* is quite unique, a text without precedent, since it is the product of writerly activities that are here integrated but that were normally, not to say invariably, considered as distinct.[50] Moreover, before the *Vita nova*, sustained self-commentary that expressly made recourse to the forms of scholastic criticism was completely unknown in Western literary culture.[51] To complicate matters further, the idea that vernacular texts were worthy of commentary was, at the very least, highly challenging. The *Vita nova* thus quickly defines both itself and its author as exceptional. At the same time, and as will become common in Dante's oeuvre, it also recognizes its roots in and debts to the tradition. The *libello* openly highlights its profound interest in exegesis by repeatedly returning to established interpretive structures, such as those of the *divisio textus*. However, as I adumbrated, this conservative analysis is restricted to the poems, whose formal and metrical character is already fixed in the tradition. Even the *novitas* of *Donne ch'avete* is to be sought in its content and not in its form: "E però propuosi di prendere per matera de lo mio parlare sempre mai quello che fosse loda di questa gentilissima" (18.9 [10.11]; And therefore I decided to take as the subjectmatter of my writing always that which would be praise of this most gentle woman). To put it simply, when it came to his poems, Dante conventionally applied the methods of traditional commentary to traditional texts.[52] Conversely, since there is little that is obviously traditional about "the book of the *Vita Nuova*," he found it necessary and appropriate to develop a new type of exegesis for the new type of literature he was forging. A type of exegesis, in fact, which found its raison d'être not outside the text, in established critical procedure, but which, as occurs in the *explicit*, emerged from within the new text itself, and which, therefore, assumed a new type of *lector* who, subtly steered by the *auctor*, would become directly involved in fashioning the new criticism. Most strikingly, the readers of the *Vita nova* no longer needed to be versed in the practices of scholastic criticism. They simply needed to allow their sensibilities and wit to be guided by the text, so that even "li più semplici" (3.15 [2.2]) could profit from it as befitted a work of salvation. At the same time, the "subtle," by exercising their learning and intelligence, would appreciate the *libello* as a work of revolutionary cultural and intellectual complexity, as well as of deliverance. The *Vita nova* is not a text written exclusively for an elite, as has been maintained for too long, but, like the Bible, and later the *Commedia*, one aimed at everyone.[53]

It is thus clear that the *Vita nova*'s originality as a metaliterary text transcends both its status as one of the first Italian vernacular translations of Latin critical language and its standing as the first self-commentary of the Western literary canon – though the significance of these attributes is, of course, considerable. In the *libello*, Dante was also intent on developing a new sort of criticism apt to clarify and accompany his new Christian vernacular literature. The *Vita nova* may not be commentary as this had been understood since the times of the ancients, but it is unquestionably profoundly interested in exegesis and in the potential of this to fuse with other textual forms while at the same time illuminating them. Indeed, the complexity, ambition, and coherence of Dante's critical enterprise can only be properly appreciated if considered in the round. As with the *Vita nova* in general, the *libello*'s metaliterary operation is also a composite. It is thus through the productive tension between the forms of the old and the new criticism that the full extent of *Dante critico*'s achievement, and hence of the *prosimetrum*'s metaliterary inventiveness, can be gauged. Just as the lyric poems are granted "new life" by being included in the *libello*, so established exegetical structures are revived by being incorporated into the *Vita nova* and vernacularized. At the same time, the traditional character of both the verses and their critical prose accompaniment is underscored by the *novitas* of the *Vita nova*'s overarching literary and hermeneutic forms. The old prepares for and is subordinated to the new; and the *libello* announces and describes the birth not just of the *homo novus* but also of the *canticum novum* and the *commentarium novum*.

V: "Incipit vita nova"

In keeping with the *Vita nova*'s heavy stress on "newness," Dante wastes no time in establishing and validating its *novitas* (thereby making his closing critique that much more disturbing and unexpected). The trope of the "book of memory," as we have begun to see, plays a key part in this initial operation. If anything, its role is actually rather more significant than Dantists have normally acknowledged. Although it is generally recognized that the metaphor exerts a controlling pull on the lexical make up of the *Vita nova*'s opening and that its force continues to be felt throughout the *libello*, scholars rarely go beyond such general formal observations.[54] Thus, the degree of the image's novelty and, more significantly, the structural and ideological implications of its original nuances have regularly been downplayed even by those who note its inventiveness,[55] although, too often and mistakenly, the metaphor has simply been dismissed as "tradizionale," as a "topos."[56] It is to Giorgio Brugnoli's great merit to have insisted on the distinctiveness of the image: "Fra le variazioni addotte del *libro*, come *libro della mente* (*Rime*, LXVII 59 e 66; *If*, II 8; *Pd*, XVII 91) e *libro del preterito* (*Pd*, XXIII 54), il formulare *libro della memoria* della *Vita nuova* sembra isolato e irripetibile e irripetuto anche al di fuori di Dante." (Among the variations of *book* adopted, such as *book of the mind* [*Rime*, LXVII 59 e 66; *If*, II 8; *Pd*, XVII 91] and *book of the past* [*Pd*, XXIII 54], the formulaic *book of memory* of the *Vita nuova* seems isolated and unrepeatable and also unrepeated outside Dante.)[57] The *libello*'s uniqueness is thus guaranteed not simply because of its personalized exclusivity ("mia"), but also due to the fact that it is a rather exceptional text – a "book of memory"; and, as I have implied, the image brings yet more in its wake that is directly relevant to the *Vita nova*.

Given the peremptory force of Brugnoli's assertion regarding the "isolation" of the "libro de la mia memoria," it comes as a surprise to learn that there are, in fact, two possible precedents for it.[58] The critic, however, dismisses both as irrelevant to Dante's "book." Brugnoli is right to reject the "tenacis memorie liber" (book of steadfast memory) evoked in the letter sent by Frederick II in early 1247 to his brother-in-law Henry III.[59] The emperor was almost certainly referring to what the philologist terms "un 'libro di famiglia'";[60] in any case, and more notably, there is no evidence to suggest that Dante had actually read the epistle. Brugnoli's reasons for refusing the validity of the second source are of a quite different order:

> Il secondo raffronto è nuovo, e mio. Ma è anch'esso sicuramente da scartare perché la locuzione non è qui in traslato, ma riferita precisamente e canonicamente al gran libro *Testamentum novum* e all'annuncio che vi è contenuto del giudizio di Dio, per cui non si capirebbe come Dante l'abbia potuta travestire per il suo libello d'amore, senza prevedere d'incorrere nel *periculum blasphemiae*.[61]

> (The second comparison is new, and mine. But it too is certainly to be discarded because the phrase is not used here metaphorically, but refers

> precisely and canonically to the great book *Testamentum novum* and to the announcement that is contained within it of God's judgment, so that it is hard to understand how Dante could have disguised it for his little book of love, without foreseeing that he would fall into the *danger of blasphemy*.)

Despite Brugnoli's energetic claims to the contrary, the second precedent deserves anything but to be "discarded." It is, in fact, hugely significant: "Malachias ... ait ..., 'Haec oblocuti sunt qui timebant Dominum, unusquisque ad proximum suum; et animadvertit Dominus et audivit: et scripsit librum memoriae in conspectu suo eis, qui timent Dominum et reverentur nomen eius' [Mal. 3:16]. Isto libro significatum est testamentum novum" (3; Malachi said, "Such were the comments uttered by those who feared the Lord, each one to his neighbour; and the Lord noticed and listened: and wrote a book of memory in his presence for those who fear the Lord and revere his name." This book signifies the New Testament). The extract is found in chapter 35, book 18 of Augustine's *De civitate Dei*[62] and provides immediate and explicit confirmation in the *Vita nova*'s very first line of the *libello*'s fundamental dependence on scripture, which the phrase "new life" then almost at once reasserts.[63] In addition, the passage helps draw attention to the *prosimetrum*'s concern with "newness," as well as to its intent to supersede the old, an idea that is central to Augustine's chapter.[64] Furthermore, just as Malachi and the other minor prophets bore witness to Christ's miraculous coming, and just as Augustine in his discussion of their prophecies draws attention to Jesus's salvific powers, so, in his "proemio," after describing the "libro" and the "libello," Dante next highlights Beatrice's celestial nature – "Ella non parea figliuola d'uom mortale, ma di deo" (2.1 [1.2]; She did not seem like the daughter of a mortal man, but of a god) – and her close ties to salvation: "la gloriosa donna de la mia mente, la quale fu chiamata da molti Beatrice li quali non sapeano che si chiamare" (2.1 [1.2]; the glorious woman of my mind, who was called Beatrice by many who did not know this to be her name). Indeed, Beatrice's proximity to Christ, which controls her treatment throughout the *Vita nova*, is made explicit if one compares her presentation in the *prooemium* to the prophets' and Augustine's discussion of the Son in chapter 35. Like Christ, Beatrice causes violent movement[65] and is termed an angel;[66] equally, like Christ, others give prominence to her name[67] and she is linked to the east.[68] As a result, Dante is also able to point to his own privileged relationship with God as Beatrice's lover and scribe. Through a system of analogy that, mutatis mutandis, recalls Beatrice's association with Jesus (*imitatio Christi*), the poet humbly hints at his ties to the last of the "minores prophetae" (*De civ. Dei* 18.35.1). He thus implies his own divinely ordained standing as *scriba Dei*, legitimating both his recourse to scripture and his need to develop a new form that could adequately serve as a vehicle for the extraordinary story of divine and human love that he had been chosen to record.

There is nothing blasphemous about Dante claiming a privileged relationship to the divine. On the one hand, it was a standard Christian belief, as the *Vita nova* confirms, that earthly existence was providentially governed and that God chose humans to do his work, whether as his representatives (Beatrice) or as his messengers (the poet); on the other hand, it was a religious commonplace to deem it a Christian's duty to imitate Christ and the saints. Chapter 35 of the *De civitate Dei* substantiates, rather than calls into doubt, the *libello*'s, and hence Dante's, orthodoxy. It provides a vital key with which to read not just the opening sentence and the rest of the "proemio," but also the *Vita nova* as a whole. The chapter focuses on God's miraculous role in history, the salvific power of Christ and his coming, and the responsibilities of those who serve as God's mouthpiece. Just as significantly, the *libello*'s dependence on the *sacra pagina* ensures that any idea regarding the purely private character of the events it describes, which the possessive *mia* ("libro de la mia memoria") might have fostered, is definitively dispelled. The *Vita nova* tells an exemplary story, whose universalizing relevance Dante highlights straightaway by presenting Beatrice both as "his lady" ("la gloriosa donna de la mia mente," 2.1 [1.2]) and as the "bearer of beatitude" to others ("la quale fu chamata da molti Beatrice li quali non sapeano che si chiamare," 2.1 [1.2]). Dante, as Beatrice's divinely ordained lover and *scriba*, certainly enjoyed a privileged relationship with her; however, Beatrice's coming, like Christ's, was for the benefit of the "many." The trope of the "book of my memory" is not "isolato e irripetibile e irripetuto," as Brugnoli would have it; indeed, if it had been, Dante could not have established the *Vita nova*'s divine credentials in the manner that he did. At the same time, there is little doubt that this trope does point to the *libello*'s uniqueness: the first modern and vernacular instance of a text whose *auctor* was speaking "ex persona Dei" (*De civ. Dei* 18.35.3). The *prosimetrum*'s formal *novitas*, as the doctrine of *convenientia* maintained, was a direct and appropriate result of the uniqueness of its message.

It is hard to deny that Augustine and his *De civitate Dei* are directly involved in the *Vita nova*'s strategy to introduce itself as a divinely inspired text. Thus, it is almost certain that Dante could only have found the quotation from Malachi that includes the allusion to the *liber memoriae* in chapter 35, since in the Vulgate the passage reads as follows: "Tunc locuti sunt timentes Dominum, unusquisque cum proximo suo; et attendit Dominus, et audivit, et scriptus est *liber monumenti* coram eo timentibus Dominum, et cogitantibus nomen eius" (Mal. 3:16 [my italics]; Then they who feared the Lord spoke, each one with his neighbor; and the Lord gave ear, and heard, and a book of remembrance was written before him for those who fear the Lord and consider his name). Augustine's wording repeats that of the Septuagint, which was unknown to Dante except indirectly, as in this instance. Indeed, the poet's debts to chapter 35 can be multiplied further. The bishop of Hippo closes his chapter in a manner that uncannily recalls the *Vita nova*'s *explicit*: "Hic est qui dicitur dies iudicii; de quo suo loco, si Deus voluerit, loquemur uberius" (3; This is the day that is called the day of judgment; about which, if God wills, I shall speak more fully in the appropriate place); and compare, "infino a tanto che io potessi più degnamente trattare di lei … sì che, se piacere sarà di Colui … io spero di dire di lei" (42.2 [31.2]; until such time as I might be able to treat of her more worthily, so that, if it pleases him, I hope to say of her). Even more suggestively, Augustine refers to Psalm 39: "De hoc quippe etiam in Psalmo dicitur: *Et eduxit me de lacu miseriae et de luto limi* [3]" (2; About this, of course, the Psalm says: *And he has led me out of the lake of misery and of the mire of mud*). Scholars have long considered the Psalm's fourth verse a likely source for Dante's religiously inflected stress on "newness" in his treatment both of the "book" of the *Vita nova* and of the "praise style": "Et immisit in os meum canticum novum" (And he placed in my mouth the new song); and compare "La mia lingua parlò quasi come per se stessa mossa" (19.2 [10.13]; My tongue spoke almost as if moved by itself). Brugnoli notes the relevance of another of the Psalm's verses: "E vi si aggiunga pure, per l'*incipit* di Dante, il sintomatico, e a mia conoscenza ancora inutilizzato, *Ps* XXXIX 8: 'tunc dixi, Ecce venio, in capite libri scriptum est de me'" (And one ought to add, as regards Dante's *incipit*, the symptomatic, and as far as I know still unused, Psalm 39:8: "Then I said, Here I come, in the heading of the book it is written about me").[69] The critic is correct to highlight the importance of the verse. In Christian thought, the verse was associated with the *liber vitae*, which relates to each person's *vita gloriae*,[70] their salvation; and salvation constitutes the *Vita nova*'s key ideological concern with respect to Beatrice ("la gloriosa donna," 2.1 [1.2]) and to her lover: "che la mia anima possa gire a vedere la gloria de la sua donna, cioè di quella benedetta Beatrice, la quale gloriosamente mira nella faccia di Colui" (42.3 [31.3]; that my soul may go and see the glory of its woman, namely of that blessed Beatrice, who gloriously looks into the face of him). In addition, the psalmist's "book" was associated with the whole of scripture, with Christ, and with "omnia necessaria homini ad salutem" (everything necessary to man for his salvation),[71] matters whose significance for the *Vita nova* does not need further elucidation. To cap it all, in Augustine's *Enarrationes*, immediately prior to his gloss on verse 8, the bishop declares: "In umbra remanserunt, solem gloriae ferre non possunt: iam nos in luce sumus, tenemus corpus Christi, tenemus sanguinem Christi. Si habemus novam vitam, cantemus canticum novum, hymnum Deo nostro" (They have remained in shadow, they cannot bear the sun of glory: we are already in the light, we hold the body of Christ, we hold the blood of Christ. If we have a new life, let us sing a new song, a hymn to our God).[72] Once more, and with his normal exemplary concision, Dante gets his cultural bearings just right.

Thanks to his recourse to scripture and to its pre-eminent *lectores*, in the very first words of the *Vita nova*, Dante provides an accurate and revealing insight into much of the *libello*. The poet was conventionally following contemporary practice on the need for a text to open with a *prooemium*, which both synthesized the work's principal interests and characteristics and offered a guide to its interpretation.[73] However, the astonishing precision and succinctness, as well as the connotative range, of Dante's initial remarks distinguish the *Vita nova*'s "proemio" from the prefatory comments normally found in classical and medieval texts. At the start of his *prosimetrum*, as occurs with other parts of the *Vita nova*, Dante began by drawing on the tradition only to leave it quickly and effectively behind. Indeed, as I have begun to demonstrate elsewhere,[74] the quality and quantity of the introductory information that, in the "proemio," Dante provided in a carefully structured manner is hugely impressive for its relevance and scope. The prologue, like the *libello* as a whole, is unique. Dante alludes to three prologues in the *Vita nova*. The first (19.15–6 [10.26–7])[75] and third references (31.3–4 [20.3–4]),[76] which bookend the allusion to the "proemio che precede questo libello" (28.2 [19.2]), help highlight the *novitas* of the *libello*'s *prooemium* given the standardized manner in which they introduce their canzoni. Yet again, the traditionalist poetics and the mechanistic, pedestrian exegesis of the poetry foreground the originality of the macrotext.

The "libro de la mia memoria" thus exerts a powerful influence not only on the vocabulary and imagery of the *Vita nova* but also on its identity and interpretation. The "book," in fact, serves as a trigger to interpretation. Beyond its fundamental scriptural connotations, the "book of memory" raises challenging questions about its exact relationship to the *Vita nova*. If, on the one hand, it is evident that the *libello* forms a "part" of the larger "book," on the other, the problem remains as to what textual elements might precisely constitute the generic "words" that Dante is "copying." To put it differently: to what extent is the *Vita nova* an accurate copy of "quella parte del libro de la mia memoria," which appears after the "rubrica la quale dice: *Incipit vita nova*"? Thus, to what extent, as discussed above, does the layout of the *libello* reflect that of the main text? It is not unusual to limit the "parole" simply to the poems. However, it seems reductive, not to say illogical, to exclude the narrative sections of the prose, given that the events these describe so obviously belong to Dante's memories. Indeed, reutilizing the term "parole," the poet himself indicates that what he is transcribing includes not just the poetry but also the narration of events: "E trapassando molte cose le quali si potrebbero trarre de l'essemplo onde nascono queste [the preceding prose account], verrò a quelle parole le quali sono scritte ne la mia memoria sotto maggiori paragrafi. // III [II] Poi che fuoro passati tanti die ..." (2.10–3.1 [1.11–2]; And passing over many things that could be taken from the original from which these originate, I will come to those words that are written in my memory under larger paragraphs. // III [II] Then after many days had passed ...). In keeping with the technical value of "sentenzia" as "interpretation, meaning," it is the processes of clarification and of selection of the verse and the prose of the "libro de la mia memoria" that are unique to the "libro della *Vita Nuova*." The "book of memory," therefore, is already a *prosimetrum*; and it is not unlikely that Dante was keen to obscure the boundaries between the two "books."[77] An especially significant effect of this act of blurring is that it allowed the poet to create a rigorous coherence between "internal" and "external," between what was in his mind and its formal linguistic expression. By the 1290s, it had long been a commonplace, regularly exploited also by Dante in his oeuvre, for writers to lament the disjuncture between their thought and its artistic expression. In the *Vita nova*, by maintaining that he was copying directly from his "mente" (2.1 [1.2]), Dante presents himself as having overcome the traditional dichotomy,[78] thereby claiming an extraordinary consistency for his work. As *scriptor*, *compilator*, *commentator*, and *auctor*, Dante is in almost perfect control of his *materia* and *ars*. The *Vita nova* thus stands as a magisterial *exemplum* of how life can effectively be fixed and textualized,[79] so that the lessons of experience, especially if that experience has been touched by the *digitus Dei*, can be a source of communal benefit. Sung by the *homo novus* in "loda" (18.9 [10.11]) of the divine and for the profit of a changing world, in which the vernacular was increasingly asserting its prerogatives, the *Vita nova* resounds yet again as the *canticum novum*.

VI: "E lo primo che cominciò a dire"

I do not believe that it is an exaggeration to assert that the *Vita nova* constitutes a new literary genre. It shares, of course, characteristics with a number of long-established and broad archgenres, such as the *prosimetrum* and the *comentum*, as well as with a variety of other clearly recognizable textual forms. At the same time, it cannot conveniently and tidily be subsumed under any of these. Thus, its metaliterary vigour and its tight integration of prose and verse have no precedent in canonical prosimetrical works such as Boethius's *Consolatio Philosophiae*, Martianus Capella's *De nuptiis Philologiae et Mercurii*, and Alan of Lille's *De planctu Naturae*. Equally, conventional commentaries lack the narrative and critical coherence of the *Vita nova* and were never, as we have seen, the result of an act of self-commentary. Bob Hollander is correct to note that the *libello* "has no precise or certain model in Western literature. … The *Vita nuova* is, as one can rarely say with such certainty, unique. Nothing in the tradition of Dante's Romance predecessors, or indeed of any precursors, serves as a sufficient model."[80] Yet, scholars persist in trying to squeeze Dante's youthful masterpiece into inappropriately restrictive textual cages, claiming that its primary, and therefore controlling, influences are to be sought in elegy, in glossed manuscripts of Ovid, in the Occitan *razos* and *vidas*, in Cicero's *De amicitia*, in Romance narrative and lyric works, in Augustine's *Confessions* and *Retractationes*, in hagiography, in Brunetto Latini's *Rettorica*, and in the various other texts and traditions that have suggestively been put forward as antecedents of Dante's "little book."[81] Most of these proposed models and sources, to a lesser or greater extent, do indeed lie behind the *libello*. However, not one of them is able on its own to account either for the *Vita nova*'s ambitious ideological aims or for its formal range and quality. The only texts that come close to achieving this are the glossed manuscripts of some of the poetic scriptural books, specifically the Lamentations of Jeremiah, the Psalter, and the Song of Songs.[82] The annotated *Canticum* in particular, thanks to its blend of verse and narrative and exegetical prose, as well as its emphasis on love, salvation, and large-scale metaliterary reflection, offered Dante an alluringly rich and complex model to follow as he endeavoured to create a new and totalizing text that could establish the potential of the vernacular as a language of culture. Yet, even Solomon's great epithalamium cannot do proper justice to the *Vita nova*'s remarkable literary range and rigour. Thus the Song and its gloss lack the *libello*'s intertextual breadth and its powerful structural cohesiveness,[83] namely, its capacity to fuse the plurality of its antecedents into a logically unified, evolving narrative and ideological whole – a whole, in fact, that is confidently greater than the sum of its parts.

The *Vita nova*, as its mix of prose and poetry immediately signals, is a hybrid, the juncture where different artistic and intellectual currents meet and merge. However, it is a hybrid that, unlike Horace's monster at the start of the *Ars poetica*, is harmoniously and originally put together. It is not the kind of "liber / ... cuius, uelut aegri somnia, uanae / fingentur species, ut nec pes nec caput uni / reddatur formae" (book whose empty fancies are like the dreams of a sick man, so that neither foot nor head can be restored to a single form).[84] Rather the *libello*'s linguistic and stylistic plurilingualism and its wide-ranging engagement with an extensive array of texts and traditions, the buildingblocks of its composite character, are effectively controlled by a strong and consistent narrative development, and, more significantly, by the coherence of its ideological and cultural interests. Thus, the lesson on spiritual salvation is complemented by the declaration of literary *renovatio*: "onde, se alcuna figura o colore rettorico è conceduto a li poete, conceduto è a li rimatori" (25.7 [16.7]; hence, if [Latin] poets are permitted any rhetorical figure or color, these are permitted to [vernacular] rhymsters). Both concerns announce the need for and the possibility of renewal; and, just as salvation entails a radical transformation, so the shift from Latin to the vernacular requires an equally sweeping process of change, which, as with the coming into being of the *homo novus*, affects every area of life. Consequently, the *Vita nova*'s plurilingualism and rich intertextuality are also signs of its effort to engage with the full complexity of the contemporary world. The *libello* thus ranges from science to philosophy, from exegesis to theology, from scholastic logic to linguistic theory, from symbolism to scripture, and from the classics to Romance literature. To treat the *Vita nova* essentially as a love story or even as a meditation on the literature of love is, I believe, to miss its point and to curtail its novelty and ambition.[85] At the end of the duecento, love in its Christian and secular ramifications was a vital and multifaceted concept, which touched on many areas of experience. It was, therefore, the ideal hook on which to hang the *libello*'s overarching religious and cultural reassessment. For Dante, love is a point of departure rather than of arrival. The principal trajectory of the *Vita nova* plots and reveals the vernacular's capacity to deal with the spiritual and intellectual complexity of reality, of which love, for all its significance, is just one aspect. In fact, the "little book" does rather more than this: by eliding the differences between prose and poetry, it innovatively confirms the vernacular's ability to accommodate and integrate the density of the real in a new, flexible, stratified, and overarching textual form: "il libro della *Vita Nuova*."

The most strikingly original feature of the *libello*, therefore, as is also the case with the *Commedia*, is its formal structure and organization and its stylistic register: to put it medievally, its *forma tractatus* and its *forma tractandi*. As I stated earlier, the *Vita nova* marks the birth of a new genre. Given the *libello*'s totalizing scope and its preference for the vernacular, Dante could only have deemed established (Latin) genres as insufficient for his purpose. At the same time, in keeping with his assessment of vernacular poetry in light of the classical *auctores* in chapter 25 [16], the poet was determined to establish clear links between his experimental text and the tradition. In this regard, his decision to base the new "book," however freely, on the conventions of the *comenta* is more than understandable. Commentary was highly flexible, not in its structures, which by the end of the thirteenth century were rigidly codified, but in its ability to deal with any subject. Despite the Middle Ages' compilatory tendencies, there were actually few summative forms. In fact, as is well known, medieval poetics relied heavily on the Horatian doctrine of the *genera dicendi*[86] and overwhelmingly preferred to compartmentalize literature into discrete and largely self-sufficient *stili*. A work such as the *Vita nova*, and after it the *Commedia*, which strove to achieve formal and intellectual openness, was normally deemed to be transgressive, since its syncretic pluralism went against the canonical rules of writing. It was thus imperative for Dante to legitimize his experimentation in ways that would be accessible to his audience. His reliance on the structures of commentary indicated that the *libello*'s encyclopedism did indeed have precedents, and hence legitimacy, and that the "booklet," for all its seeming eccentricities, was nonetheless interpretable.[87] Even more important for Dante's effort to justify the *Vita nova* is the privileged relationship that he established between the *libello* and scripture. The only text that could unquestionably and completely account for its hybrid and plurilingual aims and identity was the Bible, which, according to standard medieval belief, drew on every language and every *genus* in order to portray its providential account of salvation through a harmonious mix of prose and verse. The supreme prosimetrical work of the Middle Ages was God's book; and no other text is as visibly and extensively present in the "little book." It is thus more than fitting that, in addition to the *Vita nova*'s register and ideology, the Bible should also legitimize its most obvious formal feature.

Thanks to the commanding recourse he made to scripture, Dante was also able to confirm the structural and stylistic integrity of his hybrid *Vita nova*. For its ideological and cultural *intentiones* to carry weight, no doubts could be raised with regard to its textual coherence and authenticity. The threat of Horace's *monstrum* lurked close to every text. Thus, as medieval proemial convention dictated, Dante affirmed the *libello*'s consistency and uniqueness from the very start of the *Vita nova*. The poet made clear that the source of both these fundamental attributes is to be sought in two closely related elements: first, in the *proemio*'s distinctly biblical register, which resounds with scriptural echoes, and second, just as significantly, in the "libro de la mia memoria," specifically in "quella parte" where "si trova una rubrica la quale dice: *Incipit vita nova*" (1.1 [1.1]; book of my memory, in that part where the heading is found that says: *The new life begins*). Dante claimed that he was not inventing anything but simply copying from (*assemplare*) and glossing ("la loro [of the words] sentenzia") a pre-existing, scripturally inflected text,[88] whose unity is guaranteed by its being a "book"[89] – and not just any book but one worthy of dissemination and commentary – the distinctiveness of which is assured by the possessive "mia." Furthermore, as the *Vita nova* progresses, and as we become increasingly aware of the providential character of the story that we are reading, reinforced as this is by the *libello*'s insistent recourse to scripture, it becomes ever more apparent that its ultimate author and primary *causa efficiens*, as the Aristotelian *accessus* would have put it, is God.[90] The "book of memory" and "la divina scrittura" (*Par*. 29.90) have a supreme and unimpeachable common origin, which, in the last instance, unproblematically accounts for the former's close dependence on the latter. What we are reading is a divine *signum*, the work of an inspired *scriba Dei*. No doubts can thus reasonably be entertained about the *libello*'s logic and exceptionality.[91]

VII: "E nel fine"

"And in the end," I can only return to Amil. The *Vita nova*, with its emphasis on friendship, is a fitting text through which to honour and remember my friend. Interpretation, too, as a theme, in light of our shared profession, does not seem out of place. Moreover, as I wrote this chapter, I became increasingly better aware of the complexity of our dealings as scholars. Like Dante in the *Vita nova*, I too have regularly alluded to those – near and far, known and unknown, alive and dead – with whom I share my intellectual life. To commemorate Amil, I had to draw on the support of colleagues. Rarely have footnotes meant so much. At our best, we are a community; and few of us have been as sensitive to the needs of that community as Amil. His collegiality was a badge of his humanity. In the "book of my memory," it is Amil's generosity that is writ large. It is the man more than the scholar that lives on in me: Amil reading, with a mischievous serenity, a book of children's poetry to our four-year-old daughter, Anna Matilde …

NOTES

1 G. Contini, "Introduzione alle Rime di Dante," in *Varianti e altra linguistica* (Turin: Einaudi, 1970), 320.

2 D. De Robertis, *Il libro della "Vita Nuova"* (Florence: Sansoni, 1961); a second amplified edition appeared under the same imprint in 1970.

3 R. Hollander, *Allegory in Dante's "Commedia"* (Princeton: Princeton University Press, 1969).

4 A.A. Iannucci, "Autoesegesi dantesca: la tecnica dell' 'episodio parallelo,'" in *Forma ed evento nella "Divina Commedia"* (Rome: Bulzoni, 1984), 109.

5 The first was published in *Dante Studies* 91 (1973): 1–25, while the second appeared in *NEMLA Italian Studies* 1 (1977): 17–28. The latter was expanded and rewritten in Italian with the title "Autoesegesi dantesca: la tecnica dell' 'episodio parallelo,'" *Lettere italiane* 33 (1981): 305–28. The articles are reprinted in Iannucci, *Forma ed evento*, 13–50, 83–114, from which I cite. All translations are my own.

6 Iannucci, *Forma ed evento*, 91.

7 It goes without saying that, over the last forty or so years, there has been a steady number of studies on the *libello*'s self-reflective characteristics. Their principal limitation, as I have just noted, is that they tend to discuss its metaliterary and metacritical aspects in somewhat too partial and unstructured a manner, thereby downplaying the fact that, in the *prosimetrum*, we have "l'incorporazione nell'opera della dimensione metatestuale della stessa," so that the "*Vita nova* definisce il proprio percorso comunicativo dall'interno." M. Pacioni, "L'*auctoritas* poetica e il personaggio Cavalcanti nella *Vita Nova*," in *Auctor / Actor: Lo scrittore personaggio nella*

letteratura italiana, 61, special issue, online journal *Studi (e testi) italiani* 17 (2006); Pacioni's article and J. Steinberg's chapter cited below are the best recent studies on the *Vita nova* that I have read. Noteworthy exceptions to the critical trend I have just sketched are: J. Ahern, "The Reader on the Piazza: Verbal Duels in Dante's *Vita Nuova*," *Texas Studies in Language and Literature* 32 (1990): 18–39; and J. Ahern, "The New Life of the Book: The Implied Reader of the *Vita Nuova*," *Dante Studies* 110 (1992): 1–16; A.R. Ascoli, *Dante and the Making of a Modern Author* (Cambridge: Cambridge University Press, 2008), 178–201; S. Botterill, "'Però che la divisione non si fa se non per aprire la sentenzia de la cosa divisa' (V.N., XIV, 13): the *Vita Nuova* as Commentary," in *"La gloriosa donna de la mente": A Commentary on the "Vita Nuova,"* ed. V. Moleta (Florence: Olschki, 1994), 61–76; F. Brugnolo and R. Benedetti, "La dedica tra Medioevo e Rinascimento: testo e immagine," in *I margini del libro: Indagine teorica e storica sui testi di dedica*, ed. M. Antonietta Terzoli (Rome and Padua: Antenore, 2004), 30–7; S. Cristaldi, *La "Vita Nuova" e la restituzione del narrare* (Soveria Mannelli: Rubbettino, 1994); A. D'Andrea, "La struttura della *Vita Nuova*: le divisioni delle rime," *Yearbook of Italian Studies* 4 (1980): 13–40, and "Dante interprete di se stesso: le varianti ermeneutiche della *Vita Nuova* e il *Convivio*," in *Strutture inquiete* (Florence: Olschki, 1993), 53–83; De Robertis, *Il libro*; O. Holmes, *Assembling the Lyric Self: Authorship from Troubadour Song to Italian Poetry Book* (Minneapolis and London: University of Minnesota Press, 2000), 120–44; T. Levers, "The Image of Authorship in the Final Chapter of the *Vita Nuova*," *Italian Studies* 57 (2002): 5–19; P. Nasti, *Favole d'amore e "saver profondo": La tradizione salomonica in Dante* (Ravenna: Longo, 2007), 53–85; C. Paolazzi, *La "Vita Nuova": Legenda sacra e historia poetica* (Milan: Vita e pensiero, 1994); M. Picone, *"Vita Nuova" e tradizione romanza* (Padua: Liviana, 1979); and Picone, *Percorsi della lirica duecentesca* (Fiesole: Cadmo, 2003), 219–65; E. Sanguineti, "Per una lettura della *Vita nuova*," in *Dante reazionario* (Rome: Editori Riuniti, 1992), 3–33; J. Steinberg, *Accounting for Dante: Urban Readers and Writers in Late Medieval Italy* (Notre Dame: University of Notre Dame Press, 2007), 61–94; T.C. Stillinger, *The Song of Troilus: Lyric Authority in the Medieval Book* (Philadelphia: University of Pennsylvania Press, 1992), 2–5, 8–10, 23–72, 85–94; M.G. Tassinari, "Metalingua e metadiscorso: prospettive sulla base di un'analisi della *Vita Nuova* di Dante," *Lingua e stile* 23 (1988): 71–94; F. Tateo, "Aprire per prosa," in *Questioni di poetica dantesca* (Bari: Adriatica, 1972), 51–75. On the *Vita nova*'s metaliterary character, see also F.J. Ambrosio, *Dante and Derrida: Face to Face* (New York: State University of New York Press, 2007), 15–49; L. Amtower, *Engaging Words: The Culture of Reading in the Later Middle Ages* (New York and Basingstoke: Palgrave, 2000), 90–105; G. Cappello, "La *Vita*

Nuova tra Guinizzelli e Cavalcanti," *Versants* 13 (1988): 47–66; D.S. Cervigni, "' … ricordandomi di lei, disegnava uno angelo sopra certe tavolette'" (*VN* 34. 1): realtà disegno allegoria nella *Vita nuova*," *Letture classensi* 35–6 (2007): 19–34; D. De Robertis, "Storia della poesia e poesia della propria storia nel XXII della *Vita Nuova*," *Studi danteschi* 51 (1978): 153–77; G. Elata-Alster, "Gathering the Leaves and Squaring the Circle: *Recording, Reading* and *Writing* in Dante's *Vita Nuova* and *Divina Commedia*," *Italian Quarterly* 24 (1983): 5–26; W. Ginsberg, *Dante's Aesthetics of Being* (Ann Arbor: University of Michigan, 1999), 20–77; L. Jenaro-MacLennan, "Autocomentario in Dante y comentarismo latino," *Vox Romanica* 19 (1960): 82–123; Elena Landoni, *Il "libro" e la "sentenzia": Scrittura e significato nella poesia medievale: Iacopone da Todi, Dante, Cecco Angiolieri* (Milan: Vita e Pensiero, 1990), 83–140; E. Livorni, "Il proemio de *La Vita Nuova*: impostazione del discorso dantesco," *L'Alighieri* 29 (1988): 3–10; M.R. Menocal, *Writing in Dante's Cult of Truth: From Borges to Boccaccio* (Durham and London: Duke University Press, 1991), 12–50; S. Roush, *Hermes' Lyre: Italian Poetic Self-Commentary from Dante to Tommaso Campanella* (Toronto, Buffalo, and London: University of Toronto Press, 2002), 25–51; R. Stella, "La *Vita nuova* de Dante: stratégie de la citation," *Cahiers d'études romanes*, n.s., 5 (2001): 19–31; E. Trevi, "Amore, figura e intendimento: Osservazioni sull'allegoria in Cavalcanti e nella *Vita Nuova*," *La cultura* 27 (1989): 143–54. I have been unable to consult I. Abramé-Battesti, "Les fonctions du meta-discours poétique chez Dante, de la *Vita Nuova* au *Convivio*," in *Dire la création: la culture italienne entre poétique et poïétique*, ed. D. Budor (Lille: Presses Universitaires de Lille, 1994), 69–76.

8 The present contribution represents the first segment of a two-part study of the *Vita nova*'s metaliterary interests. Its focus is primarily on what can loosely be termed macrostructural issues: the *libello*'s form, the ideological and literary implications of its overarching concern with *novitas*, and its (self-) exegetical structures. The second contribution will assess the *Vita nova*'s treatment of the institution of literature, namely, of the various elements that make up the literary system. As a consequence, it examines the ways in which the *prosimetrum* can be read both as a history of literature and as a neo-Horatian "manual on writing," a sort of *poetria*, in fact, which thus anticipates both the *Convivio*'s and the *De vulgari eloquentia*'s lessons on poetics. Naturally, as might be expected, Dante's broad historical and perceptive engagement with literature once again serves, in the first instance, as self-commentary. Ultimately, my research is meant to cast light on the structured complexity both of the *Vita nova*'s appreciation of literature and of its metaliterary discourse. When I started to think about this project, I naively assumed that I would be able to fit my discussion

into a single study. Dante being Dante, however, things soon began to "get out of hand." I apologize to my readers for failing to keep together what, in truth, should have remained whole. In addition, both halves ought, ideally, to be read in light of my earlier contributions on the *Vita nova*'s Horatian and plurilingual characteristics: "'Valentissimo poeta e correggitore de' poeti': A First Note on Horace and the *Vita nova*," in *Letteratura e filologia tra Svizzera e Italia: Miscellanea di studi in onore di Guglielmo Gorni*, ed. M.A. Terzoli, A. Asor Rosa, and G. Inglese (Rome: Edizioni di Storia e Letteratura, 2010); and "The Roots of Dante's Plurilingualism: 'Hybridity' and Language in the *Vita nova*," in *Dante's Plurilingualism: Authority, Knowledge, Subjectivity*, ed. S. Fortuna, M. Gragnolati, and J. Trabant (Oxford: Legenda, 2010), 98–121.

9 Barański, "The Roots of Dante's Plurilingualism."

10 On the complex wealth of the *Vita nova*'s prose, see I. Baldelli, "Lingua e stile delle opere in volgare di Dante," in *Enciclopedia dantesca*, appendix, 82–8; Barański, "The Roots of Dante's Plurilingualism." Baldelli stresses the range of the *Vita nova*'s prose, highlighting its use of technical vocabulary, of Latinisms, and of terms with concrete associations (82–3, 86–7), before concluding "lo spessore della prosa della *Vita Nuova* appare dunque assai ampio" (88). See also G. Bertoni, "La prosa della *Vita Nuova* di Dante," in *Lingua e cultura (Studi linguistici)* (Florence: Olschki, 1939), 167–222; B. Terracini, "La prosa poetica della *Vita Nuova*," in *Analisi stilistica: Teoria, storia, problemi* (Milan: Feltrinelli, 1966), 207–49.

11 All quotations from and references to the *Vita nova* are taken from Dante Alighieri, *Vita Nuova*, ed. D. De Robertis (Milan and Naples: Ricciardi, 1980), which, as is well known, reprints Barbi's 1932 critical edition. As is equally well known, since the publication of Gorni's edition in 1996 (Dante Alighieri, *Vita Nova*, ed. G. Gorni [Turin: Einaudi, 1996]), the decision as to which text of the *libello* to cite is no longer straightforward. My situation is made more difficult by the fact that, on the one hand, I prefer Barbi's text, while, on the other, I find Gorni's divisions more persuasive. S. Carrai finds himself in a similar position to mine: Dante Alighieri, *Vita nova*, ed. S. Carrai (Milan: Rizzoli, 2009); see especially his "Nota al testo," 25–30. To reflect my ambivalence, when citing, I first provide Barbi's numbering, but then give Gorni's in square brackets. A further complication relates to the *libello*'s title. The philological evidence in support of the form *nova* rather than the traditional *nuova* is strong. I thus refer throughout to the *Vita nova*. In quotations, I naturally cite the form of the title used by the author on whom I am drawing.

12 Henceforth, whenever I use the designation *Vita nova*, I refer to the *libro* in its entirety.

13 On the universalizing qualities of the "book of memory," see subsection 5 below.

14 "Che il primo prosimetro della letteratura italiana si sia sviluppato come una sorta di autoantologia poetica, commentata e integrata da brani in prosa, è detto esplicitamente da Dante, com'è noto, nel lapidario esordio." S. Carrai, "Introduzione," in Dante Alighieri, *Vita nova*, ed. Carrai, 18.

15 Dante's reference to "the most simple" is obviously scriptural in character: "In illo tempore respondens Iesus dixit: Confiteor tibi, Pater, Domine caeli et terrae, quia abscondisti haec a sapientibus, et prudentibus, et revelasti ea parvulis" (Matt. 11:25; and cf. Luke 10:21; 1 Cor. 1:26–7). Indeed, the whole sentence – "Lo verace giuducio del detto sogno non fue veduto allora per alcuno, ma ora è manifestissimo a li più semplici" (3.15 [2.2]) – recalls John's phrase: "Haec non cognoverunt discipuli eius primum: sed quando glorificatus est Iesus, tunc recordati sunt quia haec erant scripta de eo, et haec fecerunt ei" (12.16). These and the many other scriptural allusions present in the *libello* – the Bible is without doubt the *Vita nova*'s primary source – point to a special relationship between God's book and Dante's *libro*. As ought to become evident during the course of this study, the Bible exerted a fundamental influence on the *Vita nova*'s ideological make up, its formal composition, and its exegesis. On the *Vita nova*'s debts to the Bible and Christian culture, see Barański, "The Roots of Dante's Plurilingualism"; V. Branca, "Poetica del rinnovamento e tradizione agiografica nella *Vita Nuova*," in *Studi in onore di Italo Siciliano* (Florence: Olschki, 1966), 1:123–48; and V. Branca, "Tradizione francescana del linguaggio agiografico della *Vita Nuova*," in *Letteratura italiana e ispirazione cristiana*, ed. C. Ballerini (Bologna: Patron, 1980), 17–43; S. Carrai, *Dante elegiaco: Una chiave di lettura per la "Vita nova"* (Florence: Olschki, 2006), 54; De Robertis, *Il libro*, esp. 86–128; Giuseppe Di Scipio, *The Presence of Pauline Thought in the Works of Dante* (Lewiston, Queenston, and Lampeter: Edwin Mellen Press, 1995), 1–28; A. Marigo, *Mistica e scienza nella "Vita Nuova" di Dante: Le unità di pensiero e le fonti mistiche, filosofiche e bibliche* (Padua: Drucker, 1914); Nasti, *Favole d'amore*; B. Nolan, "The *Vita Nuova*: Dante's Book of Revelation," *Dante Studies* 88 (1970): 51–77; M. Pazzaglia, "La *Vita Nuova* fra agiografia e letteratura," in *L'armonia come fine* (Bologna: Zanichelli, 1989), 73–96; P. Rigo, *Memoria classica e memoria biblica in Dante* (Florence: Olschki, 1994), 11–32; C.S. Singleton, *An Essay on the "Vita Nuova"* (Baltimore and London: Johns Hopkins University Press, 1977);

Stillinger, *The Song of Troilus*. I shall have something to say on the seeming contradiction between "subtlety" and "simplicity" in due course. For an important reading of the radical hermeneutic reverberations of Dante's claim that the dream is accessible to "li più semplici," see G.B. Stone, "Dante's Averroistic Hermeneutics (On 'Meaning' in the *Vita Nuova*)," *Dante Studies* 112 (1994): 133–59.

16 I examine both the remit of the "book of memory" and the status of the author-protagonist below; see subsections 5 and 4 respectively.

17 This essay goes on to argue this point below; see subsection 4.

18 Steinberg, *Accounting for Dante*, 2, 62–6, 81.

19 I base the discussion that follows primarily on five of the six complete fourteenth-century manuscripts of the *Vita nova*: Chigi L. VIII. 305; Martelli 12; Magliabechiano Cl. VI. 143 (normally termed the Strozziano on the basis of its earlier provenance); Toledo, Archivo y Biblioteca capitulares, MS Zelada 104.6; and Chigiano L. V. 176. I also make the occasional reference to the three trecento manuscripts that include fragments of the *libello*: Laurenziano Acquisti e Doni 224; the Trespiano preserved in S. Maria degli Angeli in Florence; and Biblioteca nazionale centrale di Firenze, Tordi 339. I have not consulted the manuscripts directly but have relied on the reproductions in Dante Alighieri, *La Vita Nuova*, ed. M. Barbi (Florence: Bemporad, 1932); and in H.W. Storey, "Following Instructions: Remaking Dante's *Vita Nova* in the Fourteenth Century," in *Medieval Constructions in Gender and Identity: Essays in Honor of Joan M. Ferrante*, ed. T. Barolini (Tempe: MRTS, 2005), 127–30. In addition I have consulted *Il codice Chigiano L. V.176 autografo di Giovanni Boccaccio*, introduction by D. De Robertis (Rome: Archivi Edizioni and Florence: Fratelli Alinari, 1974); and *Mostra di manoscritti, documenti e edizioni (VI centenario della morte di G. Boccaccio)*, 2 vols. (Certaldo: a cura del Comitato promotore, 1975). I have also made extensive use of the semidiplomatic transcriptions of the manuscripts made available on "I testimoni della *Vita Nova*" website, http://vitanova.unipv.it/. I have not considered the sixth fourteenth-century manuscript, Verona, Biblioteca Capitolare, MS 445, since this was copied between 1375–1400, and thus after Boccaccio's influential resystematization of the text of the *Vita nova*; see Storey, "Following Instructions," 126.

20 For descriptions of the manuscripts, see M. Barbi, "Introduzione," in Dante Alighieri, *La Vita Nuova*, xix–lxxxviii; also the excellent updated and detailed descriptions found at http://vitanova.unipv.it. See also P. Trovato, *Il testo della "Vita Nuova" e altra filologia dantesca* (Rome: Salerno, 2000).

21 Boccaccio does the same in his other autograph manuscript of the *Vita nova*, the Chigiano L. V. 176, which postdates the Toledano.

22 "Il Chigiano L. VIII. 305, fiorentino, scritto verso la metà del Trecento, che oltre a essere il più antico è anche il più fededegno, in quanto si dimostra conservativo di aspetti della lingua tardoduecentesca e anche del fiorentino dell'epoca." S. Carrai, "Nota al testo," in Dante Alighieri, *Vita nova*, ed. Carrai, 25–6.

23 The first initial capital, since it marks the *incipit*, is more elaborate than the three subsequent initial capitals.

24 Barbi, "Introduzione," xxiv.

25 *Mostra di manoscritti*, 1: 103.

26 C. Giunta, "Sul rapporto tra prosa e poesia nel Medioevo e sulla frottola," in *Storia della lingua e filologia: Per Alfredo Stussi nel suo sessantacinquesimo compleanno*, ed. M. Zaccarello and L. Tomasin (Florence: Edizioni del Galluzzo, 2004), 36, 38. See also M.C. Camboni, "Le rime di Antonio di Cecco da Siena," *Nuova rivista di letteratura italiana* 8 (2005): 30.

27 E. Pasquini, "Intersezioni fra prosa e poesia nelle *Lettere* di Guittone," in *Guittone d'Arezzo nel settimo centenario della morte*, ed. M. Picone (Florence: Cesati, 1995), 179.

28 The exception is the Strozzi manuscript. The verse in the fragments is also copied as if it were prose.

29 See the following paragraph.

30 "Si torna a capo, oltre che per il principio delle poesie e per il riprendere poi della prosa, anche dopo il termine delle divisioni" (Barbi, "Introduzione," xxviii).

31 Storey, "Following Instructions," 122. Pacioni makes a similar point: "Con piena consapevolezza di appesantire il testo, Dante fornisce continuamente punti di riferimento del corpo dei componimenti, in modo tale da renderne più difficile lo smembramento e la confusione con la parte in prosa durante la copiatura. ... Come già mostra l'enfatizzazione del *titulus* (*incipit Vita nova*), Dante costruisce una mappa interna al 'libello' che garantisce l'integrità materiale nella trasmissione del testo" ("L'*auctoritas* poetica," 60).

32 This device has a similar function to the initial and final *rime rilevate*, which mark the boundaries of each canto of the *Commedia*.

33 Storey, "Following Instructions," 125. Storey also notes that, when compared to "the most typical forms of the medieval book ... Dante's *Vita Nova* stands as one of the more problematic puzzles ... in the history of manuscript production" (117). As I hope has already become clear, the present subsection is deeply indebted to W. Storey's excellent article.

34 See R. Black and G. Pomaro, *La "Consolazione della Filosofia" nel Medioevo e nel Rinascimento italiano: Libri di scuola e glosse nei manoscritti fiorentini* (Tavernuzze: SISMEL-Edizioni del Galluzzo, 2000); and *Codices*

Boethiani: A Conspectus of Manuscripts of the Works of Boethius. III: Italy and the Vatican City, ed. M. Passalunga and L. Smith with V. Longo and S. Magrini (London: The Warburg Institute and Turin: Nino Aragno Editore, 2001); both volumes contain many reproductions of manuscript folios. See also F. Troncarelli, *Boethiana Aetas: Modelli grafici e fortuna manoscritta della "Consolatio Philosophiae" tra IX e XII secolo* (Alessandria: Edizioni dell'Orso, 1987). In addition, see C. Leonardi, "I codici di Marziano Cappella," *Aevum* 34 (1960): 1–99 and 411–524.

35 One effect of the allusion to the "altro chiosatore" – "e però lascio cotale trattato [discussing Beatrice's death] ad altro chiosatore" (28.2) – is to stress that the exegetical passages in the macrotext have a different status than a conventional commentary, which, unlike Dante's *divisiones*, was always presented as distinct from the work it was glossing.

36 See M. Irvine, *The Making of Textual Culture: "Grammatica" and Literary Theory 350–1100* (Cambridge: Cambridge University Press, 1994), 371–93. See also M. Picone, "L'Ovidio di Dante," in *Dante e la "bella scola" della poesia*, ed. A.A. Iannucci (Ravenna: Longo, 1993), 110–13.

37 No one is more aware than I am of the limitations of the preceding analysis. In order to assess fully the status and implications of the *Vita nova* manuscripts, it would be necessary to examine these also in light of manuscripts of the scriptural poetic books (in particular, the Song of Songs; P. Nasti informs me that normally the Canticle was conventionally distinguished from its gloss); of Occitan manuscripts in which poems are accompanied by *vidas* and *razos* (though, as is well known, there are noteworthy differences between the layout of the *Vita nova* and Occitan lyric manuscripts, not least because of the major differences in scale of their respective prose sections); see W. Burgwinkle, "The *Chansonniers* as Books," in *The Troubadours: An Introduction*, ed. S. Gaunt and S. Kay (Cambridge: Cambridge University Press, 1999), 248; and of manuscripts that bring together Guittone's prose and poetic works (I shall return to the relationship between Guittone manuscripts and the *Vita nova* in the companion piece to this study; for the present, see R. Leporatti, "Il 'libro' di Guittone e la *Vita Nova*," *Nuova rivista di letteratura italiana* 4 (2001): 41–150. See also H.W. Storey, *Transcription and Visual Poetics in the Early Italian Lyric* (New York and London: Garland, 1993), 171–92; Pasquini, "Intersezioni"; Holmes, *Assembling the Lyric Self*, 47–69. Despite the partiality of my treatment, I hope I have at least managed to raise some valid questions about the original form and appearance of the *Vita nova*.

38 As is often the case with Dante's experimentation, he was not the first to begin to develop a specifically vernacular "look." It is enough to think of organizational and scribal developments and innovations in the formation

of anthologies of Romance lyric poetry. What distinguishes Dante's efforts from those of his contemporaries are the greater boldness and coherence of his inventions.

39 Irvine, *The Making of Textual Culture*, 389.

40 Storey notes that, in the *Vita nova*, "the reading orientation of poems … is not referenced by their relative positions in the macrotext [as in the *Rerum vulgarium fragmenta*]. … The narrative continuum of the *Vita Nuova*, arranged by the dominant 'chapters', supersedes its poetic structures" (*Transcription*, 339–40).

41 In this regard, whatever other meanings the term *libello* might have in the *Vita nova*, it literally refers to the small number of pages on which the *Vita nova* is written; Storey hypothesizes that the original version "would have consisted materially of no more than two quinternions (10 bifolia / 20 *chartae*), or perhaps even two quaternions (8 bifolia or 16 *chartae*)" ("Following Instructions," 120). On the technical value of *libellus / libello*, see R. Hanna III, "Booklets in Medieval Manuscripts: Further Considerations," *Studies in Bibliography* 39 (1986): 100–11; P. Robinson, "The 'Booklet': A Self-Contained Unit in Composite Manuscripts," in *Codicologia 3: Essais typologiques*, ed. A. Gruys and J.P. Gumbert (Leiden: Brill, 1980), 46–69; Storey, "Following Instructions," 118–21. See also F. Dolbeau, "Noms de livres," in *Vocabulaire du livre et de l'écriture au moyen âge*, ed. O. Weijers (Turnhout: Brepols, 1989), 79–99; M. Teeuwen, *The Vocabulary of Intellectual Life in the Middle Ages* (Turnhout: Brepols, 2003), 178–9. I intend to examine the implications of the designation *libello* in the second instalment of this research.

42 Storey, "Following Instructions," 122–5; Pacioni, "L'*auctoritas* poetica," 59–61.

43 I should like to express my warmest gratitude to my friend and colleague, Kenneth Clarke, for his help, advice, and support as I researched and wrote this subsection. I am just sorry that I have not been able to include and develop his many invaluable observations, as these fell outside the immediate narrow remit of my discussion.

44 In the subsection that follows, I assess at some length the key role of the *proemio* in introducing the *Vita nova*. At this juncture, and in line with Gorni and Carrai, I should like simply to note that I believe that the prologue stretches well beyond the two-sentence opening chapter of the Barbi edition of the *libello*. For a fuller discussion of my reasons, see Barański, "The Roots of Dante's Plurilingualism," where I argue that the *prooemium* actually extends beyond the limits proposed by the *Vita nova*'s two most recent editors. As far as I am concerned the *proemio* embraces Barbi's 1–3.15, namely Gorni's 1–2.2.

45 But see Levers, "The Image of Authorship."
46 Dante's creation of a new readership can be compared to his fashioning of a new form for the *Vita nova*.
47 Amtower overstates the amount of interpretive freedom that Dante grants the reader; see *Engaging Words*, 98.
48 In the present study, I mention issues of *auctoritas* only in passing, since these have been thoroughly examined by A. Ascoli and by M. Pacioni. See also Amtower, *Engaging Words*; M. Picone, "La teoria della *auctoritas* nella *Vita Nova*," *Tenzone* 6 (2005): 173–91.
49 See Barański, "The Roots of Dante's Plurilingualism."
50 See Ascoli, *Dante*, 6.
51 I am far from certain that the vast majority of Dante scholarship has even taken cognizance of this revolutionary fact, never mind begun to consider its implications. R. Hollander is among the few who note the uniqueness of the *Vita nova*: "It remains true that we possess no earlier example in the history of Western literature of a writer who gathered *his own* poems into a collection and then wrote commentaries on them." *Dante: A Life in Works* (New Haven and London: Yale University Press, 2001), 14.
52 Indeed, as I suggested earlier, Dante claims to be offering the definitive explanation of the poems. In this way, readers are invited not to expend their critical energy on the poems, as there is really nothing more to say about them, but to focus their exegetical attention on the new text that the poet has fashioned for them.
53 Pacioni, too, refers to the *Vita nova*'s "ambizione a un pubblico più vasto," as confirmed by Dante's reference to "tutte le persone" (26.15 [17.15]) ("L'*auctoritas* poetica," 58–9).
54 But see E. Fenzi, "Il libro de la memoria," in *Dante in lettura*, ed. G. De Matteis (Ravenna: Longo, 2005), 15–38; Singleton, *An Essay*, 25–54.
55 "La designazione della 'memoria' come 'libro' nel quale sono scritti e si leggono … gli avvenimenti passati … individua un preciso campo semantico su cui si struttura l'intero proemio, con un'ampiezza e perspicuità di sviluppi … che va ben al di là delle puntuali indicazioni dei modelli … e che rappresenta un vero punto e a capo della tradizione: con conseguenze interne imponenti, non solo per il riflesso sul linguaggio dell'intero libro, ma per come l'immagine viene a prefigurare la realtà oggettiva, la dimensione dell'opera, del libro, la sua dimensione di 'storia'" (De Robertis, *Vita Nuova* [ed.], 27). See also E.R. Curtius, *European Literature and the Latin Middle Ages* (London and Henley: Routledge and Kegan Paul, 1979), 326.
56 M. Corti, *Percorsi dell'invenzione: Il linguaggio poetico e Dante* (Turin: Einaudi, 1993), 39, 40.

57 G. Brugnoli, "Un libello della memoria asemplato per rubriche," *La parola del testo* 1 (1997): 56.
58 But see note 63 below.
59 *Historia diplomatica Friderici Secundi* ..., ed. J.L.A. Huillard-Bréholles (Paris: Plon, 1852–61), 6.1: 502.
60 Brugnoli, "Un libello della memoria," 57.
61 Brugnoli, "Un libello della memoria," 58.
62 I cite the *De civitate Dei* from the *Patrologia Latina* (henceforth *PL*), 41.
63 E. Fenzi, with his customary impeccable erudition, cites several other instances of the image of the "book of memory," though not the passage from the *De civ. Dei* ("Il libro de la memoria," 19). Fenzi's meticulous research certainly points to the "diffusione" of the image. At the same time, it is far from certain that Dante would have known any of the texts he cites. In any case, none brings with it the wealth of pertinent cultural reverberations of *De civ. Dei* 18.35. See below.
64 "Novum procul dubio Testamentum debemus accipere, ubi sempiterna, non Vetus, ubi temporalia sunt promissa" (*De civ. Dei* 18.35.3).
65 "*Haec dicit Dominus exercituum: Adhuc unum modicum est, et ego commovebo caelum et terram et mare et aridam, et movebo omnes gentes, et veniet desideratus cunctis gentibus* [Hag. 2:6]. Haec prophetia partim completa iam cernitur, partim speratur in fine complenda. Movit enim caelum angelorum et siderum testimonio, quando incarnatus est Christus; movit terram ingenti miraculo de ipso virginis partu; movit mare et aridam, cum et in insulis et in orbe toto Christus annuntiatur: ita moveri omnes gentes videmus ad fidem" (*De civ. Dei* 18.35.1); and compare, "Apparve ... . In quello punto dico veracemente che lo spirito de la vita, lo quale dimora ne la secretissima camera de lo cuore, cominciò a tremare sì fortemente ... e tremando disse" (2.3–4 [1.4–5]).
66 "Nec mirandum est, quia Domini omnipotentis angelus dictus est Christus Iesus" (*De civ. Dei* 18.35.3); and compare, "Io cercasse per vedere questa angiola giovanissima" (2.8 [1.9]).
67 "*Ab ortu enim solis usque ad occasum magnum nomen meum in gentibus, et in omni loco sacrificabitur et offeretur nomini meo oblatio munda; quia magnum nomen meum in gentibus, dicit Dominus* [Mal. 1:10]" (*De civ. Dei* 18.35.3); and compare, "la quale fu chiamata da molti Beatrice li quali non sapeano che si chiamare" (2.1 [1.2]).
68 "*Ab ortu enim solis* [Mal. 1:10]" (*De civ. Dei* 18.35.3); and compare, "Ella era in questa vita già stato tanto, che ne lo suo tempo lo cielo stellato era mosso verso la parte d'oriente" (2.2 [1.3]).
69 Brugnoli, "Un libello della memoria," 58.

70 P. Lombard, *Sententiae in IV libris distinctae* (Grottaferrata: Editiones Collegii S. Bonaventurae ad Claras Aquas, 1971–81), 3.31.1.1; T. Aquinas, *Scriptum super libros Sententiarum magistri Petri Lombardi episcopi Parisiensis*, ed. M.F. Moos, 2 vols., bk. 3 (Paris: P. Lethielleux, 1956), 3.31.1.2. See also Fenzi, "Il libro de la memoria," 17–18.

71 *Super Heb.* 10.1, in T. Aquinas, *Super epistolam ad Hebraeos lectura*, ed. R. Cai (Turin and Rome: Marietti, 1953), 335–506; and T. Aquinas, *Summa theologica* (Paris: Migne, 1864), 1.39.8.5.

72 Augustine, *Enarrationes in Psalmos* 39.13 (*PL* 36).

73 On medieval prologues, see E. Gallo, "Matthew of Vendôme: Introductory Treatise on the Art of Poetry," *American Philosophical Society Proceedings* 118 (1974): 59–60; D. Kelly, "Theory of Composition in Medieval Narrative Poetry and Geoffrey of Vinsauf's *Poetria nova*," *Medieval Studies* 31 (1969): 117–48; H. Lausberg, *Handbuch der literarischen Rhetorik* (Munich: Max Hueber Verlag, 1960), 1:150–63; D.V. Smith, *The Book of the "Incipit": Beginnings in the Fourteenth Century* (Minneapolis and London: University of Minnesota Press, 2001).

74 Barański, "The Roots of Dante's Plurilingualism."

75 "Questa canzone, acciò che sia meglio intesa, la dividerò più artificiosamente che l'altre cose di sopra. E però prima ne fo tre parti: la prima parte è proemio de le sequenti parole; la seconda è lo intento trattato; la terza è quasi una serviziale de le precedenti parole. La seconda comincia quivi: *Angelo clama*; la terza quivi: *Canzone, io so che*. La prima parte si divide in quattro: ne la prima dico a cu' io dicer voglio de la mia donna, e perché io voglio dire; ne la seconda dico quale me pare avere a me stesso quand'io penso lo suo valore, e com'io direi s'io non perdessi l'ardimento; ne la terza dico come credo dire di lei, acciò ch'io non sia impedito da viltà; ne la quarta, ridicendo anche a cui ne intenda dire, dico la cagione per che dico a loro. La seconda comincia quivi: *Io dico*; la terza quivi: *E io non vo' parlar*; la quarta: *donne e donzelle*."

76 "Io dico che questa cattivella canzone ha tre parti: la prima è proemio; ne la seconda ragiono di lei; ne la terza parlo a la canzone pietosamente. La seconda parte comincia quivi: *Ita n'è Beatrice*; la terza quivi: *Pietosa mia canzone*. La prima parte si divide in tre: ne la prima dico perché io mi muovo a dire; ne la seconda dico a cui io voglio dire; ne la terza dico di cui io voglio dire. La seconda comincia quivi: *E perché me ricorda*; la terza quivi: *e dicerò*."

77 Ginsberg, too, observes that "the nature of this [between the two books] … is hard to specify precisely" (*Dante's Aesthetics*, 22). It might be argued, though I am not certain that I would want to go as far, that since the

acts of selection and interpretation are, in the first instance, necessarily intellectual operations, they too must have a place in Dante's "book of memory."

78 But see E. Fichera, "Ineffabilità e crisi poetica nella *Vita Nuova*," *Italian Quarterly* 42 (2005): 5–22.

79 See Menocal, *Writing in Dante's Cult of Truth*, 16. For a different analysis of the relationship between life and poetry in the *Vita nova*, see De Robertis, "Storia della poesia."

80 Hollander, *Dante*, 13–14. See also L.C. Rossi, "Postfazione," in Dante Alighieri, *Vita Nova*, ed. Luca Carlo Rossi (Milan: Mondadori, 1999), 246–7.

81 I aim to discuss several of these texts and traditions in the companion piece to this essay.

82 See R.L. Martinez, "Mourning Beatrice: The Rhetoric of Threnody in the *Vita nuova*," *Modern Language Notes* 113 (1998): 1–29; Nasti, *Favole d'amore*; Stillinger, *The Song of Troilus*.

83 I should like to stress that I am speaking here in strictly literary and not in medieval theological terms. Naturally, I am well aware that, in the Middle Ages, the Bible was deemed to embrace and integrate every form, style, language, and subject; and the same claim was made as regards each of the books of scripture. At the same time, individual books were especially associated with particular *genera*. The Song of Songs, for instance, was closely tied to comedy. It is the case, as I shall shortly discuss, that, in light of medieval sacred poetics, the Bible is the text that the *Vita nova* is most obviously and suggestively imitating. And yet faith is one thing, literary structures are quite another.

84 *Horace on Poetry: The "Ars Poetica,"* ed. C.O. Brink (Cambridge: Cambridge University Press, 1971), lines 6–9.

85 See also Barański, "The Roots of Dante's Plurilingualism."

86 See F. Quadlbauer, *Die antike Theorie der "Genera dicendi" im lateinischen Mittelalter* (Vienna: Hermann Böhlaus Nachf., 1962).

87 The problem of the *Vita nova*'s interpretability has received limited attention in Dante scholarship. Most discussions of the *libello*'s exegetical character have concentrated on its traditionalist analysis of the poems; but see D'Andrea, "Dante interprete di se stesso," 498–9; R. Hollander, "Dante 'Theologus-Poeta'," in *Studies in Dante* (Ravenna: Longo, 1980), 55–8; as well as Hollander, "*Vita Nuova*: Dante's Perceptions of Beatrice," *Dante Studies* 92 (1974): 1–18; Holmes, *Assembling the Lyric Self*, 132; E. Jager, *The Book of the Heart* (Chicago and London: The University of Chicago Press, 2000), 74–7. Although it is extremely important to Dante's strategy to present himself as deserving of commentary, namely as authoritative, as

I remarked earlier, such conventional analysis barely touches the "book of the *Vita Nuova*." What is striking and essential as regards the *libello*'s interpretability are the new intrinsic exegetical structures that Dante developed to explain and legitimize his work – structures, in fact, which subsequently serve as the basis of the *Commedia*'s metaliterary system. It is these structures that are the fulcrum around which this essay is organized.

88 Since Dante is "copying," the obvious implication is that the *libello*'s scriptural tenor is already a feature of the "book of memory," thereby offering a further early clue of the extraordinary character of the events that the protagonist experienced in his "new life."

89 "L'idea della memoria personale come *libro*, storia organica o insieme coerente di esperienze." M. Ciccuto, in Dante Alighieri, *Vita Nuova*, ed. M. Ciccuto (Milan: Rizzoli, 1984), 87.

90 Divinely motivated literature had two authors: God provided the inspiration, while the human *scriba* was responsible for the textual execution; see A.J. Minnis, *Medieval Theory of Authorship*, 2nd ed. (Aldershot: Scolar Press, 1988), 90–102.

91 Nor can any doubts be entertained about the outstanding capabilities of its human author. There was no more effective way for Dante to establish his authoritativeness than to present himself as a divinely inspired writer. Indeed, he not only highlighted his extraordinary literary abilities, but, as a correlative of these, he also immediately pointed to his unique human attributes: "E però che soprastare a le passioni e atti di tanta gioventudine pare alcuno parlare fabuloso, mi partirò da esse" (2.10 [1.11]). It was a commonplace of writing on the *scribae Dei* and on the *auctores* to underscore the exceptional nature of their artistic and personal qualities.

2 A Cavalcantian *Vita nuova*: Dante's Canzoni *Lo doloroso amor che mi conduce* and *E' m'incresce di me sì duramente*

TEODOLINDA BAROLINI

I remember with pleasure and sadness the many wonderful occasions to talk of Dante with Amilcare Iannucci. This essay, adapted from my commentary on Dante's lyrics, *Rime giovanili e della "Vita Nuova"* (Milan: Rizzoli, 2009), with the addition of original translations of the canzoni by Richard Lansing, is offered as a small tribute to how much we learned from Amilcare during the years that we were privileged to share with him.

As clearly indicated by its first words, the canzone *Lo doloroso amor* is about "painful love": "doloroso amor." Barbi places *Lo doloroso amor* immediately after the other great early canzone of tormented and sorrowful love, *E' m'incresce di me sì duramente*.[1] Contini follows Barbi with respect to placement, here as elsewhere, noting however that "in an ideal chronology of the *rime dolorose* for Beatrice, this canzone is certainly the oldest" (in una cronologia ideale delle rime dolorose per Beatrice la nostra canzone occupa certo il posto più antico).[2] Foster and Boyde pick up on the implicit suggestion in Contini's comment, placing *Lo doloroso amor* first among Dante's *rime dolorose*, including those from the *Vita nuova*.[3] In this way, Foster and Boyde place *Lo doloroso amor* literally in the "posto più antico" of this thematic group and take advantage of the programmatic quality of the *incipit*.

In order to explain my placement of *Lo doloroso amor*, I will need briefly to remind the reader of the basic issues of the editorial history of Dante's *rime*.[4]

Dante did not order his *rime*. Hence, every editorial attempt to order them – whether it be an order that seeks an approximate chronology, like that of Barbi, Contini, Foster and Boyde, and myself, or an order that follows in the footsteps of the editorial tradition, like that of

De Robertis – is necessarily an invention: editorial, not authorial. All editors of Dante's *rime* are working in the absence of an authorial ordering, with the exception of the authorial orderings that we find in Dante's hybrid texts of prose mixed with poetry: the *Vita nuova* and *Convivio*.[5]

In the absence of a Dantean ordering of the *rime*, various editorial solutions have been proposed in the course of the centuries-long commentary tradition. The poems were traditionally divided by genre, the *canzoni* isolated from the sonnets and *ballate*; more recently, in the last century, the ordering by genre gave way to the attempt to put the poems in a chronological order. Even more recently, De Robertis has returned to the traditional ordering by genre and has availed himself of Boccaccio's transcription and ordering of the canzoni. In other words, De Robertis places the canzoni first, as is traditional in ancient anthologies, and with respect to their order, he follows Boccaccio, who transcribed fifteen of Dante's canzoni. These are the so-called "canzoni distese," an expression that derives from the phrase with which Boccaccio concludes his transcription in codex Chigiano L.V.176 ("finiscono le canzoni distese di Dante").

In other words, Boccaccio – or someone before him, according to a recent proposal[6] – chose the ordering of the canzoni that we find in De Robertis's edition. But Boccaccio omitted the canzone *Lo doloroso amor* from his collection. Given the noninclusion of *Lo doloroso amor* among Boccaccio's fifteen *canzoni distese*, the canzone is placed by De Robertis in the sixteenth position in his edition, after the fifteen canzoni transcribed by Boccaccio. This position is given to *Lo doloroso amor* despite the fact that it is, according to the unanimous consensus of Dante's editors (including De Robertis), an early canzone.

I cannot endorse De Robertis's editorial solution, which puts *Lo doloroso amor* in a marginal position, suspended between the late canzone *Amor, da che convien* and the nonexistent canzone (cited in *De vulgari eloquentia*), *Trag[g]emi de la mente Amor la stiva*. Nor do I follow Foster and Boyde, who separate *Lo doloroso amor* from its sister canzone, *E' m'incresce di me*, to place it first among the *rime dolorose*. Rather, I take this opportunity to place *Lo doloroso amor* immediately before *E' m'incresce di me*, to produce a reading of maximum ideological cohesion.

Foster and Boyde consider *Lo doloroso amor* an archaic canzone, stylistically linked to *La dispietata mente*, a canzone with Sicilian features but "not specifically Cavalcantian" (72). I, on the other hand, consider *Lo doloroso amor* profoundly Cavalcantian. Moreover, it is a canzone to whose Cavalcantian matrix theologized elements are added, exactly as seen in the sonnet that precedes it in my order, *Ne le man vostre*, and as will be seen again in the canzone that follows it, *E' m'incresce di me*, where we encounter not just generically theologized elements but elements pertaining to the *Vita nuova*. In fact, the canzoni *Lo doloroso amor* and *E' m'incresce di me* are hermeneutically linked and lend themselves to a unitary interpretation, as Barbi suggested by placing them next to one another in his edition (but in inverted order, with *E' m'incresce di me* coming first). Given the elements typical of the *Vita nuova* that can be found in *E' m'incresce di me*, these canzoni suggest a reading based on the nonlinearity of Dante's progression towards what only in retrospect is his inevitable destination: they dramatize Dante's experimentation with an ideological and poetic path that he subsequently discarded. Specifically, a commentary that connects *Lo doloroso amor* and *E' m'incresce di me* allows us to see that Dante experimented with what seems retrospectively like an ideological oxymoron: a Cavalcantian *Vita nuova*.

The great interest that the canzoni *Lo doloroso amor* and *E' m'incresce di me* hold for readers lies precisely in their relationship with the *Vita nuova*, the text from which they were excluded and which their very existence helps us to better comprehend. These canzoni clearly demonstrate that Dante imagined a course antithetical to the one that he later followed in the *libello*. On the basis of these canzoni, we can infer that Dante conceived of an experience that could be defined in the oxymoronic terms of a Cavalcantian *Vita nuova*. Cavalcanti's hold on Dante's imagination is still very strong – and we should not forget that his hold extends beyond the *Vita nuova*: Dante wrote mature lyrics that are Cavalcantian.[7]

The canzoni *Lo doloroso amor* and *E' m'incresce di me* offer interpretive clues fundamental for the reconstruction of Dante's itinerary up to the threshold of the *Vita nuova*. They provide tools with which to understand the creation of the figure of Beatrice: they show us that the making of Beatrice as she is presented in the *Vita nuova* was a gradual process, a *gradatio* that we can, to some degree, reconstruct. In these canzoni we witness an unholy matrimony: on the one hand there are the traces of an event that is already conceived of as miraculous, hyperbolic, and theologized, but on the other hand these innovations are presented against a background whose ideology is still courtly and / or Cavalcantian.

Lo doloroso amor che mi conduce
a·ffin di morte per piacer di quella
che lo mio cor solea tener gioioso,
m'ha tolto e toglie ciascun dì la luce
ch'avean li occhi miei di tale stella
che non credea di lei mai star doglioso;

e 'l colpo suo, c'ho portato nascoso,
omai si scuopre per soverchia pena,
la qual nasce del foco
che m'ha tratto di gioco,
sì·cch'altro mai che male io non aspetto; 11
e 'l viver mio – omai de' esser poco –
fin a la morte mia sospira e dice:
"Per quella moro c'ha nome Beatrice." 14

Quel dolce nome, che mi fa il cor agro,
tutte fiate ch'i' lo vedrò scritto
mi farà nuovo ogni dolor ch'i' sento; 17
e della doglia diverrò sì magro
della persona e 'l viso tanto afflitto
che qual mi vederà n'avrà pavento. 20
E allor non trarrà sì poco vento
che non mi meni, sì ch'io cadrò freddo;
e per tal verrò morto,
e 'l dolor sarà scorto
co·ll'anima che se ·n girà sì trista, 25
e sempre mai co·llei starà ricolto
ricordando la gioia del dolce viso
a che nïente pare il paradiso. 28

Pensando a quel che d'amor ho provato,
l'anima mia non chiede altro diletto,
né il penar non cura il quale attende; 31
ché poi che 'l corpo sarà consumato
se n'anderà l'amor che m'ha sì stretto
co·llei a Quel ch'ogni ragione intende; 34
e se del suo peccar pace no i rende,
partirassi col tormentar ch'è degna,
sì·cche non ne paventa,
e starà tanto attenta
d'inmaginar colei per cui s'è mossa, 39
che nulla pena averà che ella senta;
sì·cche, se 'n questo mo[n]do l'ho perduto,
Amor nell'altro me ·n darà tributo. 42

Morte, che·ffai piacere a questa donna,
per pietà, innanzi che·ttu mi discigli,

va' da·llei, fatti dire
perché m'avien che la luce di quegli
che mi fan tristo mi sia così tolta.
Se per altrui ella fosse ricolta,
fa' ·lmi sentire, e trarra'mi d'errore,
e assai finirò con men dolore.[8]

(The painful love that leads me to my end
in death because a willing act of her
who used to fill my heart with joy
has robbed and robs me still each day of light
my eyes were used to claiming from her star
that made me think she'd never make me sad:
This wound, which I have kept concealed from view,
can now be seen because of my deep pain,
engendered by the fire
that robbed me of my joy,
so that I now expect just pain alone.
My life (what little now remains of it)
will sigh to me right to my death and say:
"I die for her whose name is Beatrice."

The sweet name that embitters so my heart
each time I see it written down someplace
will make the pain I feel renew itself;
I think I will become so changed by grief,
my body wasted and my face distraught,
that those who see me will recoil in fear.
And it will then take but a little breeze
to sweep me off so that I fall down dead;
so that is how I'll die,
my anguish to escort
my sullen soul that must now fade away;
and it will always keep her company,
remembering the joy of her sweet face,
beyond compare of even paradise.

Reflecting on what love has made me feel,
my soul desires no other happiness,
nor will it fear the torment it awaits;
for once my body has been turned to dust,

the love that's bound me so to it will rise
aloft to him who comprehends all things;
and should he grant its sin no amnesty,
it will depart with torments that are just,
but which it does not dread;
it will be so intent
on contemplating her who made it leave
that there will be no pain that it might feel;
and thus if I have lost it in this world,
Love in the other will repay me well.

Death, you who implement this lady's will,
for pity's sake, before you ruin me,
go up to her and ask
why is it that the light of those fair eyes
that sadden me has been withdrawn this way.
If someone else instead receives this light,
end my illusion now by telling me,
so I can suffer death less painfully.)[9]

The beloved lady in *Lo doloroso amor* is explicitly called Beatrice, but the Beatrice in question retains the features of Cavalcanti's lethal lady.[10] From this we can deduce that Dante found the name "Beatrice" before arriving at a final decision on how to take advantage of the meaning of that name. Even more remarkable, the canzone indicates that Dante was originally quite capable of treating the *Vita nuova*'s principle "nomina sunt consequentia rerum" (*Vita nuova* 13.4) ironically and of linking the *nomen* Beatrice to an explicitly nonbeatifying *res*. She is, in fact, not a giver of life but of death: the verse in which Dante names her – the name "Beatrice" is present only here in the lyrics excluded from the *Vita nuova*[11] – is "Per quella moro c'ha nome Beatrice" (14; I die for her whose name is Beatrice). Here Dante does not name Beatrice casually, as he names Violetta, Fioretta, or Lisetta, other ladies in his lyrics; rather, he records her name as the structural equivalent of his own death. The extraordinary verse in which he does so – "Per quella moro c'ha nome Beatrice" (14) – is the concluding verse of the first stanza.

When, in *Purgatorio* 27, Dante writes of "il nome che ne la mente sempre mi rampolla" (41–2; the name that's always flowering within my mind), we should think, apropos the "always" in "*sempre* rampolla," of *Lo doloroso amor*: the first recorded flowering of the name "Beatrice" in Dante's mind occurs in this early canzone. But this is a perverse flowering, for in the canzone we learn that though the name of Beatrice may be sweet, yet it makes his heart bitter, and he experiences this bitterness every time that he sees it written (interesting proof of the intense writerliness of our poet, confirmed by the supporting metaphor of the self as glossator in the *Vita nuova*): "Quel dolce nome che mi fa il cor agro, / tutte fïate ch'i' lo vedrò scritto / mi farà nuovo ogni dolor ch'i' sento" (15–17; The sweet name that embitters so my heart / each time I see it written down someplace / will make the pain I feel renew itself). These verses begin the second stanza, and they underline the concluding message of the preceding stanza. In the event that the reader did not sufficiently grasp verse fourteen's affirmation regarding the name that does not function as it ought to, the *incipit* of the second stanza reinforces the antithesis *Beatrice / moro* with the chiasmus *dolce-nome / cor-agro*, which underlines it.

Dante places this play *in malo* on the name "Beatrice" in a position of high relief, in the concluding verse of the first stanza. The first stanza provides in this way a model that will serve for the whole canzone, insofar as it will be typical of *Lo doloroso amor* to begin the stanzas in a fairly conventional manner and then to conclude them with material that is more hyperbolic than normal, more theologized. Thus the first stanza begins with a sorrowful love, conventionally lethal, that is retroactively radicalized by the introduction of the name "Beatrice" in the final verse. That the poet suffers from a "doloroso amor che mi conduce / a·ffin di morte per piacer di quella / che lo mio cor solea tener gioioso" (1–3; painful love that leads me to my end / in death because a willing act of her / who used to fill my heart with joy) is not particularly notable; nor is it notable that the effect of the lady on the lover is antithetical to her *senhal* (think of Guittone's *bella gioia*, who brings him so much *noia*). What is notable is the radicalization of these conventional motifs brought about by their contamination with theological motifs, as happens through the introduction of the name "Beatrice."

From this point of view, *Lo doloroso amor* anticipates *Donne ch'avete intelletto d'amore*, where a conventionally erotic discourse is also projected onto a theological backdrop and in this way radically transformed. The major difference between *Lo doloroso amor* and *Donne ch'avete* is that in the first canzone the theologized material is used in a systematically deviant manner: in this perverse variant of the *Vita nuova* (a label that can be applied even more rigorously to *E' m'incresce di me*), "nomina NON sunt consequentia rerum" and Beatrice is not a principle of life but of death. *Lo doloroso amor* and *E' m'incresce di me* give the impression that Dante posed himself the problem of making the sum Guinizzelli +

Cavalcanti to see what the result would be: to the Guinizzellian strategy of theologizing the erotic-courtly code is added the theme of lethal love presented in a hyper-Cavalcantian key (and in fact not even Guido addresses a *congedo* to "Morte," as Dante does uniquely in *Lo doloroso amor*).

The second stanza of *Lo doloroso amor* prolongs the initial antithesis ("Quel dolce nome che mi fa il cor agro") with the idea that the name of the lady will give the lover not new life and hope but instead (in a motif that will be dear to Petrarch) renewed pain: "mi farà nuovo ogni dolor ch'i' sento" (17). The suffering continues as the dominant motif in a canzone that opens with "Lo doloroso amor che mi conduce / a·ffin di morte" and that closes when the lover imagines himself having arrived at the death to which love has led him: the circle closes as it opened, and the last word of *Lo doloroso amor* is "dolore."

In the second stanza, where the lover is still continuing the journey towards the death addressed in the *congedo*, the poet documents the afflictions that consume him, leaving him "sì magro / della persona" (18–19; my body [so] wasted) that "non trarrà sì poco vento / che non mi meni, sì ch'io cadrò freddo" (21–2; and it will then take but a little breeze / to sweep me off so that I fall down dead [literally, so that I fall down cold]). These verses, which include the only occurrence in Dante's lyrics of *magro* (or its variant *macro*), will be remembered in the *Commedia*: in the *Paradiso*, it is the "poema sacro," rather than *doloroso amor*, "che m'ha fatto per molti anni macro" (*Par.* 25.1–3; sacred poem ... that made me thin through many years). In the context of paradise, thinness assumes the odour not of sexual passion but of holiness: St Peter and St Paul are "magri e scalzi" (*Par.* 21.128; thin and barefoot). In the canto of *Inferno* dedicated to lust, we find instead a situation similar to that of our canzone. The "bufera infernal" that "mena li spirti" (*Inf.* 5.31–2; infernal whirlwind [that] drives the spirits) echoes the "vento / che non mi meni" of *Lo doloroso amor*, and the concluding verse, "E caddi come corpo morto cade" (*Inf.* 5.142; and I fell as a dead body falls), recalls "sì ch'io cadrò freddo" of the canzone. Moreover, the first verses of our canzone, "Lo doloroso *amor* che mi *conduce* / a·ffin di *morte* per *piacer* di quella," are echoed in Francesca's celebrated verses: in "mi prese del costui *piacer* sì forte" (*Inf.* 5.104; seized me with his beauty so strongly) and above all in "*Amor condusse* noi ad una *morte*" (*Inf.* 5.106; Love led us to one death), which strips away "doloroso" and "a·ffin" to arrive at the essential building blocks of *amore*, *condurre*, and *morte*. *Lo doloroso amor* and its companion canzone, *E' m'incresce di me*, where these building blocks are also present,[12] served as incubators for an ideology that Dante will reject, but to which he will also give voice through Francesca, whose culminating

"Amor condusse noi ad una morte" is imprinted on the opening of *Lo doloroso amor* syntactically, lexically, and above all ideologically.

It is curious that this same second strophe of *Lo doloroso amor*, which endures in the memory of the great eschatological poem that is the *Commedia*, should conclude by introducing into the canzone its own erotic eschatology. Here Dante follows in the footsteps of Giacomo da Lentini (thus also recalling the canzone *La dispietata mente*, which also engages in significant dialogue with the Sicilian poet), whose sonnet *Io m'aggio posto in core a Dio servire* avails itself of the *paradiso / viso* rhyme and makes it emblematic of the interior struggle of the poet, who feels *diviso* between God ("Io m'aggio posto in core a Dio servire, / com'io potesse gire in *paradiso*" [1–2; I placed it in my heart to serve God, so that I might go to paradise]) and his lady ("Sanza mi *donna* non vi voria gire, / quella c'à blonda testa e claro viso" [5–6; Without my lady I wouldn't want to go, she of the blonde head and bright face]). Using the same *paradiso / viso* rhyme used by Giacomo to indicate the same internal division, Dante openly declares that paradise is worth nothing in comparison with the memory of the sweet face of his lady: "ricordando la gioia del dolce *viso* / a che nïente pare il *paradiso*" (27–8; remembering the joy of her lovely face / against which paradise seems nothing).

And that is not all: the third and last strophe of *Lo doloroso amor* delineates the drama of the lover against a backdrop that is more and more exaggeratedly eschatological and theologized. Here the poet takes up again the dilemma of Giacomo, *diviso* – the dilemma of the courtly world – and in the strongest and most explicit manner aligns himself not on the side of God but on that of the lady: "Pensando a quel che d'amor ho provato," the poet declares that "l'anima mia non chiede altro diletto" (29–30; Reflecting on what love has made me feel, / my soul desires no other happiness). Further, the love that he felt in life protects him from fear of the beyond ("né il penar non cura il quale attende" [31; nor will it fear the torment it awaits]), since when he dies, love will accompany his soul to God. The phrase "l'*amor* che m'ha sì *stretto*" (33; the love that's bound me so to it), which in the canzone is rhymed with "l'anima mia non chiede altro *diletto*" (30), constitutes another echo of *Lo doloroso amor* destined for the fifth canto of *Inferno*, where we find the proximity of "diletto" not with the past participle of *stringere* ("stretto") but with the *passato remoto* "strinse": "Noi leggiavamo un giorno per diletto / di Lancialotto come *amor* lo *strinse*" (127–8; We were reading one day, for pleasure, of Lancelot and how Love bound him).

In the third strophe, Dante creates a perverse variant of the famous *congedo* of Guido Guinizzelli's *Al cor gentil rimpaira sempre amore*, where the Bolognese poet imagines having to justify his love for his lady before a divine tribunal, declaring: "Tenne d'angel sembianza / che fosse del Tuo regno; / non me fu fallo, s'in lei posi amanza" (58–60; She had an angelic look, as if from your kingdom; it was no fault in me, if I placed my love in her). Here the theologizing of the amorous discourse serves to elevate the earthly (the "vano amor" of which God accuses the poet) towards the divine and thus to exculpate the poet: it is not a "fault" to love the lady precisely because she belongs to the divine kingdom; indeed, if fault exists, it is God's, who created women so similar to the angels of his kingdom. But even if Guinizzelli indulges in the daring game of throwing back at the Creator the accusation that was leveled at himself, we still remain in a context in which God – not the lady – is the point of reference.

In *Lo doloroso amor*, Dante inverts the terms, making the lady the point of reference instead. The poet details the situation of his soul, which has, as in Guinizzelli's *congedo*, arrived before the divine tribunal: if God does not pardon the soul its sins, it will depart with the punishments it deserves ("e se del suo peccar pace no i rende, / partirassi col tormentar ch'è degna" [35–6; and should he grant its sin no amnesty, / it will depart with torments that are just]), but in such a way as to not be afraid ("sì·cche non ne paventa" [37; but which it does not dread]). How can it be that the soul of the poet will not be afraid of the punishments of hell? Because, in another reprise of Giacomo, this time of the Sicilian topos of the image of the lady painted in the heart of the lover, the poet explains that his soul will be so intent on imagining his lady that it will not feel any pain: "e starà tanto attenta / d'inmaginar colei per cui s'è mossa, / che nulla pena averà che ella senta" (38–40; it will be so intent / on contemplating her who made it leave / that there will be no pain that it might feel).

In an overturning of the normative hierarchy between Creator and creature, here the poet makes the lady the absolute point of reference of his universe. She is, in fact, "colei per cui [l'anima sua] s'è mossa" (39), the one for whom his soul set forth on the path of desire: the journey of his life, the journey towards the death described by the canzone, the spiritual motion of his soul – all of it is as a function of her, defined as "colei per cui s'è mossa." Intent and concentrated on imagining his lady, the poet will be immunized to the punishments of hell, pains that in fact he will not even feel. The old topos of the *guiderdone* finds in these verses a new and eschatological vitality: here finally is the true recompense lavished by Love on the faithful! If Love was sparing with him in this life, "'n questo mo[n]do" (41), it will instead be generous in the next: "sì·cche se 'n questo mo[n]do i' l'ho perduto, / Amor nell'altro me ·n darà tributo" (41–2; and thus if I have lost it in this world, / Love in the other will repay me well).

The importance of *Lo doloroso amor* derives in great part from the strong eschatological bent of this last strophe, by the underlined contrast between this world and the other world: "questo mondo" and "l'altro [mondo]." Dante is here experimenting with the same theologized elements, of Guinizzellian heritage, that will make the style of *Donne ch'avete intelletto d'amore* "new." But, given the sorrowful theme of *Lo doloroso amor*, these elements here take on a perverse and nonnormative colouring.

The eschatological elements in *Lo doloroso amor* have a history in Dante's repertory, one that extends beyond *Inferno* 5 all the way to the seventh canto of *Paradiso*, where we find the same combination of the name of Beatrice, first divided "pur per *Be* e *ice*" (*Par.* 7.14) and then written whole in verse 16, with the hyperbole of the lover who does not feel the punishments of hell:

> Ma quella reverenza che s'indonna
> di tutto me, pur per *Be* e per *ice*,
> mi richinava come l'uom ch'assonna.
> Poco sofferse me cotal Beatrice
> e cominciò, raggiandomi d'un riso
> tal, che nel foco faria l'uom felice ... (*Par.* 7.13–18)

> (But that reverence that lords over all of me, even just with *Be* and with *ice*, made me bow like a man falling asleep. Beatrice didn't leave me in this state for long, and she began, shining on me with the rays of such a smile as would make a man happy in the fire.)

Here are the vestiges of *Lo doloroso amor*: the courtly world invoked in the neologism "s'indonna," a verb denoting "to lord over someone as feudal mistress or *donna*" (*Par.* 7.13); the name made sign by the division into syllables, *Be* and *ice*, as though "written," as stipulated in the words of *Lo doloroso amor*, "Quel dolce nome che mi fa il cor agro, / tutte fïate ch'i' lo *vedrò scritto*" (15–16); and above all the description of the lady's smiling countenance, capable of immunizing her lover from the pains of hell: "un riso / tal, che nel foco faria l'uom felice" (*Par.* 7.17–18).

Lo doloroso amor is important in reconstructing Dante's ideological path because its key verse, "Per quella moro c'ha nome Beatrice" (14), is antithetical to the values of the poet who Dante became, whose epigraph could well be "Per quella vivo c'ha nome Beatrice." *Lo doloroso amor* thus executes an ideological oxymoron: it anticipates on the one hand the Beatrician and theologized *Vita nuova* and on the other the fatal love of the *rime petrose*, as though the lethal lady of the *rime petrose* were called not "stone" but "she who makes happy, she who gives *beatitudine*." The extremism of *Lo doloroso amor* lies in its commingling of elements that will be antithetical in the Dantean universe as ultimately scripted.

In conclusion, a note on the transmission of *Lo doloroso amor*. In this most existential of contexts, that of the poem's material transmission, *Lo doloroso amor* holds a very particular position, one of precarious marginality with respect to Dante's other canzoni. *Lo doloroso amor* is, as De Robertis notes, "estravagante tra le estravaganti" (an outsider among the outsiders),[13] and in fact the history of its transmission is the history of its absence. As I noted earlier, this canzone was not a part of the fortunate group of fifteen canzoni copied by Boccaccio, a group destined to be transmitted as a corpus in their Boccaccian order. Excluded from Boccaccio's *canzoni distese*, *Lo doloroso amor* was then excluded from the first printed edition of Dante's lyrics, the Giuntina of 1527.[14] Given its exclusion from what De Robertis calls "la grande tradizione" of Dante's lyric poems, *Lo doloroso amor* has had a less privileged transmission than Dante's other canzoni: "The codices, for this canzone, are not counted in the hundreds as for the other canzoni, or in tens, if we count, as we must, the vast Boccaccian tradition as a single witness (but one with enormous influence for almost two centuries); rather they are counted on the fingers of one hand."[15] The absence of *Lo doloroso amor* from Boccaccio's *canzoni distese* has thus contributed to its marginal position, a marginality ironically reified by De Robertis in his recent edition, as though *Lo doloroso amor* were less canonical, less Dante's canzone, than the others.

It is difficult to repress the suspicion that it is precisely the verse "Per quella moro c'ha nome Beatrice" that created strong doubts in the copyists, including Boccaccio, and in this way damaged the transmission of the canzone that contains it. If that were the case, one could say that in a certain sense the copyists showed themselves to be shrewd readers. They understood – and attempted to eliminate – the challenge posed by *Lo doloroso amor* to the dominant myth of his persona that Dante so ably constructed and passed on to posterity.

E' m'incresce di me sì duramente,
ch'altrettanto di doglia
mi reca la pietà quanto 'l martiro,
lasso, però che dolorosamente
sento contra mia voglia
raccoglier l'aire del sezzaio sospiro
entro 'n quel cor che' belli occhi feriro
quando li aperse Amor co· le sue mani
per conducermi al tempo che mi sface.
Oïmè, quanto piani,
soavi e dolci ver' me si levaro
quand'elli incominciaro
la morte mia, che tanto mi dispiace,
dicendo: "Nostro lume porta pace."

"Noi darem pace al core, a voi diletto"
diceano agli occhi miei
quei della bella donna alcuna volta;
ma poi che sepper di loro intelletto
che per forza di lei
m'era la mente già ben tutta tolta,
co· le 'nsegne d'Amor dieder la volta;
sì che la lor vittorïosa vista
poi non si vide pur una fïata:
ond'è rimasa trista
l'anima mia che n'attendea conforto;
ed ora quasi morto
vede lo core a cui era sposata,
e partir la conviene innamorata.

Innamorata se ne va piangendo
fora di questa vita
la sconsolata, che la caccia Amore.
Ella si move quinci sì dolendo,
ch'anzi la sua partita
l'ascolta con pietate il suo Fattore.
Ristretta s'è entro 'l mezzo del core
con quella vita che rimane spenta
solo in quel punto ch'ella se ·n va via,
ed ivi si lamenta
d'Amor che for d'esto mondo la caccia,

e spessamente abraccia
li spiriti che piangon tuttavia,
però che perdon la lor compagnia.

L'imagine di questa donna siede
sù nella mente ancora,
là ove la puose quei che fu sua guida;
e non le pesa del mal ch'ella vede,
anzi vie più bella ora
che mai e vie più lieta par che rida,
ed alza gli occhi micidiali, e grida
sovra colei che piange il suo partire:
"Vanne, misera, fuor, vattene omai!"
Questo grida il disire
che mi combatte così come suole,
avegna che men duole,
però che 'l mio sentire è meno assai
ed è più presso al terminar de' guai.

Lo giorno che costei nel mondo venne,
secondo che si truova
nel libro della mente che vien meno,
la mia persona pargola sostenne
una passïon nova,
tal ch'io rimasi di paura pieno;
ch'a tutte mie virtù fu posto un freno
subitamente, sì ch'io caddi in terra
per una luce che nel cuor percosse;
e se 'l libro non erra,
lo spirito maggior tremò sì forte
che parve ben che morte
per lui in questo mondo giunta fosse;
ma or ne 'ncresce a quei che questo mosse.

Quando m'aparve poi la gran biltate
che sì mi fa dolere,
donne gentili a cui i' ho parlato,
quella virtù c'ha più nobilitate,
mirando nel piacere,
s'accorse ben che 'l suo male era nato;
e conobbe il disio ch'era creato

per lo mirare intento ch'ella fece,
sì che piangendo disse a l'altre poi:
"Qui giugnerà, in vece
d'una ch'i' vidi, la bella figura
che già mi fa paura,
che sarà donna sopra tutte noi
tosto che fia piacer degli occhi suoi."

I' ho parlato a voi, giovani donne
ch'avete gli occhi di bellezze ornati
e la mente d'amor vinta e pensosa,
perché raccomandati
vi sian li detti miei ovunque sono;
e 'nnanzi a voi perdono
la morte mia a quella bella cosa
che me n'ha colpa e mai non fu pietosa.

(I feel such deep compassion for myself
that pity makes me bear
in equal measure sorrow and great pain,
and so excruciatingly, alas,
I feel unwillingly
the final sigh swell up within my heart
that those alluring eyes of hers struck hard
when Love with his own hands first opened them
to lead me to the hour of my demise.
How gentle and how kind,
how tender was the look that they displayed
the day they undertook
to bring about my death, so painfully,
and said to me: "Our light will bring you peace."

"We'll bring peace to your heart, and joy to you,"
her eyes said to my eyes,
the ones my lady used to show at times;
but once they knew, by their own reasoning,
that through her power my mind
had been entirely torn away from me,
they turned and fled beneath Love's gonfalon,
so that the look they had in victory
was never to be seen again, not once:

and so my soul now grieves
when it expected comfort from their light,
and must now look upon
my heart near death, to which it once was wed,
and has to take its leave still full of love.

Still full of love my soul, disconsolate,
departs this life of ours
with tears of sorrow, driven out by Love.
In going forth it suffers so much pain
that, just before it leaves,
its Maker hears its plea with sympathy.
The soul retreats inside the inner heart
to join what little life remains to fade
the very instant that it takes its leave.
And there it censures Love,
who forces it to leave this world behind,
embracing more than once
the spirits that lament unceasingly
the painful loss of its sweet company.

The image of this lady still holds sway
within my intellect,
where it was placed by him who was her guide.
But it's not troubled by the harm it sees,
indeed she's lovelier
than in the past and smiles with greater joy;
and as she raises up her murderous eyes,
she castigates my soul that weeps for death:
"Get out of here, you wretch, now go away."
Such words desire speaks,
assailing me as it has always done,
though now the pain is less
because my power to feel is less intense
and is far closer to the end of woe.

The day on which she came into this world,
according to the book
of memory that falters more and more,
my youthful body was subjected to
a feeling so unusual

I sank into a state of fearfulness;
and it arrested all my faculties
so suddenly I fell right to the ground,
because a light had pierced me in the heart:
and if this book is right,
the greater spirit trembled with such force
that it became quite clear
that death was just about to claim its life.
But he who did ordain this now repents.

When I first saw her wondrous loveliness
that brings such pain to me,
dear noble ladies who've now heard me speak,
the faculty that stands above the rest,
while gazing on her face,
perceived that its affliction had been born
and recognized the yearning brought to life
by having gazed on her so steadfastly;
and so it told the other faculties, in tears:
"In place of her I saw
will come the lovely image of that one,
which I already fear
and who will reign as mistress of us all,
as soon as it is pleasing to her eyes."

Young ladies, I have spoken now to you,
whose eyes hold beauty as an ornament
and who are ruled by painful thoughts of love,
in order that my poem
commend itself to you where it is heard:
before you, I forgive
that lovely one for having caused my death,
who bears all blame, yet never showed me pity.)

Whether or not as a result of its scandalous thematic content, *Lo doloroso amor* experienced an anomalous reception with respect to the group of heavily anthologized and thus more fully "canonical" canzoni. In the case of *E' m'incresce di me*, such marginalization does not occur, but this canzone, also sorrowful, also theologized (if anything, even more theologized, with features that approach the *Vita nuova*), joins its fellow in the ability to provoke scholarly anxiety. Such anxiety was expressed in the futile *querelle* on the identity of the murderous lady of *E' m'incresce di me*, and in the prolonged refusal to concede the obvious: that this lady is Beatrice.[16] This occurred because *E' m'incresce di me* does not contain a verse, like "Per quella moro c'ha nome Beatrice" (*Lo doloroso amor*, 14; I die for her whose name is Beatrice), that renders the identity of the lethal lady undeniable.

In any case, exegetes concur with Barbi's formulation according to which, like *Lo doloroso amor*, *E' m'incresce di me* "should be placed in the period of strong love, of painful love, a love represented in the *Vita nuova* only by the four sonnets of chapters XIII–XVI."[17]

E' m'incresce di me begins in a strongly Cavalcantian key, delineating the self-pity that the lover feels for himself because of the death inflicted on him by his lady's eyes, eyes that will be protagonists throughout the canzone. In this primordial moment of the drama, they are "belli occhi" (7; alluring eyes) that seem "piani, / soavi e dolci" (10–11; gentle, kind, and tender); but later they will be "occhi micidiali" (49; murderous eyes), and in the last stanza her dominion will be sealed by a gaze bestowed by those same eyes: "che sarà donna sopra tutte noi / tosto che fia piacer degli occhi suoi" (83–4; who will reign as mistress of us all, / as soon as it is pleasing to her eyes). If in the first stanza her eyes "incominciaro / la morte mia" (12–13; undertook / to bring about my death), in the second they leave him for dead on the battlefield that is love. From the moment that the lady's eyes take in their victory "di loro intelletto" (18; by their own reasoning), demonstrating an "intelletto d'amore" of a very different order than that possessed by the ladies of *Donne ch'avete intelletto d'amore* they depart with the banners of Love, with the result that "è rimasa trista / l'anima mia che n'attendea conforto" (24–5; my soul now grieves / when it expected comfort). The abandoned soul is the protagonist of the third stanza, where it is depicted as dejected, crying, and disconsolate, in a typically Cavalcantian register: "Innamorata se ne va piangendo / for di questa vita / la sconsolata, che la caccia Amore" (29–31; Still full of love my soul, disconsolate, / departs this life of ours / with tears of sorrow, driven out by Love). The Cavalcantian tone, melancholic and elegiac, is prolonged for the whole third strophe:

Ristretta s'è entro 'l mezzo del core
con quella vita che rimane spenta
solo in quel punto ch'ella se· n va via,
ed ivi si lamenta
d'Amor che for d'esto mondo la caccia,

e spessamente abraccia
li spiriti che piangon tuttavia,
però che perdon la lor compagnia. (*E' m'incresce di me*, 35–42)

(The soul retreats inside the inner heart
to join what little life remains to fade
the very instant that it takes its leave.
And there it censures Love,
who forces it to leave this world behind,
embracing more than once
the spirits that lament unceasingly
the painful loss of its sweet company.)

In the third stanza we note the recurrence of the verb *cacciare*, used twice to denote existential exile in a context of markedly Cavalcantian register: the soul is literally hunted "out of this life" ("fora di questa vita / la sconsolata, che la *caccia* Amore," 30–1) and "out of this world" by Love ("ed ivi si lamenta / d'Amor che for d'esto mondo la *caccia*," 38–9). If the exilic locutions "fora di questa vita" and "for d'esto mondo" are of a Cavalcantian timbre, the verb *cacciare* is not; to the contrary, it imports into the Cavalcantian melancholy a vitality and robustness that are instead very Dantean and anticipates the idiosyncratically and innovatively Dantean tone of the fourth and fifth stanzas.

Moreover, the double presence of the verb *cacciare* in the third stanza of *E' m'incresce di me* has a bearing on the complex drama between Dante and his "primo amico," Guido Cavalcanti. One wonders if Dante, writing in *Purgatorio* of Guido Guinizzelli, Guido Cavalcanti, and himself that "così ha tolto l'uno a l'altro Guido / la gloria de la lingua; e forse è nato / chi l'uno e l'altro *caccerà* del nido" (*Purg.* 11.97–9; thus has one Guido taken from the other the glory of our language, and perhaps he is born who will chase one and the other from the nest), and using the verb *cacciare* to designate himself as the one who will aggressively chase ("caccerà") Guinizzelli and Cavalcanti from the poetic nest, did not recall what is plausibly his first use of the verb, in the youthful Cavalcantian canzone *E' m'incresce di me*.[18] Certainly a Love that "hunts" breaks with Cavalcanti, who never uses the verb *cacciare* in his love poems. Interestingly, Guido uses *cacciare* only in two correspondence sonnets, one to Guido Orlandi and the other precisely to Dante, the sonnet *I' vegno 'l giorno a te*, in which he harshly reproves his friend for "la vil tua vita" and concludes in this way: "Se 'l presente sonetto spesso leggi, / lo spirito noioso che·tti *caccia* / si partirà dall'anima invilita" (12–14; If you read the present sonnet often, the noisome spirit that chases you will depart from your vilified soul). Perhaps this rather aggressive suggestion on the part of his friend in a poem addressed to him is what Dante remembered as he penned his own aggressive verses in *Purgatorio* 11.

E' m'incresce di me is divided into two halves of three strophes each, as the narrative emphasis shifts from the lover to the lady, or, in Contini's words, "from a subjective, internal point of view" to "an objective, historical point of view."[19] The fourth stanza opens with the imposing figure of the victorious lady who installs herself in the mind of the lover (the word *mente* will be used four times in *E' m'incresce di me*, more than in any other of Dante's poems; here it anticipates the "libro della mente" of the next stanza): "L'imagine di questa donna siede / sù nella mente ancora" (43–4; The image of this lady still holds sway / within my intellect). Onto the scene erupts a lady-assassin who "raises up her murderous eyes" (49; alza gli occhi micidiali) and celebrates her absolute dominion with a shout, whose sadistic content is registered through the immediacy of direct discourse: "e *grida* / sovra colei che piange il suo partire: / 'Vanne, misera, fuor, vattene omai'" (49–51; she castigates my soul that weeps for death: / "Get out of here, you wretch, now go away").[20] The verb *gridare*, which Dante uses again in the following verse ("Questo *grida* il disire" [52; Such words desire speaks]), could not be less Cavalcantian, literally, given that Cavalcanti never uses it. The same could be said of the adjective *micidiale* used by Dante for the "occhi micidiali" of the lady, another word that does not appear in the more restricted diction – calmer, more resigned – of Cavalcanti.

The fourth stanza of *E' m'incresce di me* marks the birth of a new poetics of passion. Moving away from the calm, rational desperation of Cavalcanti, Dante here is inventing the diction and the register of erotic aggression that he will exploit with so much success in the *rime petrose*, in the prose treatises, and ultimately in the *Commedia*: passion and aggression are essential to Dante's poetics. Dante is as hot and impassioned, even when dealing with the intellect, as Cavalcanti is detached and cold, even – above all – when dealing with passion. The verb *gridare* and the adjective *micidiale* appear together in *E' m'incresce di me* and again in the most aggressive of the *petrose*, *Così nel mio parlar*, in which the lover struggles with a lady who is "micidiale e latra" (58; murderous and thieving).

At this point, it might seem that Dante had already accomplished enough in this canzone, but in fact it is the fifth stanza that moves the poet most significantly along his poetic itinerary. The fifth stanza of

E' m'incresce di me is essentially a trial run for the *Vita nuova*, in the sense that the lady, this same aggressive, cruel, and lethal lady, will be presented as a being who is special and miraculous in absolute terms, not only within the subjectivity of the lover but objectively and historically. Situating his narration on a stage that now encompasses the whole world, the poet takes an enormous step backwards in history in order to return to the day of the birth of his lady and to the effects of this birth on his child's body. He says that he is able to read these effects "in the book of memory" (nel libro della mente):

Lo giorno che costei nel mondo venne,
secondo che si truova
nel libro della mente che vien meno,
la mia persona pargola sostenne
una passïon nova,
tal ch'io rimasi di paura pieno. (*E' m'incresce di me*, 57–62)

(The day on which she came into this world,
according to the book
of memory that falters more and more,
my youthful body was subjected to
a feeling so unusual
I sank into a state of fearfulness.)

Here, in stanza five of *E' m'incresce di me*, we see elements of the miraculous and theologized history of the *Vita nuova* still linked syntactically to the Cavalcantian love that provokes fear and death. For instance, in verse 59, "nel libro della mente che vien meno," the image of the "libro della mente," which before too long will adorn the prose opening of the *Vita nuova*, is destabilized by the Cavalcantian faltering of "vien meno"; similarly, the "passïon nova" that the lover feels is not such as to cause ecstasy but "such that I remained full of fear" (61–2; tal ch'io rimasi di paura pieno). If on the one hand the poem affirms, as does the *Vita nuova*, an experience that is absolutely new and different, that can miraculously make itself felt by the child's body of the poet in the moment of her birth, on the other hand it is still about a passion that causes fear and trembling and that carries the soul towards death:

e se 'l libro non erra,
lo spirito maggior tremò sì forte

che parve ben che morte
per lui in questo mondo giunta fosse;
ma or ne 'ncresce a quei che questo mosse. (*E' m'increse di me*, 66–70)

(And if this book is right,
the greater spirit trembled with such force
that it became quite clear
that death was just about to claim its life.
But he who did ordain this now repents.)

In the last verse of the fifth stanza, the death of the self awakens pity in the ordainer of these events, God, ("or ne 'ncresce a quei che questo mosse"), already invoked in verse 34, where "ascolta con pietate il suo Fattore" (34; its Maker hears its plea with sympathy). *E' m'increse di me* thus moves from self-pity in its first verse to God's pity: Dante's field has broadened. But she who is born with such cosmic effects in *E' m'increse di me* is not yet the Beatrice of *Donne ch'avete intelletto d'amore*; to the contrary, in this canzone the intellective faculty of the lover realizes "che 'l suo male era nato" (76; its affliction had been born). We are still dealing with the Beatrice of *Lo doloroso amor*, of whom the poet wrote "Per quella moro c'ha nome Beatrice" (14). The canzoni *Lo doloroso amor* and *E' m'increse di me* are evidence of an interior drama: they show that the road Dante followed to arrive at the Beatrice of the *Vita nuova* was far from overdetermined. Dante experimented with various formulas, and *E' m'increse di me* was one of these experimentations, a canzone in which the poet combines Cavalcanti's lethal love with a new erotic aggression all Dante's own and then sets the whole drama in a cosmic and supernatural frame. The result is a fascinating, ideological aporia: a lady who is miraculous but also Cavalcantian.

NOTES

1 See *Rime*, ed. M. Barbi, in *Le opere di Dante: testo critico della Società Dantesca Italiana* (Florence: Bemporad, 1921), followed by the posthumous commentary, *Rime della "Vita Nuova" e della giovinezza*, ed. M. Barbi and F. Maggini (Florence: Le Monnier, 1956).
2 *Rime*, ed. G. Contini (Turin: Einaudi, 1946; repr. 1965), 67.
3 *Dante's Lyric Poetry*, ed. K. Foster and P. Boyde, 2 vols. (Oxford: Oxford University Press, 1967).

4 For a more detailed discussion of the editorial history, see the introduction to *Rime giovanili e della "Vita Nuova,"* ed. T. Barolini (Milan: Rizzoli, 2009), 6–40.

5 See the introduction to my commentary for the implications regarding authorial order that can be derived from these hybrids. The *Commedia* too can qualify as a hybrid because of Dante's insertion of the *incipit*s from three of his lyrics.

6 G. Tanturli has promoted the idea that the collection of fifteen *canzoni* existed before Boccaccio; see Tanturli, "L'edizione critica delle *Rime* e il libro delle canzoni di Dante," *Studi danteschi* 68 (2003): 250–66.

7 On this theme and for an examination of Cavalcantianism among Dante's lyrics and beyond, see my essay "Dante and Guido Cavalcanti (On Making Distinctions in Matters of Love): *Inferno* 5 in its Lyric and Autobiographical Context," *Dante Studies* 116 (1998): 31–63; repr. in *Dante and the Origins of Italian Literary Culture* (New York: Fordham University Press, 2006), 70–101.

8 The texts of the canzoni *Lo doloroso amor* and *E' m'incresce di me* are taken from the edition of Dante Alighieri, *Rime*, ed. D. De Robertis, 3 pts., 5 vols., *Le opere di Dante Alighieri*, Edizione Nazionale, ed. Società Dantesca Italiana (Florence: Le Lettere, 2002). The five volumes (technically, three parts consisting of five *tomi*) are not paginated sequentially throughout. Rather, part I, *I documenti*, consists of two *tomi* (volumes) comprising one unit; part II, *Introduzione*, consists of two *tomi* comprising a second unit; and part III, *Testi*, consists of one *tomo* comprising a third unit. Most of my citations of De Robertis in this essay come from vol. 2 of *Introduzione*, where the critical material is located.

9 These original translations of *Lo doloroso amor* and *E' m'incresce di me* are by R. Lansing, whose translations of the *rime* will accompany the poems in *Dante's Lyric Poetry: Poems of Youth and of the "Vita Nuova,"* ed. and comm. T. Barolini (Toronto: University of Toronto Press, 2014).

10 Hence De Robertis comments that *Lo doloroso amor* is "testimone fondamentale della dialettica beatitudine / non-beatitudine, nonché dell'avvicinamento alla *Vita Nova*" (II, 2:1152).

11 In the lyrics that do not belong to the *Vita nuova*, the name "Beatrice" appears only in *Lo doloroso amor*; in those belonging to the *Vita nuova* it appears twice in the canzone *Li occhi dolenti* and once in the sonnet *Oltre la spera*, while the sonnet *Deh pellegrini* contains the noun "beatrice." The diminutive "Bice" appears only in the sonnet *Io mi senti' svegliar*, placed in the *Vita nuova*.

12 *E' m'incresce di me* offers verses that use the building blocks *amore*, *condurre*, and *morte* exactly as in the opening of *Lo doloroso amor*, although here *morte* is described by periphrasis as "il tempo che

mi sface": "quando li aperse Amor co· le sue mani / per conducermi al tempo che mi sface" (*E' m'incresce di me*, 8–9). These building blocks appear again in the lyrics only in a poem that is constructed as the precise antithesis to *Lo doloroso amor*, the canzone *Amor che movi tua vertù dal cielo*, where we find a virtuous "disio che mi conduce" (20). In *Amor che movi*, the poet prays to Love *not* to permit the situation delineated in *Lo doloroso amor*: "non soffrir che costei / per giovanezza mi conduca a morte" (56–7).

13 See De Robertis, *Rime*, II, 2:756. In the field of Dantean philology, the word *estravagante* is used to refer to poems not included in the *Vita nuova* or the *Convivio*, poems viewed as being kept "outside," constrained by authorial exclusion to wander without a home. See my essay "Editing Dante's *Rime* and Italian Cultural History," 2004, repr. *Dante and the Origins of Italian Literary Culture*, 245–80, for a discussion of the term *estravagante* applied to Dante's lyrics. I do not believe it to be at all "neutral" and "philological" but rather a witness to cultural issues embedded within *filologia dantesca*.

14 The name Giuntina refers to the collection of *Sonetti e canzoni di diversi antichi autori toscani* (*Sonnets and canzoni of diverse ancient Tuscan authors*), printed by the publishing house of the Giunti brothers in Florence in 1527. The Giuntina, as it is known in the critical literature, is the first printed edition of the lyrics of Dante and other "antichi autori toscani."

15 "I codici, per questa canzone, non si contano a centinaia come per le altre, a decine comunque facendo della copiosissima tradizione boccaccesca, come si deve, un'unica testimonianza (ma, s'è detto, con una sua voce in capitolo per quasi due secoli), bensì sulle dita di una mano" (De Robertis, *Rime*, II, 2:1152).

16 See Barbi, *Le opere di Dante*, 244–56.

17 "La canzone va posta nel periodo dell'amor forte, dell'amor doloroso, della quale nella *Vita Nuova* furono accolti soltanto i quattro sonetti dei capitoli XIII–XVI" (Barbi-Maggini, *Rime*, 256).

18 The use of *cacciare* in the *Commedia* that most recalls the early use in *E' m'incresce di me* describes the soul of Boethius, driven from its body: "Lo corpo ond' ella fu cacciata giace / giuso in Cieldauro" (*Par.* 10.127–8; The body from which she was driven lies below in Cieldauro). Except for a use of *scacciare* in the sonnet *Onde venite voi così pensose?* ("sì·mm'ha in tutto Amor da·ssé *scacciato*," 10), the other uses both of the verb *cacciare* and of the noun *caccia* in Dante's lyrics come from more mature poems. In the canzone *Amor che movi tua vertù dal cielo*, the poet describes the actions

of Love, as in *E' m'incresce di me*, but as a Love that acts not cruelly but virtuously: "tu *cacci* la viltà altrui del core" (7). In the sonnet to Cino, *I' ho veduto già senza radice*, Dante advises his friend not to pursue the "giovane donna": "parmi che·lla tua *caccia* [non] seguer de" (14). In the canzone of exile, *Tre donne*, *cacciare* is found in the political *congedo*: "canzone, *caccia* con li neri veltri" (102).

19 Contini, *Rime*, 61 ("dal punto di vista soggettivo, interno ... un punto di vista oggettivo, storico").

20 It is altogether unusual for the courtly lady to speak, let alone to shout, although it is true that we are dealing here with a discourse that could be placed in the mouth of Love and that is not at all indicative of the subjectivity or the interiority of the lady. The use of *gridare* in Dante's lyrics is discussed further in the introductory essay to *Donne ch'avete*; see Barolini, *Rime giovanili e della "Vita Nuova,"* 307.

3 Dante's Cato Again*

ROBERT HOLLANDER

Why return to this old problem, unresolved after nearly seven centuries of debate? Even more than a century ago, Dantists were apparently exhausted by the endless quarrels about this looming and perplexing figure in the *Commedia*. Witness Charles Grandgent, who joins the fray by quoting Orazio Bacci: "E speriamo che anche del Catone non si ritorni a parlare troppo presto" (And let us hope that we will be spared too prompt a return to the discussion of Cato).[1] One reason for disregarding Bacci's hope is that among the few things about which most students of the problem are likely to agree is that there exists no commonly accepted solution. A second reason is that Dante's choice of Cato seems to have been deliberately problematic, forcing us to consider his reasons for making such an astounding decision. A third is to acknowledge that Dante's inclusion of Cato in the community of Christians must be considered as particularly challenging, given his position as the first saved human soul encountered by the protagonist. His decision to promote the Stoic republican from pagan suicide to Christian hero is indeed extraordinary. There is, in short, sufficient reason to return to one of the most controversial presences in Dante's afterworld.

At his first appearance, he is indeed meant to be recognized as the soul of Cato of Utica (that name reflects the place of his suicide in 46 BC, in his fiftieth year). That is perhaps the only aspect of the problem his presence here creates about which most will agree. It is also vital to understand that no one other than Dante was of the opinion that Cato's virtues were specifically Christian, much less that he was destined for salvation. Most

* The many references in this paper to Amilcare Iannucci's work reflect a desire to acknowledge his interest in several of the subjects with which it engages and, indeed, on one occasion, in the very concerns that lie at the heart of the issue addressed here.

early (and many later) commentators balk at one or both of these notions; as a result, they attempt to deal with Cato as representing one abstract quality or another rather than a historical figure, as we shall see.

Before Cato appears in the text, the second canticle has begun with relative authorial dispatch.[2] The *Inferno* had opened with background narrative – a shadowy history of the poet / protagonist's lostness – in twenty-seven verses. Only later begins the tale of the journey itself, in which the poet first tells of his failed attempt at escape and of the appearance of a beneficent shade, who will shortly thereafter identify himself as Virgil. As a result, the poet's initial transaction with his authorities and his audience is delayed until the third tercet in canto 2, verses 7–9, his invocation found only in the first of these, his asseveration of mnemonic capability in the last two. By contrast, the *Purgatorio* begins with twelve verses of poetological prologue, first announcing authorial intent (1.1–6) and then invoking the aid of the *sante Muse*, and in particular *Calliopè*, as Muse of epic poetry.[3] Most commentators identify Calliope as the ninth and greatest of the Muses (because she represents epic poetry).[4] Dante was surely aware of her being summoned both by Virgil (*Aen.* 9.525)[5] and by Ovid (*Met.* 5.338–40), the last as a part of the lengthy tale of the gods' revenge on the nine daughters of Pierus, who, in their presumption, imagined themselves better singers than the Muses and challenged them to a vocal contest. Doubly rash, they chose to sing of the rebellion of the giants (see *Inf.* 31.91–6); the Muses sang of the goodness of the goddesses Ceres and Proserpina. In Ovid's world of divine assertion and vengeance, it is not difficult to imagine who won. The nine girls were turned into raucous-sounding magpies. Identifying himself with the pious Calliope, Dante, fully aware of his potential presumption in putting himself forward to sing God's justice, makes a gesture of humility. The precarious balance that a poet of divine revelation must manage is never far from his (or our) concern. Iannucci discusses the two contrasting songs implicitly referred to in this opening passage (*Purg.* 1.1–12), that of the Pierides as contrasted with that of Calliope.[6] His point is that their juxtaposition prepares the reader to be aware of the conflicting nature of the two songs of the next canto (2.46 and 2.112) – a point not made by any of us who argue for the antithetical nature of those two later musical expressions. That the two songs focus a reader's attention on the importance of this conflict is underlined by the fact that, in these first two cantos, the verb *cantare* (1.4 and 2.47) and the noun *canto* (1.10; 2.107; 2.131) have a dense combined presence. Here we see five of their eventual 108 appearances, eclipsed – perhaps unsurprisingly – only by all the references to singing heard in Eden (*Purg.* 27–9): a total of thirteen in three cantos (as well as by the four in 150 verses between *Inferno* 19.118 and 21.2, as an anonymous reader for the Press has pointed out).

This exordium and invocation of *Purgatorio* combined occupy the first twelve lines; in *Paradiso* these will be trebled to thirty-six. The narrative proper begins at verse 13 with two phrases, *dolce color* and *orïental zaffiro* (sweet hue and oriental sapphire), that we would not expect in descriptions of anything seen in hell. With the adjective *dolce* of that first phrase we encounter a key word of *Purgatorio* and realize that we are in the promised land – or at least its vestibule. This part of God's kingdom, for all the pain of the penance described in it, is surely a far happier place than the one the protagonist has left behind. The opening narrative is concerned with what Dante raised his eyes to see far above him: the glow of the celestial Venus, with the constellation of Pisces – fish were traditionally emblematic of Christ – fittingly visible, if veiled by her effulgence, above her; and then that of four stars in the Southern Hemisphere,[7] representing the infused virtues[6] possessed by Adam and Eve alone among mankind;[9] and, finally, in vain towards the necessarily absent Big Dipper. And now, returning his gaze to earth, he sees Cato. Hardly anyone has wondered about *which* classical figure Dante chose to present as the warder of *Purgatorio*.[10]

My concern here is to reopen an unresolved and vexed question:[11] Why did Dante choose to begin *Purgatorio* with Cato of Utica? He is granted, in no uncertain terms, custody of the entire penitential space of the mountain, from its shore to just before its summit, where his authority is apparently replaced by that of Matelda (in *Purg*. 28). The fact that we see him only as a liminal figure, at the lower border of the magic mountain, should not remove the force of Virgil's acknowledging his authority over the entire mountainside: "Intendo mostrar [Dante] quelli spirti / che purgan sé sotto la tua balìa" (*Purg*. 1.65–6; I intend to show [him] those spirits / who cleanse themselves within your charge).[12] We might also reflect on the fact that, after the disturbance caused by Dante himself, we never see any inhabitant of the mountain misbehave in any way. Should anyone ever do so, Cato, we may assume, might reappear in a moment, as he does in canto 2, to set that renegade back on track. That we never see or hear of him again does not necessarily indicate that he has no duties anywhere else on the mountain but only that there has never been a need for him to exercise them.

Unlike Charon, the first infernal guardian, named three times in the third canto of *Inferno* (3.94–128), Cato is not named after he appears to the visitors. While no commentator has actually denied that this figure is supposed to represent Cato, disbelief that Dante could have intended him to be among the saved has encouraged some wild speculation as to his meaning. Indeed, we have heard his name twenty cantos earlier (and we will not hear it again), when the protagonist has just left the forest in which he has been observing the suicides:

Lo spazzo era una rena arida e spessa,
non d'altra foggia fatta che colei
che fu da' piè di Caton già soppressa. (*Inf.* 14.13–15)

(It was an expanse of deep and arid sand,
much like the sand pressed long ago
beneath the feet of Cato.)

Had Dante been planning Cato's custodianship of the Mount of Purgatory even then? We will probably never be able to resolve that question.[13] One notes that Cato is associated, by proximity, at least, with the sin of suicide (it is perhaps significant that he is presented as being in motion across a desert – but then so are some of the sinners Dante will soon be observing in this canto [24]). While it would be difficult to support the notion that Dante had planned Cato's role at the foot of the mountain by the time he was composing this brief reminiscence, Porcelli, discussing the absence of Cato's name from the first two cantos of *Purgatorio* in which he is "on stage," errs in the other direction when he does not mention Cato's presence in this earlier passage.[14]

If there exist numerous treatments of Cato in Latin literature, no one has ever doubted (or should doubt) that Dante's major source for his treatment of Cato was Lucan.[15] However, at least by the time of the first version of the commentary of Dante's son Pietro (1340), we find annotators insisting on fashioning an allegorical understanding of Cato's conceptual identity,[16] doubtless stirred by understandable dismay that the Great Poet had possibly intended to present as redeemed a man never before understood as being other than a pagan – and a pagan who was guilty of the sin of suicide. It is also true that his rebellion was *contra imperium romanum*, at least in the incorrect understanding, shared by Dante, that Julius was the first emperor (we should probably not forget that we have seen two of his co-conspirators, Brutus and Cassius, in two of Lucifer's mouths in the canto immediately preceding this one).[17] And this is not to mention his at least unusual living arrangements with his wife, Marcia.[18] Nonetheless, Cato is destined for eternal life in paradise: "non ti fu per lei amara / in Utica la morte, ove lasciasti / la vesta ch'al gran dì sarà sì chiara" (*Purg.* 1.73–5; since death in Utica / did not seem bitter, there where you left / the garment that will shine on that great day).[19]

The most vexing problem is simply this: no one, whether historian, *literatus*, or theologian, has ever said (or perhaps even imagined) that Cato was a Christian. How could Dante have thought, much less said, that he was? It is a scandal, one that has agitated most Dantists. How are we to understand that Dante had contrived to conceive this Christianized pagan, this "Saint Cato"?[20] His own son Pietro was perhaps the first (and for a long time remained the last) to insist that, when Christ harrowed hell, not only the believing Hebrew patriarchs and matriarchs were included but also Cato.[21] However, one has the sense that Pietro was subject to considerable scolding for these words since, in the third redaction of his commentary (*Purg*. 1.70–84), he turns tail completely, embracing Augustine's harsh views of Cato's suicide.[22] Nonetheless, even in his first treatment Pietro tried to diminish the effect of his own judgment, allegorizing Cato as *l'Onestà*. Here are his words: "umbram Catonis Uticensis: ipsam umbram accipiendo hic sub tipo honestatis, et ab ipsa dirigi cum Virgilio – idest cum ratione" (1.28–69; the shade of Cato of Utica, being here to be understood as exemplary of honesty, and as being directed by it along with Virgil, representing Reason). Cato is thus dissociated from that scandalous suicide and is rather to be considered a personification of a quality (as is Virgil, representing Reason). This way of reading the poem persists even in our day, for example, the phrase in a recent commentary characterizing Virgil as "la guida della ragione umana" (the guidance of human reason). However, it is also clear that Dante expects us to read only his allegorical characters (e.g., *la Fortuna* [*Inf*. 7], *la Povertà* [*Par*. 11]) "allegorically," all others "historically." The fourteenth-century commentators, as well as some more recent ones, understood Cato abstractly (for example, "the holy life," "liberty," "virtue"), because interpreters simply do not want to believe that Dante actually considered Cato a Christian and – *mirabile dictu* – a saved one, at that.[23] In fact, the centuries-long unhappiness caused by the presence of Cato the Younger here is both amusing and instructive.[24]

Cato had been present in Dante's work prior to the *Commedia*. In *Convivio* he was treated variously, first as having been noble in his actions (3.5.12; 4.5.16; 4.6.10; 4.17.3) and then as meant to be understood "allegorically" (4.21.9; 4.27.16; 4.28.6, 13–16 [four occurrences], 17–18 [twice]). In the *Commedia*, Dante goes beyond the fairly abstract moralizing allegory of the penultimate chapters of *Convivio*; his later version of Cato becomes less allegorical than historical. In *Monarchia*, almost certainly written after the completion of *Purgatorio*, he is treated only as historical (*Mon.* 2.5.15 and 17). In the first of these passages (*Mon.* 2.5.15) we hear what would seem to be an echo of *Purgatorio* 1.71, "*libertà* va cercando" (in search of liberty he makes his way): "illud inenarrabile sacrifitium severissimi vere *libertatis* tutoris Marci Catonis" (and that sacrifice, words cannot express it, of the most stern guardian of liberty, Marcus Cato).[25] In the second passage, Dante quotes Cicero's *De officiis*: "moriendum potius quam tyrampni vultus aspiciendus fuit" (It was fitting that he should die rather than have had to set eyes on the face of the tyrant).[26]

While it is true that Dante had, from at least early in the fourteenth century, greatly admired Cato (he is first mentioned in *Conv.* 3.5.12), in none of the earlier expressions of admiration is there more than a possible hint that he considered him as being among the elect. Cato is treated in surprisingly positive terms in *Convivio* 4, first reappearing in sections 5, 6, and 10, where he receives accolades of a lofty and Christian-sounding sentiment, and then his name appears nine times in chapters 27 and 28, reaching its highest pitch in 28.15: "E quale uomo terreno più degno fu di significare Dio che Catone? Certo nullo" (What man on earth was more worthy of signifying God than Cato? Surely none). A reader of this much-cited and certainly surprising opinion of Cato's worth should probably examine it more closely, noting its distance from a statement of fact; it would rather seem a statement of philological similarity. The Cato of *Convivio* 4 is capable of "signifying" God, of having an allegorical significance, one lodged in verbal resemblance. Turning to the first canto of *Purgatorio*, however, we find a series of clues, all suggestive rather than stated forthrightly, that make *us* responsible for Dante's shocking decision – as is usual in any number of such passages in the poem.[27] Here we find Cato "signifying" Christ in his suicide. That he also variously "signifies" Moses and Paul, as will eventually be indicated, below, not only fails to dislodge that figural resemblance, it almost certainly enhances it.

In writings of St Augustine (*De civitate Dei* 1.17, 20) cited by Benvenuto (comm. vv. 28–33) Dante might have found both a way to understand certain acts of suicide positively (when "by divine inspiration it happens that the act gives an example of fortitude in the disdain for death") and a specific denial that Cato's was such an act (*De civ. Dei* 1.23, where Cato's suicide is regarded as deriving from weakness and not from fortitude). Has Dante perversely conflated these two opinions, disagreeing with their author by making Cato the positive exemplar that we find here?[28] Dante, if he was thinking of the passage, might have smiled at the opportunity that the very question allowed a later discussant. This, then, would offer another example of Dante's continuing debate with the bishop of Hippo over the meaning of Roman history,[29] which Augustine sees as without redeeming value, while Dante believes it essential to our understanding of God's purposes in the world.

Purgatorio, Canto 1

Turning to Cato's first presence in the opening scene of the new *cantica*, we find the following:

> vidi presso di me un veglio solo,
> di tanta reverenza in vista,
> che più non dee a padre alcun figliuolo.
> Lunga la barba e di pel bianco mista
> portava, a' suoi capelli simigliante,
> de' quai cadeva al petto doppia lista.
> Li raggi de le quattro luci sante
> fregiavan sì la sua faccia di lume,
> ch'i' 'l vedea come 'l sol fosse davante. (*Purg*. 1.31–9)

> (I saw beside me an old man, alone,
> who by his looks was so deserving of respect
> that no son owes his father more.
> His beard was long and streaked with white,
> as was his hair, which fell
> in double strands down to his chest.
> The rays of those four holy stars
> adorned his face with so much light he seemed
> to shine with brightness of the sun.)

(1.31–3) We can only wonder what a first-time reader would make of this description, so trained are we to recognize Cato from our memories of adolescent schoolrooms, of college lecture halls, or from other venues of instruction in the *Commedia*. Whatever our first and subsequent instructors in the worlds of the poem told us about why he is here, what he was doing here, or where he eventually would spend his afterlife, they all (correctly) told us this was the shade of Cato the Younger.

He is presented as a father, with an overtone of being in a paternal role to Dante.[30] In what does his authority exist? In verses 1.65–6 it is Virgil who informs Dante (and us) that Cato supervises the spirits "che purgan sé, sotto la [s]ua balìa." There is a certain amount of dispute about the limits of Cato's *balìa*.[31] To many readers, he seems rather to be serving as God's legate, the governor of the entire mountain up through the seventh terrace, and not merely the beach alone or the beach and the *Ante-purgatorio*.[32] It seems fairly obvious that normally Cato has no reason to intervene, since all the others who come to his island are moved only by joy in their redemption and, once welcomed by him, simply follow his instruction (if he must give them any) and make their way upward. Thus, it seems possible that we never see or hear of Cato's leaving the shore except for this one intervention in the second canto because no one but the living Dante (and temporary visitor, Virgil) ever misbehaves on the magic mountain. Had Dante not been here, Casella would not have sung "Amor che ne la mente" and the pilgrims' progress in ascending the mountain would not have been interrupted. If anyone should ever misbehave, Cato might have to become a more mobile guardian. As things stand, he is more like a cop in a kindergarten than a guard in a maximum security prison. It is only Dante, we probably are meant to infer, who needs to descend the slope for purification and then, in the next scene, who causes a delay in the ascent of these new arrivals. There is no evidence in the rest of the *canti* dedicated to purgation (3–27) of even a small fault committed in them by any penitent. In each of the opening two, we are shown that Dante is first less "pure" than the post-mortem penitents and then more stained by sin than they. We may thus assume that, if Cato is the warden of the entire mountain, base to summit (with Eden alone outside his purview), he never has to leave base camp because there is never a need for his correction. Thus his function would seem usually to be greeter rather than guard. It is perhaps only these two interlopers, whom he at first assumes to have arrived without divine permission and to be attempting to storm Olympus from the depths of hell, who have ever caused any trouble on the mountain. At any rate, we have no evidence on which to base any other assumption.

(1.34–6) The "doppia lista" of Cato's hair "cadeva al petto" (fell to his chest).[33] Moses, in medieval iconography, wore *la barba bifida*, a forked beard. One reason that he was presented in this guise was probably that, because of Jerome's possible mistranslation[34] (his face "horned" instead of "shining with light"), he was for centuries pictured as wearing a forked beard to make his chin and his horned forehead "match."[35] It was in this way that Jerome's possible mishearing of the words of the Holy Spirit changed the representation of Moses's physical appearance for centuries. Apparently, the first correction of the trend initiated by Jerome came, unsurprisingly perhaps, from Thomas Aquinas.[36] However, Michelangelo, whether deliberately or casually, reapplied the traditional iconography descended from Jerome.[37] As early as the publication of Francesco da Buti's commentary, there was an awareness of a certain resemblance between Cato and a Hebrew patriarch.[38] Currently, several Dantists believe that Dante's Cato is not only represented as resembling Moses physically but is to be understood as being a "postfiguration," to use an exegetical term, of the Hebrew leader.[39] There will be more to say on the reappearance of Mosaic traits in the Cato of the next canto; later in this one he will be associated with the most frequent antitype of Moses, Jesus Christ.

Among the several classical texts having relevance to Dante's conception of Cato, a privileged role surely belongs to his guide's *Aeneid*, with its single reference to Cato (8.670): *his dantem iura Catonem* (Cato giving them their laws).[40] This representation of Cato is the last image described on the shield of Aeneas. Cato as "lawgiver" to the Romans enjoys a complementary role to Moses as lawgiver to the Jews. There is a further aspect, however, to Cato's meaning for Dante. When he looked at this verse he saw in it Cato's name juxtaposed – as though in a Virgilian prophecy – with his own (*his* ***dantem*** *iura*).[41] For Dante to have found his own name linked with Cato's in Virgil's poem must have seemed, to the disciple of both these classical heroes – one in contemplation, the other in the world of action – fatidic, since, on the only occasion in that first *poema sacro*[42] in which Cato's name appears, it is conjoined with his own.[43] And Dante, too, will here refer to Cato by name only once.

(1.37–9) The last verse of this passage, "ch'i' 'l vedea come 'l sol fosse davanti," was, when written, perhaps less controversial than it has become. For centuries, apparently until Paolo Costa and Bruno Bianchi in the nineteenth, all commentators insisted that the verse indicated that the rising sun was shining on Cato's countenance. The minority position of Costa and Bianchi, late to develop but perhaps more convincing, proposes that the poet indicates Cato's presence as radiant in the sight of the protagonist. In other words, the text ("ch'i' 'l vedea come 'l sol fosse davanti") reads more naturally if Cato, resplendent with the sun, is *davante a Dante* than if the sun is merely *davante a lui* (Cato). Scartazzini (comm. v. 39) presented both interpretations as equals and did not choose between them: "as though the rays of the sun were striking him in the face" or "as though I had the sun in front of me."[44] The present writer, who used to accept the more common reading, now prefers the minority opinion.[45] In either case, Cato's countenance is radiant. Some of us think of a Transfiguration, whether that of Moses (Exod. 34:29) or that of Jesus (Matt. 17:2; Mark 9:1). There is also a possibility that there is even here, in this scene of radiance that precedes the palinode found in the next canto (2.112–23), a preparation for that rejection of a wrong lady.[46]

"Or ti piaccia gradir la sua venuta:
libertà va cercando, ch'è sì cara,
come sa chi per lei vita rifiuta.
Tu 'l sai, ché non ti fu per lei amara
in Utica la morte, ove lasciasti
la vesta ch'al gran dì sarà sì chiara.
Non son li editti etterni per noi guasti,
ché questi vive e Minòs me non lega;
ma son del cerchio ove son li occhi casti
di Marzia tua, che 'n vista ancor ti priega,
o santo petto, che per tua la tegni:
per lo suo amore adunque a noi ti piega.
Lasciane andar per li tuoi sette regni;
grazie riporterò di te a lei,
se d'esser mentovato là giù degni." (*Purg*. 1.70–84)

("May it please you to welcome his arrival,
since he's in search of liberty, which is so dear,
as he well knows who gives his life for it.
You know this well, since death in Utica
did not seem bitter, there where you left
the garment that will shine on that great day.
Not by us are the eternal edicts broken,
for this man lives and Minos does not bind me,
but I am of the circle where your Marcia
implores with her chaste eyes, O holy breast,

that you still think of her as yours.
For love of her, then, I beseech you,
allow us passage through your seven kingdoms.
I will report to her your kindness –
if you deign to be mentioned there below.")

(1.70–5) The second tercet of this passage is clear in its most decisive identification of Cato yet and in its prediction of his eventual salvation.[47] The reader is informed that Cato will receive his glorified body in the general resurrection that will follow the Last Judgment. One thus wonders at the claim of Pasquazi that the issue of Cato's salvation is left unresolved.[48] Sometimes the avoidance behaviour of those who simply do not want to believe that the poet meant us to understand that Cato is saved is dumbfounding.[49] Pasquazi is, however, closer to the mark than Andreoli (comm. ad loc.), who simply denies the possibility that Cato could have been saved, arguing that Dante provides no evidence in support of such a view – an earlier example of how the force of Dante's daring treatment of Cato has escaped his readers.[50] Virgil offers the reader a first sense of Cato's resemblance to Christ, the antitype of Moses, for it is Christ who liberated both the believing Jews (including Moses, we remember) and the believing pagans (including Cato, as Dante's second son reasoned) from their bondage in Limbo.[51] If there is a single Lucanian text that might have suggested that Cato was a Christian (or at least supported Dante's decision to save him), it is surely those words uttered by Cato in reference to his willingness to give up his life for republican ideals of freedom:[52] "hic redimat sanguis populos" (*Phars.* 2.312; Let my blood ransom the people), words that surely support those who are of the opinion that Dante presents him as *figura Christi*.[53] The first typological essay by Auerbach (1944) is rightly considered groundbreaking but (as Ezio Raimondi recognized) falls short of the understanding of others who followed him (e.g., Raimondi himself).[54] For Auerbach, the historical Cato is the *figura* of the soul we meet here, the "fulfilled" Cato in the afterworld. However, Auerbach never puts the pieces of his formulation together to develop, for instance, the relationship between Cato and Christ, even though the nearly necessary result of his essay is to bring the reader to precisely that awareness.[55] Nonetheless, in some useful sense, each damned or saved soul is in figural relation to his or her own previous self.[56] Whatever the problems we may find with his treatment, Auerbach deserves credit for bringing figural allegory into play in modern Dante studies.[57]

(1.76–7) Virgil corrects the false impression that Dante and he are illegal immigrants from hell (even if it is obviously true that they have escaped from there and thus are different sorts of visitors from all the others who arrive at this shore). However, instead of explaining his role in Dante's journey, as he will to Sordello with a self-defensive statement but at least a truthful one ("Non per far, ma per non fare ho perduto / a veder l'alto Sol che tu disiri / e che fu tardi per me conosciuto" [*Purg.* 7.25–7; Not for what I did but what I did not do / I lost the vision of the lofty Sun you long for / and which I cáme to know too late]), to Cato he says, "Questi vive e Minòs me non lega" (*Purg.* 1.77; This man lives and Minos does not bind me). While the continuation of this formulation (1.78–81) makes it clear that Virgil is where Marcia is, in Limbo, we seem to be invited to think, at least momentarily, of the pagan guide as being tempted to minimize his responsibility for his own damnation. What next transpires reflects another aspect of Virgil's character: his willingness to use flattery.

(1.78–84) Virgil now makes it plain that he is a *limbicolo* and thus damned. He may have learned, we might reflect, how *captatio benevolentiae* functions in a Christian context from Beatrice, who practised it upon him (*Inf.* 2.58–60, 73–4). If such rhetoric worked on him, perhaps, he may have concluded, it will now be effective with Cato. However, and as Di Benedetto has noted, "the mention of Marcia was something of a *gaffe*."[58] Further, that Cato is not gullible even for a moment is made clear at verse 92, when he characterizes these seven verses of Virgilian pleading as flattery (*lusinghe*). Until the nineteenth century, commentators understood by his use of that word that Cato was not pleased at Virgil's choice of tactic. Eventually there began to appear a positive response to Virgil's words (see Bianchi [1868], comm. v. 1.92): "Qui in senso onesto, [il termine] vale blandimento, preghiera con dolce lode" (Here the term is used positively to mean praise, request sweetly expressed). It seems that the reality is quite different, especially from Cato's point of view. Marcia remains "beyond the evil stream" (1.88; di là dal mal fiume); it would have been better to implore Cato in the name of the living Christian Beatrice (1.91–3) than that of dead Marcia.[59] Cato's rebuke of Virgil is gentle but firm: (1) Marcia pleased me well enough when I was mortal, but after I was harrowed from Limbo in accord with the New Law of Christ, pity for the damned was no longer possible for me; (2) Beatrice's having interceded for you is all that is required; there is no need for flattery.[60] Cato, unlike Orpheus, will not look back for his dead wife. He would seem, rather, to have Christ's words in mind: "For in the resurrection they neither marry, nor are given in marriage, but are as the angels of God in heaven" (Matt. 22.30, a passage Dante cites later in this *cantica, Purg.* 19.137).

"Questa isoletta intorno ad imo ad imo,
là giù colà dove la batte l'onda,
porta di giunchi sovra 'l molle limo:
null' altra pianta che facesse fronda
o indurasse, vi puote aver vita,
però ch'a le percosse non seconda.
Poscia non sia di qua vostra reddita;
lo sol vi mosterrà, che surge omai,
prendere il monte a più lieve salita." (*Purg.* 1.100–8)

("This little island, at its lowest point,
there where the waves beat down on it,
grows reeds in soft and pliant mud.
There no other plant can leaf,
or harden to endure,
without succumbing to the battering waves.
After you are done, do not come back this way.
The sun, now rising, will disclose
an easier ascent to gain the peak.")

(1.100–1) The purgatorial mount seems to resemble a modern skyscraper rather than a mountain, and, in consequence, is much more difficult to climb for the living soul who must reach its summit.
(1.102–5) Cato's reference to the rushes (*giunchi*) sets the stage for the final scene of the canto. Francis had chosen for himself and his followers a simple belt, not leather or other potentially luxurious accoutrement but the plainest cord, of small worldly value, in order to signify and remind its wearer of humility. This new girding reminds us that, in the preceding *cantica*, the protagonist is eventually discovered to have been wearing a "corda," with which Virgil challenges Geryon at *Inferno* 16.106. This cord would seem to represent the strength to withstand the passions of incontinence and violence, since Virgil uses it to challenge the keeper of the bottom half of *Inferno*, the realm of fraud. The scene thus announces that Dante is now proof against both these classes of lesser sins and ready to take on that more challenging one. In any case,

the "giunco schietto" (1.95), the rush with which Virgil is ordered to bind his pupil, is (as Tommaseo [comm. vv. 94–6] was perhaps the first to suggest) meant to echo positively the horrifying vegetation of the forest of the suicides, described as *not* smooth and straight ("non rami schietti," *Inf.* 13.5) but contorted. One might consider the possibility that the poet is opposing the self-destroying, suicidal resolve represented by Pier delle Vigne in *Inferno* 13 with the "positive suicides" of both Christ (the obvious referent of the humble plant that regrows once it is harvested at the climactic conclusion of this canto) and of Cato, who gave themselves to death for a higher cause, a theme central to the meaning of this canto. Like them, the protagonist will henceforth proceed in humility, in imitation of Christ – and of Cato.

(1.106–8) Cato obviously intends these to be his parting words. It is important to realize that he does not anticipate having to do anything more for these two special visitors. We may wonder whether he has to interact with other newly arrived souls. It seems most unlikely that he must send the spirits down before they ascend, since he does not intervene with the one group we know something about. Apparently, he merely observes the spirits' instinctual behaviour, which is to head upward; they are, after all, unlike Dante and Virgil, saved souls. And so Cato's nonintervention with Dante and Virgil would seem to indicate the normal procedure at debarkation, an instinctual and immediate upward urgency under the watchful, approving eye of Cato of Utica.

Venimmo poi in sul lito diserto,
che mai non vide navicar sue acque
omo, che di tornar sia poscia esperto.
Quivi mi cinse sì com' altrui piacque:
oh maraviglia! ché qual si scelse
l'umile pianta, cotal si rinacque
subitamente là onde l'avelse. (*Purg.* 1.130–6)

(Now we came to the empty shore.
Upon those waters no man ever sailed
who then experienced his return.
There he girded me as pleased Another.
What a wonder it was that the humble plant
he chose to pick sprang up at once
in the very place where he had plucked it.)

(1.130–3) Unlike Ulysses (whose proclivities were measured in the twenty-sixth canto of *Inferno* and who, in his rash and prideful search for experience and knowledge, drowned a short distance from this *locus humilis*), Dante, under the guidance of Virgil, is from now on clearly associated with humility. The reminiscence of Ulysses here has enjoyed a recent surge of attention, but notice of it is as ancient as the commentary of Benvenuto da Imola (followed, as he often was, by John of Serravalle). Citing St Augustine's opinion in *De civitate Dei*, Benvenuto (comm. vv. 130–2) says that no one had lived at the antipodes who ever returned from there; he goes on to suggest that this passage reflects the failed voyage of Ulysses. Some recent writers have also pointed out that the rhyme words in the passage (*diserto, esperto; acque, piacque, nacque*) are also found in Ulysses's narrative (*Inf.* 26.98–102 and 137–41).[61] The protagonist is presented as an anti-Ulysses, a *viator in bono*.[62] Indeed, the poet here seems to be criticizing his own Ulyssean impulses in order to embrace those represented by Cato, a figure who combines both political and religious liberty and in this first canto is both a historical personage and an antitype of Moses and Christ, each of whom gave his life to seek freedom for those trusting in his purposes and leadership.

(1.134–6) The theme of resurrection is clearly present in this concluding tercet. It is obvious – and has been so for a very long time – that the classical model for Dante's *umile pianta* is found in Virgil's *ramus aureus*.[63] It seems paradoxical that the source of a Christian symbol of humility (pliant, generative multiplicity) should be one of pagan perfection (golden, rigid self-sufficiency). Pagan pride has been converted into Christian humility, at least in Dante's jaundiced view, in which Christian magic is presented as more humble but, at the same time, more powerful than that of the pagans. [64]

Purgatorio, Canto 2

The canto's beginning reveals that the spiritual condition of the two travellers tends towards the lethargic. They are compared by many, Benvenuto perhaps the first (comm. ad loc.), to pilgrims on their way to earn indulgence for their sins – but not with particular eagerness. Indeed, they seem to be hesitant. Russo cites Hebrews 11:13–6, with its insistence on the nature of life as a pilgrimage, as relevant to to this opening passage.[65] Hebrews 11, which claims that the great figures of the Old Testament were capable of faith in Christ to come, introduces the possibility that others born before Christ were equally so. These newly arrived Christian pilgrims, however, seem more at home with "Egypt" (cf. 2.46) than they are eager for the New Jerusalem, in this resembling the Hebrews in the desert (see Exod. 14:11–12; 16:2–3; 17:3), who lacked a full measure of zeal for their journey.[66]

Poi, come più e più verso noi venne
l'uccel divino, più chiaro appariva;
per che l'occhio da presso nol sostenne,
ma chinail giuso; e quei sen venne a riva
con un vasello snelletto e leggero,
tanto che l'acqua nulla ne 'nghiottiva.
Da poppa stava il celestial nocchiero,
tal che faria beato pur descripto;
e più di cento spirti entro sediero.
In exitu Isräel de Aegypto
cantavan tutti insieme ad una voce
con quanto di quel salmo è poscia scripto.
Poi fece il segno lor di santa croce;
ond' ei si gittar tutti in su la piaggia:
ed el sen gì, come venne, veloce. (*Purg.* 2.37–51)

(Then, as the heavenly bird approached,
closer and closer, he appeared more radiant,
so that my eyes could not sustain his splendour,
and I looked down as he came shoreward
with a boat so swift and light
the water did not part to take it in.
At the stern stood the heavenly pilot –
his mere description would bring to bliss.
And more than a hundred souls were with him.
"In exitu Isräel de Aegypto"
they sang together with one voice,
and went on, singing the entire Psalm.
Then he blessed them with the sign of Holy Cross.
They flung themselves upon the beach,
and he went off as swiftly as he came.)

(2.37–40) The second angel that we encounter in the poem (the first descended to breach the locked gates of Dis in the ninth canto of *Inferno*) recalls, antithetically, Charon, the ferryman of the dead across the river Acheron.[67] All, however, is changed from the third canto of *Inferno*: this voyage is undertaken with benevolent angelic intent and includes passengers who are all but saved.

(2.41–5) The holy *vaporetto*, guided by the "celestial nocchiero," has approached rapidly in a cinematic series of abrupt and decreasingly long shots. Having first seen its cargo, namely the hundred and more souls within, we now hear their voices, as the visual yields to the auditory. This configuration may suggest a first version of Dante's own ship in *Paradiso* 2.3, which makes its way, singing ("cantando varca"). And what they sing is neither surprising nor without consequence: the Psalm of the Exodus, fitting accompaniment to the completion of a journey of liberation,[68] as surely Dante himself would have agreed while composing the *Epistle to Cangrande*, at least some six years later, when he set down a theoretical justification for his poetic comportment, using this very Psalm as exemplary of his own *modus significandi*.[69]

(2.46–8) It seems superfluous to note that the text insists that *all* the Psalm was sung by the new arrivals.[70] The resulting sense of wholeness, radiance, and harmony that we, overhearing the chorus, experience is deliberately set against our sense of the next song, Casella's, which Cato's intervention will cause to break off soon after it was begun.

(2.49–51) Like the only other angel the reader has encountered (in *Inf.* 9), this one is eager to be on his way, most likely in order to ferry more souls from Ostia, who are perhaps thicker in their accumulation there because of the Jubilee year.

> Io vidi una di lor trarresi avante
> per abbracciarmi, con sì grande affetto,
> che mosse me a far lo somigliante.
> Ohi ombre vane, fuor che ne l'aspetto!
> tre volte dietro a lei le mani avvinsi,
> e tante mi tornai con esse al petto. (*Purg*. 2.76–81)

> (I saw one of them come forward
> with such affection to embrace me
> that I was moved to do the same.
> Oh empty shades, except in seeming!
> Three times I clasped my hands behind him
> only to find them clasped to my own chest.)

(2.76–81) This much-admired scene is modelled on another, but which one? Virgil's epic contains a pair of three identical lines (*Aen*. 2.792–4 and 6.700–2), each describing a failed embrace.[71] Almost all of the first commentators opt for the latter (for two thousand years the one more often remembered and cited in any context), Aeneas's attempt to hold fast to Anchises's paternal ghost. However, some have had a fresher idea, beginning apparently with the author of the *Chiose ambrosiane*.[72] John of Serravalle (comm. vv. 79–81) also thinks of Aeneas's previous (and identically described) effort to embrace the ghost of his wife, Creusa in *Aeneid* 2. He was followed by Vellutello (comm. vv. 79–87) and by Gelli (comm. *Inf.* 1.66). Modern commentators almost universally return to the more familiar scene in *Aeneid* 6, and it has been rare in the last century of glossing to find anyone even contemplating the earlier scene involving Creusa.[73] Moreover, the context, in which Casella will shortly be singing a song of love to Dante, would suggest the greater appropriateness of Creusa than of Anchises. The context of the *Aeneid*'s first failed embrace is that of a man turning back for a beloved woman who is now dead (in contrast, perhaps not coincidentally, to the Marcia-denying Cato of the last canto);[74] the context of the second is that of a man having his mission confirmed by his father's spirit. (Had the attempted embrace been of Cato, the second Virgilian scene would have been a natural association.)

"Casella mio, per tornar altra volta
Là dov'io son, fo questo vïaggio,"
Diss' io; "ma a te com' è tanta ora tolta?"
Ed elli a me: "Nessun m'è fatto oltraggio,
se quei che leva quando e cui li piace,
più volte m'ha negato esto passaggio;
ché di giusto voler lo suo si face:
veramente da tre mesi elli ha tolto
chi ha voluto intrar, con tutta pace.
Ond' io, ch'era ora a la marina vòlto
dove l'acqua di Tevero s'insala,
benignamente fu' da lui ricolto.
A quella foce ha elli or dritta l'ala,
però che sempre quivi si ricoglie
qual verso Acheronte non si cala." (*Purg.* 2.91–105)

("O Casella, I make this voyage to return
another time," I said, "here where I've come.
But why did it take you so much time to get here?"
To which he answered: "No wrong is done me

if he, who takes up whom it pleases him and when,
has many times denied me passage,
for righteous is the will that fashioned his.
It is three months now that he has taken,
acquiescent, all who would embark.
And I, finally moving towards the shore
where Tiber's waters take on salt,
was kindly gathered in by him.
To that estuary he now sets his wings,
for there the souls collect
that do not sink to Acheron.")

(2.91–3) The protagonist's easy way of referring to his probable salvation makes clear not so much his pride as his faith. Why would God, he seems to have asked himself, extend such special grace to a being were he not destined for salvation? While the commentators tend to pass over this statement without being disturbed by its hidden claim, the subject raised in his subsequent question to his musical friend has been the occasion for much debate.

(2.94–105) Casella's twelve-line response to Dante's question adds an additional *situs* to purgatory, which is thereby divided into three spaces: the mountain of purgation itself, an Ante-purgatory, and this pre–Ante-purgatory, located somewhere never described but surely meant to be understood as existing at or near Ostia. It is there that all souls destined for God's eternal kingdom are somehow gathered from everywhere on earth. It is not surprising that the poet avoids making explicit any details about this other-worldly neighbour of the Roman port city. We are told, however, that the laws of this place themselves underwent a change in the last week of 1299, for after that date *anyone* who wanted to depart for the "holy land" would be accommodated by the angel. Dante has apparently, on no authority other than his own, decided that the plenary indulgence for sinners extended to the souls of the justified dead as well. We must therefore understand that, during the past three months, Casella *did not want* to travel south towards heaven. (In *Ante-purgatorio*'s Belacqua we may discover his nonblood relation.) Given Casella's behaviour once he arrives at this shore, however, this is not totally surprising. Finally, three months after the merciful decree was made, he decided that he wanted to leave. The date: 25 March 1300, the Florentine New Year. Is it coincidence that this, the most likely date for the beginning of Dante's journey,[75] is also that on which Casella probably set out – at least in the poet's itinerary? If they do the math, readers are thus allowed to share in the delightful spectacle of these two miraculous voyagers, each starting from Italy, one gliding over the seas, the other moving under the earth, arriving at the antipodes some two days later within minutes of one another, reunited in friendship and in peace.[76]

> E io: "Se nuova legge non ti toglie
> memoria o uso a l'amoroso canto
> che mi solea quetar tutte mie doglie,
> di ciò ti piaccia consolare alquanto
> l'anima mia, che, con la sua persona
> venendo qui, è affannata tanto!"
> *Amor che ne la mente mi ragiona*
> cominciò elli allor sì dolcemente,
> che la dolcezza ancor dentro mi suona. (*Purg.* 2.106–14)

> (And I: "If a new law does not take from you
> memory or practice of the songs of love
> that used to soothe my every sorrow,
> please let me hear one now to ease my soul,
> for it is out of breath and spent,
> joined to my body coming here."
> "Love that converses with me in my mind,"
> he then began, so sweetly
> that the sweetness sounds within me still.)

(2.106–11) Dante's request of Casella is in some ways reminiscent of Virgil's request of Cato in the previous canto (1.81–4). It is an inappropriate request addressed to the right person, while Virgil's is an appropriate request put forward in inappropriate terms. There *is* a "new law" here in purgatory. It is the "law" of Grace, that freedom to which Psalm 113 has already borne witness. The New Law does not take from Casella either his memory or his musicianship. Dante's question is a foolish one. What this law does take away is the rightness of singing such songs as the second ode of *Convivio*.[77] To be sure, Casella's song is Dante's song,[78] the second *canzone* found in *Convivio*.[79] It was composed in celebration of Lady Philosophy. All that sounds innocent or even positive.[80] However, early on in *Convivio* she is specifically designated as having replaced Beatrice in Dante's affections.[81] Within the confines of *Convivio* this is not problematic. In the *Commedia*, in which Beatrice is the moving force for so much that occurs, it is.[82] Thus some discussants have taken what seems at first an unlikely position: that Dante is here denigrating his affection for that lady.[83]

(2.112–14) This passage is at the centre of the continuing controversy over conflicts found in this canto. It seems possible that the protagonist's desire to listen to his own old song is, at the very least, inappropriate to his situation, as Bernardino Daniello understood in his gloss: "In Purgatorio non si canta cose vane, & lascive; ma Hinni & Salmi in laude di Dio, & fasseli oratione" (In purgatory one does not sing of vain, lascivious matter, but offers hymns and psalms in praise of God and prays to him). Nonetheless, the majority of commentators insists that there is nothing sinful either in Dante's request or in Casella's acquiescence to it. How then should we interpret Cato's intervention (2.118–23)?[84] Barolini takes issue with Hollander for not having appreciated the softening effect achieved by the poet's exclamation in the next canto (3.7) that the cantorial behaviour is only a "picciol fallo" (3.9; small fault).[85] She has not observed the further point (made first, perhaps, but tellingly, by Venturi, in 1732 [comm. v. 7]): Virgil's fault is negligible "because the reasons for which Cato reproved those souls were not appropriate to him, since he was not in the state of purging himself in order to be able to look on God." In other words, it is a small fault only for Virgil but not for the rest of the new arrivals, including Dante, who are all saved Christians.[86] We shall return to this question shortly.

> Noi eravam tutti fissi e attenti
> a le sue note; ed ecco il veglio onesto
> gridando: "Che è ciò, spiriti lenti?
> qual negligenza, quale stare è questo?
> Correte al monte a spogliarvi lo scoglio
> ch'esser non lascia a voi Dio manifesto." (*Purg*. 2.118–23)
>
> (We were spellbound, listening to his notes,
> when that venerable old man appeared and cried:
> "What is this, laggard spirits?
> What carelessness, what delay is this?
> Hurry to the mountain and there shed the slough
> that lets not God be known to you.")

(2.118–19) Virgil, Dante, all the more than a hundred new souls, and perhaps Casella, the singer himself, are enchanted. We witness the extraordinary success of a *canzone* as if from the latest musical comedy, music by Casella and lyrics by Dante Alighieri. Only the theatre critic of the *Corriere del Purgatorio*, the great-grandson of Cato the Censor, does not surrender to its charms.[87] He is the sole presence to offer a negative judgment and leaves no doubt that the musical experience that is so pleasing to everyone is completely deleterious. It is interesting that most of the commentators, except for the first ones (notably Benvenuto da Imola [to vv. 118–23], who rebukes the protagonist harshly),[88] are of the opinion that the musical moment is a positive one. However, a mainly persuasive reading is found in the commentary of John Carroll, perhaps the finest commentator writing in English who ever published, although now he is mainly forgotten even in his own land – not to mention the English-speaking lands across the sea.[89] Carroll understands the crux of the argument as follows: "The meaning, then, seems to be that Cato refuses to allow Dante to listen to the love songs of a Philosophy which used to 'quiet all his longings.'" Exactly. This musical encounter, satisfying for the protagonist as he listens to his own words, eventually reveals itself as a deeply problematic experience.

(2.119–23) Cato's reappearance in these five concluding verses represents his sole presence in the second canto. If we return to his farewell near the end of the first, we immediately understand that the "veglio onesto" did not expect to see Virgil and Dante again. Apparently, Cato had become habituated to a *dolce far niente* as a result of his supervision of only obedient inmates. We are asked to contemplate the likelihood that, ordinarily, Cato never has occasion to leave the beach. All who arrive know how to behave except for Dante Alighieri, who wants to listen to a song for which he himself had written the words and which celebrates not his blessed Beatrice but the "woman" to whom he, unworthily, turned after Beatrice's death.

The word *scoglio* has caused (and continues to cause) considerable puzzlement. Lombardi (comm. vv. 121–2) was the first to grasp its central meaning and implications:

> Il verbo *spogliare* non permette che per *scoglio* intendasi quì ciò che comunemente a dì nostri intendesi, un masso cioè in mezzo al mare, o in riva ad esso; ma esigge quell'altro significato, a cui si rinviene anticamente essere stato da buoni Italiani scrittori esteso, d'*integumento* e di *scorza*. … Ignorando il Castelvetro cotal altro significato della voce Italiana *scoglio*, s'è mosso a censurare il presente passo dicendo, che *lo scoglio si rimove, si spezza, si rompe, si fora ec., ma non si spoglia* [*Opere crit. varie*, pag. 162]. Spogliarsi adunque l'anime dello scoglio, che non lascia loro veder Dio,

sarà togliere il sozzo velame delle colpe, che le ricopre: e sarà frase buona, anzi somigliante a quella di s. Paolo *expoliantes veterem hominem cum actibus suis* [*Ad Coloss.* 3 v. 9].

(The verb *spogliare* does not here allow that by *scoglio* may be understood that which commonly in our day is understood, that is, a reef in the middle of the sea, or rocks along the shore. Another definition is required, one which was put forth in the old days by capable writers of Italian, *integument*, or *rind*. ... Ignorant of such other signification of the Italian word *scoglio*, Castelvetro [*Opere critiche varie*, p. 162] was stirred to censure this passage, complaining that a *scoglio* might be moved, be split, be broken, have a hole put through it, but not be "spoiled." Thus for souls to *spogliarsi* of their *scogli* will be to take off the filthy veil of their sins, which covers them; and it will be a powerful phrase, indeed very like that uttered by St. Paul, "putting off the old man with his deeds" [Col. 3:9].)[90]

Thus, and as Lombardi argued well, *scoglio* here does not have the marine meaning it had in *Inferno*, but refers to the remnant of sin that the penitent must shed.

The surprisingly sparse and unimpressive response to the presence of *Amor che ne la mente mi ragiona* in the early commentaries comes as at least a minor surprise. Most of those who do report that Dante wrote the song sung by Casella (e.g., Pietro di Dante [in his third redaction], the author of the *Chiose cagliaritane*, Francesco da Buti, the Anonimo Fiorentino) are vague about its provenance. Benvenuto tries to be more specific but is totally confused, saying that the song had been written in praise of Beatrice.[91] Benvenuto at least continues by making a point worthy of a schooled commentator, speaking of Boethius's discussion of the power of music and its resultant danger.[92] His remark was echoed by his disciple from Serravalle (fifteenth century), who takes a step backwards on the question of provenance simply by asserting that this song was written by Dante, a fact that can be determined merely by looking at the text of *Purgatorio* 2. Cristoforo Landino (comm. vv. 112–17) made the first reference to the *Convivio* in this context: Dante "in his *Symposium*, or rather *Convivio*, demonstrates in this *canzone* that his love is not directed to a mortal being, but to things philosophical and theological," a reading *in bono* that is followed by Vellutello. The enthusiastic responses of these two commentators find uninterrupted support right up to and through the Romantic Momigliano, who, perhaps predictably, responds to the canzone's resonance as follows: "It fits so very well with the serenity of the listening souls and seems to reflect their distance from all earthly care."[93] Some will argue that this is exactly what the song fails to be.[94] Even Charles Singleton, who might well have been expected to understand the oppositional nature of these particular two songs, God's song of the Exodus and Dante's song of love for the enemy of Beatrice, fails to perceive that they are in conflict (comm. v. 112): "In the *Convivio* this *canzone*, like the other two there given, is interpreted allegorically as being in praise of Lady Philosophy. But such allegorical meaning is not to be conceived as belonging to the song here. This is simply a love song, set to such sweet music that it can quiet the longings of both the living and the dead." It is difficult to understand how a skilled Dantist like Singleton can avoid seeing the urgent conflict between two kinds of love for two different kinds of women. On the other hand, he is hardly alone. It is nonetheless a bit surprising to find another skilled commentator, Anna Maria Chiavacci Leonardi (comm. *Purg*. 2, *proemio*), who has read the revisionist work of Freccero[95] but downplays the opposition between the two songs, electing the following intermediate position: "But I do not believe that Dante had wanted to give this moment of abandon a strongly negative connotation. At the end of the day, it is about, as he will tell us in the next canto, a 'little flaw' or, as Cato now calls it, 'carelessness.'" Her "compromise position" resembles that struck by Barolini and by Pertile; it leaves both of them, too, with the disadvantage of ignoring the pivotal opposition insisted on by the context of the whole dramatic scene of the canto: the solemnly joyous arrival of the pilgrims, the joyful if sinful celebration of a past love, and Cato's stinging rebuke.[96] As this writer argued forty years ago, if that hypothesis is not correct, then Cato is just an amusing old fogey, or, as Bowden puts it, Cato in his anger "resembles nothing so much as a schoolmaster, fussing at the angel-boat souls who linger listening to Casella's love song instead of getting on with their assignments."[97] One wonders how Dante would answer such responses. More or less like thundering Cato, perhaps.[98]

Cato had said his adieu, having directed the new arrivals towards God without allowing for interruptions in their progress for a musical interlude or "altra vanità con sì breve uso" (*Purg*. 31.60; other novelty of such brief use); but here they are, right where he left them, on the beach. All too many readers forget to be surprised at the pilgrims' lack of movement. Those who believe we should accept Cato's severe reprimand as only a friendly reminder fail to see in it reference to the wrath of Moses against the backsliding Hebrews, when he speaks to

Aaron: "non est clamor adhortantium ad pugnam neque vociferatio conpellentium ad fugam sed vocem cantantium ego audio" (Exod. 32:18; These are not the cries of men encouraging battle, nor the shouts of those who urge retreat; what I hear are voices raised in song). The Hebrews' misplaced affective choices eventually include the worship of the golden calf (Exod. 32). Nearly forty years ago two readers suggested that Dante's second Convivial ode took on the calf's role in this replay of that Exodal moment.[99] In 1990 John Scott made a vigorous assault on this "American" position for holding that in the *Commedia* Dante reproves the "philosophical" *Convivio*. Against the view that "in Cato's words, the ode is no less than a 'slough' that prevents God from being seen by the pilgrims," Scott counters: "This equation, 'slough' = *Amor che ne la mente mi ragiona,* is – at least for me – a gratuitous innovation, which goes against the traditional (and obvious, therefore convincing) interpretation of Cato's words. The 'scoglio' ... is surely the *impedimentum* of sin, which has to be cast off on the mount: ... The fault of which Cato accuses the sinners is 'negligenza ... stare' (3.121) instead of moving towards God, and it is in no way analogous to the 'worship of the golden calf,' as Hollander seems to imply (1990, 35–36)."[100] An answer to Scott may be found in Francesco da Buti's comment to verse 75, which insists on "la loro negligenzia la quale procede da' diletti mondani" (their forgetfulness that issues from worldly pleasures), an analysis that seems closer to the mark than Scott's. That verse carries an overtone of a line in the passage from *Convivio* describing the effect of Mars as music, moving the hearers to such a state that they "quasi cessano da ogni operazione" (*Conv.* 3.13.24; cease almost all activity). The cause of this negligence is Dante's old love song. Is a reader supposed to believe that this is only coincidental?

More recent work has challenged much of what seemed obvious to traditional Dantists, for example, that Virgil is best conceived as personifying Reason, that the *dolce stil novo* was practised by Guido Guinizzelli and several other precursors of Dante, that Dante did not write the *Epistle to Cangrande*, that he *did* write *Il Fiore*, etc., etc. Dante could have chosen many deficient objects to stand in contrast with Psalm 113; however, he chose his own ode as the instrument of seducing this group of newly liberated souls and of attempting to make them again captive, now that they have so recently become free. That he chose his own old song to accomplish this task cannot be inconsequential.[101] That the second canto of *Purgatorio* uses the conflicting values of two songs to stage its crucial issue, the choice between Exodus and Egypt, would seem guaranteed by the Exodal subject of the first song and the Egyptian dalliance invoked by the response of the listeners to the second.[102] Scott's essential view was shared by Pertile, according to whom the deeper significance of the word *scoglio* (slough) is found in patristic sources, in particular in discussions of the notion of "rind" (remains), as in the shed hide or skin of a dead creature.[103] The central motif, deriving from Genesis 3:21, Colossians 3:9–10, and texts found in Gregory of Nyssa, Ambrose, and Augustine, involves the animal skins put on by Adam and Eve to hide their guilty nakedness after the Fall (thus garbing the "old man" [*Purg.* 2.119] in dead garments, symbolic of his own mortality) and the injunction of Paul to put off the old tunic of fleshliness in order to put on the new life of faith in Christ. This writer is in accord with Pertile's general interpretation of this word but continues to believe that the context of the passage, which sets the Convivial ode against Psalm 113, urges us to understand that Dante's earlier ode, by sliding away from veneration of Beatrice, is a record of his previous sinful intellectual and affective activity. Pertile scants the closeness of Dante's text to the second and third chapters of Colossians, for which this writer had argued, apparently without convincing Pertile, who does not refer to this citation.[104] This first and last post-*Inferno* use of *scoglio* (employed seventeen times previously, always to refer to the topography of hell, its reefs, or rocky protuberances) has the status of a pseudohapax. This indication has precise relevance in Dante's autobiography, that hidden but continuous thread from which the *Commedia* is woven. "Correte al monte a *spogliar*vi lo scoglio": Paul's verb *expoliare* and its context are clearly reflected here ("Nolite mentiri, invicem, *expoliantes* vos veterem hominem cum actibus suis, et induentes novum eum, qui rinovatur in agnitionem secundum imaginem eius qui creavit illum" [Col. 3:9–10; Lie not one to another: stripping yourselves of the old man with his deeds, and putting on the new him who is renewed unto knowledge according to the image of the one who created him]'). Indeed the entire context of Colossians, and especially that of chapters 2 and 3 (1–17) is apposite. A few highpoints follow in italics, which all seem more appropriate to Dante's concerns in *Purgatorio* 2 than Pertile's citations of Genesis, which are, in effect, the pre-text for Paul's remarks: the Colossians are confused as to what they should worship. Therefore, Paul must remind them of the forms of the true faith: "Hoc autem dico, ut *nemo vos decipiat in sublimitate sermonum*" (2:4; Now this I say, that no man may deceive you by loftiness of words). "Videte," he continues, "*ne quis vos decipiat per philosophiam* et inanem fallaciam secundum traditionem hominum, secundum elementa mundi et non secundum Christum" (2:8; Beware lest any man cheat you by philosophy and vain deceit, according to the tradition of men, according to the elements of the world, and not according to Christ). And this part of Paul's sermon draws towards its conclusion with the following: "Verbum Christi habitet in vobis abundanter, in omni sapientia *docentes et commoventes vosmetipsos psalmis*, hymnis et canticis spiritualibus, *in gratia cantantes in cordibus vestris Deo*" (3:16; Let the word of Christ dwell in you abundantly, in all wisdom, teaching and admonishing one another in psalms, hymns, and spiritual canticles, singing in grace in your hearts to God). Colossians 2–3 read like a commentary on *Purgatorio* 2. That is to put things the wrong way round. One is forced to admire the daring and concision of Dante, conflating in Cato the presences of Moses and Paul.[105]

Those of us who believe that the resonance of the two songs in Dante's text necessarily involves a recantation of some of his earlier views find, unsurprisingly, that this scene is filled with reminiscence of his earlier divagations from Beatrice and thus from a true way to God.[106] As the present writer has been suggesting for some time now, the second canto is divided into three parts that have a marked resemblance to the traditional rubrics of Psalm 113:[107] first, vv. 1–51, the arrival of the saved souls, having completed their exodus; second, vv. 52–119, they succumb to the temptations at the base of the mountain; and third, vv. 119–33, the harsh rebuke of "Moses" returns them to their temporarily abandoned quest for the kingdom of heaven. Even if no one else has put forward this ordering of the narrative of this canto, it still seems a reasonable hypothesis that helps explain the tensions within it.[108]

To conclude, it would surely seem that Dante had decided to develop his portrait of Cato on an understanding that the pagan hero (at least he was such according to Lucan) had grasped freedom's truest significance, which is both political and simultaneously transcends politics. Such liberty eventually came to mean making an "exodus from the slavery of worldly corruption towards the liberty of eternal glory" (exitus anime sancte ab huius corruptionis servitute ad eterne glorie libertatem), as Dante himself would later say in the *Epistola a Cangrande* 21. It would not appear to be coincidental that the text that informs this canto, Psalm 113, is the key text in that document also.[109] Was Cato's faith, in Dante's unauthorized yet inalterable view, explicit or implicit? As Grandgent may have been the first (and last) to point out (perhaps preceded and followed by still others in the *selva oscura* of *dantismo*), had Cato died a Christian, he would not have gone to hell.[110] "Where then?" we may well ask. As far as Dante tells us, there was no purgatorial abode for the saved souls until after the crucifixion. And Cato is only a relatively small (or, at least, brief) embarrassment. Where did Ripheus spend the centuries between his death in Troy and his arrival on the mountain? There is no basis in Dante's text for an answer or even perhaps for anything upon which to build a theory. It seems more or less clear, after his allegorical treatment of Cato in the fourth book of the *Convivio*, that Dante decided to attribute to the historical figure Judeo-Christian dimensions, most notably (1) as the saviour of a people (the republican army led across a desert towards freedom), figurally reminiscent of Moses leading the Hebrew people from Egypt to Jerusalem; (2) as a saviour who was not himself allowed to enjoy the fruits of the retaking of the promised land (both Moses and Cato died "in the desert"); (3) at the same time, even in death, sacrificing himself for the liberty of others ("hic redimat sanguis populos," *Phars*. 2.312), he triumphs. The martyrological tone with which Dante refers to Cato's suicide calls to mind Christ's victory over death.[111]

The reasons for Dante's risky decision may remain forever obscure. We will perhaps never know whether he decided that Cato had had implicit faith while he lived, explicit faith posthumously like Trajan (Christ, after all, had harrowed him in AD 34),[112] or perhaps even some other unspecified sort of faith. Cato's dramatic deeds, as recounted in the first two cantos of *Purgatorio*, leave us, poor readers of this richest of poems, perplexed.[113] And yet, considering Virgil's rueful response (1.70–5) to Cato's salvation, measured against his own failure in that regard, we can perhaps appreciate the pathos of his salute:

"Or ti piaccia gradir la sua venuta:
libertà va cercando, ch'è sì cara,
come sa chi per lei vita rifiuta.
Tu 'l sai, ché non ti fu per lei amara
in Utica la morte, ove lasciasti
la vesta ch'al gran dì sarà sì chiara." (*Purg*. 1.70–5)

("May it please you to welcome his arrival,
since he's in search of liberty, which is so dear,
as he well knows who gives his life for it.
You know this well, since death in Utica
did not seem bitter, there where you left
the garment that will shine on that great day.")

A rereading of a commentary tradition that has struggled so long and so hard to come to grips with Dante's seemingly unfathomable decision reveals two different but similar grounds for discomfort. Some are alarmed because their faith is called into question, others because their rationality is. As this writer has grown fond of saying, "Dante's self-presentation as Christian poet offends only two groups of readers: believers and non-believers."[114]

NOTES

1 See C.H. Grandgent, "Cato and Elijah: A Study in Dante," *Publications of the Modern Language Association of America* 17 (1902): 71–90; and O. Bacci, *Bullettino della Società Dantesca Italiana* 2 (1894): 55.

2 F. De Nicola speaks of the intense forward motion conveyed in the first dozen lines: "the continuous spiritual and psychological dynamism" of the second canticle as mirrored by the six verbs of motion found in its first dozen verses. "Osservazioni sul prologo del *Purgatorio*," in *Studi di letteratura italiana in onore di Fausto Montanari* (Genoa: Melangolo, 1980), 19.

3 On Virgil's special appeal to Calliope (*Aen*. 9.525–8) for particular help (along with the general support of her eight sister Muses) with the poet's description of the extent of the slaughter wrought by Turnus and the Trojans on the battlefield that day, see M. Pastore Stocchi, "Calliopè," *Enciclopedia dantesca* (Rome: Isituto dell'Enciclopedia Italiana, 1970–8), 1:767. The poet beseeches her (and them – the *vos* addressed in the opening verse: "Vos, o Calliope, precor, adspirate canenti" [I pray you, and particularly thee, O Calliope, inspire me as I sing]). Pastore Stocchi goes on to say that such calls for a particular Muse's assistance are usually found in appeals for aid with especially difficult or sublime passages. See also the commentaries to *Inf.* 2.7–9 of Landino, Vellutello, Portirelli, Scartazzini (to v. 9), Campi, Poletto, and some dozen twentieth-century commentators. Here and elsewhere, citations of commentators indicated by name alone derive from the online Dartmouth Dante Project. English translations of passages from the *opere minori* are as found in the online Princeton Dante Project.

4 Poletto (comm. vv. 7–12) was perhaps the first commentator to point out that Dante had used the phrase *sermo Calliopeus* (to indicate "my words in verse") in reference to his own appended sonnet in a letter to Cino da Pistoia (*Epist*. 3.4). For consideration of various potential sources for Dante's Calliope, see A. Illiano, "*Purgatorio* I, 1–31: Prologo e *Incipit Narratio*," in

Miscellanea di studi in memoria di Silvio Pasquazi, ed. A. Paolella, V. Placella, and G. Turco (Naples: Federico & Ardia, 1993), 2:456–8.

5 Her summoning by Virgil was first cited by Pietro di Dante (comm. ad loc.), with some twenty followers, the most recent of these Anna Maria Chiavacci Leonardi (comm. ad loc.).

6 A.A. Iannucci, "Casella's Song and the Tuning of the Soul," *Thought* 65 (1990): 34. See the identical and independent observation of K. Marti, "Dante's 'Baptism' and the Theology of the Body in *Purgatorio* 1–2," *Traditio* 45 (1989–90): 179.

7 For an attempt to reinvigorate the claim that these four stars represent the Southern Cross, which Dante learned about either directly or indirectly from Marco Polo, see Hollander (comm. vv. 22–4). Nonetheless, one must admit that neither Marco nor his book is ever mentioned by Dante. See G. Bertuccioli, "Marco Polo," in *Enciclopedia Dantesca*, 4:589. It is perhaps instructive to note that a recent book, *Marco Polo and the Encounter of East and West*, ed. S. Akbari and A. Iannucci (Toronto: University of Toronto Press, 2008), devoted in part to Marco's *Nachleben* in the West, does not contain an essay devoted to the question of Dante's knowledge of the explorer's writings or the notions contained in them.

8 J. Bartuschat wants to deny the notion (which he attributes solely to Singleton) that Cato's virtues were infused. "Canto I," *Lectura Dantis Turicensis: "Purgatorio,"* ed. G. Güntert and M. Picone (Florence: Cesati, 2001), 16. In this vein see also C.A. Mangieri, "Dante e la sua 'prima gente,'" *Testo*, n.s., 16 nos. 29–30 (1995): 85–8; and G. Muresu, "Le 'quattro stelle' (*Purgatorio* I 22–27)," in *L'orgia d'amore* (Rome: Bulzoni, 2008), 107–10. On the other hand, there are many more who believe the reader is meant to understand that the four cardinal virtues were innate in Cato, as they were in Adam and Eve (and only in them among humankind – see the following note). The first modern commentator to have used the adjective *innato* in this context seems to have been Chimenz (comm. vv. 23–4): "*Quattro stelle* etc.: symbolic of the four cardinal virtues, known in full only by Adam and Eve ('a,' da, 'la prima gente') because they were innate in them, before their sin." (For Dante's related concept of "innate virtue," see *Purg*. 18.62: "*innata* v'è la virtù che consiglia," the italicized word repeated at 18.68 to refer to the freedom of the will, innate in all, as opposed to the far rarer presence of the infused cardinal virtues.) Chimenz was followed by Giacalone (v. 22, v. 23); Bosco / Reggio (vv. 31–51); Pasquini / Quaglio (v. 24); Chiavacci Leonardi (v. 23); Hollander (vv. 22–4); Fosca (ibid.).

9 If, as the text suggests, one has to be in this spot to see these four stars, the only people ever to see them were the first two human souls. Once they fell from grace, they (mysteriously – and Dante never does confront the issue) ended up somewhere in or near Mesopotamia, and there began populating the earth with humankind. C.S. Singleton argues well for this view, basing his sense of the passage in what he considers Dante's understanding of the older Latin version of Gen. 3.24, in which Adam (as well as Eve) was sent "opposite Eden" right after he fell, i.e., into the antipodal hemisphere. *Dante Studies 2: A Journey to Beatrice* (Cambridge: Harvard University Press, 1967 [1958]), 146–55. And thus only Adam and Eve knew these stars. Whatever their literal significance, their symbolic valence seems plain and has so from the time of the earliest commentators. They represent the four moral (or cardinal) virtues: prudence, justice, fortitude, and temperance. What is important to understand (and for a fine exposition of the point in one of the most helpful essays on Dante's Cato ever written, see E. Proto, "Nuove ricerche sul Catone dantesco" *Giornale storico della letteratura italiana* 59 (1912): 193–248) is that these virtues were infused and not earned, which again points to Adam and Eve, the only humans born before Christ who had the cardinal virtues infused in their very making. Those who share Proto's view include G. Paparelli, "Il Canto I," in *Purgatorio: Letture degli anni 1976–'79*, ed. S. Zennaro (Rome: Bonacci, 1981), 19; N. Longo, "Il canto d'apertura del *Purgatorio*: Dalla morte dell'anima alla luce della speranza," in *Atti e memorie dell'Accademia Petrarca di lettere arti e scienze* 67–8 (2005–6): 304. Longo agrees with E. Raimondi, "Rito e storia nel I canto del *Purgatorio*," in *Metafora e storia* (Turin: Einaudi, 1970), 65–94, who points out that both Proto and Singleton, if in different ways, treat Cato's virtues as infused, an understanding that he reiterates. Among the commentators there is little early support for this idea. However, see Francesco da Buti (comm. vv. 22–7), discussing Adam and Eve, whom he takes to be the "prima gente" (first people) at v. 24. This view is supported by most who deal with the problem, e.g., M. Sansone, "Il canto I del *Purgatorio*," in *Letture e studi danteschi* (Bari: De Donato, 1975), 103, citing F. D'Ovidio, "Il primo canto del *Purgatorio*," in *Nuovi studii danteschi: Il "Purgatorio" e il suo preludio* (Milan: Hoepli, 1906), 8–148. M. Seriacopi eventually also associates them and Cato with the infused virtues. "Esegesi dei canti I e II del *Purgatorio* in un commento inedito quattrocentesco," *Tenzone: Revista de la Asociación Complutense de Dantología* 3 (2002): 249. For a recent iteration of the view, dependent upon a complex and risky series of asseverations that the phrase refers to "the ancient Romans," see Mangieri, "Dante e la sua 'prima gente.'"

10 For a convincing explanation of why the reader should not be encouraged to confuse the two homonymous figures, Cato the Censor ("The Elder") and Cato the Utican suicide ("The Younger"), despite some who indeed ventured into this hypothesis, see D'Ovidio, "Il primo canto del *Purgatorio*," 36–46. Grandgent was among the latter and also suggests that a passage by Brunetto Latini may have caused Dante's "confusion" ("Cato and Elijah: A Study in Dante," 84). Introducing a third "Cato" into the mix, N. Scarano suggests that Dante may have encountered the *Disticha Catonis* at school and believed that Cato of Utica had written them. "Come Dante salva Catone," in *Saggi danteschi* (Livorno: Giusti, 1905), 155. On the other hand, it is difficult to believe that Dante had the two historical *Catones* mixed up, since his depiction of this figure is indelibly Lucanian in origin. G. Mazzotta also speaks of the possible influence of the *Disticha* on Dante. "Opus restaurationis," in *Dante, Poet of the Desert: History and Allegory in the "Divine Comedy"* (Princeton: Princeton University Press, 1979), 58. J. Scott suggests that the distichs helped form the medieval view, including Dante's, which associated Cato with the four cardinal virtues. "Cato: A Pagan Suicide in *Purgatory*," in *Dante's Political Purgatory* (Philadelphia: University of Pennsylvania Press, 1996), 76–78. For the interesting but eventually unconvincing argument that Dante (given the fact of his allegiance to Lucan) perhaps intended his reader to think of his Cato as an amalgam of at least two *Catones*, the author of the *Disticha* and either Cato the Elder or Cato the Younger, see B. Bowden, "Dante's Cato and the *Disticha Catonis*," *Deutsches Dante-Jahrbuch* 75 (2000): 125–32.

11 For the fullest discussion in the commentaries of the possible justifications of Cato's presence in this Christian precinct, see Fosca (comm. vv. 37–9).

12 For one of the most convincing arguments that Cato's "custodianship" extends to all of the penitents, see Sansone, "Il canto I del *Purgatorio*," 133n18. In response to those who point out, as part of their argument that Cato's authority is limited to the lower part of the mountain (either the point of arrival at the shore or the shore and *Ante-purgatorio*), that there are angels in charge of the gate in canto 9 and of each cornice, Sansone says: "The contradiction is only apparent and the question pedantic: when Cato speaks of 'his' *grotte*, surely referring to all of purgatory, he does not wish to say that he is in fact in charge of the ledges or terraces of the mount – and even less that he has in his charge any sort of oversight of all the other custodian-angels (one need only consider the sense of reverence with which he speaks of these angels at vv. 97–9), but more simply that he, at the base or entrance of the mountain, is in a some sense in charge of it altogether, as we say of those who, in a city girded by walls, are assigned

the custodianship of its gates, that they are in charge of it entirely." For Porena's opposition to this view, see note 32.

13 R. Manescalchi accepts the questionable Fra Ilaro / Ferretti / Padoan thesis of an early Florentine (and thus pre-1302) version of the first seven cantos of *Inferno,* to which he adds an even more questionable hypothesis of his own: since Cato is "a *punto fermo* (necessary tenet) of the *Commedia*" his presence here was in Dante's mind even *before* Dante composed *Il Convivio*. "Una nuova interpretazione del Catone dantesco" *Critica letteraria* 36 (2008): 425–6 n22. However, even if the myth of a pre-existent version of *Inferno* 1–7 should turn out to be based in fact, a fact negates the main ground for Manescalchi's hypothesis: Cato is not mentioned in the first seven cantos (he first appears only, as we have seen, in the fourteenth canto). Thus his first appearance in the *Commedia* is in the part that Manescalchi must admit was composed post-*Convivio*. Further, were the hypothesis valid, we might expect to find that the "punto fermo" had put in his first appearance sooner than in the third treatise of *Convivio* (3.5.12).

14 B. Porcelli, "Catone e Matelda: nominazione assente e nominazione ritardata," *Il nome nel testo: Rivista internazionale di onomastica letteraria* 1 (1999): 77–86.

15 For Dante's knowledge and use of Lucan, see, among the large number of studies available, at least V. de Angelis, "… e l'ultimo Lucano," in *Dante e la "bella scola" della poesia: Autorità e sfida poetica*, ed. A.A. Iannucci (Ravenna: Longo, 1993), 145–203.

16 It is perhaps instructive to observe the following attempt to come to terms with the problem of Cato's presence. See A. Consoli: "Who is Cato? Surely not an allegory of human conscience, as R. Montano, V. Russo, and others might like, but a symbolic figura – as in Pagliaro's understanding – who maintains the heroic humanity and holy testimony of faith in the ideal of integral liberty, physical and spiritual, political and moral, pagan and Christian: universal." "Umanità del Catone dantesco," in *Dante ecumenico: Letture e postille* (Naples: Conte, 1973), 106. This is an enthusiastic step away from arid allegorization, but one step back from a historical understanding of Cato's role for Dante.

17 L. Warner points to a connection between suicide and martyrdom in Dante's reference to the "sacratissime victime Deciorum" (*Mon.* 2.5.15; those most holy victims, the Decii) in a sentence of Cicero's that also praises "illud inenarrabile sacrifitium severissimi vere libertatis tutoris Marci Catonis" (and that sacrifice [words cannot express it] of the most stern guardian of liberty, Marcus Cato). "Dante's Cato, Crusade Martyr,"

Electronic Bulletin of the Dante Society of America (August 2004). For an excellent brief review of Dante's potential sources for this conception of Cato in his Latin treatise, in addition to Cicero's *De officiis* 1.31, see Scott, "Cato: A Pagan Suicide in *Purgatory*," 70–4.

18 For a rare study devoted entirely to Marcia herself, see G. Muresu, "Dal *Convivio* alla *Commedia*: il caso Marzia," in *Tra gli adepti di Sodoma* (Rome: Bulzoni, 2002), 155–69.

19 As we shall see, there are quite a few readers who doubt that Dante meant to represent Cato as saved. However, for a resounding affirmation, see Paparelli, "Il Canto I," 24: "Salvo, dunque, Catone senza ombra di dubbi" (Cato is saved, then, without the shadow of a doubt).

20 That Virgil insists that Dante also kneel before the arriving angel in the following canto (*Purg.* 2.28) is further indication of Cato's Christianity, if any is required. See Paparelli, "Il Canto I," 23; and O. Ciacci: "The fact that Virgil should insist that [Dante kneel] before Cato is meant to inform us that Virgil thinks of Cato as a saved soul." "Problemi di critica dantesca (terza serie)," *Il Rinnovamento* 22–3 (1992–3): 3.

21 Pietro 1, comm. vv. 85–90: "when Christ freed him from Limbo, that is, from ignorance of true salvation; since it is not only possible but likely that God, who had created him so virtuous, had also inspired in him faith in Christ, His Son who will return, and thus he died contrite, and thus he was saved."

22 Pietro 3, comm. vv. 74–84: "In this passage the author is not to be understood as saying what at first blush the literal sense proposes, since it is not reasonable either to say or to believe that the soul of Cato had gone down to Limbo and thence was drawn forth by the death of Christ, and thus arriving at this place in purgatory, since Augustine in the first book of *De civitate Dei* [1.23] reproves such a death as that of Cato …; consequently, it is only rational to believe that [Cato] was damned; and thus the author must be understood, in this passage, speaking allegorically, that we must understand Cato not as himself but as the virtue of honesty figuratively present in him." What Augustine said in this passage was damning indeed: "But their own writings [i.e., those by pagans who justify suicide] authorize us to prefer Marcus Regulus to Marcus Cato. For Cato, not having conquered Caesar but defeated by him, disdained surrendering himself to him and, that he might escape such submission, killed himself" (*De civitate Dei* 1.24). The response of D'Ovidio to Augustine's objection runs as follows: "Such reticence, in the form of possible exceptions, opened the way for Dante to distance himself in this particular case from his sainted instructor. Saving Cato was the result merely of moving him from one of

Augustine's lists to another, from among those listed as guilty to among those who were worthy. Arriving at such a rebellious view was not difficult even for this orthodox poet. The question, then, is not whether Dante knew Augustine's opinion or whether he would have dared oppose it, but only what and who had provided him the incentive to oppose it" ("Il primo canto del *Purgatorio*," 105).

23 For a fairly early appreciation of the fact that the reader is supposed to understand that Cato is saved, see Scarano, "Come Dante salva Catone," 119–20; he also later (136–7) suggests that Augustine's positive views of the self-destructive Samson and of the virgin suicidal martyrs in *De civitate Dei* 1 may have also helped redeem Cato in Dante's eyes. (For Dante's desire to correct Augustine's view of Roman history, see R. Hollander, "Dante's Reluctant Allegiance to St. Augustine in the *Commedia*," *L'Alighieri* 32 (2008): 5–15). Scarano concludes this part of his argument as follows: "The sin of Cato was no sin, but a sacrificial act willed by God."

24 See, for example, the contortions of the Anonimo Fiorentino (comm. vv. 31–6): "This was Cato. Now, before we go any further, there is a doubt that must be resolved, lest it rise up against its own Author, since he puts Cato in purgatory among the souls who are intended for salvation – but he was a pagan; and that seems opposed to our faith. One may respond that the Author does not assert that this is Cato himself, but that, with respect to Cato's virtue, just as God, responding to the prayers of Saint Gregory, drew the soul of the emperor Trajan up from eternal death, just so through his power might he have saved Cato. But a better way of answering this question is to say that here the Author presents Cato as representative of the virtuous man, that in him we are to understand virtue and the virtuous man in general." Or of Cristoforo Landino (comm. 1.31–3): "This person is meant to be taken as Cato of Utica. And because it might seem to many that [Dante] had deviated from the Christian religion by putting a gentile who died without having been baptized among the saved, I reply that he does not put Cato here as the soul of Cato, which we are constrained to believe is among those of the damned, but puts him here as Liberty under his own name, because such a man as Cato, more than anyone else, was a lover of liberty." What admirable evasive energy! It is not Cato himself who is / will be saved, but only his virtue, thus creating a whole new category: salvation for abstract qualities (virtue, love of liberty) apart from the souls containing them. In trying to help Dante avoid heresy, the commentators invent their own.

25 Scartazzini (comm. v. 31) was apparently the first commentator to cite this passage.

26 For this text, see note 17.

27 See Hollander (comm. ad locos) for discussions of the theological interpretations of these passages, which hide yet reveal the poet's inadmissible claims for divine authority. Such claims are never set forth as they would have been by a visionary, frankly and insistently, but are presented in indirect, riddling ways that require a bold reader, one willing to take responsibility for the author's disturbing insistence on divine assistance. As instances, we might consider a number of matters subtly requiring "theological" interpretations: "alto ingegno" (*Inf.* 2.7; lofty genius); "quando Amor mi spira, noto" (*Purg.* 24.57; when Love inspires me, I take note); "entra nel petto mio e spira tue" (*Par.* 1.13; enter my breast and breathe in me); and "il poema sacro / al quale ha posto mano e cielo e terra" (*Par.* 25.2–3; the sacred poem / to which both Heaven and earth have set their hand).

28 See also Grandgent ("Cato and Elijah: A Study in Dante," 87), referring to the "loophole" furnished in these passages so that Dante could in better conscience "save" Cato despite Augustine's previous strongly worded condemnation of his suicide. Sansone makes essentially the same point, going on to report that Augustine was followed in this opinion by both Hugh of St Victor and Aquinas. Augustine himself later comes back to the problem (*De civitate Dei,* 19.4) when he asks, "Was it fortitude or weakness that prompted Cato to kill himself?" ("Il canto I del *Purgatorio,*"105). Augustine clearly implies that it was weakness (see note 22). For a fascinating study of Petrarch's hidden but guiding presence in certain of Benvenuto's glosses on Cato, see G. Crevatin, "'Fu vera gloria?': La *vanitas* di Catone nel *De gestis Cesaris* del Petrarca," in *Tradizioni patristiche nell'Umanesimo*, ed. M. Cortesi and C. Leonardi (Florence: Sismel-Edizioni del Galluzzo, 2000), 3–22. Benvenuto da Imola (comm. 1.73) cites the author of a history of Julius Caesar, but in fact, as Crevatin argues (22), Petrarch, as author of *De gestis Cesaris*. Thus, in this lengthy gloss Petrarch's words, which undermine the courage and disinterested quality of Cato's suicide, lie just beneath the barely controlled disgust of Benvenuto. Cato did not kill himself "pro libertate, aut honestate" (for the cause of liberty, or honesty); rather, his four motives were, first of all, envy (of Caesar); second, shame (as Augustine had said); third, wrath and indignation; fourth (and as Petrarch, unrecognized by Benvenuto, had said) out of a desire for fame: "for, and as a wise man has written, Cato seems to have sought to

die, not so much in order to escape Caesar, as a certain number of Stoics assert, but in order to make his name resound by a most criminal act." It is fortunate that Dante could not have read what he would have considered calumny. Is this yet another example of Petrarch's hostility to Dante? Would he have had such public negative thoughts about Cato had there not been Dante's Cato to defame? For two powerful revisionist studies of Petrarch's complex reaction to Dante's priority, in very much this vein, see Z. Barański, "Petrarch, Dante, Cavalcanti," in *Petrarch and Dante: Anti-Dantism, Metaphysics, Tradition*, ed. Z. Barański and T.J. Cachey, Jr (Notre Dame: University of Notre Dame Press, 2009), 50–113; and T. Cachey, "Between Petrarch and Dante: Prolegomenon to a Critical Discourse," in *Petrarch and Dante*, 3–49.

29 For the absence of and need for a global study of the presence in Dante's work of Augustine's formulations of his thought, see Hollander, "Dante's Reluctant Allegiance to St. Augustine in the *Commedia*." A happy exception is S. Marchesi, *Dante and Augustine: Linguistics, Poetics, Hermeneutics* (Toronto: University of Toronto Press, 2010).

30 Raimondi ("Rito e storia nel I canto del *Purgatorio*," 76n) calls attention to Dante's other statements of a son's indebtedness to his father: *Mon.* 3.3.18: "illa reverentia … quam pius filius debet patri" (that reverence which a dutiful son owes his father); *Mon.* 3.16.18 "illa igitur reverentia … qua primogenitus filius debet uti ad patrem" (that reverence, which a firstborn son should show his father); *Conv.* 4.24.17: "Figliuoli, obedite alli vostri padri per tutte cose, per ciò che questo vuole Iddio" (Children, obey your fathers in all things, for this is the will of God); *Ep.* 3.9 (to Cino da Pistoia): "Perlege, deprecor, *Fortuitorum Remedia*, que ab inclitissimo phylosophorum Seneca nobis velut a patre filiis ministrantur" (Read, I beg you, the *Remedies against Fortune*, which are offered to us, as though by a father to his sons, by that most famous philosopher Seneca).

31 It is more than difficult to agree with W. Wetherbee's characterizations of Cato's authority: "Cato has reappeared, removed from any living relation to humanity or history, to preside over a realm of his own ('le mie grotte' [*Purgatorio* 1.48]), whose spiritual significance, like that of Limbo, is effectively neutral." "*Poeta che mi guidi:* Dante, Lucan, and Virgil," in *Canons*, ed. R. Von Hallberg (Chicago: University of Chicago Press, 1984), 135. Wetherbee had previously characterized Cato's first act as menacing "Virgil and Dante with the very laws of hell" (134; he indicates, in particular, *Purg.* 1.40–8). He continues: "In a realm where grace is the operative power, Cato is associated emphatically with old and unalterable laws." In

a later work, Wetherbee returns to Cato's *grotte*, which now "seem to belong neither to hell nor to purgatory. It would appear, indeed, that Dante has provided the martyr of Roman liberty with a Limbo all his own." "Cato's Grotto," in *The Ancient Flame: Dante and the Poets* (Notre Dame: Notre Dame University Press, 2007), 101.

32 Cato's reference to his realm as his *grotte* (1.48) has caused problems. A. Illiano believes that these are "cavernous spaces dug into the rocky wall of a mountain." "*Purgatorio* I," in *Dante's "Divine Comedy," Introductory Readings II: "Purgatorio,"* ed. T. Wlassics (Charlottesville: UVa. Printing Office, 1993), 13. Most modern commentators understand *grotte* to refer to the entire penitential part of the mountain; that was not always so. The earliest annotators mainly paid no attention to the potentially problematic word. Benvenuto (ad loc.) is nonspecific: "*venite a le mie grotte?* that is, to the place of purgation"; Francesco da Buti, the only other fourteenth-century commentator to use the word, thinks it refers to the lower zone of the mountain: "*venite a le mie grotte*; that is to these *grotte* of this mountain, which precede purgatory proper"; Vellutello: "To my caves, or caverns, which the poet presents as being beneath the mount of purgatorio"; Lombardi: "*alle mie grotte*, plural for singular, to my cave"; Andreoli is the first to set things right: "to the mountain entrusted to my watch. *Grotta* for *roccia, ripa* (rock, embankment) was employed by Dante several times in the *Inferno*, and is still used in the mountains around Pistoia"; Bianchi agrees; Scartazzini was the first to offer the accepted modern reading: "Cato's *sette regni* (seven kingdoms), v. 82, that is, the circles of purgatorio"; and see Campi: "Cato refers to the rocky mount of purgatory as *grotte*, indicating the whole by the part. That is what I said 45 years ago in the edition I published in Padua and I do not regret having done so"; Poletto is the most imposing discussant: "If one considers closely verses 65–66 and 82, it is clear that we are to understand [that Cato has in his charge] the entire mountain." There is general agreement right through Dino Provenzal's commentary (vv. 65–6): "*sotto la tua balía*: under your command. The expression *mie grotte* has already made clear to Virgil that Cato is the custodian of purgatorio." However, just when a visitor to this gallery finds all the exhibits proffering the same message, along comes Porena to argue against the consensus: "*Le mie grotte*: that's like saying 'i miei scogli' [my reefs], that is, the lower part of the island from which rises skyward the mount of purgatory … . Cato is keeper of the approaches to purgatory. Other commentators, who believe that Cato guards and governs all of purgatory, disagree. But God's ministers in purgatory are angels, and it is not possible that Cato's authority be superior to that of these angels;

indeed, we shall hear Cato himself refer to them as being superior to him (vv. 97–99)." Porena's point is interesting but fails to override the obvious evidence that Virgil describes Cato as being in charge of the entire penitential part of the mountain. (For a challenging rejoinder to Porena's argument, see Sansone, "Il canto I del *Purgatorio*," cited in note 12). The point that Porena does not make is simpler and potentially still more troubling for the consensus found in the other commentaries from the eighteenth century on: we only see Cato here, not in any of the higher places, neither in Ante-purgatory nor purgatory itself. How does one explain that? Only Chimenz has tried: "*Le mie grotte*: the rocks, the rocky mount of purgatory (cf. *Inf.* XIV, 114; XXI, 110; *Purg.* III, 90; XIII, 45, etc.), over all of which Cato may well call himself *custode* (cf. vv. 65–66 and 82)." However, for another hypothesis that may be more pertinent, see the argument in the main text immediately following. In any case, most of the succeeding commentators pay no attention to Porena's argument (Sapegno, Giacalone, Singleton, Chiavacci Leonardi, Fosca).

33 D'Ovidio ("Il primo canto del *Purgatorio*," 46–9) gives three reasons to believe Dante added the detail that Cato's beard was not of uniform whiteness either because he was misled by a putative variant in Lucan's text (2.376), in which "maestam … barbam" read "mixtam … barbam" (describing his beard as being either "sad" or "mixed") or because Cato was not yet "ancient" (see Singleton's observation, just below). Illiano refers to the "perfect partition of the strands (*bande*) taken from the apostolic iconography and the portraits of the patriarchs in frescoes and mosaics" ("*Purgatorio* I," 9–10). However, and as Singleton says (comm. v. 31), "It should be remembered that for Dante *la senettute* (old age) begins at forty-six (*Conv.* 4.24.4)." Among the commentators, Torraca (comm. vv. 34–6) seems to have been the first to make this point.

34 Whether or not Jerome mistook "horns" for "shining with light" is still debated. Translating the Pentateuch from Hebrew (with some reflections of the Greek Septuagint) into Latin in the very late fourth or possibly early fifth century, Jerome rendered Exod. 34:29 as *cornuta esset facies sua* (his countenance was horned). That was the accepted reading well into the Renaissance, with an exception made by Aquinas (see note 36).

35 See L. Réau, *Iconographie de l'art chrétien* (Paris: Presses universitaires de France, 1955–9), 2:177–8; R. Hollander, *Allegory in Dante's "Commedia"* (Princeton: Princeton University Press, 1969), 124–6; R. Mellinkoff, *The Horned Moses in Medieval Art and Thought* (Berkeley: University of California Press, 1970); C. Kaske, "Mount Sinai and Dante's Mount Purgatory," *Dante Studies* 89 (1971): 16n4 (citing Mellinkoff, plates 58, 72, 78, 79, 82, 86); P. Armour, "The Theme of Exodus in the First Two Cantos of

the *Purgatorio*," in *Dante Soundings*, ed. D. Nolan (Dublin: Irish Academic Press, 1981), 59–99; and C. McEachern, "Why Do Cuckolds Have Horns?," *Huntingdon Library Quarterly* 71 (2008): 607–31.

36 Aquinas, in his commentary to 2 Cor. 3:6–11, at § 93, refers to this passage in Exodus, in Paul's discussion of it (2 Cor. 3:7), as follows: "It should be noted that the Apostle argues from a statement in Exodus, where our text says that Moses had his face horned, so that the people of Israel could not come near. Another version says that his face shone, and this is better. For it should not be supposed that he literally had horns, as some depict him, but he is described as horned because of the rays which seemed to be like horns" (trans. F. Larcher, OP).

37 Scarano ("Come Dante salva Catone," 113) wondered whether Dante's portrayal of Cato did not influence Michelangelo's depiction of Moses. This was perhaps the first notice of a possible resemblance between the patriarch and Dante's Cato, even if Scarano nearly certainly had the pattern of influence askew. Nonetheless, it was to be another sixty-four years until someone argued that Dante's portrayal of Cato revealed Mosaic iconography (Hollander, *Allegory in Dante's "Commedia,"* 124–6); see note 39.

38 Francesco da Buti (comm. vv. 40–8): "And [Dante] used Cato, exemplary of liberty and justice, rather than anyone else, to make his fiction trueseeming. He could not use anyone from the Old Testament as the guardian of purgatory, since they had all gone up to heaven with Christ when he harrowed Limbo." But was not Cato harrowed, too? Dante never informs us of such crucial details. For the Christological resonance of this scene, see F. Bucci, who refers to "the juxtaposition that Dante makes of the psalm and the Christian sign *par excellence*." "Dante tra *iustificatio* e liturgia," *La Cultura* 40 (2002): 240. See also Grandgent, "Cato and Elijah: A Study in Dante," 75: "The long white hair and beard are suggestive of a patriarch or a prophet."

39 See Hollander, *Allegory in Dante's "Commedia,"* 124–6; Kaske, "Mount Sinai and Dante's Mount Purgatory," 2–3; G. Mazzotta, "Opus restaurationis," 15n (citing Hollander, although it is not clear whether in agreement or not); Armour, "The Theme of Exodus in the First Two Cantos of the *Purgatorio*," 84; C.A. Cioffi, "'Dolce color d'orïental zaffiro:' a Gloss on *Purgatorio* I.13," *Modern Philology* 82 (1985): 357; Scott, "Cato: A Pagan Suicide in *Purgatory*"; Wetherbee, "Cato's Grotto," 101; P. Williams, "Cato of Utica in Cicero's *De finibus* and Dante's *Commedia*: Is He a Good Role Model or Not?," in *Dante and his Literary Precursors*, ed. J.C. Barnes and J. Petrie (Dublin: Four Courts Press, 2007), 26 (although not in agreement about the effect of the resemblance).

40 For the extraordinary importance Dante lent Virgil's poem, see N. Vaccaluzzo: "The *Aeneid* was Dante's pagan Gospel and its word had almost the authority of Scripture." "Le fonti del Catone dantesco," *Giornale storico della letteratura italiana* 40 (1902): 142. This characterization might have been made, perhaps even more forcefully, for Lucan's poem. See note 53.

41 The first to cite this Virgilian verse to help explain or justify Cato's presence in the *Commedia* was apparently Pietro di Dante (3, comm. vv. 28–69). Strange as it may seem, the next observer seems to have been Grandgent, "Cato and Elijah: A Study in Dante," 83 and then E. Auerbach, "Figura," in *Scenes from the Drama of European Literature*, trans. R. Manheim (New York: Meridian, 1959 [1944]), 66. Auerbach was followed, with notice of his priority in some cases, by Raimondi, "Rito e storia nel I canto del *Purgatorio*," 84; Mazzotta, "Opus restaurationis," 48; M. Aversano, *Il velo di Venere* (Naples: Federico & Ardia, 1984), 17n7; U. Limentani, "Purgatorio I," in *Dante's "Comedy": Introductory Readings of Selected Cantos* (Cambridge: Cambridge University Press, 1985), 69; S. Carapezza, "Legge, luce e libertà: richiami testuali ed efficacia rappresentativa nell'approdo al *Purgatorio*," *ACME: Annali della Facoltà di Lettere e Filosofia dell'Università di Milano* 57 no. 2 (2004): 285. Neither Auerbach nor any of these others, however, makes reference to the barely hidden presence of Dante's name in the verse; for such an understanding, see Hollander, *Allegory in Dante's "Commedia,"* 128–9: "There is that one further touch in Virgil which must have made Dante start and smile: the line contains his own name." This understanding is supported by Scott: "It is only possible to guess at the fascination exerted on the poet's imagination by Cato's separation from the damned [in Virgil's scene] and by the presence of his own name in the phrase" ("Cato: A Pagan Suicide in *Purgatory*," 75); and see Muresu, "Il "sacrificio" per la libertà (*Purgatorio* I)," 92n: "the verse in the *Aeneid* in which it almost seems that his own name were prophetically joined with that of this hero: 'secretosque pios, his *dantem* iura *Catonem*.'"

42 For an earlier version of this phrase describing Virgil's poem (*sacri poematis*), see Macrobius, *Saturnalia* 1.24.13.

43 See Hollander (comm. *Purg*. 30.63): "There was a tradition honored by many classical and medieval writers that one should only name oneself at the *incipit* and / or *explicit* of one's work. ... It is widely appreciated that Dante only named himself once in the body of any of his extended works, here in verse 55. What had not been noted was that his self-nomination echoed the only self-nomination found in the extended works of Virgil, indeed in the very *Georgic* (4.563, 'Vergilium') that Dante had cited a few lines earlier (vv. 525–527 at *Purg*. 30.49–51). With the publication of Trifon

Gabriele's commentary … it became apparent that at least one earlier commentator had made the same discovery in his comment to this verse, where he says that …, in naming himself, Dante wished to imitate Virgil's self-nomination ('wishing to imitate Virgil … *illo Vergilium me tempore* [I Virgil then]')."

44 Aversano (*Il velo di Venere*, 136–7) suggests a third way to construe "come il Sol fosse davanti," that is, that the Sun "fosse già sorto" (had just risen). There seems little to recommend this interpretation.

45 For others of like mind, see Paparelli, "Il Canto I," 26; and Scott, "Cato: A Pagan Suicide in *Purgatory*," 227–8n.

46 See Hollander (comm. vv. 37–9): "Dante had described the face of Lady Philosophy in the second ode of *Convivio* as overcoming our understanding as the sun overcomes weak sight. Since the next canto will introduce that ode from *Convivio* for our consideration, it may be worth considering the appropriateness of that image to this scene." Raimondi ("Rito e storia nel I canto del *Purgatorio*") suggests possible biblical sources for Cato's shining face: Apoc. 10:1, 1:16; Matt. 13:43. Mazzotta ("Opus restaurationis," 49) cites Apoc. 1:12–16, where Christ's head and hair are white as wool and His face shines like the sun.

47 L. Pertile agrees, in "Dante, lo scoglio e la vesta," in *Da una riva e dall'altra: Studi in onore di Antonio D'Andrea*, ed. D. Della Terza (Fiesole: Cadmo, 1995), 99.

48 S. Pasquazi, "Catone," *Cultura e Scuola* 13–14 (1965): 534.

49 For instance, the following passage from a recent commentator: "I believe, then, that Dante, when he chose a man of the pre-Christian era to preside over purgatorio – and the greatest, with respect to moral issues, of his era, perhaps representing the apex reached by man before the radical transformation realized in the incarnation of Christ, that Dante had wanted to give this realm an historical significance – in addition to that moral significance of the soul's purification to make itself worthy of paradise; [Cato] somehow symbolizes the history of humanity before Christ, attaining a natural fullness in knowledge and virtue (one thinks of Aristotle and of the Stoics, and, in political terms, of the years of peace under Augustus), but which has not yet been transformed by Grace; a fullness, that is, like that possessed by Adam in Eden, but not divine." Chiavacci Leonardi, proemial remarks to *Purg.* 1; cited by Longo, "Il canto d'apertura del *Purgatorio*," 305. For another recently hedged bet, see Carapezza, "Legge, luce e libertà," 291–2, where the reader is given licence to interpret verse 75 either as granting Cato salvation or not.

50 S. Pasquazi avoids choosing: "It seems to me best to leave unresolved the question" (of Cato's salvation). "Catone," in *All'eterno dal tempo*, 3rd

ed. (Florence: Bulzoni, 1985), 185. For a more recent example, see Manescalchi, "Una nuova interpretazione del Catone dantesco," 426n26: Cato's death in Utica is to be understood "not as *physical*, rather as *moral*, that is, as a renunciation *in toto* of any worldly ambition." This sort of allegorism is evident from Manescalchi's continuation of this thought: Cato's beloved liberty "has nothing to do with political *libertas*" (429). One wonders what Lucan would have replied to that – or Dante himself.

51 For Pietro's view that Cato was saved, see note 21. Some commentators have wondered why Virgil does not recognize Cato from Limbo, where they both resided, Cato for forty-six years, Virgil for the last nineteen of Cato's temporary (unlike Virgil's) stay. We might reflect that they were not lodged in the same "neighbourhood," since Cato would have been among those who blamelessly led the active life, while we have seen Virgil return to his former (and future) "home," among the poets in Limbo. Illiano, however, seems to believe that Cato has recognized Virgil from their shared time there but also suggests that "in purgatory … the rules allow no recall of earthly or Limbal acquaintances" ("*Purgatorio* I," 14). This would come as a considerable surprise to the protagonist, not to mention Casella, Belaqua, or Forese Donati. As we have seen in Limbo, Virgil's companions (*Inf.* 4.67–102) are all "contemplatives," in fact only poets. He obviously does not dwell in the company of such "active" souls who are also there, within the seven gates of the *nobile castello*, where apparently both Cato and Marcia were found, perhaps near one another (though we are not told, since Cato is no longer there). While we have no material on which to base an opinion, the most likely explanation would seem to be that Virgil had never seen Cato in Limbo and only imagines Marcia's natural, anxious desire for her discarded husband's posthumous return. However, Dante himself had imagined exactly such Marcian behaviour as he now describes (79–80) in *Convivio* (4.28.13): "The great poet Lucan, in the second book of his Pharsalia, shows us by way of an allegory that these two things are appropriate to this age of life. There he says that Marcia returned to Cato and begged and implored him to take her back in her old age. Here Marcia signifies the noble soul." And again (at 4.28.18): "Two reasons move me to say this [Marcia is imagined as speaking]: one is that after my death it may be said that I died as the wife of Cato; the other, that after my death it may be said that you did not spurn me, but, through your good will, took my hand in marriage."

52 See Carapezza, "Legge, luce e libertà," 286 (agreeing with Pasquazi, "Catone"): "Now it is necessary to deal with liberty of a theological nature." However, for a frontal attack on the notion that Cato's republican

allegiance had anything at all to do with his salvation, see G. Muresu, "Il 'sacrificio' per la libertà (*Purgatorio* I)," 131: "That Cato had been a most stalwart defender of republican ideals is for Dante a detail almost totally insignificant." Had Dante been limited by logical parameters in his political theology, Muresu might be correct. However, he was not. The republic is the best form of governance known to humankind; the *imperium* was a God-chosen instrument to replace it once it fell. This does not mean that Dante ever gave up, in his own life and writings, on the republican ideal. See R. Hollander and A.L. Rossi, "Dante's Republican Treasury," *Dante Studies* 104 (1986): 59–82.

53 See Hollander, *Allegory in Dante's "Commedia,"* 126–31 and 134–5; in agreement, see R. Lansing, *From Image to Idea: A Study of the Simile in Dante's "Commedia"* (Ravenna: Longo, 1977), 83–4. Raimondi ("Rito e storia nel I canto del *Purgatorio*," 80) also cites this verse, but, explaining what Dante found ready to hand in Lucan, to whose poem he refers as *scriptura paganorum* (*Ep.* 13.63), also notes Dante's allusion to Lucan's description of Jupiter's omnipresence: "Etiam scriptura paganorum contestat, unde Lucanus in nono: 'Juppiter est quodcunque vides, quocunque moveris'" (Dante, *Ep.* 13.63; To which also the writings of the pagans bear witness; for Lucan says in his ninth book: "Jupiter is whatever thou seest, wherever thou goest"). For our poet, this would surely be a Christian-sounding formulation. Since the passage immediately preceding this in the epistle (13.62) discusses the inspired writers of the Holy Scripture ("Dicit enim Spiritus Sanctus" [For the Holy Spirit speaks] in Jeremiah, the Psalms, Wisdom, and Ecclesiasticus), the inclusion of Lucan among such authorities should have received more attention than it has. Dante's use of the word *scriptura* tends to suggest more theological implication than the perfectly adequate translation "writing" may encourage. In fact, the first commentary included in the DDP in which reference to this passage in *De bello civili* appears is that of Trucchi (1936, comm. *Purg*. 29.4–9); and then, as one might expect, it appears several times in the commentaries of the so-called "American school" (Singleton and Hollander), whence it makes its way to Fosca. When he wrote this epistle, Dante had had some time to reformulate the dangerous claims for divine inspiration he had made in the *Commedia*; the epistle only strengthens them, which may explain why so many have attempted so urgently to dismiss it as a forgery. See also Grandgent, "Cato and Elijah: A Study in Dante," 89; and his proemial remarks (comm. *Purg*. 1), noting the probable influence on Dante of Lucan's phrasing in his description of Cato's refusal to consult the oracle of Ammon: "ille deo plenus" (*Phars*. 9.564; He is filled with the

god). Grandgent remained for the better part of a century the only Dantist ever to have remarked on that suggestive verse in, what was clearly for this poet, the holiest of pagan scriptures, the ninth book of *De bello civile*. Search of the DDP reveals no other commentator who cites it. However, see Scott ("Cato: A Pagan Suicide in *Purgatory*," 77), who not only cites these words but also the potential for a Christian understanding offered by *Phars*. 9.554–5: "Nam cui crediderim superos arcana daturos / dicturosque magis quam *sancto* vera *Catoni*?" (For to whom may I believe the gods would reveal the mysteries and proclaim their hidden truths other than to holy Cato?).

54 For an attempt to deny the usefulness of Auerbach's appropriation of biblical typology to an understanding of Dante's poem, see A. Illiano, *Sulle sponde del Prepurgatorio: Poesia e arte narrativa nel preludio all'ascesa ("Purg." I–III, 66)* (Fiesole: Cadmo, 1997). Illiano is not alone in taking this position.

55 E.g., Raimondi, "Rito e storia nel I canto del *Purgatorio*," 82, referring to Cato as "a shade that, from a distance and within the limits of an undeveloped hint, nonetheless announces the coming of Christ the liberator." R. Manescalchi goes so far as to argue for Dante's interpreting Cato's offer of his own blood as a boastful countering of Christ, who died sorrowing on the cross. "Il 'Cristo lieto' (Dante *Pg*. XXIII, 74) e il 'Cristo risorto' di Piero della Francesca," *"Porti di Magnin": Periodico di Arti, Scienze e Cultura* 58 (2009): 89. In his view, *Purg*. 23.74 becomes a rebuff of Lucan's Cato, by depicting Jesus dying joyfully on the cross – an ingenious but possibly fanciful response. And for the reflection, "For me it is difficult to believe that Lucan is not referring to Jesus Christ in these verses," see Manescalchi, "Una nuova interpretazione del Catone dantesco," 443.

56 For some theoretical shortcomings in Auerbach's discussion of figuralism / typology as it applies to the *Commedia*, see Hollander, *Allegory in Dante's "Commedia,"* 48–9.

57 For the astounding failure of Charles Singleton to cite any of Auerbach's work in this area in his own discussions, see Hollander (comm. *Par*. 31.79–81): It is "shocking that Singleton, who only mentions Auerbach once in his commentary, not even on that occasion (his gloss to *Purg*. 12.40–42) refers to Auerbach's discussions of Dante's figural technique (something Singleton never did in any of his publications)." And, for Singleton's bad habits as translator, see R. Hollander, "Charles Singleton's Hidden Debts to Thomas Okey and John Sinclair," *Electronic Bulletin of the Dante Society of America* (February 2006). See also Hollander (comm. *Par*.

21.29) for notice of Paolo Amaducci's pioneering (if flawed) work in this area, almost totally forgotten, even by those of us who follow the basic tenets of the school that he half-discovered in the early twentieth century (but see E. Esposito, "Amaducci, Paolo," in *Enciclopedia Dantesca*, 1:193–4). As for the early commentators, who do not generalize their observations at the theoretical level, there are "figural" moments in the commentaries of Guido da Pisa and Francesco da Buti. However, a most interesting exception is present in the uncompleted (we have only his treatment of the first canto) commentary of Filippo Villani; for discussion of his figural view of the *Commedia*, see Hollander, *Allegory in Dante's "Commedia,"* 49, 80–1n, 262–3n, 266–8, and esp. 290–6.

58 A. Di Benedetto, "Simboli e moralità nel II canto del *Purgatorio*," *Giornale storico della letteratura italiana* 162 (1985): 175.

59 Virgil's promise to reward Cato by presenting his gratitude (for permission to climb the seven terraces with Dante) to Marcia provides still further evidence that we are not to understand that the poet encourages his readers to believe in any likelihood at all of Virgil eventually being saved. For disagreement with Nicolae Iliescu, Mowbray Allen, and Zygmunt Barański, all of whom maintain that Virgil's eventual eternal "address" is meant to be understood as an open question, see Hollander (comm. *Par.* 19.106–8 and 109–114).

60 Muresu ("Dal *Convivio* alla *Commedia*: il caso Marzia," 161) criticizes Raimondi ("Rito e storia nel I canto del *Purgatorio*," 85) for considering Cato's rebuke as being marked by "tenerezza" (tenderness); he goes on to say that many others share this faulty notion.

61 For the former passage, see D. Thompson, *Dante's Epic Journeys* (Baltimore: The Johns Hopkins University Press, 1974), 47; for the latter, R. Hollander, "*Canto* II: The New Song and the Old," in *Dante's "Divine Comedy." Introductory Readings II: "Purgatorio,"* 32. P. Rigo points out that Benvenuto had already noted the similarities between *Inf.* 26.139–41 and these verses. *Memoria classica e memoria biblica in Dante* (Florence: Olschki, 1994), 48. G. Santangelo notes the presence of an Ulyssean echo here but adds a curious comment, describing it as "the echo that careless readers fail to notice." "La nostalgia dell'Eden nel proemio del Purgatorio," in *Letteratura e critica: Studi in onore di Natalino Sapegno*, ed. W. Binni, A. Castellani, P. Chiarini, G. Melchiori, M. Praz, and C. Salinari (Rome: Bulzoni, 1974–7), 4:38. In fact, it has been a frequent feature of treatments of this canto; see, for example, G.R. Sarolli, *Prolegomena alla "Divina Commedia"* (Florence: Olschki, 1971), 60–2; F. Masciandaro, "The Recovery of the Way

to Eden: Rites of Expulsion and Reconciliation in *Purgatorio* I," in *Dante as Dramatist: the Myth of the Earthly Paradise and Tragic Vision in the "Divine Comedy"* (Philadelphia: University of Pensylvania Press, 1991), 136–41.

62 For the poet's opposition of Cato and Ulysses, see J. Scott, *Dante magnanimo: Studi sulla "Commedia"* (Florence: Olschki, 1977), 152–6; Paparelli, "Il Canto I," 37–8; and W. Stull and R. Hollander, "The Lucanian Source of Dante's Ulysses," *Studi Danteschi* 63 (1997): 1–5, 28–33. And see M. Pastore Stocchi, "Da Ulisse a Catone: Una lettura del canto I del *Purgatorio,*" *Rivista di Studi Danteschi* 6 (2006): 3–24, who concludes by arguing that Cato is a character precisely antithetic to Ulysses. When one considers that Ulysses is the major classical figure encountered after Limbo in the infernal descent and that Cato is the first and most imposing classical figure whom we encounter in *Purgatorio* (at the very least until we encounter Statius), his remarks make sense – and are further supported by the references to Ulysses at the conclusion of *Purgatorio* 1. See also C. Bon, who somehow omits reference to Stull and Hollander's 1997 article, just mentioned above. "Lucano all'*Inferno,*" in *La divina foresta: Studi danteschi*, ed. F. Spera (Naples: M. D'Auria, 2006), 97–104.

63 See *Aen*.6.143–4: "Primo avulso non deficit alter / aureus" (When the first is plucked, a second gold one is not lacking in its place). The first to cite this fairly obvious borrowing was the poet's second son (Pietro 1, comm. vv. 134–6). He has been followed frequently, first by Benvenuto da Imola (comm. ad loc.). See also M. Bambeck, "Dantes Waschung mit dem Tau und Gürtung mit den Schilf," in *Wiesel und Werwolf: Typologische Streifzüge durch das romanische Mittelalter und die Renaissance*, ed. F. Wolfzettel and H.-J. Lotz (Stuttgart: Steiner, 1990), 15–16, citing H. Gmelin, *Kommentar* (Stuttgart: Klett, 1955): 43–4. M. Picone argues, unconvincingly, that the more pertinent source is the Homeric *moly*, *Od.* 10.302–6, as found translated in Ovid, *Met.* 14.291–4. "Dante riscrive Ovidio: la metamorfosi purgatoriale," *Rassegna europea di letteratura italiana* 21 (2003): 16–20. K. Marti ("Dante's 'Baptism,'" 171) suggests that Dante may have also been thinking of the *iuncus* in Isaiah 35:7, as well as the reflorescent tree in Job 14:7.

64 For the *Schilf*, or *giunco*, as "typologically" significant of Christ, see Bambeck, "Dantes Waschung mit dem Tau und Gürtung mit den Schilf," 20–5.

65 V. Russo, "Il canto II del *Purgatorio,*" in *Nuove letture dantesche* (Florence: Le Monnier, 1969), 3:243.

66 For a discussion of the hesitance that suffuses this canto, see G. Gorni, "Costanza della memoria e censura dell'umano nell'Antipurgatorio,"

Studi Danteschi 54 (1982): 53–70. As Poletto (comm. ad loc.) was perhaps the first to note, the phrasing here reflects that of *Vita nuova* 12.6, where, in a simile, Dante is unsure about the path he should pursue.

67 R. Bertacchini is not alone in considering this *angelo nocchiero* as "answering" the *nocchier de la livida palude*, Charon (*Inf.* 3.98). "Il canto II del *Purgatorio*," *L'Alighieri* 30 (1989): 36–8.

68 D.J. Tucker sees the Psalm's liturgical connections reflected here. "*In exitu Isräel de Aegypto*: the *Divine Comedy* in the Light of the Easter Liturgy," *The American Benedictine Review* 11 (1960): 43–61. Iannucci makes a further distinction of a liturgical nature, citing Wingell, who points out that the text would seem to suggest that the saved souls have been singing (Easter) Sunday Vespers, which service begins with Psalm 109 and concludes with 113. "Casella's Song and the Tuning of the Soul," *Thought* 65 (1990): 36–7. Iannucci concludes: "The angelic voyage has taken no longer than it takes to chant five psalms" (125).

69 Unlike those who bypass the issue without mentioning it (for a recent example, see A. Roncaccia, "*Memoria rerum* e *memoria verborum* nel canto II del *Purgatorio*," in *Musaico per Antonio [Stäuble]*, ed. J.-J. Marchand [Florence: Cesati, 2003], 35–68), Picone expresses the view that Dante's *Epistola a Cangrande* is explicative of this second canto and of the whole poem. "Canto II," in *Lectura Dantis Turicensis: Purgatorio*, 34–5. Raimondi ("Rito e storia nel I canto del *Purgatorio*," 67–8) makes a similar point, employing the Exodus itself and Psalm 113 to do so. It seems permissible, in light of recent discoveries, particularly those of L. Azzetta, "Le chiose alla *Commedia* di Andrea Lancia, l'*Epistola a Cangrande* e altre questioni dantesche," *L'Alighieri* 21 (2003): 5–76, to treat the document as genuine until such time as one or another of the previous arguments for inauthenticity (or a new one) is made in more convincing form than we find in the interrogations or negative findings that have heretofore been offered. See note 109 for some recent discussions.

70 For the understanding that these pilgrims to this holy land sang the entirety of Psalm 113, see Hollander: "That this was understood in Dante's time is evidenced by the commentary to *Purgatorio* II of Pietro di Dante, which cites the Psalm by means of its opening and concluding verses (1–3 of our 114 and 17–18 of our 115)." "Cato's Rebuke and Dante's *scoglio*," *Italica* 52 (1975): 356.

71 The poet's remembrance of his affectionate but foolish behaviour clearly seems to be reminiscent of a similar moment, when Dante first experiences first-hand the incorporeal nature of shades: "lor vanità che par

persona" (*Inf.* 6.36; their emptiness that seems real bodies). It seems remarkable that it was only with Tommaseo in the nineteenth century (comm. vv.79–81) that a commentator heard this echo.

72 See the *Chiose ambrosiane* to v. 80, ca. 1355. It is not possible to determine which passage Benvenuto, Landino, Gabriele, or Venturi had in mind, as each only cites the text of the line itself without a clear reference to its context in Virgil's poem. The failure to provide precise identification may, however, indicate adherence to the more usually cited passage in *Aen.* 6. For the notion of a double reference, that is, to *both* passages, see G. Economou, "Self-Consciousness of Poetic Activity in Dante and Langland," in *Vernacular Poetics in the Middle Ages*, ed. L. Ebin (Kalamazoo: Medieval Institute Publications, 1984), 180. And now see W.W. Yeo, "Embodiment in the *Commedia*: Dante's Exilic and Poetic Self-Consciousness," *Dante Studies* 121 (2003): 92n48, in agreement with Economou.

73 One exception is found in M. Gragnolati, "Nostalgia in Heaven: Embraces, Affection and Identity in the *Commedia*," in *Dante and the Human Body* (Dublin: Four Courts, 2007), 123. One would expect, perhaps, that commentators would at least discuss their options. Such, however, is not often the case. See Gorni ("Costanza della memoria e censura dell'umano nell'Antipurgatorio," 53), who surprisingly does not even consider the other and better alternative. Hollander, however, presents reasons for the relevance of the less favoured source: the poet will later and unmistakably refer to Aeneas's attempted embrace of Anchises (*Par.* 15.25–7); it would be less than likely for him to do so here as well since he had two such moments to choose from, and the context works for Creusa ("Cato's Rebuke and Dante's *scoglio*," 349; and "*Purgatorio* II: The New Song and the Old," 38).

74 See Hollander, "*Purgatorio* II: The New Song and the Old," 39.

75 See Hollander, commentary to *Inf.* 1.1; *Inf.* 1.11; *Purg.* 1.19–21.

76 For one of the very few recognitions that, whatever Dante's reason for the contrivance of Casella's delayed departure between Christmas, 1299 (the date to which Boniface had retrodated his bull, promulgated 22 February 1300, of the *anno santo* [or Jubilee] and Easter), that delay conveniently deposits Casella and Dante at the Purgatorial shore within moments of one another, see Muresu, "Casella, il 'passaggio negato' e il Giubileo (*Purgatorio* II 94–105)," in *Tra gli adepti di Sodoma*, 241n–42n. For other recent discussions of the much-discussed but not very important "problem" of Casella's delayed departure, see L. Peirone, "Casella," *Enciclopedia Dantesca*, 1:856a–58b; and L. Cassata, "L'indulgenza giubilare nell'episodio di

Casella (*Purg*. II, 91–105)," in *Dante e il Giubileo: Atti del convegno, Roma, 29–30 novembre 1999*, ed. E. Esposito (Florence: Olschki, 2000), 149–51.

77 See Hollander, "Cato's Rebuke and Dante's *scoglio*," 350.

78 For a discussion of whether or not Casella actually composed a musical setting for the *canzone*, see Picone, "Canto II," 35–9. It is probably fair to say that this is impossible to know, but that it would have been unusual for a musician to set a poem of this length and of such a philosophical bent. Most current students of the issue lean towards the opinion that the poet imagines the magical nature of purgatory to have enabled Casella's spontaneous composition. It was S. Plona who reignited the controversy begun by Aristide Marigo quite some time before, when she asserted that it was unlikely that such a poem had actually been set to music. "Forse Casella non cantò," *Nuova Antologia* 1833 (1953): 93–6. See the welcoming response to her article of M. Marti, "Dolcezza di memorie ed assoluto etico nel canto di Casella (*Purg*. II)," in *Studi su Dante* (Galatina: Congedo, 1984 [1962]), 81–8. And see Giacalone (comm. vv. 86) for a skeptical review of the question, which restores some balance and puts both arguments in a proper limbo: "The question of whether or not Casella were capable of singing a philosophical ode is utterly beside the point." In short, while it is unlikely that Casella had actually composed the song, it was Dante's decision to have him do so on the spot, here in the afterlife. This does not mean that Casella had not composed a melodic accompaniment, but it does not require that he had not.

79 Iannucci points out that "Casella's song is the only example of profane music present in *Purgatorio*." "Musica e ordine nella *Divina Commedia* (*Purgatorio* II)," in *Studi americani su Dante*, ed. G.C. Alessio and R. Hollander (Milan: Franco Angeli, 1989), 110.

80 See A. Pézard, who believes that this song would have been innocent if sung on earth but warns that "the conscience of him who aspires to eternal life must be more exigent than that of an *honnête homme* who lives in this world." "Dante et les âmes en peine," in *Dans le sillage de Dante* (Paris: Société d'études italiennes, 1975), 453–61.

81 For the startling notion that the treatment of love found in *Convivio* is an improvement, from the poet's retrospect in the *Commedia*, over that found in the *Vita nuova*, even though it replaces Beatrice with the *gentile donna*, see J. Freccero: "The 'Amore' celebrated here marks an advance over the 'Amore' of Francesca's verses in the same measure that the *Convivio* marks an advance over the *Vita Nuova*." "Casella's Song (*Purg*. II, 112)," in *Dante: The Poetics of Conversion*, ed R. Jacoff (Cambridge: Harvard University

Press, 1986 [1973]), 188. And see Bertacchini ("Il canto II del *Purgatorio*," 48), in a similar vein, extolling the treatment of the *canzone* in the prose of *Convivio* that deals with the poem, originally a "stilnovistic" and juvenile poem for Beatrice [*sic*], in a manner more "Boethian" and thus "correct."

82 For a brief history and bibliography of the response to v. 112, see Hollander, "Cato's Rebuke and Dante's *scoglio*," 360–1n9. Benvenuto's moralizing reading (shared by Francesco da Buti, who refers, more briefly, to the "empty pleasure offered by the song") is worth having, since it will become a rarity (comm. vv. 121–3): "And take note of how much artistry our poet here employs. First he sets forth his own utter delight and then Cato's stinging rebuke. Wherefore I wish to draw your attention to a further point, that is, notwithstanding the commendation of music that he had made, the poet here is justifiably chided by Cato: first, because he was no longer young; second, because here he was returning to a song concerning matters of love, in which he had once been only too much involved; third, because he now was headed toward penitence, whence it were better now to advance in tears toward joy than in song to come to lamentation." Such a stern, moralizing reading is mainly absent from the commentary tradition. From its earliest days there have been those who find that it is the listening rather than the song that is at fault, since the pilgrims should be moving upward. From Landino on, a second group finds the song actually laudable, with Cato's rebuke either neglected or, if noticed, treated as being overzealous. A fairly typical instantiation of this rose-hued view is found in K. Foster and P. Boyde: "It is exquisitely appropriate that, to evoke a like contemplative 'moment' at the foot of Mount Purgatory, this canzone will be sung by Dante's friend Casella." *Dante's Lyric Poetry* (Oxford: Clarendon, 1967), 2:174. Responding to M. Marti ("Dolcezza di memorie ed assoluto etico nel canto di Casella (*Purg.* II)," 90) and arguing strongly for the moral imperative represented by Cato's intervention, G. Cavallini is of the opinion that Casella and Cato represent "two fundamental aspects of the pilgrim Dante's state of mind in this new realm, without however marking any contradiction between the two, between his human abandon, his rapt ecstasy, and his moral duty." "Il Canto II del *Purgatorio* e il rito di riconoscimento," *Rivista di letteratura italiana* 20 (2002): 19.

83 For this argument, see A. Hallock, "Dante's *selva oscura* and Other Obscure *selvas*," *Forum Italicum* 6 (1972): 72–4; and Hollander, "Cato's Rebuke and Dante's *scoglio*," 353–5. For a restatement of the more traditional view, see I. Baldelli, "Linguistica e interpretazione: l'amore di Catone, di Casella, di Carlo Martello e le canzoni del *Convivio* II e III," in *Miscellanea di*

studi linguistici in onore di Walter Belardi, ed. P. Cipriano, P. Di Giovine, and M. Mancini (Rome: Il Calamo, 1994), 2:535–55, esp. 549. It was over a half century ago that F. Montanari interpreted the scene as being structured on the two songs it contains ("Il canto secondo del *Purgatorio*," *Humanitas* 10 [1955]: 359–63), a reading that was redeveloped (usually without notice of Montanari's contribution) in the 1970s by Freccero, "Casella's Song (*Purg*. II, 112)," 186–94; and by Hollander, "Cato's Rebuke and Dante's *scoglio*"; and followed by several others, including Gorni, "Costanza della memoria e censura dell'umano nell'Antipurgatorio," 55 ("The opposition between these two *incipit* is decisive"); T. Barolini, *Dante's Poets: Textuality and Truth in the "Comedy"* (Princeton: Princeton University Press, 1984), 31–40; and E. Sanguineti, "Infernal Acoustics: Sacred Song and Earthly Song,"*Lectura Dantis virginiana* 6 (1990): 74–7. See also Sarolli (*Prolegomena alla "Divina Commedia,"* 52–4), who was perhaps the first to grasp fully the crucial antithetical relationship between the songs, which he understands in terms of the "conflict, both poetic and theological, between the *personification* of a consoling *Philosophia* … and the *historicity* of *Beatrice*, *type* or *figure* by analogy." See further F. Salsano, "*Purgatorio*: Canto II," in *Lecturae Dantis* (Ravenna: Longo, 2003 [1984]), 108; Hollander, "*Purgatorio* II: The New Song and the Old"; Iannucci, "Casella's Song and the Tuning of the Soul," 42–4; Picone, "Canto II," 40; L. Scorrano, "Casella e il dramma della volontà imperfetta (il canto II del *Purgatorio*)," in *Versi controversi*, ed. D. Cofano and S. Valerio (Foggia: Edizioni del Rosone, 2008), 178–81. Marti ("Dante's 'Baptism,'" 178–90) devotes the larger part of his study to the opposition of the two songs, with reference to none of his predecessors. For general disagreement with such ways of reading the episode, see Baldelli, "Linguistica e interpretazione"; and G. Muresu, "L'inno e il canto d'amore (*Purgatorio* II)," *Rassegna della letteratura italiana* 104 (2000): 5–48, offering several sharp disagreements with Hollander; for another rejoinder to Hollander, see Pertile, "Dante, lo scoglio e la vesta," 91.

84 While several Dantists believe that the nature of the relationship between the singing and the rebuke is one of urgent antithesis, more accept the view that the actions of Dante, Virgil, and the newly arrived pilgrims are simply inoffensive and excusable dallying. Several others try to find a middle ground, arguing that the behaviour is not what it should be but is not really terribly culpable either.

85 Barolini, *Dante's Poets*, 34n. For a fairly recent expression of the traditional palliative response to Virgil's "fault," see A. Di Benedetto: "*Picciol fallo* [only a small fault] is that of Virgil, who is reason and therefore [represents] Dante himself … The *picciol fallo* is that of Dante and of the other

souls. We are not the audience for a repeat performance of the Augustinian conflict between a spiritual seduction and a sensual one, both brought on by music." "Simboli e moralità nel II canto del *Purgatorio*," *Giornale storico della letteratura italiana* 162 (1985): 179–80. See, however, the study of A. Levitan, "Dante as Listener, Cato's Rebuke, and Virgil's Self-Reproach," *Dante Studies* 103 (1985): 37–55, which concludes by examining some ironic implications of Virgil's *rimorso*.

86 Against the argument that the remembered sweetness of his own song is proof that it should not be considered a negative experience, Hollander ("Cato's Rebuke and Dante's *scoglio*," 350) observed: "The poet himself, remembering the moment even as he records it, is still moved by its sweetness, as he was 'grieved again' in remembering his interview with Ulysses (*Inf*. 26.19: 'Allor mi dolsi, e ora mi ridoglio')." And see Hollander, "*Purgatorio* II: The New Song and the Old," 40.

87 Nor did his successor, Benvenuto da Imola, who will have nothing to do with the "soft school" of music criticism. See note 82.

88 See, again, note 82.

89 Carroll's work may be consulted on the electronic pages of the Dartmouth Dante Project.

90 This gloss has been accepted by nearly everyone for the meaning of the noun (see discussion in Pertile, "Dante, lo scoglio e la vesta"), arguing that the *scoglio* of *Purg*. 2 is a different word from the seventeen uses of *scoglio* found in *Inferno*. Pertile goes on to point out (independently of Baldelli, "Linguistica e interpretazione," 545n), that Lombardi (1791) was the first to point to *iscorza* and *iscoglia* ("pelle morta di serpente" [dead skin of a serpent]), as defined in the *Vocabolario della Crusca* (in 1612, 1691, and 1747): s.v. *scoglia*, "the skin, that a snake sheds every year. Lat. *spolium*." For the relevance of Col. 3:9, see the commentaries (ad loc.) of Tommaseo, Scartazzini, Campi, Hollander, and Fosca, the latter pointing out that the passage in Augustine includes reference to this passage in Colossians. It is not easy to understand Pertile's choice of Genesis over Colossians as source text; Pertile points to another biblical source, Gen. 3:21, and the *tunicas pelliceas* (garments of skins) that Adam and Eve are given just before they are driven from the Garden. However, it is quite obvious that when the phrase *espogliare lo scoglio* (cited by Lombardi in his gloss) is so close to Paul's phrasing (*expoliantes veterem hominem*) that, at the very most, a combination of the two biblical sources poses a possible solution.

91 Benvenuto (comm. vv. 112–17): "Casella began to sing, a cause for utter delight, one of Dante's odes celebrating his love for Beatrice."

92 Boethius has an obvious presence in this scene, as several scholars have noted, e.g., W. Vernon: "Boethius was so deeply absorbed in the sweet singing of [Lady] Philosophy, that when she had concluded, he still remained listening fixedly," citing *Cons.* 3.1: "Iam cantum ille finiverat … mulcedo defixerat." *Readings on the "Purgatorio" of Dante, Chiefly Based on the Commentary of Benvenuto da Imola* (London: Macmillan, 1889), 73n. See also Freccero, "Casella's Song (*Purg.* II, 112)," 189–90; Hollander, "Cato's Rebuke and Dante's *scoglio*," 353–5; Bertacchini, "Il canto II del *Purgatorio*," 51–3; Iannucci, "Casella's Song and the Tuning of the Soul," 35, passim. And for the central study of the impact of Boethius on European letters, see P. Courcelle, *La "Consolation de Philosophie" dans la tradition littéraire* (Paris: Études Augustiniennes, 1967). For Boethius in Dante, the only "global" study remains that of R. Murari, *Dante e Boezio* (Bologna: Zanichelli, 1905). See also W. Kranz, "Dante und Boethius," *Romanische Forschungen* 63 (1951): 72–8; E. Scuderi, "Dante e Boezio," *Orpheus* 9 (1962): 105–7; M.T. D'Alverny, "Notes sur Dante et la Sagesse," *Revue des études italiennes* 11 (1965): 5–24; A. Gualtieri, "Lady Philosophy in Boethius and Dante," *Comparative Literature* 23 (1971): 141–50. And see F. Tateo, "Boezio," *Enciclopedia Dantesca*, 1:654a–658a.

93 For the (similar) opinion that the Casella episode is "among the most affectionate found in the poem," one that is characterized by its "lovely and delicate harmony," see Cavallini, "Il Canto II del *Purgatorio* e il rito di riconoscimento," 13–14.

94 For a contemporary history of the debate over the performance of the *canzone* here, see M. Fiorilla, "*Amor che nella mente mi ragiona* tra ricezione antica e interpretazione moderna," *Rivista di Studi Danteschi* 5 (2005): 141–54.

95 See his groundbreaking – at least for American Dantists – article "Casella's Song." However, for a significantly different American view, see D.W. Robertson, Jr: "This personification is basically the same lady who appears in *The Consolation of Philosophy* of Boethius, in the books of Wisdom and Ecclesiasticus in the Vulgate Bible, and in a number of medieval and Renaissance poems. She is, for example, the inspiration for Dante's Beatrice." *The Literature of Medieval England* (New York: McGraw-Hill, 1970), 218n. Robertson tends to reduce all medieval literature to the same paradigm and never accepted the concept that Dante's allegory was different in kind from that which he considered normative, taking as his premise exactly that which is at issue.

96 Barolini, *Dante's Poets*, 40; and Pertile, "Dante, lo scoglio e la vesta."

97 Bowden, "Dante's Cato," 126.

98 For a similar view, see G. Federzoni: "The reason for the reference to the *canzone* here is that the amatory life, to which the spirits encountered in this planet [Venus] offered themselves, the Epicurean existence condemned by the austerity of the Christian religion, is, on the contrary, justified by pagan philosophy, the philosophy that Dante himself celebrated in the second treatise of the *Convivio* and most of all in this very *canzone*." *La "Divina Commedia" di Dante Allighieri commentata per le scuole e per gli studiosi da Giovanni Federzoni* (Bologna: L. Cappelli, 1921–3), to *Par*. 7.36–9. This gloss is remarkable for at least two reasons: first, no one else during this period was offering anything even vaguely similar to this stark observation; second, it is close to various modern formulations, e.g. those put forward by R. Montano, "Caratteristiche del *Purgatorio*: Catone personificazione di una natura riscattata dall'umana debolezza," in *Storia della poesia di Dante* (Naples: Quaderni di Delta, 1963), 7–36; Freccero, "Casella's Song (*Purg*. II, 112)"; Hollander, "Cato's Rebuke and Dante's *scoglio*" (and now see his comm. *Par*. 7.34–9); Hollander, "Dante's *Paradiso* as Philosophical Poem," *Italica* 86 no. 4 (2009): 574–8; and recently quite a few others, perhaps most insistently by A. Gagliardi, *La tragedia intellettuale di Dante: Il "Convivio"* (Catanzaro: Pullano, 1994); Gagliardi, "Dalla Commedia al *Convivio*: Catone e Casella," *Tenzone: Revista de la Asociación Complutense de Dantología* 3 (2002): 59–107 (where he refers to "the *Convivio* and its reversed mirror image in the *Commedia*" [61]); and Gagliardi, "Dante e Averroè: il desiderio di (vedere) Dio," in *"E 'n guisa d'eco i detti e le parole": Studi in onore di Giorgio Bárberi Squarotti*, ed. F. Cattina, M.I. Grasso, and B. Sancin (Alessandria: Edizioni dell'Orso, 2006), 2:23–39. On occasions such as these, we see how a minimally consulted commentator, as was and is Federzoni, relatively ignored even in his own time and later virtually unknown, may surface with crucial observations that, in themselves, give a lifetime's middling effort focus and reward. Iannucci notes that *De vulgari eloquentia* (2.6.6) also mentions this *canzone*. He points out that even those critics (predominantly North American) who see the problem of the Convivial setting of the *canzone* do not mention its presence in *De vulgari eloquentia*, where it is praised for its aesthetic form, while its failing moral content is not mentioned ("Musica e ordine nella *Divina Commedia* [*Purgatorio* II]," 109; and "Casella's Song and the Tuning of the Soul," 41–2).

99 See Kaske, "Mount Sinai and Dante's Mount Purgatory," 13; Hollander, "Cato's Rebuke and Dante's *scoglio*," 351; and Hollander, "*Purgatorio* II: The New Song and the Old," 35–6.

100 J. Scott, "Dante and Philosophy," *Annali d'italianistica* 8 (1990): 274–5.

101 See Hollander, "Cato's Rebuke and Dante's *scoglio*," 348: "Casella's song is a Siren's song." And see Aversano, *Il velo di Venere*, 159: "Casella's song thus has the same effect, fascinating and paralyzing, as does the Sirens' song." For a much earlier and similar view, see Carroll (comm. vv. 118–23): "Read thus in the light of the *Convito*, what Cato rebukes is the Philosophy whose sweet music once held Dante in captivity. This may seem to corroborate the view of those writers who hold that the unfaithfulness of which Beatrice convicts Dante on the Mountain-top was simply his devotion at one period of his life to Philosophy in preference to herself, the Heavenly Wisdom (*Purg*. 30, 31)."

102 Baldelli opposes this view; he mentions Hollander, "Cato's Rebuke and Dante's *scoglio*" and "*Purgatorio* II: The New Song and the Old," as well as Barolini, *Dante's Poets*, as those with whom he disagrees and summarizes his position as follows: "The actuality 'Casella's song / Cato's rebuke' is not, thus, comparable to other situations in which we find condemnation of things gravely sinful, as is the case with the dream of the *femmina balba* (the stuttering woman), *la dolce serena* (the sweet siren), *l'antica strega* (the ancient witch–*Purg*. 29, 1–69); or like the accusations of Dante by Beatrice [referring to *Purg*. 30–1, one imagines]. … The entirety of the stylistic structure and the verbal actuality of these scenes is absolutely antithetic to that referred to in Casella's loving song" ("Linguistica e interpretazione," 545n, 549). Why this could or should be true is left unexpressed; a reading of the text itself does not offer confirmation, since the context is one of a confrontation highly similar to those that Beatrice does understand in this way – or else Cato must have been meant to be perceived as a meddling old fool.

103 Pertile, "Dante, lo scoglio e la vesta." Kaske ("Mount Sinai and Dante's Mount Purgatory," 13), following Pietrobono, opts for "veil" as the meaning of the word. Singleton's brief discussion (comm. ad loc.) adduces Augustine's suggestion that the snake that sheds its skin resembles the "new man" (*De doctrina Christiana* 15.24). This reference to Augustine is also found in the commentaries ad loc. of Campi, Singleton, Chiavacci Leonardi, and Fosca. That Augustine makes specific reference to Col. 3:9–10 seems helpful in ascertaining exactly which meaning of *scoglio* Dante had in mind.

104 See Hollander, "Cato's Rebuke and Dante's *scoglio*," 357.

105 For the Pauline references, see also Rigo, *Memoria classica e memoria biblica in Dante*, 93–4.

106 For the question of Dante's retrospective view of his earlier *Convivio*, focusing on the positions of Freccero and Hollander as contrasted with

those of Scott and Pertile, see A. Ascoli, *Dante and the Making of a Modern Author* (Cambridge: Cambridge University Press, 2008), 276–7.

107 See Hollander, "Cato's Rebuke and Dante's *scoglio*," 356 and comm. vv. 46–8: "For the pertinence of typical medieval rubrics to the Psalm, which divide it into three parts (the miracle of the Exodus, the Hebrews' back-sliding worship of the Golden Calf, reaffirmation of God's continuing support of them), a division that is seen as paralleling the three scenes of the canto (completion of the 'exodus' of the arriving souls, Casella's song as 'idolatrous,' Cato's insistence on the pilgrims' devotion to God), see Hollander, '*Purgatorio* II: The New Song and the Old,' 35–6. Each of these moments is assigned, as it were, a single simile that reflects its central action, the arrival of the ship (vv. 13–18), Dante's unique status as still living in the flesh (vv. 70–74), Cato's rebuke (vv. 124–132)." Two sets of rubrics found accompanying this Psalm are arrestingly appropriate to the tripartite organization of the events depicted in the second canto of *Purgatorio*; see Hollander, "Cato's Rebuke and Dante's *scoglio*," 362–3n29: [1] "Miracula Dei, Isräelem ex Aegypto educentis" (The miracles of God, leading Israel out of Egypt). [2] "Vana gentium idola" (Vain idols of the Gentiles); [3] "Deus verus omnium piorum praesidium" (God true protector of all the devout); and [1] "Miracula in exitu de Aegypto patrata enarrantur" (The telling of the miracles achieved during the flight from Egypt); "Deoque," [2] "non inanibus vero idolis," [3] "gloria tribuenda est, ab eoque solo sperandum auxilium" (To God, and not to the indeed vacuous idols, is glory due; from him alone is aid to be hoped for). (Both these rubrics contain a variant of the phrase "vana" [or *inana*] "idola" for the "simulacra gentium" of the biblical text [Ps. 134:15].) Ibid., 361n12 attributes his first awareness of this fairly obvious reference (at least it is once it is observed) to the observation of a student, A.S. Fehsenfeld, Jr (Princeton '72). And, in a similar vein, if without the same precision, see Mazzotta, "Opus restaurationis," 64: "Dante views Cato's journey through the desert of temptation, his shunning the tyranny of the idols, his self-sacrifice for mankind, and his quest for freedom as elements that make Cato's redemption the secular reenactment of Exodus."

108 Hollander, "*Purgatorio* II: The New Song and the Old," 41: "The second canto of the *Purgatorio* dramatizes the need for interpretation by presenting two songs to its audience, the arriving pilgrims. It is clear that we comprise a still more crucial audience. Most of us have chosen to follow the lead of the one whom we take to be our leader, Dante himself. (His several intellectually or morally flawed responses as he moved through *Inferno* have not, apparently, been cogent enough sign of his frequent

inadequacy as guide to our reactions.) He, lost in the beauty of his own old song, either fails to understand or else forgets the message of the new song which he has heard first, and which should have served as a rein on his enthusiasm. It is as old as Exodus and as new as the dawn which brings it, this Easter Sunday morning on the shore of the mountain. Even its angelic sanction has not prevented most of us from leaving the theater humming the other song, that lovely little Italian air, *Amor che ne la mente mi ragiona*. One can only imagine Dante's reaction as he hears us go out, back into the night."

109 This writer is fully cognizant that there remain a few Dantists who resist the increasing likelihood that Dante was the sole author of the epistle. See some further arguments for confirming its Dantean nature in the most recent of his several treatments of the authenticity of the *Epistle*: Hollander, "Is 'The Verse' Milton's Response to the *Epistle to Cangrande*?," *Electronic Bulletin of the Dante Society of America* (April 2009), now in an extended version, "Milton's Elusive Response to Dante's *Comedy* in *Paradise Lost*," *Milton Quarterly* 45 (2011): 1–24; and Hollander, "Due recenti contributi al dibattito sull'autenticità dell'*Epistola a Cangrande*," *Letteratura italiana antica* 10 (2009): 541–2. For a (favourable) review of the latter, see G. Puletti, "Schede e segnalazioni," *Studi Danteschi* 75 (2010): 378–81.

110 Grandgent, "Cato and Elijah," 86.

111 See the observation of G. Bàrberi Squarotti that Cato finally takes on the role of a lay figure of Christ. "Ai piedi del monte: il prologo del *Purgatorio*," in *L'arte dell'interpretare: Studi critici offerti a Giovanni Getto* (Cuneo: L'Arciere, 1984), 33. A less cautious interpretation is offered by Bambeck ("Waschung mit dem Tau und Gürtung mit den Schilf," 9): "This Cato is no longer the Cato of Utica, the Cato of Roman history, but instead a Cato residing in the Christian afterlife." See also Paparelli, "Il Canto I," 24; Sanguineti, according to whom Cato is "a figure, finally, of Christ the Redeemer" ("*Purgatorio* I," in *Dante reazionario* [Rome: Editori Riuniti, 1992], 133); and Scott, "Cato: A Pagan Suicide in *Purgatory*," 76.

112 According to Illiano (*Sulle sponde del Prepurgatorio*, 27), Dante probably imagined that Cato's "conversion" was the result of "the direct vision of Christ descended into Limbo to administer his sacrament of baptism." This hypothesis has the merit of avoiding the problem of a Cato converted during his earthly pilgrimage, in which case his initial presence in Limbo might seem scandalous. Still, the many Hebrew saints (in 1300 there are several more Hebrews in heaven than Christians – shocking as that fact may seem – as we discover in *Par.* 32) had to wait Christ's

coming in Limbo, so that if Cato was there, he would have been in excellent company. There seems to be no other hypothesis that is as acceptable as that Cato had to spend some eighty years in hell, followed by a total of 6466 in purgatory; for the calculation that for Dante there are some 5200 years left to run until the end of the world, see Hollander, "The World-historical Meaning of *Inferno* 1.1 as Confirmed by *Paradiso* 9.40," *Electronic Bulletin of the Dante Society of America* (November 2009).

113 For example, E. Bigi, who takes Dante's "historical" Cato as being, in Auerbachian mode, a "figura" of the warden of purgatory; however, allegorically speaking (and Bigi clearly is applying the "allegory of the poets") he is "the allegory of that spiritual attitude by which the soul becomes dramatically conscious both of the gravity of the step taken toward gaining freedom from sin and of the responsibilities that such a new condition brings with it." "Il canto I del *Purgatorio*," in *Forme e significati nella "Divina Commedia"* (Bologna: Cappelli, 1981), 134.

114 See Hollander, "*Purgatorio* II: The New Song and the Old," 28.

4 "Che libito fe' licito in sua legge": Lust and Law, Reason and Passion in Dante

ELENA LOMBARDI

Amilcare Iannucci's essay "Forbidden Love: Metaphor and History" is one of the most significant contributions to the endless and tormented exegesis of *Inferno* 5 because it helps to historicise the canto in a very original way, identifying within the episode of Francesca a marked historical metaphor.[1] Iannucci locates Dante's episode within a literary trend that records the "joining of two irrational and destructive forces, love and war" (94). This model originates in the myth of Ares and Aphrodite as recounted in the eighth book of the *Odyssey* (8.266–369). The beautiful deities of love and war carry on an illicit affair at the expense of the deformed Hephaestus, who captures the lovers in a fine net, inviting the other gods to deride them, until Poseidon appeals to set them free. Iannucci points out that the Ares and Aphrodite structure is most directly embedded in the story of Troy, where the Olympian laughter is turned into destruction and madness. Both the Olympian and the earthly story are articulated in three phases: they both begin with marriage, representing balance and harmony, which is then troubled by the adulterous affair: "Passion overwhelms reason, and the law is broken" (95). The wronged husband and his allies then re-establish peace and the law through violence. Thus, adultery deranges the course of history and exposes its mad and violent side.

This structure is replicated in countless medieval romances, including that of Lancelot and Guinevere. Iannucci shows that this model is also reproduced in the story of Francesca, at least as it is told by early commentators, notably Boccaccio, and argues that Dante's moral conclusion in *Inferno* 5 is that passion leads to disorder, not only in the individual but also in society. Thus, Iannucci brings to light an understudied aspect of the episode, namely the "societal implications of unchecked passion" (98), and shows an important yet rarely emphasized continuity between canto 5 and the two contiguous cantos: canto 6, the first political canto of *Hell*, and Limbo, which is featured as a battle between reason and passion, Rome and Babylon, in another of Iannucci's remarkable and enduring interpretations.[2]

As is well known, but so easily forgotten, the complete story of the love between two handsome youths, Francesca da Rimini and Paolo Malatesta, as well as their tragic death by the hand of Francesca's husband and Paolo's brother, the deformed Gianciotto, is a fabrication of early commentators. As Teodolinda Barolini notices, Dante, who is Francesca's "historian of record," only gives four very bare indications of the plot: her name is Francesca (*Inf.* 5.116); she was born near the Po delta (5.97–9), which is, as many commentators agree, a very vague reference to the city of Ravenna; she and her lover were "cognati" (6.2) or sister and brother in law, and were killed by one of their kin (5.108).[3] Historians of the canto and of medieval Romagna explain that Francesca is a very minor player in the historical context. Her marriage to Gianciotto (John the Lame), the son of the emerging leader of Rimini, Malatesta da Verucchio, sealed the alliance between two powerful families, the Da Polenta from Ravenna and the Malatesta from Rimini. There is no historical evidence of the romance between Francesca and Paolo, Gianciotto's younger brother. Her death along with Paolo's, which occurred between 1283 and 1286, did not revoke the alliance between the Polentani and the Malatesta or even hinder further intermarriage between the two families. Francesca is a footnote in history,[4] poeticized by Dante and made legendary by the work of the commentators.

Iannucci points out that the enhancements of the commentary tradition, chiefly Boccaccio's, serve precisely to "mythologize" the story of Paolo and Francesca. While the details of the marriage by proxy and the burial in a single tomb are famously derived from the story of Tristan and Iseult, "the figure of the informer, the deformed husband, the imagery of the net-like trap, he [Boccaccio] took from the adultery of Venus and Mars" (97). Iannucci explains that Boccaccio "recognizes in it [canto 5] an archetypal pattern and proceeds to reproduce it through narrative amplification and embellishment" (97). The Ares and Aphrodite structure is embedded in one crucial moment of the canto, the so-called catalogue of the Queens:

La prima di color di cui novelle
tu vuo' saper, mi disse quelli allotta,

fu imperadrice di molte favelle.
A vizio di lussuria fu sì rotta,
che libito fé licito in sua legge,
per tòrre il biasmo in che era condotta.
Ell' è Semiramìs, di cui si legge
che succedette a Nino e fu sua sposa:
tenne la terra che 'l Soldan corregge.
L'altra è colei che s'ancise amorosa,
e ruppe fede al cener di Sicheo;
poi è Cleopatràs lussurïosa.
Elena vedi, per cui tanto reo
tempo si volse, e vedi 'l grande Achille,
che con amore al fine combatteo.
Vedi Parìs, Tristano; e più di mille
ombre mostrommi e nominommi a dito,
ch'amor di nostra vita dipartille. (*Inf.* 5.52–69)

(The first of them about whom you would hear, he then replied, was empress over many tongues. She was so given to the vice of lechery she made lust licit in her law to take away the blame she had incurred. She is Semiramis, of whom we read that she, once Ninus's wife, succeeded him. She held sway in the land the Sultan rules. Here is she who broke faith with the ashes of Sichaeus and slew herself for love. The next is wanton Cleopatra. See Helen, for whose sake so many years of ill rolled past. And see the great Achilles, who battled, at the last, with love. See Paris, Tristan; and he showed me more than a thousand shades, naming as he pointed, whom love had parted from our life.)

These lustful lovers are distinguished by their lofty historical and / or literary status. The dames and knights of old not only embody extremely important texts that are the "background library" of this episode (*Iliad*, *Aeneid*, the *Romance of Tristan*) but also play central roles in large-scale historical events, mostly violent in nature. Iannucci points out that tales of love and war are implicitly invoked in these lines. Semiramis (*Inf.* 5.52–60), empress of many people, recalls the Babylonian expansion wars in Asia Minor; Dido (5.61–2) prefigures the Carthaginian wars of the Roman Republic; and Cleopatra (5.63) augurs the civil wars at the onset of the empire. The devastation and mourning brought about by the Trojan War is implied in the figures of Helen (5.64), Achilles (5.65), and Paris (5.67), and the turmoil in Cornwall is evoked by Tristan (5.67).

Iannucci explores in particular the figure of Semiramis and her origins in Orosius (*Historiae* 1.4.7–8), Ovid (*Metamorphoses* 4.58), and Augustine (*De civitate Dei* 18.2). These intertexts make her an image for the corrupt *civitas mundi*, and the type of "lawlessness, or better, how passion creates its own laws" (100). The first sinner to be mentioned by name, Semiramis not only typifies (as all other damned in hell do) the realization of one corrupt earthly self but also the fulfilment of Babylon, of the corruption of the earthly city. As such, she is a true synecdoche of hell.

Following Iannucci's lead, this essay explores the relation between lust and law – famously recalled in canto 5's description of Semiramis, who "made lust licit in her law" (*Inf.* 5.56; "che libito fé licito in sua legge") – and, more generally, between passion and reason in Dante's oeuvre, and emphasizes the threat that lust/passion posits not only to the well-being and salvation of the individual self but also to the political stability of society.

One of the many purposes of the catalogue of the Queens is to convey the transition and, indeed, to emphasize the continuity between the sin of lust and the spiritualized and poeticized experience of love. On the one hand, Dante emphasizes the sin with the customary lust of Semiramis, "che libito fé licito in sua legge" (5.55) and with Cleopatra, described as "lussuriosa" (5.63). On the other hand, the theme of lust is interwoven with that of love. Dido is "amorosa" (5.61); Achilles "con amore al fine combatteo" (5.66; battled, at the last, with love); all the other souls in this rank were departed from our life because of love, "amor di nostra vita dipartille" (5.69).

It is my argument that lust is indeed the unstable and destabilizing interface between many discourses in medieval culture. It transcends the narrow definition of sexual desire and the tight category of sin of the flesh to inhabit the realm of love and interact with pillars of the medieval moral world, such as reason and the law. Lust is a problematic sin because it is both quintessentially spiritual (so much so that some equated it with original sin) and yet fundamentally embodied, because it is connected to two central features of the human condition, reproduction and love, and because it has societal as well as individual consequences. Lust is constructed in very different ways in theological, monastic, and pastoral environments and involves such different disciplines as canon law and medicine.[5] Traditionally lust is divided into six categories. For instance, Aquinas (*Summa theologiae* 2a–2ae.153–4) breaks lust down into simple fornication (any intercourse that is not geared towards reproduction), adultery (extramarital), incest (among relatives), seduction (the illicit deflowering of a virgin), rape (violence on an abducted woman), and sin against nature (masturbation, bestiality, homosexuality, and improper use of sexual organs). To these, tradition often adds sacrilege (among those who have taken vows) and understands fornication as intercourse with widows, concubines, and prostitutes.

Luxuria is the official name of lust as vice, whereas *concupiscientia* or *cupiditas* indicates its theological manifestation as the "disordered affectivity, the tendency of natural desires and appetites to pursue their own objects in disregard to the proper order of reason."[6] Other inflections of lust are *libido, lascivia, incontinentia,* and the more philosophical *intemperantia.* Both terminologically and ideologically there is a very fine line between "impulse" and "sexual impulse," lust being always conceived as the primary consequence and illustration of inordinate desire.[7]

The position of lust between soul and body, its dangerous naturality, and the fact that the sexual drive has important implications for attraction, love, thought, and memory combine to make it a very difficult sin to define. The compiler of the *Fasciculus morum*, a fourteenth-century Franciscan handbook for preaching, provides four diverging definitions of the sin: spiritual intemperance, bodily incontinence, desire, and the blinding of reason. He writes:

> Circa primum est sciendum quod a diversis diversimode diffinitur. Quidam enim dicunt primo sic: "Luxuria est anime perverse amantis corporeas voluptates neclecta temperancia." Secundo alius sic: "Luxuria est incontinencia corporis ex pruritu carnis nascens vel originem habens." Tercio per alium sic: "Luxuria est concubitus desiderium supra modum et contra racione effluens." Quarto, Bernardus: "Luxuria est sitis ebria, deflacio momentanea, amaritudo eterna; lucem odit, tenebras appetit, totam hominis depredatur mentem."
>
> (On the first point we should know that lechery is variously defined by various authors. Some say: "Lechery is the failure to observe moderation in a soul that perversely loves bodily pleasures." Another author says: "Lechery is bodily incontinence, which is born of or has its origin in the itching of our flesh." Yet another definition is this: "Lechery is the desire to have sex, which rises beyond measure and against reason." And a fourth definition, according to Bernard, declares: "Lechery is drunken thirst, a

momentary outburst, eternal bitterness; it shuns the light, seeks darkness, and entirely plunders man's mind.")[8]

The idea that lust is a fundamentally spiritual sin, turning the rational soul against itself and making it blind, and reducing humans to mere bestiality, resonates strongly in the theological and monastic context. In places like monasteries where the occasion for sinning is removed, lust resides in thoughts, desires, memories, and the illusions and seductions of the world, which must be fought with both bodily and spiritual discipline. The theological discourse on lust revolves mainly around the connection between the spiritual and the bodily aspects of the sin, on its being natural and necessary to the continuation of the species, and on its declensions. Finally, in the world lust is a very bodily sin, indeed the only sin, as Carla Casagrande and Silvana Vecchio observe, to involve all the senses: primarily vision, but also hearing (seduced by words and music), smell (overwhelmed by perfumes), taste (lured by food and wines), and touch (enticed by inappropriate contact). Moreover, it was held that lust infected the body with all sorts of diseases (among which leprosy is often mentioned), that it manifested itself through a fetid stench, and, according to Robert Grosseteste, potentially involved every body fluid or excretion.[9] Medieval doctors were busy finding remedies for the "disease of love" (*hereos*), while Greek and Arabic medical texts, first appearing in translation in the twelfth and thirteenth centuries, treated sexuality as a phenomenon of the human body, with its own causes, effects, benefits, and remedies.[10]

Besides being a sin and a disease, lust was also a crime.[11] It appears to be, indeed, the only sin of incontinence that is of concern for medieval canonists due to its societal consequences and its intersection with marriage law. Lust features prominently in Gratian's *Decretum*, where we find five kinds of "illegal coitus," which become the five or six traditional declensions of lust (*fornicatio*, *stuprum*, *adulterium*, *incestus*, and *raptus*).[12] Any sexual behaviour that deviated from marriage and reproduction (or threatened the celibacy of the religious) was perceived as a menace to society. Strikingly, adultery was considered the most relevant sexual crime, even the benchmark of major sexual offences, and sexual offences committed by women were considered more reprehensible than those committed by men.[13]

At the beginning of *Inferno* 5, Virgil defines the sinners in the second circle in an apparently plain manner as those "who make reason subject to desire" (5.39; che la ragion sottomettono al talento). However, Dante's definition is truly ambivalent. On the one hand, it is very fitting for lust, as poignantly represented by the *contrapasso* in the first circle. The storm, the main meteorological passion, drags the hopeless sinners in a completely irrational fashion "di qua, di là, di su, di giù" (*Inf.* 5.43; here and there, down and up). On the other hand, this definition fits well all sins of incontinence, and sin in general (as a blinding of reason in favour of evil) as Boccaccio cleverly points out in his commentary.[14] The characterization of lust clearly resembles that of *cupiditas*, the inordinate desire at the root of every human evil. More problematically, this definition is also very fitting for love, as Teodolinda Barolini has shown by gathering many examples in the love lyrics of Dante's time.[15] In calling into question *ragione* and *talento*, Dante signals that lust is the trigger of a larger discourse and the unstable subheading of a wider philosophical clash. Dante taps into one of the greatest debates of ancient and medieval philosophy and poetry, the conflict between reason and passion. Reason leads to ascent, order, and social cohesion whereas passion leads to debasement, disorder, and subversion of the social fabric. Passion is always associated with the sensible world of matter, the body, movement, change, and pleasure. Lust, although sometimes a minor subheading of a larger category, represents a powerful and problematic example of the tyranny of passion over reason.

From Plato's *Phaedo* through Aristotle's *Nicomachean Ethics* and *De anima*, Cicero's *Tusculan Disputations*, Aquinas's *Summa theologiae*, and all the way to Erasmus's *Enchiridion*, ancient and medieval philosophy regularly contrast passion and reason; the latter needs to subjugate (Plato), repress (Cicero and the Stoics), or minimally cultivate and direct (Aristotle and Aquinas) the former in order for both the individual and the society to function. The relation between the two is articulated by two main metaphors: that of the battle, whereby the human soul is presented as a battleground of mind and reason versus appetite and passion, and that of horse riding: reason, the horseman, must rein in and govern passion, the horse. While the first image implies the necessity of the extinction of passion, the second hints rather at its taming and suggests the usefulness of passion: if well directed and correctly spurred, desire may become a useful and faithful carrier for the self.

The relations between reason and passion also feature prominently in love poetry. Here, the balance between the two radically shifts in favour of love; one of the tenets of love literature is precisely the fact that love overcomes reason. Here too the image of the restive horse characterizes the need to rein in passion and appears in both the classics and the medieval romance tradition. It is found, for instance, in Ovid's *Amores*, where the unrestrained horse is compared to the "wind of lust" carrying the poet away,[16] and it is a recurrent theme in Petrarch's *Canzoniere*.[17]

Aristotle's *Nicomachean Ethics* contains one of the most elaborate projects of reconciling desire and pleasure to reason, with a view to moral and philosophical happiness, in which temperance (ἀκρασία, the moderate use of bodily pleasures such as sex and food) and its opposite (ἀκολασία) play a crucial role. In the tenth book of the *Ethics* in particular, Aristotle outlines a program of aligning happiness (the pursuit of pleasure) with intelligence and the contemplative life (and with politics). The medieval sense of irony does not spare the Philosopher. A common medieval story, drawing on eastern folktales possibly first popularized in the West by Jacques de Vitry (thirteenth century), has Aristotle lecture his pupil Alexander on the dangers of Eros, only to find himself subsequently stalked by Phyllis, the very courtesan that Alexander abandoned at the teacher's suggestion. Aristotle eventually gives in to all of her whims, including letting her ride him and whip him like a horse, thus subverting the traditional image of reason riding and reining in passion. When caught in this embarrassing position by his pupil, the Philosopher at least gets the last word; his situation proves the difficulty of fighting desire, shows its horrid consequences, and justifies the sternness of the teacher's lecture.[18] In the story of Aristotle and the courtesan, lust stands as the line of least resistance for the rational self, the point of breakage that triggers the revenge of passion. Lust appears as the grotesque opposite of wisdom and knowledge, but the ironic target of the story is philosophy's attempt to overcome every passion or desire in general.

Aristotle is not the only victim of lust's revenge. In the Middle Ages similar stories circulated concerning wise men, characters such as Solomon and Virgil, caught in unphilosophical situations with attractive young women. Even Boccaccio's statement about Dante's own lust in the *Trattatello*, in the context of praise of the poet's virtue and knowledge, must be best read along these lines.[19] Young Dante's own problem with the excesses of love is traditionally related to his extravagant (i.e., not collected in the *Vita nuova*) lyrical poetry. Thus, we still read in ancient and modern commentaries alike that in *Inferno* 5 Dante faces "his own sin," which strangely encompasses both tragic love and disorderly poetry.

Lust, love, and love poetry inhabit the same neighbourhood, as *Inferno* 5 clearly demonstrates. In one of the sequences depicted on the ceiling in the main room of the Chiaramonte Palace in Palermo (ca. 1380), we find a powerful illustration of the mingling of the three elements. A series of tableaux recounting episodes of the story of Tristan and Iseult are immediately followed by a depiction of Aristotle being ridden by the courtesan. There is no distance, the painter suggests, between the idealistic and poetic expansion of the great love stories and the comically grotesque example of the philosopher being reduced to beast.[20]

Dante suggests something similar in the terrace of the lustful in purgatory (*Purg.* 26), where he gives a more traditional definition of lust, including both homosexual and heterosexual love (which are famously and problematically displaced in hell, sodomy being enlisted as a sin of violence against nature). This canto is possibly even more metapoetic than *Inferno* 5, featuring as speakers two poets of the courtly love tradition: Guido Guinizzelli and Arnaut Daniel. The definition of heterosexual lust in *Purgatorio* 26 emphasizes the two opposite aspects of bestiality and legality. After describing the homosexual ranks as those who share Caesar's inclination, Guinizzelli illustrates the excesses of the heterosexual ranks with the example of Pasiphaë's coupling with the bull:

> Nostro peccato fu ermafrodito
> ma poiché non servammo umana legge,
> seguendo come bestie l'appetito
> in obbrobrio di noi, per noi si legge,
> quando partinci, il nome di colei
> che s'imbestiò ne le 'mbestiate schegge. (*Purg.* 26.82–7)

> (Hermaphroditic was our sin. Because we did not follow human law, but ran behind our appetites like beasts, when, in our disgrace, we move off from the others, we shout her name who made herself a beast inside the beast-shaped rough-hewn wood.)

In this passage, Dante rephrases the notions of *ragione* (reason) and *talento* (desire) from *Inferno* 5 through their amplifications – "human law" and "bestiality." The expression "umana legge" (83; human law) is unanimously glossed as "reason" in the light of *Inferno* 5.39 "submitting reason to desire" and of a passage in *Convivio* 2.7.4, where Dante states, "Chi da la ragion si parte, e usa pur la parte sensitiva, non vive uomo ma vive bestia" (He who departs from his reason and uses merely his sensitive part lives not as a man but as a beast). However, the excerpt from *Convivio* points to the fact that being or becoming "like a beast" is the consequence of sin in general and not of lust in particular. Yet, here bestiality stands for one of the subspecies of lust (species crossing): according to Aquinas, bestiality is by far the worst form of lust, as it is a sin that goes beyond the bounds of humanity (*Summa theologiae* 2a–2ae.154, 12). If referred to the example of Pasiphaë, "human law" might be rephrased as "the law of nature which supervises human intercourse." If we refer to Guido Guinizzelli and Arnaut Daniel, who, as poets of the courtly love tradition, celebrated extramarital love, this excess might then be waged not only against reason but also against the laws of society, namely against matrimony.[21] Thus, by having Guido Guinizzelli illustrate the powerful example of Pasiphaë, Dante seems to draw the reader's attention to the ultimate similarity *sub specie aeternitatis* of two extreme happenings of what in *Inferno* 5 he discusses ambiguously as "love": on the material/bodily side, the extreme sexual choice of "species crossing"; on the intellectual/spiritual side, the extreme expansion of courtly poetry. Much like the illustrations of Palazzo Chiaramonte, Dante reveals that the distance between heroic love stories sung by the lofty words of the poets and the horrid example of Pasiphaë is very short.[22]

The struggle between reason and passion is a central topic in Dante's work, where these very terms fluctuate between the realms of the philosophical and the erotic. In the remainder of this essay, I shall explore the dynamics of lust/passion versus reason/the law in Dante, with focus on the image of horse riding, and show how the conflation of the erotic and the philosophical leads, quite unexpectedly, to the political. The breaking of the law that supervises human intercourse affects not only the individual self (lust as sin) and the very fabric of society (lust as crime) but also the mechanisms that regulate human interrelations, such as societies and nations.

Throughout his early work and in the *Vita nuova*, Dante explores the erotics of passion, eventually locating *eros* under the strict control of reason. In the description of his first meeting with Beatrice at the age of nine (*Vita nuova* 2.9–10), the reader is informed that the love that sprang forth then was, and always would be, accompanied by "the faithful advice of reason" (2.9; lo fedele consiglio de la ragione).[23] At the end of the *libello*, the attraction to a woman other than (dead) Beatrice is stigmatized as the "enemy of reason" (39.1; avversario de la ragione).[24]

One of Dante's most subtle strategies in the rational appropriation of love is found in the sonnet *Amore e il cor gentil sono una cosa*, which is very much in the background of *Inferno* 5. In this sonnet, Dante first quotes Guido Guinizzelli and his poem *Al cor gentil* as authorities for his own definition of love: "Amore e 'l cor gentil sono una cosa, / sì come il saggio in suo dittare pone" (1–2; Love and the gracious heart are a single thing, as Guinizelli tells us in his poem). Whereas Guinizzelli had illustrated the relation between love and the gentle heart with a series of images drawn from nature (bird, fire, and stone), Dante here provides a more Aristotelian simile, comparing the relation between love and the gentle heart to that of reason and the rational soul: "e così esser l'un sanza l'altro osa / com'alma razional sanza ragione" (3–4; One can no more be without the other than can the reasoning mind without its reason), thus suggesting the interdependence of the erotic and the rational.

The philosophical battlefield between reason and passion in Dante's oeuvre is the discussion of natural desire in the *Convivio*. Dante posits that the use of reason is the very definition of the human being ("vivere nell'uomo è ragione usare," *Conv.* 4.7.11) and that to live like an animal is equivalent to being dead.[25] The way the relation between desire and reason is established in the *Convivio* is as unproblematic as the condemnation of lust appears to be at the beginning of *Inferno* 5 and in *Purgatorio* 26: whoever abandons the route of reason lives the life of a beast, is dead to the higher aspects of life, and even potentially damned.

When reason is discussed in relation to natural desire, however, Dante's argument becomes much more nuanced and complex. Natural desire is the irrational, innate, and spontaneous instinct that drives all things – inanimate and animate alike – towards their own good. Dante first describes natural desire in *Convivio* 3.3.1–11, in the context of his claim that the "love that discourses in my mind" in the song that opens the third treatise is not a base or sensible type of love (it is not lust), but the rational love for the truth. In a passage reminiscent of Augustine's notion of the *pondus amoris* (weight of love), but also of several other theological and philosophical authorities, such as Thomas Aquinas and Albert the Great, Dante states that each thing has its "speziale amore" (*Conv.* 3.4.1; special love). Simple bodies such as earth and fire always tend to one direction (earth downwards, fire upwards), mixed bodies, such as minerals, privilege the place where they were created, plants manifest their love in their choice of different places (humid, dry, etc.), animals in the choice of both place and species (natural desire in reproduction, "natural lust"). The human being, the most complex creature of all, shares all these loves.[26] It is driven to gravity, to the place and time of its generation, to food, and to both an animal desire for reproduction (which in the human being becomes a very powerful drive that needs to be controlled) and a rational love for truth and friendship.[27]

Dante returns to the theme of natural desire towards the end of the fourth book of the *Convivio* (4.21 and 22),[28] while discussing human goodness and happiness. Likely relying on Cicero's *De finibus*, Dante defines this desire as *hormen*, which he first translates as "appetito d'animo" (4.21.13) and then as "appetito d'animo naturale" (4.22.4). This desire is indeed very similar to the natural desire analysed in the third treatise of *Convivio*, but here it is presented as divinely instituted in human beings and, therefore, differing from the desire of inanimate objects, plants, or animals.[29] Although initially similar to all other desires, the *hormen* diversifies itself from them and finds its rational route, electing the soul as the part of the human being that is best and, therefore, most worthy of love.[30] The relation between reason and passion is presented once again as obvious and natural (the natural desire of the human being is to cultivate the rational part of the self), although the rhetoric of the self's love for its rational part is strongly erotic. The text then moves into a digression on the ways the "root" can turn out badly and how this can be rectified through the cross-pollination effected by correction and education (4.22.12).

Later in the book Dante returns to the theme of the *hormen*, describing it as an instinctual drive. Like a horse, the *hormen* pursues and flees in order to lead the human being to perfection.[31] Thus, it needs to be reined in by reason:

> Veramente questo appetito conviene essere cavalcato dalla ragione; ché sì come uno sciolto cavallo, quanto ch'ello sia di natura nobile, per sé, sanza lo buono cavalcatore, bene non si conduce, così questo appetito, che irascibile e concupiscibile si chiama, quanto ch'ello sia nobile, alla ragione obedire conviene, la quale guida quello con freno e con isproni, come buono cavaliere. (*Conv.* 4.26.6)
>
> (Nevertheless this appetite must be ridden by reason, for just as a horse set loose, however noble it may be by nature, cannot act as its own guide without a good rider, so the appetite, which is called irascible or concupiscible, however noble it may be, must obey reason, which guides it with bridle and spurs like a good horseman.)

In an Aristotelian fashion, the restrictive element of reason (*il freno*) is the virtue of temperance, while the spurring element (*lo sprone*) is magnanimity.[32] The exemplar is Aeneas, who was unrestrained like a horse ("infrenato") in his early adulthood. Thus, he needed to be "bridled in" when it came to Dido and spurred in the case of the journey in the underworld. Reason restricts lust and incites knowledge:

> E così infrenato mostra Virgilio, lo maggiore nostro poeta, che fosse Enea, nella parte dello Eneida ove questa etade si figura: la qual parte comprende lo quarto, lo quinto e lo sesto libro dello Eneida. E quanto raffrenare fu quello, quando, avendo ricevuto da Dido tanto piacere quanto di sotto nel settimo trattato si dicerà, e usando con essa tanto di dilettazione, elli si partio, per seguire onesta e laudabile via e fruttuosa. (*Conv.* 4.26.8)
>
> (Vergil, our greatest poet, shows that Aeneas was unrestrained in this way in that part of the Aeneid in which this age of life is allegorized, the part comprising the fourth, fifth, and sixth books of the Aeneid. How great was his restraint when, having experienced so much pleasure with Dido, as will be recounted below in the seventh book, and having derived from her so much gratification, he took his departure from her to follow an honorable, praiseworthy and profitable path.)

One can only lament the absence of the seventh book of the *Convivio*, in which Dante claimed he would have expanded on this point. Dante's meditation on natural desire continues in the *Comedy*. Initially it dovetails again with the erotic and the lyrical, albeit in the context of the severe infernal condemnation of "those who submitted reason to desire." In line with a long tradition of love-lyric that involves young Dante himself, Francesca characterizes erotic love as instinctual and, therefore, innocent and ineluctable:

> Amor, ch'al cor gentil ratto s'apprende,
> prese costui de la bella persona
> che mi fu tolta; e 'l modo ancor m'offende.
> Amor, ch'a nullo amato amar perdona,
> mi prese del costui piacer sì forte,
> che, come vedi, ancor non m'abbandona. (*Inf.* 5.100–6)
>
> (Love, quick to kindle in the gentle heart, seized this man with the fair form taken from me. The way of it afflicts me still. Love, which absolves no one beloved from loving, seized me so strongly with his charm that, as you see, it has not left me yet.)

In the first line Francesca notably echoes Guinizzelli's *Al cor gentil*, as well as Dante's own echoes of Guinizzelli in *Amore e il cor gentil*, but she also indicates the point at which love spins out of control and becomes a bestial passion that subjugates reason: it is the velocity implied in the word *ratto*, which defies the control of reason and propels the lovers "onto one death" (*Inf.* 5.107; ad una morte). While Francesca's somewhat rushed reading appears as a justification of courtly tenets, the poet's placement of the lovers in hell appears as a straightforward censure of the same assumptions. This seemingly plain scenario conceals its own complexity, which is made explicit in Dante's reflection on natural desire at the centre of purgatory, where the philosophical discourse on natural desire from the *Convivio* and the erotic meditation on the lyric tradition from *Inferno* 5 converge. In purgatory, Dante glosses courtly principles (that love is innate in the human being, that it derives from the sight of the beloved object, and that it is powered by desire) with a largely Thomistic framework, thus depriving those tenets of their singularity, and de-eroticizes love by framing it in the wider question of reason, passion, and free will. At the heart of the second *cantica* Dante radically rewrites the courtly and *stilnovo* notion that love is inevitable (and praiseworthy) because it is natural by firmly harnessing this natural inclination to free will.

Dante's theory of love in purgatory is articulated through the three arguments laid out in cantos 16–18. The discourse on natural desire begins quite surprisingly with a civil/political question in canto 16, where Dante asks Marco Lombardo the reason for the current unrest and evilness of earthly affairs. Marco puts the blame on human beings: as creatures endowed with free will, they have sole responsibility for what happens on earth. Marco then famously describes the newly embodied human soul as a playful little girl, who intuitively longs to return to her creator, yet follows inordinately every little object of desire, and is forever at risk of falling into sin.[33] Recalling the horse-riding image, Marco explains that the law and the prince are the only means of bridling (*freno*) and directing (*guida*) the innocent but inordinate natural desire:

Di picciol bene in pria sente sapore;
quivi s'inganna, e dietro ad esso corre,
se guida o fren non torce suo amore.
Onde convenne legge per fren porre;
convenne rege aver, che discernesse
de la vera cittade almen la torre. (*Purg.* 16.91–6)

> (At first it tastes the savor of a trifling good. It is beguiled by that and follows in pursuit if guide or rein do not deflect its love. Therefore, there was need that laws be set to act as curbs, need for a ruler to discern at least the tower above the one true city.)

The antidote to inordinate desire, which in the *Convivio* and *Inferno* 5 is human reason, is here rephrased as human law and imperial authority – one that is sadly absent in Dante's contemporary Italy, and in the whole world, since both the imperial and papal authorities, "Rome's two suns," are at the moment obscured.[34]

In canto 17, however, the focus turns steadily on love, the centre of the Christian world, where "né Creator né creatura mai fu sanza amore" (*Purg.* 17.91–2; neither Creator nor his creature … was ever without love). In the human being a fundamental distinction is traced between the natural, instinctual side of love ("amore … natural," 17.93), which is free of guilt ("sempre senza errore," 17.94) and the elective side of love ("amore … d'animo," 17.93), which carries the possibility of error. Natural love is the sign of divinity within the human being, the confused suggestion that there is a goal of all desires.[35] Elective love is the seed of every virtue (when it pursues the first intuition that God is the end of all desires) and vice (when it diverges from it).[36]

In the next canto Dante provides a rational demonstration of the nature of love, with the intention of dispelling the mistakes of "the blind who make themselves guides" (i.e., the poets and theorists of courtly love; *Purg.* 18.18). Love, a potentiality of the human soul, "ch'è creato ad amar presto" (18.19; which is created quick to love) takes place in three steps. First, it is stirred by the pleasure deriving from a beautiful object ("cosa che piace," "piacer," 18.20–1). The pleasant object is then abstracted by the faculty of apprehension, causing the soul to bend towards it and bind itself to the beloved object within the human self.[37] Finally, the captive soul holds on to the beloved object by means of desire, a restless motion of the soul, which is compared to fire.

Virgil's explanation of the nature of love ends abruptly with the image of expanded and relentless desire; the master seems convinced that he has dispelled the mistakes of courtly poets and theorists and their belief that if love is in itself innate and good, so every love must be so.[38] Yet the pupil (and the reader) remains quite confused about why there are sinful dispositions in a love that is innate and to which the soul is inevitably drawn and asks for more. Virgil raises the stakes by stating that he can answer Dante only insofar as human reason is concerned. Only Beatrice will be able to illuminate fully the subject according to faith.[39] Human reason, which in *Vita nuova, Convivio,* and *Inferno* 5 served to restrain passion, proves itself unable to understand passion and requires, therefore, a supernatural support.

In his rational explanation, Virgil looks back to Marco Lombardo's point on the primal desires of the human soul and free will. He relates the scholastic notion that the human soul has some specific virtues that are understood only in operation, just as the specificity of the tree is seen through its foliage.[40] The specific virtue of the human soul is to have principles of knowledge (*notizia*) and desire (*affetto*). These principles are (mysteriously to the pagan guide) innate to the soul, and they incline it towards some universal objects of desire ("i primi appetibili," *Purg*. 18.57). These first desires are beyond sin and virtue ("questa prima voglia / merto di lode o di biasmo non cape," 18.59–60), like the impulse of the bee to produce honey ("come studio in ape / di far lo mele," 18.58–9). Another virtue that is innate to the rational soul is "la virtù che consiglia" (18.62; the faculty that counsels), which has the capacity to oversee the homology between the first natural desire towards the supreme good and all the other, secondary desires.[41] Classical philosophers already noticed this innate freedom ("innata libertate," 18.68), which counteracts the theory of the ineluctability of appetites. Only Christianity, here emphatically embodied by Beatrice, explicitly understands this faculty as free will: "la nobile virtù Beatrice intende / per lo libero arbitrio" (18.73–4; this noble virtue Beatrice understands as the free will), which, as Bruno Nardi explains "is the free judgment of reason on action, not obstructed by appetite."[42]

At the centre of purgatory, then, we witness a circular strategy that encloses lust/love/natural desire within the perimeters of reason, will, and the law. First (in canto 16), Marco Lombardo joins free will (as the root of all evil in the world) to natural desire and establishes the law and imperial authority as the curbing elements for natural desire, and therefore, as the corrective measure against the degeneration of human will. Then (at the beginning of canto 18), Virgil elaborates philosophically on the courtly assumptions about the naturalness and ineluctability of love. Finally (at the end of canto 18), Virgil returns to Marco's premise by deepening the discourse on natural desire and putting it under the control of an already rectified free will and under the aegis of a glorified (adulterous) lover, Beatrice.

Interestingly, an uncommon image of horse riding follows the explanation on the nature of love. The rush of the slothful towards purgation is compared to the fury of the Bacchic revelers in Thebes:

> E quale Ismeno già vide e Asopo
> lungo di sè di notte furia e calca,
> pur che i Teban di Bacco avesser uopo,
> cotal per quel giron suo passo falca,
> per quel ch'io vidi di color, venendo,
> cui buon volere e giusto amor cavalca. (*Purg*. 18.91–6)

> (As once the rivers Ismenus and Asopus saw a furious throng of revelers crowd their banks on any night, the Thebans felt the need for Bacchus, such a throng cut their way, as does a sickle, around that circle, and I could tell that right will and just love drove them on.)

Dante conflates two contrasting images in this simile. On the one hand, the orgiastic Bacchic rites bring to mind the sacralization, one may say even the politicization, of passion and lust: they are indeed "lust made licit."[43] On the other hand, in the second half of the simile, a new image of horse riding emerges, signalled by expressions such as *cavalcare* (to ride) and *falcare*, describing the striding pace of a galloping horse (technically "falcade" or "curvet").[44] This image partially reverses the traditional illustration of "reason on top," and, at the same time, verifies the theory of love put forth at the centre of purgatory. Although love, and not reason, is in the saddle and rides the purging spirits, the consequence is not any grotesque reverse in line with the Aristotle-courtesan imagery (implicitly recalled by the blinding of reason in the Bacchic orgies). There are indeed two riders of the penitent self: a rightful love and *buona volontà*, the already rectified will.

This image shifts the emphasis from unbridled natural desire (as in *Vita nuova*, *Convivio* 3 and 4, *Inferno* 5, and the beginning of *Purgatorio* 18), which needs to be regulated and "mounted" by reason, to the role of the will. Although in purgatory the will is truly free and unconstrained, on earth, as Marco Lombardo states at the beginning of this episode, it needs to be reined in by the law.

The constellation lust-reason-will steers towards the civil and the political. A passage from the fourth book of the *Convivio* frames this transition with extraordinary clarity. By introducing imperial authority as the perfection of human life and "the regulator and the ruler" of all human operations (*Conv.* 4.9.1), Dante breaks down human activities into two categories: those that are supervised by reason and those that are supervised by the will. Examples of the latter kind of activity are "offendere e giovare, sì come star fermo e fuggire alla battaglia, sì come stare casto e lussuriare" (*Conv.* 4.9.7; giving offence or assistance, standing ground or fleeing in battle, and remaining chaste or yielding to lust). Such activities are fully subject to the human will, and they define one as good or evil.[45] Justice is the human aim of such activities and, in order to foster it, "the written reason" (i.e., Roman law) was established.[46] In this passage, lust is taken as an illustration of a human sin or vice that hampers justice and requires the law, which is in turn presented as the highest achievement of human reason, indeed reason itself written down. Lust's subversion of reason becomes here much more a civil than an individual matter. This challenge requires a very special horseman, the emperor himself.[47]

> Sì che quasi dire si può dello Imperadore, volendo lo suo officio figurare con una imagine, che elli sia lo cavalcatore della umana volontade. Lo quale cavallo come vada sanza lo cavalcatore per lo campo assai è manifesto, e spezialmente nella misera Italia, che sanza mezzo alcuno alla sua gubernazione è rimasa! (*Conv.* 4.9.10)
>
> (Thus we might say of the Emperor, if we were to describe his office with an image, that he is the one who rides in the saddle of the human will. How this horse pricks across the plain without a rider is more than evident, especially in wretched Italy, which has been left with no means whatsoever to govern herself.)

This segment anticipates directly two passages in purgatory: Marco Lombardo's speech (canto 16), which articulates the relation between natural desire, free will, and the law, and the political invective in *Purgatorio* 6, where Italy, a destitute prostitute ("non donna di province, ma bordello" [*Purg.* 6.78; no mistress over provinces but a harlot]), is compared to a horse left for too long without a rider, which is now impossible to tame:

> Che val perché ti racconciasse il freno
> Iustinïano, se la sella è vòta?
> Sanz' esso fora la vergogna meno.

Ahi gente che dovresti esser devota,
e lasciar seder Cesare in la sella,
se bene intendi ciò che Dio ti nota,
guarda come esta fiera è fatta fella
per non esser corretta da li sproni,
poi che ponesti mano a la predella.
O Alberto tedesco ch'abbandoni
costei ch'è fatta indomita e selvaggia,
e dovresti inforcar li suoi arcioni. (*Purg.* 6.88–99)

(If there is no one in your saddle, what good was it Justinian repaired your harness? Your shame would be less great had he not done so. Ah, you who should be firm in your devotion and let Caesar occupy the saddle, if you but heeded what God writes for you, see how vicious is the beast not goaded and corrected by the spurs, ever since you took the bridle in your hands. O German Albert, who abandon her now that she is untamed and wild, you who should bestride her saddle-bow.)

This is perhaps the most complex horse-riding metaphor in Dante's work. Italy is compared to a horse, which was tame in the past, thanks to the harness adjusted by Justinian (the *Corpus iuris civilis*). However, the main seat of the emperor (saddle, saddle-bow) is empty, and no corrective or punitive measures (spurs) are in place. Therefore, she becomes a wild and indomitable beast ("fiera … fella … indomita e selvaggia," 6.94, 98). The church tries to handle the horse by holding it near the bridle ("predella," 6.96), and lead it on foot, but to no avail.

The horse-riding image recurs one more time in Dante's work, at the very culmination of Dante's political treatise, the *Monarchia*. The two aims of the human being, earthly and celestial happiness, are ruled by the imperial and religious authority, symbolized by "human reason" (*Mon.* 3.15.9) and the Holy Spirit. They are the bit and bridle that govern the unruly human mind, which, like a horse, would give in to bestiality (*bestialitas*), falling into all sorts of inordinate desire (*cupiditas*), if not sternly ridden by these two authorities:

Has igitur conclusiones et media, licet ostensa sint nobis hec ab humana ratione que per phylosophos tota nobis innotuit, hec a Spiritu Sancto qui per prophetas et agiographos, qui per coecternum sibi Dei filium Iesum Cristum et per eius discipulos supernaturalem veritatem ac nobis necessariam revelavit, humana cupiditas postergaret nisi homines, tanquam equi, sua bestialitate vagantes "in camo et freno" compescerentur in via. (*Mon*. 3.15.9)

(These ends and the means to attain them have been shown to us on the one hand by human reason, which has been entirely revealed to us by the philosophers, and on the other by the Holy Spirit, who through the prophets and sacred writers, through Jesus Christ the son of God, coeternal with him, and through his disciples, has revealed to us the transcendent truth we cannot do without; yet human greed would cast these ends and means aside if men, like horses, prompted to wander by their animal natures, were not held in check "with bit and bridle" on their journey.)

In conclusion, the exploration of the legal dimension of lust in canto 5 brings to the fore a complex discourse in which lust/love/passion is linked to political instability and is matched by reason, in turns linked to justice, law, the figure of the emperor, and eventually that of the pope. Not surprisingly, one of the most powerful images of lust in the whole *Comedy*, indeed the only proper image of lust in the poem, is political. Dante's powerful rewriting of the biblical *meretrix magna* (Apoc. 17:1–5) brings us a picture of unbridled sexual desire, for once detached from love and love poetry. During the complex allegorical drama staged at the top of purgatory (*Purg*. 30–3), the chariot of the church, formerly ridden by Beatrice and guided by the griffin (symbolizing Christ, i.e., the church's lawful husband) metamorphoses into a monstrous animal ridden by a lustful prostitute ("una puttana sciolta," 32.149, the antithesis of Beatrice) and by her cruel lover ("drudo," 32.155, adulterous lover, clearly opposed to Christ as lover/spouse):[48]

Sicura, quasi rocca in alto monte,
seder sovresso una puttana sciolta
m'apparve con le ciglia intorno pronte;
e come perché non li fosse tolta,
vidi di costa a lei dritto un gigante;
e basciavansi insieme alcuna volta.
Ma perché l'occhio cupido e vagante
a me rivolse, quel feroce drudo
la flagellò dal capo infin le piante. (*Purg*. 32.148–56)

(Secure, like a fortress on a towering mountain, I saw a disheveled harlot sitting there, casting provocative glances this way and that. I saw a giant who stood beside her, perhaps to prevent her being taken from him. They kissed each other again and again. But because she turned on me her lustful, roving eye, that savage lover thrashed her body from head to foot.)

The woman (the church) looks around herself with lustful eyes and makes love to the giant (the king of France). The verb is *basciare*, which famously recurs in the episode of Francesca (as the kiss of erotic love) and in *Purgatorio* 26 (as the kiss of Christian peace between the repentants). The woman looks lasciviously at Dante. This is truly a mysterious detail, very difficult to interpret outside of Dante's penchant for always putting himself in the centre of the picture (albeit as a representative of the average Christian)[49] – unless we read it, with Iannucci, as a reminder of the tight grip, and the tragic effect, of lust on both the individual/lyrical self and the member of the political community.

NOTES

1 A. Iannucci, "Forbidden Love: Metaphor and History (*Inferno* V)," in *Dante: Contemporary Perspectives*, ed. A. Iannucci (Toronto: University of Toronto Press, 1997), 94–112.

2 Limbo is one of the main focuses of Iannucci's scholarship. See at least: "Limbo: the Emptiness of Time," *Studi Danteschi* 52 (1979–80): 69–128; "Il limbo dei bambini," in *Sotto il segno di Dante: Scritti in onore di Francesco Mazzoni*, ed. L. Coglievina and D. De Robertis (Florence: Le Lettere, 1998), 153–64; and "Dante e il Vangelo di Nicodemo: la discesa di Beatrice agl'Inferi," *Letture classensi* 12 (1983): 39–60. For the Rome/Babylon theme see, "*Paradiso* XXXI," in *Lectura Dantis Virginiana*, III, supplement, *Lectura Dantis* 16–17 (1995): 470–85; and "Firenze, città infernale," in *Dante da Firenze all'aldilà*, ed. M. Picone (Florence: Cesati, 2001), 217–32.

3 T. Barolini, "Dante and Francesca da Rimini: Realpolitik, Romance, Gender," *Speculum* 75 (2000): 5.

4 As Barolini points out, the first reference in contemporary historical documents (a bare allusion to Francesca's dowry within Malatesta da Verucchio's will in 1311) postdates Dante's work, and the earliest chroniclers to mention the story of the lovers from Romagna, both postdating Dante's

death and familiar with Dante's text, severely downplay the event and never mention Francesca's name ("Dante and Francesca da Rimini," 25–6).

5 For lust in the Middle Ages, see C. Casagrande and S. Vecchio, *I sette vizi capitali: Storia dei peccati nel medioevo* (Turin: Einuadi, 2000), 149–72; B. Kent, "On the Track of Lust: *Luxuria*, Ockham, and the Scientists," in *In the Garden of Evil: the Vices and Culture in the Middle Ages*, ed. R. Newhauser (Toronto: Pontifical Institute of Medieval Studies, 2005), 349–70; P. Payer, *The Bridling of Desire: Views of Sex in the Late Middle Ages* (Toronto: University of Toronto Press, 1993). For lust and its challenge to reason in Dante, see E. Lombardi, *The Wings of the Doves: Love and Desire in Dante and the Middle Ages* (Montreal: McGill Queens University Press, 2012), 51–85. For an overview of lust, see S. Blackburn, *Lust* (Oxford: Oxford University Press, 2004).

6 Payer, *The Bridling of Desire*, 48.

7 See, for instance, Augustine, *De civitate Dei* 14.16: "Cum igitur sint multarum libidines rerum, tamen, cum libido dicitur neque cuius rei libido sit additur, non fere assolet animo occurrere nisi illa, qua obscenae partes corporis excitantur."

8 *Fasciculus morum: A Fourteenth-Century Preacher's Handbook*, ed. and trans. S. Wenzel (University Park: Pennsylvania State University Press, 1989), 648–733, quotation on 648–9; quoted by Kent, "On the Track of Lust," 362.

9 Casagrande and Vecchio, *I sette vizi capitali*, 152–7.

10 D. Jacquard and C. Thomasset, *Sexuality and Medicine in the Middle Ages* (Princeton: Princeton University Press, 1988), esp. 116–38; M. Ciavolella, *La malattia d'amore dall'antichità al Medioevo* (Rome: Bulzoni, 1976); and Ciavolella, "L'amore e la medicina medievale," in *Guido Cavalcanti tra i suoi lettori*, ed. M.L. Ardizzone (Florence: Cadmo, 2003), 93–102.

11 For the legal aspect of lust, see J. Brundage, *Law, Sex and Christian Society in the Middle Ages* (Aldershot: Variorum, 1993).

12 Gratian, *Decretum* 2.36 1.2: "Sed non omnis illicitus coitus, nec cuiuslibet illicita defloratio raptus appellatur. Aliud enim est fornicatio, aliud stuprum, aliud adulterium, aliud incestus, aliud raptus. Fornicatio, licet uideatur esse genus cuiuslibet illiciti coitus, qui fit extra uxorem legitimam, tamen specialiter intelligitur in usu uiduarum, uel meretricum, uel concubinarum. Stuprum autem est proprie uirginum illicita defloratio, quando uidelicet non precedente coniugali pactione utriusque uoluntate uirgo corrumpitur, patre iniuriam ad animum statim post cognitionem non reuocante. Adulterium uero est alieni thori uiolatio. Unde adulterium dicitur quasi ad alterius thorum accessio. Incestus est consanguinearum

uel affinium abusus. Unde incestuosi dicuntur qui consanguineis uel affinibus suis abutuntur. Raptus admittitur, cum puella a domo patris uiolenter ducitur ut corrupta in uxorem habeatur, siue puellae solummodo, siue parentibus tantum, siue utrisque uis illata constiterit; hic morte mulctatur."

13 J. Brundage, *Law, Sex and Christian Society in the Middle Ages*, 374–7. See also 370: "Where medieval canonical records have been published and analyzed, they show with monotonous regularity that a major part of the routine business of the canonical courts consisted in routine prosecutions of fornicators and adulterers, many of them recidivist, interspersed with occasional actions against perpetrators of other sexual offences."

14 Boccaccio, DDP, *ad Inf.* 5.39: "Intesi ch'a così fatto tormento: Qui, poi che l'autore ha posta la qualità del tormento, dichiara quali sieno i peccatori a' quali questo tormento è dato, e dice che intese, da Virgilio si dee credere, che a così fatto tormento, come disegnato è, Eran dannati i peccator carnali, Che la ragion sommettono al talento, cioè alla volontà. E come che questo si possa d'ogni peccatore intendere, per ciò che alcun peccatore non è che non sottometta, peccando, la ragione alla volontà, vuol nondimeno l'autore che per quel vocabolo carnali s'intenda singularmente per li lussuriosi."

15 T. Barolini, "Dante and Cavalcanti (On Making Distinctions in Matters of Love): *Inferno* V in Its Lyric Context," *Dante Studies* 116 (1998): 42. Barolini has noted references to Guido delle Colonne, *Amor che lungiamente m'hai menato*, 48–9: "forza di senno è quello che soverchia / ardir di core"; Guittone d'Arezzo, *Or si parrà s'eo saverò cantare*, 10–11: "che 'n tutta parte ove distringe Amore / regge follore in loco di savere"; and Guido Cavalcanti, *Donna me prega*, 33: "che la 'ntenzione per ragione vale." For the discussion of other sources of Dante's definition of lust, see Lombardi, *The Wings of the Doves*, 65–7.

16 ut rapit in praeceps dominum spumantia frustra
frena retentantem durior oris equus;
ut subitus, prope iam prensa tellure, carinam
tangentem portus ventus in alta rapit –
sic me saepe refert incerta Cupidinis aura,
notaque purpureus tela resumit Amor. (*Amores* 2.9b.29–35)

17 *Canzoniere* 6, 47, 48, and 236, of which see at least sonnet 6:
Sí traviato è 'l folle mi' desio
a seguitar costei che 'n fuga è volta,
e de' lacci d'Amor leggiera et sciolta
vola dinanzi al lento correr mio,

che quanto richiamando piú l'envio
per la secura strada men m'ascolta:
né mi vale spronarlo, o dargli volta,
ch'Amor per sua natura il fa restio;
Et poi che 'l fren per forza a sé raccoglie,
i' mi rimango in signoria di lui,
che mal mio grado a morte mi trasporta:
sol per venir al lauro onde si coglie
acerbo frutto, che le piaghe altrui,
gustando afflige piú che non conforta.

On these sonnets, see E. Lombardi, "'I desire therefore I am': Petrarch's *Canzoniere* between the medieval and modern notion of desire," in *Early Medievalism: The Interplay between Scholarly Reflection and Artistic Production*, ed. A. Montoya, S. van Romburgh, and W. van Anrooij (Leiden: Brill, 2010), 33–6.

18 On this theme, see G. Sarton, "Aristotle and Phyllis," *Isis* 14 (1930): 8–19. One of the most popular versions of this story is the *Lai d'Aristote*, formerly attributed to Henri D'Andeli and now to Henri de Valenciennes. See the text in *Les Dits d'Henri d'Andeli*, ed. A. Corbellari (Paris: Champion, 2003), 73–90.

19 D. Comparetti, *Virgil in the Middle Ages* (London: Swan Sonnenschein, 1895), 325–39. On Boccaccio, see M. Papio, "Editor's notes," *Helitropia* 2, no. 1 (2004), http://www.brown.edu/Departments/Italian_Studies/heliotropia/02-01/papio.shtml.

20 The tableau can be seen in F. Bologna, *Il soffitto della sala magna allo Steri di Palermo* (Palermo: Flaccovio, 2002), 136 and in the illustrations, appendix, fig. 16.

21 In the commentary tradition (DDP, *ad Purg*. 26.83) only Benvenuto da Imola and Robert Hollander contemplate this possibility.

22 For the connection between Pasiphaë and Francesca, see M. Gragnolati, "*Inferno* V," in *Lectura Dantis Bononiensis*, vol. 2, ed. E. Pasquini and C. Galli (Bologna: Bononia University Press, 2012), 7–12.

23 *Vita nuova* 2.9: "E avvegna che la sua imagine, la quale continuatamente meco stava, fosse baldanza d'Amore a segnoreggiare me, tuttavia era di sì nobilissima vertù, che nulla volta sofferse che Amore mi reggesse sanza lo fedele consiglio de la ragione in quelle cose là ove cotale consiglio fosse utile a udire."

24 *Vita nuova* 39.1–2: "Contra questo avversario de la ragione si levoe un die, quasi ne l'ora de la nona, una forte imaginazione in me, che mi parve vedere

questa gloriosa Beatrice con quelle vestimenta sanguigne co le quali apparve prima a li occhi miei; e pareami giovane in simile etade in quale io prima la vidi. Allora cominciai a pensare di lei; e ricordandomi di lei secondo l'ordine del tempo passato, lo mio cuore cominciò dolorosamente a pentere de lo desiderio a cui sì vilmente s'avea lasciato possedere alquanti die contra la costanzia de la ragione: e discacciato questo cotale malvagio desiderio, sì si rivolsero tutti li miei pensamenti a la loro gentilissima Beatrice."

25 *Conv.* 4.7.11: "Sì come dice Aristotile nel secondo dell'Anima, 'vivere è l'essere delli viventi'; e per ciò che vivere è per molti modi (sì come nelle piante vegetare, nelli animali vegetare e sentire e muovere, nelli uomini vegetare, sentire, muovere e ragionare o vero intelligere), e le cose si deono denominare dalla più nobile parte, manifesto è che vivere nelli animali è sentire - animali, dico, bruti -, vivere nell'uomo è ragione usare."

26 *Conv.* 3.4.1–5: "Onde è da sapere che ciascuna cosa, come detto è di sopra, per la ragione di sopra mostrata ha 'l suo speziale amore. Ché le corpora simplici hanno amore naturato in sé allo luogo propio, e però la terra sempre discende al centro; lo fuoco ha [amore a]lla circunferenza di sopra, lungo lo cielo della luna, e però sempre sale a quella. Le corpora composte prima, sì come sono le minere, hanno amore allo luogo là dove la loro generazione è ordinata, e in quello crescono e [d]a quello [ricevono] vigore e potenza: onde vedemo la calamita sempre dalla parte della sua generazione ricevere vertù. Le piante, che sono prima animate, hanno amore a certo luogo più manifestamente, secondo che la complessione richiede; e però vedemo certe piante lungo l'acque quasi cansarsi, e certe sopra li gioghi delle montagne, e certe nelle piagge e da piè de' monti: le quali se si transmutano, o muoiono del tutto o vivono quasi triste, sì come cose disgiunte dal loro amico. Li animali bruti hanno più manifesto amore non solamente alli luoghi, ma l'uno l'altro vedemo amare. Li uomini hanno loro propio amore alle perfette ed oneste cose. E però che l'uomo, avegna che una sola sustanza sia, tutta fia[ta la] forma, per la sua nobilitade, ha in sé [e] la natura d'ognuna [di] queste cose, tutti questi amori puote avere e tutti li ha."

27 *Conv.* 3.4.10–11: "E per la natura quarta, delli animali, cioè sensitiva, hae l'uomo altro amore, per lo quale ama secondo la sensibile apparenza, sì come bestia; e questo amore nell'uomo massimamente ha mestiere di rettore per la sua soperchievole operazione, nello diletto massimamente del gusto e del tatto. E per la quinta e ultima natura, cioè vera umana o, meglio dicendo, angelica, cioè razionale, ha l'uomo amore alla veritade e

alla vertude; e da questo amore nasce la vera e perfetta amistà, dell'onesto tratta, della quale parla lo Filosofo nell'ottavo dell'Etica, quando tratta dell'amistade."

28 On the theme of reason and natural desire in *Convivio* 4, see E. Gilson, *Dante et la philosophie* (Paris: Vrin, 1939); B. Nardi, *Nel mondo di Dante* (Rome: Edizioni di Storia e Letteratura, 1944); the commentary to book 4 by C. Vasoli, *Convivio*, in *Opere minori*, vol. 1, pt. 2 (Milan and Naples: Ricciardi, 1979); and P. Falzone, "Desiderio naturale di sapere, nobiltà dell'anima e grazia divina nel IV trattato del *Convivio*," in *Dante the Lyric and Ethical Poet*, ed. Z. Barański and M. McLaughlin (Oxford: Legenda, 2010), 24–55.

29 *Conv.* 4.22.5: "E sì come nelle biade che, quando nascono, dal principio hanno quasi una similitudine nell'erba essendo, e poi si vengono per processo [di tempo] dissimigliando; così questo naturale appetito, che [de]lla divina grazia surge, dal principio quasi si mostra non dissimile a quello che pur da natura nudamente viene, ma con esso, sì come l'erbate quasi di diversi biadi, si simiglia. E non pur [nel]li uomini, ma e nelli uomini e nelle bestie ha similitudine; e questo [in questo] appare, che ogni animale, sì come elli è nato, sì razionale come bruto, se medesimo ama, e teme e fugge quelle cose che a lui sono contrarie, e quelle odia."

30 *Conv.* 4.22.7–8: "Dico adunque che dal principio se stesso ama, avegna che indistintamente; poi viene distinguendo quelle cose che a lui sono più amabili e meno, e più odibili [e meno], e séguita e fugge, e più e meno, secondo [che] la conoscenza distingue, non solamente nell'altre cose, che secondamente ama, ma eziandio distingue in sé, che ama principalmente. E conoscendo in sé diverse parti, quelle che in lui sono più nobili, più ama quelle; e con ciò sia cosa che più [nobile] parte dell'uomo sia l'animo che 'l corpo, quello più ama. E così, amando sé principalmente, e per sé l'altre cose, e amando di sé la migliore parte più, manifesto è che più ama l'animo che 'l corpo o che altra cosa: lo quale animo naturalmente più che altra cosa dee amare."

31 *Conv.* 4.26.5: "Qui adunque è da reducere a mente quello che di sopra, nel ventiduesimo capitolo di questo trattato, si ragiona dello appetito che in noi dal nostro principio nasce. Questo appetito mai altro non fa che cacciare e fuggire; e qualunque ora esso caccia quello che e quanto si conviene, e fugge quello che e quanto si conviene, l'uomo è nelli termini della sua perfezione."

32 *Conv.* 4.26.7: "Lo freno usa quando elli caccia, e chiamasi quello freno Temperanza, la quale mostra lo termine infino a[l] quale è da cacciare; lo

sprone usa quando fugge, per lui tornare allo loco onde fuggire vuole, e questo sprone si chiama Fortezza o vero Magnanimitate, la quale vertute mostra lo loco dove è da fermarsi e da pungare."

33 Esce di mano a lui che la vagheggia
prima che sia, a guisa di fanciulla
che piangendo e ridendo pargoleggia,
l'anima semplicetta che sa nulla,
salvo che, mossa da lieto fattore,
volontier torna a ciò che la trastulla. (*Purg*. 16.85–90)

34 Le leggi son, ma chi pon mano ad esse?
Nullo, però che 'l pastor che procede,
rugumar può, ma non ha l'unghie fesse;
per che la gente, che sua guida vede
pur a quel ben fedire ond' ella è ghiotta,
di quel si pasce, e più oltre non chiede.
Ben puoi veder che la mala condotta
è la cagion che 'l mondo ha fatto reo,
e non natura che 'n voi sia corrotta.
Soleva Roma, che 'l buon mondo feo,
due soli aver, che l'una e l'altra strada
facean vedere, e del mondo e di Deo.
L'un l'altro ha spento; ed è giunta la spada
col pasturale, e l'un con l'altro insieme
per viva forza mal convien che vada. (*Purg*. 16.97–111)

35 *Purg*. 17.127–9: "Ciascun confusamente un bene apprende / nel qual si queti l'animo, e disira; / per che di giugner lui ciascun contende."

36 Mentre ch'elli è nel primo ben diretto,
e ne' secondi sé stesso misura,
esser non può cagion di mal diletto;
ma quando al mal si torce, o con più cura
o con men che non dee corre nel bene,
contra 'l fattore adovra sua fattura.
Quinci comprender puoi ch'esser convene
amor sementa in voi d'ogne virtute
e d'ogne operazion che merta pene. (*Purg*. 17.97–105)

37 L'animo, ch'è creato ad amar presto,
ad ogne cosa è mobile che piace,
tosto che dal piacere in atto è desto.
Vostra apprensiva da esser verace

tragge intenzione, e dentro a voi la spiega,
sì che l'animo ad essa volger face;
e se, rivolto, inver' di lei si piega,
quel piegare è amor, quell'è natura
che per piacer di novo in voi si lega. (*Purg.* 18.19–27)

38 Or ti puote apparer quant' è nascosa
la veritate a la gente ch'avvera
ciascun amore in sé laudabil cosa;
però che forse appar la sua matera
sempre esser buona, ma non ciascun segno
è buono, ancor che buona sia la cera. (*Purg.* 18.34–9)

39 *Purg.* 18.46–8: "Ed elli a me: Quanto ragion qui vede, / dir ti poss' io; da indi in là t'aspetta / pur a Beatrice, ch'è opra di fede."

40 Ogne forma sustanzïal, che setta
è da matera ed è con lei unita,
specifica vertute ha in sé colletta,
la qual sanza operar non è sentita,
né si dimostra mai che per effetto,
come per verdi fronde in pianta vita. (*Purg.* 18. 49–54)

41 *Purg.* 18.61–3: "Or perché a questa ogn' altra si raccoglia, / innata v'è la virtù che consiglia, / e de l'assenso de' tener la soglia."

42 Nardi, *Nel mondo di Dante*, 295–305.

43 Francesco da Buti (DDP, *ad Purg.* 18.91–3) suggests the slight incompatibility between the purgatorial environment and the simile of the Bacchic rites, pointing out that the Thebans committed "furious and lustful" acts under the influence of wine: "E fa una similitudine, dicendo che questa gente andava in furia e in caccia, come andavano li Tebani lungo li loro fiumi; cioè Ismeno et Asopo, quando faceano sacrificio a Baco loro iddio, per avere dell'acqua per le loro vigne, dicendo così: *E quale furia e calca Ismeno et Asopo*; che sono due fiumi in quello di Tebe, *già vidde Lungo di sè di notte*: imperò che di notte, lungo li ditti fiumi, andavano li Tebani correndo e cantando le lode di Baco, quando voleano che piovesse; e però dice: *Pur che i Teban di Baco avesser uopo*; cioè bisogno de la deità di Baco, a dare loro dell'acqua per le loro vigne: imperò che quando volean altro, andavano a fare lo sacrificio vestiti di pelle co l'aste in mano su per lo monte Citeron e co le fiacule, per ch'era di notte. Bacco era nato di Tebe; cioè di Semele tebana e di Giove, e però li Tebani aveano devozione in lui, et a lui ricorreano per tutte le cose et in tutti li loro bisogni, facendo li loro sacrifici di notte,

e con naccari, tamburi et al tri istrumenti, e con aste in mano e vestiti di pellicce, come ditto è, facendo atti furiosi, et atti disonesti di lussuria, come fa fare la briachessa." See also Nicola Fosca, DDP, *ad Purg.* 18.91–3.

44 The horse-riding metaphor is not evident in the translation, which privileges instead the image of the sickle (*falce*) inherent in the horse-riding term *falcare*, literally to impress a curving movement similar to that of a sickle. See Anna Maria Chiavacci Leonardi, DDP, *ad Purg.* 18.94.

45 *Conv.* 4.9.7: "Sono anche operazioni che la nostra [ragione] considera nell'atto della volontade, sì come offendere e giovare, sì come star fermo e fuggire alla battaglia, sì come stare casto e lussuriare; e queste del tutto suggiacciono alla nostra volontade; e però semo detti da loro buoni e rei, perch'elle sono propie nostre del tutto, perché, quanto la nostra volontade ottenere puote, tanto le nostre operazioni si stendono."

46 *Conv.* 4.9.8: "E con ciò sia cosa che in tutte queste volontarie operazioni sia equitade alcuna da conservare e iniquitade da fuggire (la quale equitade per due cagioni si può perdere, o per non sapere quale essa si sia o per non volere quella seguitare), trovata fu la ragione scritta e per mostrarla e per comandarla. Onde dice Augustino: Se questa – cioè equitade – li uomini la conoscessero, e conosciuta servassero, la ragione scritta non sarebbe mestiere; e però è scritto nel principio del Vecchio Digesto: La ragione scritta è arte di bene e d'equitade."

47 The image of the emperor riding the human will has an interesting resonance with a pseudo-Augustinian passage quoted by Aquinas, in which grace is the rider of human will. See *Summa theologiae* 1a. 2ae. q. 110, a. 4 a. 1: "Videtur quod gratia non sit in essentia animae sicut in subiecto, sed in aliqua potentiarum. Dicit enim Augustinus, in Hypognost., quod gratia comparatur ad voluntatem, sive ad liberum arbitrium, sicut sessor ad equum. Sed voluntas, sive liberum arbitrium, est potentia quaedam, ut in primo dictum est. Ergo gratia est in potentia animae sicut in subiecto."

48 For a close reading of this episode, with emphasis on the relation between the bride of the Song of Songs and the whore, see L. Pertile, *La puttana e il gigante: Dal Cantico dei Cantici al Paradiso terrestre di Dante* (Ravenna: Longo, 1998), 203–25. Pertile importantly notices that "la feroce parodia etico-politica ha dunque la stessa matrice fantastica delle dolcezze dello stilnovo. Il lirico e il politico sgorgano dalla stessa fonte e si servono dello stesso linguaggio" (225). Robert Hollander points out that the word *drudo* recurs also in *Inferno* 28 to identify the lover of the prostitute Thais. On

this, and for another interpretation of the characters in the allegorical scene, see Hollander, DDP, *ad Par.* 12.55.

49 The commentary tradition relates an alternative interpretation; that Dante here stands for the supporter of the German Emperor Albert (see *Purgatorio* 6), to whom the church turns in a desperate attempt to free herself from the king of France.

5 The *Vulgata* in the *Commedia*: Self-Interpreting Texts

CAROLYNN LUND-MEAD

In "Autoesegesi dantesca," Amilcare Iannucci suggested that Dante's use of prose commentary in the *Vita nuova* and *Convivio* continues in the *Commedia* by means of what Iannucci called the "parallel passage," through which Dante forges intratextual links between not only words and phrases but also whole episodes.[1] The second of the two texts furnishes the interpretative key to the first. As an example, Iannucci discussed the relation between Dante's encounters with the writer Brunetto Latini in *Inferno* 15 and with the miniaturist Oderisi da Gubbio in *Purgatorio* 11–12. For Iannucci, Oderisi's critique silences commentators who would believe that Dante shares Brunetto's vision.[2] Returning to these two important episodes and building on Iannucci's insight into parallel passages, I expand his inquiry into new territory in this essay by exploring the role that scripture plays in the development of Dante's critical art of autoexegesis in the *Commedia*. Many of what Iannucci termed as Dante's "precise internal echoes"[3] come from the Bible. The poet's carefully selected allusions awaken an echo chamber of responses within the self-interpreting texts known as the scriptures. The exchange is reciprocal. While Dante gives new life and presence to this source text, he, in turn, gains authoritative, critical illumination from the divinely appointed opus of the medieval Christian world. The validation granted by this alliance is crucial for the success of Dante's literary project.

As Iannucci noted, the implementation of parallel passages as a critical technique has its antecedents in medieval Biblical exegesis, in which one passage of the Bible must be interpreted by means of another.[4] Dante follows this method in the *Monarchia* in order to refute the papal interpretation of the significance of "the two swords" that Peter offers to Christ in the Gospel of Luke: "Domine ecce gladii duo hic" (Lc. 22:38;

Lord, behold here are two swords).[5] Dante rejects the claim that the two swords represent Christ's gift of temporal and ecclesiastical power to St Peter and his successors ("quod omnino negandum est" [*Mon.* 3.9.2; which must utterly be denied]). According to Dante, this reading not only fails to take into account the larger context of Luke's passage but also misses clues within correspondent biblical texts. In Luke, Peter spontaneously offers his swords to Jesus in response to the Master's advice to his twelve disciples to prepare themselves for defence now that he will be taken from them. (All four Gospels record that one of Jesus' followers later used his sword to cut off the ear of a servant of the high priest, in defence of Jesus [Mt. 26:51; Mk. 14:47; Lk. 22:50; Io. 18:10].) The episode of Peter's two swords, Dante explains, must be read as part of a process of revealing Peter's complex character. Dante proves in this discussion in the *Monarchia* that he knew how to use biblical interpretative methods for the purpose of critical debate.

In the *Commedia*, however, Dante creates self-interpreting parallel passages to serve a more complex purpose. The text becomes "at the same time an act of poetic creation and a critical reflection."[6] This statement applies equally well to the text of the Bible. As scholars have long recognized, parallel stories further the biblical plot: scripture rewriting scripture characterizes the development of Israel's sacred texts. This is particularly true in fundamental stories, such as the creation of the world and the giving of the law. The Bible opens with two stories of the creation of heaven and earth. According to the first version, God said, "faciamus hominem ad imaginem et similitudinem nostram" (Gen. 1:26; Let us make man to our image and likeness). In the second, "formavit igitur Dominus Deus hominem de limo terrae / et inspiravit in faciem eius spiraculum vitae" (Gen. 2:7; The Lord God formed man of the slime of the earth: and breathed into his face the breath of life). The second account complements the Creator as absolute commander in the first with the Creator as master craftsman. In Deuteronomy, the narrator rewrites the teachings of the law-giver Moses (which first appear in the book of Exodus), forcing the reader to shift between "that day" of Moses and "this day" of the Deuteronomist.[7] In this passage on divine law, the narrator sets the perimeters for the subsequent history of God's people in the Promised Land, where they will succeed if they follow God's law and will fail if they do not. Moses's law "then" becomes their law "now." In each of these instances, second versions create new possibilities without cancelling or diminishing earlier ones.[8]

New Testament texts carried on this already well-established practice, thus assimilating the older datum of the Hebrew scriptures (by then translated into the Greek Septuagint) into a new whole. The opening of the Gospel of John, for instance, reinterprets the creation texts of Genesis as, "In principio erat verbum" (Io. 1:1; In the beginning was the Word), thus expressing a new beginning that occurs in the incarnation: "Et Verbum caro factum est et habitavit in nobis" (Io. 1:14; And the Word was made flesh and dwelt among us). In the Gospel of Matthew, Jesus as the "new Deuteronomist" rewrites the law for his day: "Omnia ergo quaecumque vultis ut faciant vobis homines et vos facite eis / haec est enim lex et prophetae" (Mt. 7:12; In everything do to others as you would have them do to you; for this is the law and the prophets). From a canonical perspective, the scriptures form a "contextual construction" (a term Iannucci applied to the *Commedia*)[9] offering the possibility of a retrospective vision. When Dante alludes to biblical episodes, therefore, he conjures up a network of meanings and taps into an expansive, self-generating process. He also aligns himself with God, the author of the canonical scriptures: "Nam quanquam scribe divini eloquii multi sint, unicus tamen dictator est Deus" (*Mon.* 3.4.11; For although there were many writers of the divine words, God alone, nevertheless, is the one who spoke them). God's words, knowledgeably interpreted and recreated, bequeath particular authority to Dante's text.

In his encounter with Brunetto Latini, Dante sets up parallel points of comparison not only between his own texts, as Iannucci points out,[10] but also between biblical episodes and biblical hermeneutics. When Dante meets Brunetto, Dante addresses him as "ser" (*Inf.* 15.30) but dares not descend to place himself on a level beside his old master, explaining:

Io non osava scender de la strada
per andar par di lui; ma `l capo chino
tenea com' uom che reverente vada. (*Inf.* 15.43–5)

(I did not dare to leave the higher path
to walk the lower with him, but I kept
my head bowed, like one who walks in reverence.)

Brunetto, however, reaches out to close the space between them and, as Dante reports, took him by the hem: "me prese / per lo lembo" (*Inf.* 15.23–4). The gesture recalls an important scriptural scene.[11] In the story of the kings of Israel, Saul, upon learning from Samuel that God has rejected him, grasps the prophet by the border of his robe (1 Sm. 15:27;

apprehendit summitatem pallii eius) and begs him not to turn away. Turning back to the king, the prophet first pronounces judgment on him, but then agrees to prevent Saul's public humiliation by accompanying him and standing beside him before the elders and all the nation to worship God together (1 Sm. 15:28–31).

This scene is recalled in later biblical episodes in which it takes on greater significance. When Saul grasps the prophet's robe, the hem of Samuel's garment tears in his hand (1 Sm. 15:27; et scissa est). Samuel interprets this action as a sign of God's wrenching the kingdom from Saul: "scidit Dominus regnum Israhel a te hodie" (1 Sm. 15.27–8; The LORD has torn the kingdom of Israel from you this very day [*NRSV*]).[12] The gesture becomes even more clearly associated with political schism in the reign of King Solomon, in which the prophet Ahijah, taking hold ("aprehendens") of Jeroboam's new garment, tears it into twelve pieces (3 Rg. 11:30). This, says Ahijah, is a sign that he will tear ("scindam") the kingdom from the hand of Solomon and will give ten tribes to Jeraboam (3 Rg. 11:31). Much later, during the time of the rebuilding of the Jerusalem temple after the return from the Babylonian exile, the prophet Zechariah converts this image of tragic *scissum* into an expression of universal hope for a unified Jewish nation (Za. 8:23). He prophesies a future Jerusalem, purified and triumphant, with God in its midst:

> haec dicit Dominus exercituum
> in diebus illis in quibus adprehendent decem homines ex omnibus linguis gentium
> et adprehendent fimbriam viri iudaei dicentes:
> ibimus vobiscum audivimus enim quoniam Deus vobiscum est
>
> (Thus says the Lord of Hosts: In those days ten men from every nation of every language shall take hold of a Jew, grasping his garment saying, "Let us go with you, for we have heard that God is with you." [*NRSV*])

According to the Gospel of Mark, Jesus finds himself besieged by the sick wherever he goes. They beg him "that they might touch even the fringe of his cloak and all who touched it were healed" (Mc. 6:56, *NRSV*). The original version of the rending of the kingdom of Israel from Saul, the divinely anointed ruler in Israel's past, metamorphoses into a prophetic hope for her future unity through the return of the Babylonian exiles to rebuild the city of Jerusalem. In the New Testament, hope is embodied in the man Jesus, who represents his people Israel in their continued search for wholeness.

The general parallels between Dante's scene and the Bible reveal the larger pattern inherent in the relation between Dante and his teacher. The divine power that created the portal of hell (*Inf.* 3.6) displaces Brunetto as Dante's leader, even as the Lord dethrones Saul, the first king of Israel (1 Sm. 15:28). Samuel and Dante each mourn the loss of a personally chosen leader. As Samuel continues to grieve (1 Sm. 15:35; lugebat) over this young man of promise until the day of his death, so Dante mourns his master, now lost to him. Brunetto's dear and kind paternal image is fixed in the pilgrim's memory ("che 'n la mente m'è fitta") and now wounds his heart ("e or m'accora," *Inf.* 15.82–3). If Dante's prayer were fulfilled, Brunetto would not yet be banished from human nature (*Inf.* 15.79–81).[13] By submitting to divine will in spite of personal grief, however, both Samuel and Dante open themselves up to the emergence of a stronger, more capable leader: King David in the former instance, and Cacciaguida in the latter. In Dante's story as in the history of Israel, the image of the grasped hem is connected with a schism (*scissum*) that will be converted into wholeness.

Dante's use of biblical sources further distinguishes him from his teacher and contributes to an understanding of the necessity of Brunetto's displacement and even damnation. Brunetto Latini seems unaware of the resonances of his gesture of greeting within its broad biblical context. As Dante would have been aware, Brunetto knew the Bible well: his *Tresor* includes brief biographies of major biblical characters, as well as an outline of biblical events and their relation to universal history.[14] Yet Dante suggests that Brunetto misses the deeper meaning of these stories. In 1 Samuel, Saul's reaching out to the prophet is a sign of humility. Similarly, in Matthew, a woman who has suffered for twelve years with a hemorrhage of blood touches the hem of Jesus's garment (Mt. 9:20; tetigit fimbriam vestimenti eius) in the belief that it will make her well; turning to her, Jesus tells her that her faith has made her whole.

When Dante turns to see who has touched his hem, he sees Brunetto – naked, burnt, and reduced in physical standing, an image of brokenness and humility. Dante's respectful, sympathetic response is immediate and moving. Yet, in spite of initial appearances, Brunetto gradually reveals that rather than an expression of humility or a means of seeking wholeness, his contact with Dante is an attempt to reaffirm his own pride. This becomes obvious in his last words, which are for the survival not of his soul, but of his work. Like his initial gesture, his final request, while humbly couched, is audacious: "Siete raccomandato il mio Tesoro, / nel qual io vivo ancora, e più non cheggio" (*Inf.* 15.119–20; Let my Treasure, in which I still live on, / be in your mind – I ask for nothing more). Although Brunetto chooses phrases such as *siete raccomandato* and *più non cheggio* to express restraint, under his polite language lies a defiant ambition: he wishes to perpetuate himself through Dante. Latini's expression of faith in continuing renown in his own work reflects a passage in his *Tresor* where he championed "glorie … la bone renomee" (the glory of good repute). Earthly fame, Brunetto went on to say, is the reward for those "de grant afere, ou de savoir bien son art" (*Tresor* 2.120.1; who have accomplished great things, or known their art well). Ironically, of course, few read the *Tresor* anymore; if Brunetto lives on, it is as Dante's damned character.

The reduced but arrogant Latini has much in common with the repentant proud in *Purgatory* 11 – creative artists bowed down under the weight of a great stone. Yet their response to suffering differs greatly from that of the defiantly self-asserting Brunetto. While the last words that Dante hears in *Inferno* 15 are Brunetto's recommendation of his *Tresor,* the first words that he hears in *Purgatorio* 11 are the beginning of the Paternoster. As often noted, the prayer of the penitents is Dante's own expanded paraphrase of the prayer that Jesus teaches his disciples in the Gospel of Matthew (Mt. 6:9–15). Brunetto places emphasis on personal pronouns:[15] "il *mio* Tesoro, / nel qual *io* vivo ancora" (*Inf.* 15.119–20; *my Treasure* in which *I* still live on); a chorus of voices opens *Purgatorio* 11 with a collective request addressed to a shared spiritual parent, "*Our* Father": "Pater *noster* qui in caelo es … panem *nostrum* supersubstantialem da nobis hodie" (Mt. 6:9, 11; *Our* father who is in heaven, … Give us this day *our* supersubstantial bread). Dante's version reads: "O padre *nostro*, che ne' cieli stai, … / Dà oggi *a noi* la cotidiana manna" (*Purg.* 11.1, 13; *Our* Father, you who dwell in the heavens[16]… Give *us* this day the daily manna). Once competitive individuals, these chanting artists signal their change of focus from personal status to collective, by repeating the first person plural pronouns of a ritual prayer. Giuseppe Giacalone emphasizes also that Dante's choice of the word *stai*, positioned at the end of the first line (*Purg.* 11.1), evokes the yearning for repose of the weary penitents.[17] Staggering along under the weight of great stones, they cannot be perceived, as Dante observed Brunetto about to race off to join a contest (*Inf.* 15.121–4).

Dante's decision not only to translate but also to expand each line of the original prayer has elicited remarkably divergent responses from commentators. Mark Musa approvingly comments that Dante's additions to the original text of the prayer "consistently and fittingly emphasize humility."[18] Our Father is elaborated to include "non circunscritto, ma per più amore / ch'ai primi effetti di là sù tu hai" (*Purg*. 11.2–3; circumscribed only by the greater love / you have for your first works on high). Manfredi Porena argues that this remark shows Dante's humble recognition that God loves man less than the angels.[19]

Not all readers approve of Dante's adaptations, however. Some compare Dante's style unfavourably with the original. Others express discomfort with the fact that Dante has changed such a well-known original. In his notes on the opening of this canto, John Sinclair observes that "it is apt to strike us as a singular lapse that Dante should exchange the sublime simplicity of the Lord's Prayer" for this "scholastic and homiletic elaboration ... even if allowance be made for the fact that such paraphrasing of Scripture was a common practice of the time and would hardly seem out of place to his contemporaries."[20] Allen Mandelbaum offers a possible defence, arguing that it is "that remarkable concentration on humility that redeems what might otherwise have seemed a somewhat over ingenious, advanced artificer's expansion on a prayer that is already indelible in itself."[21]

Concerns about the appropriateness of Dante's paraphrase suggest a more fundamental problem. How was it possible for the poet to open the first canto of the purgation of pride with his own rewriting of the authoritative words of Jesus, particularly when this terrace includes the vainglory of human artistry ("O vana gloria de l'umane posse" [*Purg*. 11.91; the first or gravest of the mortal sins]),[22] which Oderisi specifically teaches Dante pilgrim to renounce? How could a poet who might be perceived as an "advanced artificer" have elaborated the words of the Lord's Prayer in order to teach humility to the penitents of purgatory?

Dante is conscious of this problem. After leaving behind the circle of the proud, he speaks of "la paura onde' è sospesa / l'anima mia del tormento di sotto" (*Purg*. 13.136–7; the fear that fills my soul with dread of the torment below). Dante imagines the weight of pride becoming his eternal punishment, "che già lo 'ncarco di là giù mi pesa" (*Purg*. 13.138; I can almost feel their weight upon me now). In his paraphrase of the Lord's Prayer in the opening of *Purgatorio* 11, Dante submits his own artistry to biblical sources so that his voice, like that of the penitents, is absorbed into a communal song. His interpretation of the passage shows a close and careful reading of the scriptures, while simultaneously altering the canonical text so that the reader sees and hears the text anew. By choosing the best-known communal prayer in Christian worship, one deeply ingrained in the liturgy of the church, Dante draws attention to the act of revision.[23] His adaptation draws on the biblical art of reinterpretation. With the authority of the Deuteronimist and the author of John's Gospel behind him, Dante demonstrates how a writer respectfully illuminates a present experience in terms of an earlier sacred text, making it alive "now."

Dante clearly bases his adaptation of the Lord's Prayer on the text of Matthew. His opening, "O Padre nostro, che ne' cieli stai" (*Purg*. 11.1; Our Father, you who dwell in the heavens) follows closely the Vulgate: "Pater noster qui in caelis es" (Mt. 6:9; Our Father who is in heaven). Dante's variation on the original, however, allows him to bring out elements of biblical intertextuality. While the word that Jesus himself uses for "bread" in Matthew and elsewhere is *panis*, Dante requests, "Dà oggi a noi la cotidiana *manna*" (*Purg*. 11.13; Give us this day the daily *manna*), adding, "sanza la qual per questo aspro diserto / a retro va chi più di gir s'affanna" (*Purg*. 11.13–14; without which he who labours to advance / goes backward through this bitter wilderness). He thus makes explicit the link between the Lord's Prayer "now" in purgatory and the dependence of God's people "then" in their wilderness journey to the Promised Land. In Exodus, God promises the Israelites, "ecce ego pluam vobis panes de caelo" (Ex. 16:4; Look, I will rain bread from heaven for you), and according to the psalmist, "et pluit illis manna ad manducandum" (Ps. 77:24; and he rained down manna upon them to eat).[24] The Gospel of John recalls this episode when a crowd, gathered at Capernaum, demand a sign from Jesus. They remind Jesus that their fathers ate bread sent by God from heaven: "panem de caelo dedit eis manducare" (Io. 6:3; He gave them bread from heaven to eat). Jesus answers, "*Ego sum* panis vitae" (Io. 6:35, 48; *I am* the bread of life); "*Ego sum* panis vivus qui de caelo descendi" (Io. 6:51; *I am* the bread of life sent down from heaven). Repeating God's famous self-description in Exodus 3:14 ("dixit Deus ad Mosen ego sum qui sum" [God said to Moses, I AM WHO AM]), Jesus reinterprets the Old Testament manna, which fed the body only ("Patres vestri manducaverunt in deserto manna et mortui sunt" [Io. 6:49; Your fathers did eat manna in the desert and are dead]), as himself, the new bread of eternal life ("si quis manducaverit ex hoc pane vivet in aeternum" [Io. 6:52; If any man eat of this bread, he shall live forever]).

But Dante may be paying particular attention to Matthew. The Vulgate version of this Gospel is unique in its insertion of the adjective "supersubstantial" into the description of the daily bread, "*panem* nostrum *supersubstantialem*" (6:11), making clear that this is spiritual bread.[25] In choosing the word "manna," Dante reinterprets Matthew's supersubstantial bread by means of the story of Exodus and the Gospel of John, according to which Jesus is the spiritual bread of eternal life.

Dante's rewriting of the Lord's Prayer verifies his participation in and understanding of biblical intertextual construction. His paraphrase, like his journey, is both personal and communal, just as his *Commedia* is a highly original literary creation born of incorporated, revised texts, especially the Bible. The prayer of the proud is a communal effort – something that Dante produced not alone, but through a complex relation with multiple biblical texts and with the process of biblical intratextuality. The result is a paradoxical, self-effacing, self-promoting conspicuously placed text.

This communal prayer for manna, the daily food of eternal life, creates the setting for Dante pilgrim's reassessment of the eternal life, which was the goal of Brunetto Latini. In *Inferno* 15, Dante claims that he is grateful to his old master who taught him "come l'uom s'etterna" (15.85; how man makes himself immortal). Brunetto supported his belief in artistic immortality through his own reading of scriptural authorities. In his *Tresor*, Brunetto (mis)interpreted the words of Jesus's maxim in Matthew 18 in order to claim that one achieves life eternal (*pardurable*) by choosing the active life over the contemplative: "et si oculus tuus scandalizat te / erue eum et proice abs te bonum tibi est unoculum in vitam intrare / quam duos oculos habentem mitti in gehennam ignis" (Mt. 18:9; And if your eye scandalize you, pluck it out and cast it from you. It is better for you having one eye to enter into life, than having two eyes to be cast into hell fire). For Brunetto, the offending eye represents the contemplative life, "s'ele courust en erreur" (if it should be corrupted by error). It is better, he argues, "garder celi de l'active, si k'il aille por ses oevres a la vie pardurable, que aler au feu d'infer" (*Tresor* 2.123.4–5; to keep the eye of the active life, so that a person might through his works achieve life everlasting rather than go to the fire of hell). Brunetto's manipulation of Jesus's maxim is eccentric and clearly self-justifying.

Unlike Brunetto, who expounds upon this maxim as a proof text of a particular doctrine, Jesus employs this saying as a hyperbolic, rhetorical technique (in the manner of his day) to evoke a response and force the reader to consider the message in which it is embedded. Jesus's message is in response to a question posed by his disciples: "Who do you think is the greater in the kingdom of heaven?" (Mt. 18:1). Setting a child before him, Jesus defines true greatness not as rank, as his disciples had expected, but as humility; the corollary of this definition is that the humble must not be offended. Adding a warning to his corollary, Jesus uses a rhetorical technique to say, "Pay attention, you who perceive rank as greatness. You are in danger of trampling down the humble, who are the truly great; it is better that you rid yourself of this vision, no matter how painful, because the penalty for this offence is hell." Ironically, Brunetto chooses to comment upon a biblical passage that refutes not only his literary interpretation but also his lifelong goal of greatness. Brunetto is bold in interpreting Jesus's maxim to redefine the nature of the active and passive life. He stumbles, however, in not realizing, as Craig S. Keener says, that we are dealing with "catchy phrases of Jewish speech rather than developed doctrinal pronouncements."[26] As Dante demonstrates in *Monarchia* 3.9.2, a biblical passage cannot be understood in isolation. Without the necessary humility required to recognize and submit to the discipline of biblical hermeneutics, Brunetto damns himself by his own failure as both reader and reviser.

Dante's last image in *Inferno* 15 confirms the irony. As Brunetto speeds away, he seems to Dante as one who wins, not as one who loses (*Inf.* 15.122; non colui che perde), the green cloth in the footrace in Verona. Dante's image of Brunetto's illusory victory exposes the fantasy inherent in the master's expectation of the triumph of virtue expressed in his *Tresor*: "et si comme li sages canpions et fors ki se combat et vaint et enporte la courone de victoire, tot autresi li bons et beates a le guerredon e le loenge de la vertu k'il fait et moustre veraiement par ses oevres" (2.7.2; Just as a good and strong champion fights and triumphs and carries the crown of victory, in the same way the good and beatific man has the reward and praise for the virtue he does and displays truly through his works). By adding the phrase "non colui che perde" to his image of the retreating Brunetto, Dante reveals his disappointment, his disbelief in the fact that the one who wrote the above words does not win "le guerredon de la beatitude" (*Tresor* 2.7.2; the reward of beatitude).

In the purgatorial canto of the proud, however, Dante's meeting with Oderisi allows him to reassess and reimagine his relation to Brunetto

Latini. Dante greets Oderisi, the acclaimed miniaturist, as "l'onor d'Agobbio" (*Purg.* 11.80; the honour of Gubbio). Oderisi responds by promoting not his own work but that of Franco Bolognese, by whom he claims to have been surpassed. As a member of the community that chants together a revised version of the Lord's Prayer, Oderisi is learning that son follows father in the natural order of artistic achievements. In the world of literature, he points out, "Così ha tolto l'uno a l'altro Guido / la gloria de la lingua" (*Purg.* 11.97–8; Thus has the one Guido taken from the other / the glory of our tongue). Moving into the present and future, Oderisi predicts: "e forse è nato / chi l'uno e l'altro caccerà del nido" (*Purg.* 11.98–9; And he, perhaps, is born / who will drive one and then the other from the nest). Oderisi subtly puts Dante on notice that he, too, shall one day be surpassed by another.[27] Oderisi presents Dante with the choice of artistic development through supersession, a choice that will move him forward towards paradise, as opposed to Brunetto's concern with personal survival, which traps him in hell among the sodomites, without a literary heir.

Unlike Brunetto, who turns Jesus's maxim about the need for humility into a recommendation of the personal achievement of glory, Oderisi chooses biblical references to underline the brevity of human glory. He exclaims, "com'poco verde in su la cima dura" (*Purg.* 11.92; How briefly lasts the crowning green of glory), noting also that "la vostra nominanza è color d'erba, / che viene e va" (*Purg.* 11.115–16; Your renown is but the hue of grass, / which comes and goes). Oderisi's phrasing draws on a common biblical pattern of imagery.[28] In Psalm 89, the psalmist writes, "mane sicut herba transeat mane floreat et transeat / vespere decidat induret et arescat" (Ps. 89:6; In the morning, just as the grass, let it pass away, in the morning, let it flourish and pass away; in the evening, let it fall down, grow hard and dry up [my translation]). In Isaiah 40:6–7, a voice orders the prophet to cry out: "omnis caro faenum / et omnis gloria eius quasi flos agri / exsiccatum est faenum et cecidit flos / quia spiritus Domini sufflavit in eo" (All flesh is grass and the glory thereof as the flower of the field. / The grass is withered and the flower is fallen, because the spirit of the Lord has blown upon it). The short-lived greenery that represents man's brief glory recalls the green cloth of the footrace in Verona that Dante imagines Brunetto to be winning. Dante now recognizes the healing power in Oderisi's words: "Tuo vero dir m'incora / bona umilità, e gran tumor m'appiani" (*Purg.* 11.118–19; Your true words pierce my heart / with fit humility and ease a heavy swelling). The pilgrim's "gran tumor" may represent Dante's own vainglory of artistry, called into question by the poet's bold opening of this terrace of humility.

The encounter with Oderisi thus enables us to see his meeting with Brunetto Latini as part of a process in which Dante reassesses the road to eternal life. Latini and Oderisi are related to one another as Dante's mentors in the stages of his journey. By means of scriptural allusions, each calls into play biblical intertextual references that add literary and historical authority to Dante's experience. This process reaches its climax in *Paradiso* 15 when Dante meets Cacciaguida, his ancestor and spiritual father, who has become a light of everlasting glory, a "star," "resplendent" in his constellation: "un astro / de la constellazion che lì resplende" (*Par*. 15.20–1). Like Brunetto, Cacciaguida is an advocate of the active life. After serving as a knight of the Church Militant fighting for the cause of the Holy Roman Empire, he now dwells in the realm of the hero-saints of Mars. Brunetto's promise of personal fame had been countered by Oderisi's emphasis on the transfer of fame from generation to generation; Cacciaguida further adds personal evidence of shared beatitude. Cacciaguida is one bright spot in a constellation contained within the shape of a cross that Dante observes flashing forth "Christ" ("quella croce chè lampeggiava Cristo," *Par*. 14.104). This cross marks the boundaries of Cacciaguida's ambition for glory. His goals are achieved within the communal cause of a shared divinity. Moved by the exquisite music of Cacciaguida's realm, Dante becomes acutely aware of the difference between this form of everlasting life and one that does not endure eternally ("non duri / etternalmente," *Par*. 15.11–12). Dante has moved a long way from belief in Brunetto's promise of man's ability to make himself eternal ("come l'uom s'etterna," *Inf*. 15.85).

Cacciaguida's relation to Dante is more intimate than that of his previous mentors. He notes that his son was the first to bear Dante's family name. As Cacciaguida also explains, the first Alighieri is still circling the terrace of pride (*Par*. 15.91–4). Vainglory, Dante learns, is clearly a family failing. Yet Cacciaguida is justly proud of his descendent, whom he greets as a branch of his family tree in whom he is well pleased: "O fronda mia in che io *compiacemmi*" (*Par*. 15.88). The phrasing recalls God's well-known acknowledgment of Jesus: "hic est Filius meus dilectus in quo mihi *conplacui*" (Mt. 3:17; This is my beloved son, in whom I have been well pleased).[29] For Cacciaguida, Dante is the branch of which he was the root: "O fronda mia … io fui la tua radice" (*Par*. 15.88–9; O bough of my tree … I was your root). The image is based on Isaiah, "et egredietur virga de radice Iesse et flos de radice eius ascendet" (Is.

11:1; And there shall come forth a shoot out of the root of Jesse, and a flower shall rise up out of his root).[30] This biblical prophecy of the branch and root was later interpreted as foretelling the return of the Messiah, glossed in the Apocalypse as the conqueror: "ecce vicit leo de tribu Iuda radix David" (Apc. 5:5; Behold the lion of the tribe of Judah, the root of David, has prevailed). In these allusions, Dante presents the model of the son who fulfils the father.

Cacciaguida's rewriting of biblical language in personal terms connects his lineage by analogy with biblical prophetic history from Isaiah to the Apocalypse. In the *Inferno*, Brunetto lays the groundwork for Cacciaguida's prophecy. Brunetto's description of Dante marks his prodigy as a remnant of the noble Roman Empire (the other branch of the poet's parental texts). He describes Dante through the image of a fruit-bearing, sweet fig tree placed among the bitter sorb trees on the dung heap of Florence. In the fig tree "riviva la sementa santa / di que' Romani" (*Inf.* 15.76–7; lives on the holy seed of those few Romans) who remained in the city. Once again, Brunetto seems unaware of the larger context of the biblical references he has incorporated into his image. The *semen sanctum* in the Bible represents God's people Israel. In dramatizing the danger to the sweet fig tree from contamination with the bitter trees that surround it, Brunetto echoes God's concern that his holy seed be contaminated by foreign influences, given that "commiscerunt semen sanctum cum populis terrarum" (1 Ezra 9:2; The holy seed has mixed itself with the peoples of the land). Brunetto warns Dante to cleanse himself of the customs of the Fiesolan heirs in Florence (*Inf.* 15.69). He suggests that Dante is a precious remnant of the noble Roman Empire, who has been chosen for a unique future. The image of a chosen remnant as seed in a tree comes from Isaiah. In chapter 6, the prophet has a vision of God, enthroned in his temple, explaining the necessity of diminishing his remnant until the holy seed (Is. 6:13; semen sanctum) remains only in the felled stump of a tenebinth or an oak tree. God marks Isaiah as his prophet and sends him out with this stern message to his people.[31] Isaiah's vision contains a liturgical foreshadowing of a Judeo-Christian future in the cry of the seraphim who are in attendance above God's throne: "sanctus sanctus sanctus" (Is. 6:3; Holy, holy, holy). This acclamation is the origin of the Jewish Kedusha, the western Christian Sanctus, and its Orthodox analogue, the Trisagion. Yet, Brunetto appears unaware of the relation between the Isaiah who first carries the message of the holy seed to God's people and the Dante who later embodies that seed.

In the *Paradiso*, moreover, Cacciaguida confirms and elaborates Brunetto's claim that Dante will carry on the blood of the Roman Empire, when he greets Dante as, "O sanguis meus" (*Par*. 15.28; O blood of mine), lines that echo Virgil's *Aeneid* 6.835, "sanguis meus." In Virgil, Aeneas is reunited with his father in the underworld. But Dante and his father meet in heaven, as Cacciaguida immediately makes clear: "sicut tibi cui / bis unquam celi ianüa reclusa" (*Par*. 15.29–30; To whom as to you was heaven's gate ever opened twice?). The answer is, of course, the apostle Paul, who was "caught up into paradise" (2 Cor. 12:4; raptus est in paradisum). Mixing Virgilian and biblical elements, Cacciaguida christens Dante as a new Aeneas and a new Paul, confirming the identity that Dante failed to recognize earlier: "Io non Enëa, io non Paulo sono" (*Inf*. 2.32–3; I am not Aeneas, nor am I Paul). In this greeting, Cacciaguida embraces Dante's Roman-Judean-Christian heritage, glosses Brunetto's prophecy, and replaces Latini as Dante's true prophetic father.

The process of revelation for Dante's future, nevertheless, clearly begins with Brunetto. In spite of his personal failure, Latini passes on prophetic pronouncements that Dante writes in his memory: "Ciò che narrate di mio corso scrivo" (*Inf*. 15.88; What you tell of my future I record), and especially, "serbolo a chiosar con altro testo" (*Inf*. 15.89; and keep for glossing along with other texts). Brunetto's words are essential building blocks for Cacciaguida's later reinterpretation. Out of such renewal, Dante creates his story and his *Commedia*. A biblical echo from the book of Proverbs adds authority to Brunetto's pronouncements. In Proverbs 7:3, the sage-narrator tells a young man, "scribe illam in tabulis cordis tui" (Prv. 7:3; Write it [my words, precepts and law] upon the tables of your heart).[32] In the *Commedia*, Virgil's response to Brunetto Latini also highlights the teacher's special role in foreshadowing Dante's future: he turns to Dante, looks at him, and when he has his attention says, "Bene ascolta chi la nota" (*Inf*. 15.99; He listens well who takes in what he hears). Virgil's words echo the beginning of the Apocalypse, in which John the Divine informs his audience, "beatus qui legit et qui audiunt verba prophetiae" (Apc. 1:3; Blessed is he who reads and those who hear the words of this prophecy [my translation]).[33] The disparity between John the Divine (as well as the sage in Proverbs) and Brunetto is striking. Brunetto, nonetheless, is a chosen voice of prophecy. Cacciaguida makes clear that in his predictions of Dante's future he is glossing the words that Dante recorded in the *Inferno*: "Figlio, queste son le chiose / di quel che ti fu detto" (*Par*. 17.94–5; Son, these are the glosses / on what was told you). Unworthy father though he remains, Brunetto contributes to the revelation of Dante's true father. Cacciaguida ratifies Dante's vision and urges him to share it with others despite the resistance he may encounter. He explains: "Ché se la voce tua sarà molesta / nel primo gusto, vital nodrimento / lascerà poi, quando sarà digesta" (*Par.* 17.130–2; For if your voice is bitter at the first taste, / it will later furnish vital nourishment / once it has been swallowed and digested).

The words of Cacciaguida, Dante, and the Bible converge. In Ezekiel and the Apocalypse, the two prophets are each told to eat a scroll on which appear God's written words of prophecy. Each prophet must then deliver the words to his people: Ezekiel to the house of Israel, John to the churches (Ez. 2:8–3:7; Apc. 10:8–11). For the prophet, the act of receiving God's words is sweet, even though the words themselves, which predict judgment for his own people, are bitter to digest:[34] "et dicit mihi accipe [librum] et devora illum / et faciet amaricare ventrem tuum / sed in ore tuo erit dulce tamquam mel" (Apc. 10:9; And he said to me: Take the book and eat it up: and it will make / your belly bitter, but in your mouth it will be sweet as honey). Cacciaguida's reworking of this biblical image places Dante in the lineage of prophets that stretches back through John the Divine and Ezekiel.

In retrospect Brunetto Latini seems likely to be among the souls in the "valle dolorosa" (*Par.* 17.137; the woeful valley) that Cacciaguida claims are known by fame, "l'anime che son di fama note" (*Par.* 17.138). Such souls become what Cacciaguida calls an example (*Par.* 17.140; essempro) whose root (*Par.* 17.141; la sua radice) will be known to those who will read Dante's poem (*Par.* 17.136–42). Brunetto thus becomes one whose witness adds to the authority of Dante's *Commedia*. Latini stands as a figure of consequence in the *Inferno* and in Dante's background. The full complexity of Brunetto's role in the *Commedia*, in keeping with the pilgrim's growing understanding, extends beyond the parallel passage of Oderisi to the episode of Cacciaguida. With this triform complement of incidents, Dante displays his art of autoexegetical re-evaluation within the trinitarian construction of his *Commedia*, a composition that serves as witness to his belief in the "Three in One" as a symbol of the divine mystery of being.

As Iannucci demonstrated, Dante uses the techniques of *autoesegesi* to create a poem that comments upon itself. Dante pilgrim moves away from acquiescence to Brunetto's theory of eternal life through personal fame supported by a biblical misinterpretation. Hunched over with

Oderisi under the weight of his stone of pride, Dante learns the lesson of shared participation in renown under the eye of a God for whom a thousand years is but a short space of time: "un mover di ciglia" (*Purg.* 11.107; the blinking of an eyelid); "sicut dies hesterna quae pertransiit" (Ps. 89:4; like yesterday, which is past).[35] Cacciaguida, by means of biblical allusions, welcomes Dante to his role as a participant in the scriptural lineage of the Son of God and his prophets. In his revision of the Lord's Prayer on the terrace of pride, Dante puts into practice his new understanding of his role as a writer of shared renown and his responsibility as inheritor of scriptural legacy by merging his voice with that of God. This paraphrase stands as a reminder of the distance that Dante has travelled and of the weakness of which he must always be mindful.

NOTES

1 A. Iannucci, "Autoesegesi dantesca: la tecnica dell' 'episodio parallelo' (*Inferno* XV – *Purgatorio* XI)," in *Forma ed evento nella "Divina Commedia"* (Roma: Bulzoni, 1984), 83–114. As Iannucci was aware, commentators from the beginning of the history of criticism "hanno cercato di 'commentare Dante con Dante'" (93). More recently William Franke discusses the ways in which interpretation within the *Commedia* "operates constantly upon narrative in textually determined ways." *Dante's Interpretive Journey* (Chicago: University of Chicago Press, 1996), 91. Zygmunt G. Barański also notes that " Dante's reflections on literature show perfect timing, not least because they bring together so effectively the literary and the critical, and merge these with his other concerns." "Dante Alighieri: Experimentation and (Self-) Exegesis," *The Cambridge History of Literary Criticism*, ed. A. Minnis and I. Johnson, vol. 2, *The Middle Ages* (Cambridge: Cambridge UP, 2005), 581. See also the extensive "Bibliography on Latin and Vernacular in Italian Literary Theory," also in *The Cambridge History of Literary Criticism*, 2:798–810; and Barański, "Dante and Medieval Poetics," in *Dante, Contemporary Perspectives*, ed. A.A. Iannucci (Toronto: University of Toronto Press, 1997), 3–22.

2 Iannucci, "Autoesegesi dantesca," 104.

3 Ibid., 94.

4 See Iannucci, "Autoesegesi dantesca," 92; and B. Smalley, *The Study of the Bible in the Middle Ages* (Notre Dame, IN: University of Notre Dame Press, 1970), 34.

5 All biblical quotations are from the *Biblia Sacra iuxta vulgatam versionem*, ed. B. Fischer et al., intro. Roger Gryson (1969; Stuttgart: Bibelgesellschaft, 2007). Abbreviations of biblical books and the numbering of the Psalms are also from this text: Quotations from the Psalms in the *Biblia Sacra* are from the *Liber psalmorum iuxta Septuaginta emandatus*. Unless otherwise noted, biblical translations are from the *Douay-Rheims Version*, trans. from the Latin Vulgate, rev. Bishop R. Challoner, 1749–52 (Baltimore: John Murphy, 1899; Rockford: Tan, 2000), with my modernization of archaic terms.

6 Iannucci, "Autoesegesi dantesca," 94.

7 R. Polzin, *Moses and the Deuteronomist: a Literary Study of the Deuteronomic History, Part One: Deuteronomy, Joshua, Judges* (New York: Seabury, 1980), 331–2.

8 See M. Fishbane, *Biblical Interpretation in Ancient Israel* (Oxford: Clarendon, 1985), 351–3.

9 Iannucci, "Autoesegi dantesca," 93.

10 Ibid., 93.

11 G. Gorni further perceives in Brunetto Latini's gesture a parody of the following biblical incidents: 1 Rg. 15:27; Za. 8:23; Mt. 9:20–1; Mc. 6.56. *Lettera, nome, numero: L'ordine delle cose in Dante* (Bologna: Molino, 1990), 324–35.

12 *The New Oxford Annotated Bible: New Revised Standard Version (NRSV)*, ed. Michael D Coogan (1973; Oxford: Oxford University Press, 2001).

13 Iannucci points out that "la discrepanza tra il contesto infernale in cui l'incontro tra Dante e Brunetto ha luogo e l'atteggiamento riverente e affezionato del pellegrino verso il suo antico maestro rende estremamente difficile formulare un giudizio critico" ("Autoesegesi dantesca," 98). Charles Davis attributes this ambivalence to Brunetto's embodiment of the contrasting extremes of public patriotism and private self-indulgence. "Brunetto Latini and Dante," *Studi medievali*, 3rd ser. (1967): 431–50. For Davis, the poetic and moral ambivalence of Brunetto adds immeasurably to the imaginative and rhetorical effectiveness of the poem (449). Anna Chiavacci Leonardi accounts for the "violent contradiction" in Brunetto's story by perceiving Brunetto as a symbol, an emblem of Dante's conception of Christian salvation in conflict with Greco-Roman values. "Il maestro di morale," in *La guerra della pietate: saggio per una interpretazione dell'Inferno di Dante* (Napoli: Liguori, 1979), 111–37. Massimilliano Chiamenti provides a sexual-psychological interpretation of conflicting emotions awakened in Dante when he finds himself unexpectedly facing his childhood master (*erastes*). *Dante Sodomita*, <http://www.nuovorinascimento.org/> 2009.

14 For details of Brunetto's historical sources, see F.J. Carmody, "Introduction," in *Li livres dou Tresor*, ed. Francis J. Carmody (Berkeley: University

of California Press, 1948), xxvi. All quotations of Brunetto Latini's *Tresor* are from Carmody's edition. Translations are from *The Book of the Treasure*, trans. P. Barrette and S. Baldwin (New York: Garland, 1993).

15 All emphasis in this essay is my own.

16 I have used Mandelbaum's translation, "you who dwell in the heavens," for Dante's clause, "che ne' cieli stai" in order to make clear in English that Dante has intentionally altered the canonical words of the prayer so that the reader sees and hears them anew. *The "Divine Comedy" of Dante Alighieri*, *"Purgatorio,"* trans. and intro. A. Mandelbaum (Berkeley: University of California Press, 1980; New York: Bantam, 1982).

17 G. Giacalone, in his note to *Purg*. 11.1 (DDP).

18 Dante Alighieri, *The Divine Comedy*, trans. and comm. M. Musa, vol. 2, *Purgatory* (1981; New York: Penguin, 1985), 122, note for lines 1–21.

19 M. Porena, in his note to *Purg*. 11.2–3 (DDP).

20 *The "Divine Comedy" of Dante Alighieri*, trans. and comm. J. Sinclair (1939; New York: Oxford University Press, 1961), 151.

21 Mandelbaum, *The Divine Comedy*, 342, note for lines 1–24.

22 Dante, *The Divine Comedy*, trans. and comm. C.S. Singleton, vol. 2, *Purgatorio* (Princeton: Princeton University Press, 1970–5), 235n91.

23 For a similar foregrounding of revisionary practices in Dante's relation to classical sources, see Kilgour's essay in this volume, "Dante's Ovidian Doubling," 174–214 below.

24 The reference to Exodus was recognized soon after Dante's death in the Codice cassinese, in the note to *Purg*. 11.15 (DDP).

25 The *Oxford English Dictionary* refers the word *supersubstantialis* to this late Latin usage in Matthew's Gospel, the only Gospel in which it occurs.

26 See C.S. Keener, *A Commentary on the Gospel of Matthew* (Grand Rapids: Eerdmans, 1999), 55.

27 On this passage, see also Kilgour, "Dante's Ovidian Doubling," 199–200 below.

28 Commentators have indicated the following references, in addition to Ps. 89:6 and Is. 40:6–7: Ps. 128:6; Sir. 14:18; Is. 28:4; and Iac. 1:10–11. Carolyn Lund-Mead and Amilcare A. Iannucci list the relevant commentators under the entry for *Purg*. 11. 92, 115. *Dante and the Vulgate Bible* (Rome: Bulzoni, 2012).

29 See also Mt. 17:5; Mc. 1:11; and Lc. 3:22, which vary slightly from Mt. 3–17. This reference was first recorded in the fourteenth century by Benvenuto da Imola and was thereafter noted by commentators in the nineteenth century (DDP).

30 G.A. Scartazzini (1874–82) and Giacomo Poletto noted this reference in the nineteenth century (DDP); Jeffrey Schnapp in the twentieth. *The Transfiguration of History at the Center of Dante's "Paradise"* (Princeton: Princeton University Press, 1986), 209.

31 1 Ezra 9:2 was recognized as an allusion of this text by Niccolò Tommaseo (1865, DDP); G. Marzot, *Il linguaggio biblico nella "Divina Commedia"* (Pisa: Nistri-Lischi, 1956), 141; and D. Mattalia (1960, DDP); Is. 6:13 was recognized by Mattalia.

32 Another nineteenth-century discovery by Scartazzini (1874–82, DDP); followed in the twentieth by C.H. Grandgent (DDP); G. Vandelli (1929, DDP); and Singleton, *The Divine Comedy*, 267n88.

33 Noted by Grandgent (DDP); N. Mineo, *Profetismo e apocalittica in Dante* (Catania: Università di Catania, 1968), 217; and Singleton, *The Divine Comedy*, 268n99.

34 D. Gibbons comments that the significance of metaphors of alimentation and digestion from the Bible ("Dante's single most important source" [693–4]) comes from the fact that God used these metaphors himself. "Alimentary Metaphors in Dante's *Paradiso*," *Publications of the Modern Language Association* 96 (2001): 693–706.

35 First noted by Pietro di Dante in his note to *Purg*. 11.91–3 (DDP).

6 Dante's Ovidian Doubling

MAGGIE KILGOUR

Elli givan dinanzi, e io soletto
di retro, e ascoltava i lor sermoni,
ch'a poetar mi davano intelletto.

(They went along in front and I, alone,
came on behind, listening to their discourse,
which gave me understanding of the art of verse.) (*Purg.* 22.127–9)

Like Dante listening in on Virgil and Statius, I hope to learn something about the nature of poetry, particularly Dante's poetry, by eavesdropping on some conversations among an expanding circle of writers: Dante and Ovid, and later Dante, Ovid, Virgil, and, briefly, Statius. In walking this route, I follow with gratitude in the footsteps of Amilcare Iannucci, who generously cleared the path for so many of us interested in Dante's self-reflection and his relations with his sources. My primary focus will be on how Dante uses the master of metamorphosis, Ovid, not only to chart the conversion experience of the *Commedia* but also to meditate on the transformation of classical forms and on the nature of artistic creation in general.

1. Putting Ovid in His Place

Dante's relation to the classics has been generally assumed to be competitive and ultimately corrective. In one of his many treatments of the topic, Iannucci argued that when Dante copies pagan authors he is driven by "the impulse to rewrite and transform his classical models by inserting them in a new ideological context" and, in particular, a

Christian one that reveals their limitations.[1] The assumption that Dante aspired to and succeeded in surpassing the ancients was a central premise of the early commentators, who compared his writings to those of the past and found the latter inferior. So Benedetto Buonmattei argued that Dante's poetry "è tanto maggiore di quelli, (non ci lasciamo accecar dalla 'nvidia) quanto è maggiore il concetto da lui spiegato, quanto è più nobile il Cielo della Terra, quanto le cose eterne, e invisibili, delle temporali, e visibili son più pregiate" (is so much greater than those [the ancients], if we are not letting ourselves be blinded by envy, as his conception is greater, as heaven is nobler than earth, as things eternal and invisible are more honoured than the temporal and visible).[2] From this perspective, imitation is basically a typological process, in which classical types are fulfilled when converted into Christian poetry.[3] In particular, Dante seems to use Ovid to create a form of "negative typology" in which Ovidian characters such as Ulysses, Phaethon, Hippolytus, Narcissus, and Arachne are contrasted with his own "corrected" versions.[4] Ovid himself becomes an ante-, and indeed *anti-*, type of Dante. While earlier scholars had assumed that Dante's knowledge of Ovid was limited to the *Metamorphoses*, recent critics have suggested that Dante was familiar with a range of Ovid's works, especially the last poetry in which Ovid gave an account of his own life and told the story of his final exile to the Black Sea.[5] Hinting that Augustus had been offended by his early erotic poetry, the poet complained that he had been destroyed by his own art, wryly writing his own epitaph in *Tristia* 3.3.73–4: "hic ego qui iaceo tenerorum lusor Amorum / ingenio perii Naso poeta meo" (I, who lie here, with tender loves once played, Naso the bard, whose life his wit betrayed).[6] The exiled Ovid himself, as well as his characters, therefore provide negative examples against which the exiled Dante defines himself; they serve as cautionary tales that warn Dante against poetic and moral error.[7] The spectre of Ovid's fate haunts *Inferno* 26, where, leaving the circle of the thieves, Dante exercises particular caution: "e più lo 'ngegno affreno ch'i' non soglio, / perché non corra che virtù nol guidi," (26.21–2; and more than is my way, I curb my powers lest they run on where virtue fail to guide them). The need of restraint at this specific point is understandable, as Dante is between two Ovidian encounters: the meeting with the metamorphosing thieves and that with the eloquent and persuasive Ulysses, whom Ovid had praised for his ability to tell the same story in different ways ("Ille referre aliter saepe solebat idem" [*Ars Amatoria* 2.123–8; Often would he tell the same tale in other words]). Ovid's Ulysses is a double for Ovid himself, who constantly retells old stories in novel ways.[8] In the exilic works too, the homesick Ovid identifies with the epic traveller determined to return to his homeland.[9] As is often noted, in the *Inferno*, Ulysses is equally an authorial figure, whose doomed voyage to purgatory mirrors the journey of the pilgrim.[10] However, Dante's Ulysses appears, as Peter Hawkins puts it, "a counter-type for the poet of the *Commedia*," an alternative author figure from whom Dante needs to hold himself back as he rises to paradise.[11] While Ovid identifies with Ulysses, Dante in the *Inferno* detaches himself from Ulysses and thus too from Ovid, restraining especially the Ovidian characteristic of *ingenium-ingegno* that got the Roman poet into trouble. Ovid's genius led only to Tomis; Dante's, it is already implied, will lead him to heaven itself.

However, this strategy of detachment is more complex than may first appear. For one thing, as Teodolinda Barolini argues, although through the poem "the pilgrim learns to be unlike Ulysses, the poet becomes ever more conscious of being *like* him."[12] Moreover, as the figure of Ulysses suggests, the kind of doubling Dante uses is itself highly Ovidian. Recent studies of Ovid's "self-conscious muse" have noted his habit of creating surrogate figures for himself, through whom he explores the nature and consequences of art.[13] With a few exceptions (most notably, if debatably, Pygmalion), Ovid's artists meet notoriously nasty ends: Philomela, Arachne, Orpheus, Niobe, and Marsyas are only the most obvious examples. By using such figures, Ovid indicates the perverse proximity between the creative and destructive urges. Eleanor Leach has argued, moreover, that Ovid's tragic artists serve as scapegoats to contrast with and foreground the author's superior authority, which, at the end of the *Metamorphoses*, enables him to assert that his art has made him immortal.[14] For Ovid, as for Dante, the author is a corrected version of his tragic characters; his climactic ascent above the stars in the last lines of the *Metamorphoses* presents him as a successful Phaethon.

However, the relation between Ovid and his doubles changes from the perspective of exile. As Ovid reviews his work and life, he notes that his fate seems to *copy* that of the fictions he has made. He too has been transformed: "inter mutata referri / fortunae vultum corpora posse meae" (*Tristia* 1.1.119–20; The aspect of my own fate can now be reckoned among those metamorphosed figures). In his life, the stories have come true. The artist, destroyed by his creations, now identifies with tragic figures such as Phaethon and Icarus (*Tristia* 3.4.21–30).[15] Ovid's last poetry thus reveals his likeness to rather than difference from his authorial doubles, as he too is a creator who has created the means of his own destruction. By making the poet himself a final example of the stories he told, the exilic verse suggests the fragility of the boundary between fantasy and reality. It brings to a climax Ovid's lifelong exploration of illusion, and especially of the insistent urge of the imagination to realize its own fantasies. While the story of Pygmalion entices us with the glory of the imagination's transformative power to turn dream into reality, that of Narcissus, who mistakes shadow for reality, reminds us of its dangers.[16]

In using Ovid and Ovidian figures as foils for his own progression, Dante is thus adapting a characteristically Ovidian method of self-creation through contrast, which, however, the exilic poetry reveals to be illusory. To read Dante as always "correcting" Ovid prevents us from seeing how Dante is developing a deeply Ovidian technique. Moreover, it overdetermines interpretation by making the pagan past inevitably, and sometimes only, Dante's "other"; as Barolini has noted, "Our insistence on Dante's corrections of classical antiquity, which began as an attempt to replace impressionistic critical enthusiasms with more rigorous assessment of the poem's intertextuality, now risks binding the text's paradoxes in a straightjacket of medieval orthodoxy that is every bit as confining and impoverishingly unilateral."[17] Looking at Dante's relation to Virgil, Winthrop Wetherbee has recently argued also that many earlier critics "tend to foreclose the possibility of our viewing Dante as first and foremost a sympathetic reader of Vergil's poetry for its own sake and on its own terms."[18] This may be even truer in the case of Ovid, whom Wetherbee names as possibly "Dante's most important model, the greatest challenge to *aemulatio*, the poet he perhaps sees as most like himself. The very theme of the *Commedia* is metamorphosis."[19] As critics have increasingly noted, Ovid is an important presence in the *Purgatorio* and *Paradiso*.[20] To describe his ascent to paradise, Dante draws first on Ovid's story of Marsyas (*Par.* 1.19–21) and then on that of Glaucus (1.67–9), which helps him convey the ineffability of the experience in which "transumanar significar *per verba* / non si poria" (*Par.* 1.70–1; To soar beyond the human cannot be described in words). Ovidian figures, as well as the process of revising and reimagining Ovid, help Dante reach his most radical and profound vision of change. Dante's use of Ovidian doubles shows that he is an attentive reader of Ovid, sensitive to the implications for his own project of Ovid's complex exploration of art and the troublingly double nature of creativity.

2. Changing Ovid

I want therefore to approach Dante's treatment from a slightly different angle, returning to the famous episode that, as I noted, appears to demonstrate Dante's sense of his own difference from Ovid: the circle of the thieves in *Inferno* 24 and 25. The episode begins in *imitatio*, as Dante uses Ovidian metamorphoses to describe the punishment of the thieves, condemned forever to lose and regain their form in a perverse kind of snake dance.[21] Dante seems to be drawing broadly on the allegorical tradition in which Ovidian stories were read as proving that sin makes a man a beast. If the canto generally invokes the general atmosphere of Ovidian change, Dante uses several specific and famous passages in the *Metamorphoses*: the transformation of men into snakes recalls closely that of Cadmus in *Metamorphoses* 4.563–604; the change of Vanni Fucci in *Inferno* 24.103–11 is compared to that of the phoenix (*Met*. 15.391–407) and also invokes the story of Io from *Metamorphoses* 1; the description of Agnolo de' Brunelleschi in *Inferno* 25.48–78 draws in some detail upon the metamorphosis of Hermaphroditus (*Met*. 4.361–5). I will return to the significance of this particular combination of stories a bit later.

Having rather ostentatiously used Ovid to set the scene, Dante, however, abruptly boasts that he has imagined a new form of change that surpasses all those of the master of metamorphosis:

> Taccia di Cadmo e d'Aretusa Ovidio,
> ché se quello in serpente e quella in fonte
> converte poetando, io non lo 'invidio
> ché due nature mai a fronte a fronte
> non trasmutò sì ch'amendue le forme
> a cambiar lor matera fosser pronte. (*Inf*. 25.97–102)
>
> (Let Ovid not speak of Cadmus or Arethusa,
> for if his poem turns him into a serpent
> and her into a fountain, I envy him not,
> for never did he change two natures, face to face,
> in such a way that both their forms
> were quite so quick exchanging substance [translation slightly modified].)

While the episode begins in *imitatio*, Dante breaks from his model, asserting that the changes he now describes, in which men and beasts trade forms, are completely different from anything Ovid might have been able to imagine.

Much of the criticism of the episode has assumed that Dante is right, and has tried to explain how Dante's metamorphoses are different from and indeed superior to those of his pagan precursor. One answer is to argue that while Ovid can only describe superficial variations of forms, the Christian poet will, by the end of his poem, achieve a complete revolution of reality. Ovidian change is superficial, fictional – mere "poetando" (25.99); in contrast, Dante's expanding poetic vision brings about substantial and radical change.[22] As Lawrence Baldassaro argued, the canto thus epitomizes the opposition between pagan metamorphosis and Christian conversion.[23] For Barolini also, "Dante is using classical material to suggest a type of negative or infernal metamorphosis that leads nowhere, that is repetitive, rather than redemptive."[24] From a Christian perspective, Ovidian change in general is the essence of hell, an infernal world without end in which forms are seen to change and transmute (*Inf.* 25.143; mutare e trasmutare) eternally.[25] Christianity is superior by its leap of the imagination. Dante's assertion of difference points towards his ultimate revision of Ovidian metamorphosis as the spiritual conversion and rebirth that is the subject of the *Commedia*.

However, while critics have generally supported Dante's claims to difference and superiority, many have been made uncomfortable by his exaggerated "overgoing" of Ovid. Dante's boast seems to imply his own momentary lapse into pride, like that of Vanni Fucci; after all, in *Purgatorio* 13.136–8 he admits to being prone to that sin. Richard Terdiman argued that for a moment Dante is, like Ovid, carried away with his own wit and forgets his spiritual purpose.[26] For Peter Hawkins, however, the lapse is intended to show once more the error that Ovid represents: "Dante deliberately loosens the grip on his genius and in his subsequent flight shows the tendency of all poets to become a Phaeton, an Icarus, a Ulysses."[27] The poet's very awareness of danger ensures that he will avoid it. Rachel Jacoff and Jeffrey Schnapp see a further and particularly deft Ovidian twist to this strategy, arguing that:

> In *Inferno* 25, the theme of imaginative freedom is linked to a virtuoso poetics of self-display fraught with moral and artistic perils. Dante enters into a poetic competition with Ovid … Dante's claim to have outdone Ovid in the act of "poetando" is presented with a braggadochio more in keeping with the spirit of infernal self-aggrandizement than with Christian humility. The grandstanding of this episode is itself an Ovidian device that replays Ovid's own obsession with technique, an aspect of his

> poetic identity acknowledged and criticized even in antiquity ... The attempt to outdo Ovid is a momentary capitulation that retrospectively both dramatizes and exorcises seductive tendencies associated with the figure of the Ovidian artist.[28]

If Dante seems to succumb to the temptation of rhetorical self-indulgence, which critics had identified in Ovid, it is only in order to hoist Ovid by his own petard. By acknowledging his own pride and potential for Ovidian "self-aggrandizement," he frees himself from it.

In general, these arguments depend again on the assumption that Dante uses Ovid as a kind of double or projection of his own errors in order to free himself from them. In contrast to the "grandstanding" artist or the egotistical Vanni Fucci, who serves a similar function, Dante in this episode seems deeply dependent on others, especially Virgil. But such dependence shows Dante's need for the classics, even as he seems to detach himself from them. The presence of Virgil in this canto might, however, suggest that classical influences themselves split into antithetical poetic routes: Ovid leads to hell, and Virgil towards heaven. As Baldassaro notes, Dante draws particular attention to the process by which the pilgrim and Virgil come to this new circle (24.22–63). By emphasizing the difficulty of the ascent, Dante both recalls the opening of the *Commedia* and looks forward to the *Purgatorio*, where he will highlight "the need for the pilgrim to move continuously forward."[29] From the start of his journey, though, the pilgrim is resistant to change; like Vanni Fucci, he clings to himself and needs Virgil to prod him into action.[30] In this respect, and despite his earlier protest that "io non Enëa ... sono" (*Inf.* 2.32; I am not Aeneas), the pilgrim is rather like Virgil's Aeneas, who also resists change in his journey, desiring to stay and die in Troy like a Homeric hero, and has to be taught to move forward to his new home.[31]

Dante's denial of likeness with his classical model covers up further important parallels. Aeneas's journey is originally impeded by his father Anchises, who at first refuses to leave his native land and is only persuaded to leave by a divine sign. Taken up on Aeneas's shoulders and carried out of the burning city, the father represents the burden of the past that Aeneas must carry from the old world to the new. However, in death, Anchises is transformed into a force who propels Aeneas into the future, which he shows his son in book 6, where he announces Aeneas's definitive metamorphosis from a Trojan into a Roman, as he is famously now called for the first time (*Aen.* 6.851). In Dante also, the classical past is imagined as a potential impediment, dragging the Christian pilgrim back into the circles of endless metamorphoses of *Inferno* 24–5. Nevertheless, it also pushes him forward, as Virgil does here. But it is not just Virgil who drives him upwards. From the retrospective of the higher levels, Ovidian metamorphosis appears not as a danger from which Dante must distance himself but as a crucial part of the very energy that fuels his own transformative vision.

3. Double Trouble

Jacoff and Schapp's identification of Dante's "grandstanding" as Ovidian is a good reminder that for Dante, and for other artists of this time, Ovid is not simply a bunch of stories or myths of change. His influence is slippery; while it is most obviously traceable in later reworkings of his tales, it can be glimpsed frequently also in the construction of authorial personae.[32] More generally, Ovid offers a set of concerns, primarily about the nature of art and its relation to desire and change. Ovid has always been the poet's poet, identified with the power of the aesthetic. Through all his works he foregrounds himself and his own creative act, reflecting on the origins, nature, and effects of creation. Like other artists, Dante thus seems especially drawn therefore to figures and places through which Ovid reflects on the powers and meaning of art.[33]

The metamorphosis of the thieves is part of a larger web of Ovidian elements through which Dante self-consciously foregrounds the process of poetic creation. The episode opens with a simile that introduces its concerns:

In quella parte del giovanetto anno
che 'l sole i crin sotto l'Aquario tempra
e già le notti al mezzo dì sen vanno,
quando la brina in su la terra assempra
l'imagine di sua sorella bianca,
ma poco dura a la sua penna tempra,
lo villanello a cui la roba manca,
si leva, e guarda, e vede la campagna
biancheggiar tutta; ond' ei si batte l'anca,
ritorna in casa, e qua e là si lagna,
come 'l tapin che non sa che si faccia;
poi riede, e la speranza ringavagna,
veggendo 'l mondo aver cangiata faccia

in poco d'ora, e prende suo vincastro
e fuor le pecorelle a pascer caccia. (*Inf.* 24.1–15)

(In that season of the youthful year
when the sun cools his locks beneath Aquarius
and the dark already nears but half the day,
and when the hoarfrost copies out upon the fields
the very image of her snowy sister –
although her pen-point is not sharp for long –
the peasant, short of fodder, rises,
looks out, and sees the countryside
turned white, at which he slaps his thigh,
goes back indoors, grumbling here and there
like a wretch who knows not what to do,
then goes outside again and is restored to hope,
seeing that the world has changed its face
in that brief time, and now picks up his crook
and drives his sheep to pasture.)

Critics have debated the relation between this lengthy extended simile and the main action.[34] In many ways it seems an extravagant and self-contained display that draws attention to the poet's mastery of rhetoric – it is "Ovidian" in its ostentatious display of wit, *ingenium*. However, the passage also introduces central themes that are more deeply Ovidian and that set the scene for what follows: change, art, the relation between appearance and reality, and artistic rivalry. The main action of the simile involves a misreading of the nature of change, as the "villanello" first despairs when he sees what he thinks is snow once more on the ground, and then rejoices when he sees it melt and knows that spring is indeed coming. What at first appears to be no change at all turns into a promise of renewal and new life. The revision of perception anticipates Dante's recognition of Ovid as a creative force for imaginative transformation rather than one of stagnant regression. Moreover, the vocabulary turns nature into a scene of artistic creation, as the frost is represented as a writer, whose "imagine" melts on the ground. The simile draws attention to the fragility, insubstantiality, as well as deluding, nature of creations. As Hawkins further suggests, the melting of the frost shows the self-destructive potential for creativity, representing "an artist destroyed in his own work" – as Ovid himself had been.[35]

The simile also prepares us for a canto in which the layering of Ovidian figures links change and writing. To convey the speed of the dissolution and then reconstitution of Vanni Fucci, Dante draws on a metaphor close at hand to a writer: "Nè *O* sì tosto mai né *I* si scrisse, / Com' el' s'accese e arse, e cener tutto / Convenne che cascando divenisse" (*Inf.* 24.100–2; Neither has "o" nor "i" been writ so quick as he caught fire and burned, turned, in the very act of falling, into ashes). Now supernatural change as well as natural change becomes a form of writing. The significance of the particular letters formed works on two levels: the Italian *io* suggests the self that Vanni Fucci both asserts and constantly loses; but the Latin *Io* refers to one of Ovid's earliest tales of transformation, which is also a story of the origins of writing. In *Metamorphoses* 1, the nymph Io, transformed into a cow but retaining human consciousness, tries to communicate with her father by writing letters in the sand with her hoof; her changed form brings about a changed form of communication as she substitutes "littera pro verbis" (1.649; letters for words).[36]

Dante's combination of the two meanings of Io – ego and inventor of letters – creates a very Ovidian identification of selfhood with writing. This scene of writing is followed up in *Inferno* 24.103–11 by the image of the phoenix, which looks back to *Metamorphoses* 15.391–407 where the bird's eternal rebirth anticipates the poet's own projected self-perpetuation in his poem. Furthermore, as Jessica Levenstein notes, in *Amores* 1.3.19–26 Io is also linked to the poet's hope of immortality through art,[37] a hope that Dante parodies in the thieves' endless change. Dante's layering of Ovidian figures continues in *Inferno* 25, which revises Ovid's transformation of Hermaphroditus to emphasize the act of writing. In *Metamorphoses* 4, the merging of boy and girl is mediated through an elaborate series of similes, in which the metaphorical transformation of the couple into other figures – ivy, a serpent, an eagle, and a squid (4.361–7) – foreshadows their final change. Dante only copies one of these, the ivy (*Inf.* 25.58–60), replacing Ovid's animal imagery with figures of melting wax (25.61) and burning paper (25.64–6). Carol Ann Cioffi believes that Dante is thinking of the famous image of wax used by Pythagoras in *Metamorphoses* 15 to describe the principle of eternal flux that rules all things and makes them immortal:[38]

> utque novis facilis signatur cera figuris
> nec manet ut fuerat nec formas servat easdem,
> sed tamen ipsa eadem est, animam sic semper eandem
> esse, sed in varias doceo migrare figuras. (*Met.* 15.169–72)

(And, as the pliant wax is stamped with new designs, does not remain as it was before nor keep the same form long, but is still the selfsame wax, so do I teach that the soul is ever the same, though it passes into ever-changing bodies.)[39]

Wax here becomes a central image for an identity that undergoes superficial changes while remaining essentially the same; for Dante, it helps characterize the infernal immortality of the thieves whose change is no change at all. By constantly being transformed, they resist the ultimate and radical transformation of conversion.

But the image of wax appears in other places in Ovid, where it is connected to the theme of writing or creation more generally. Ovid's description of the death of Narcissus may be especially on Dante's mind:[40]

sed ut intabescere flavae
igne levi cerae matutinaque pruinae
sole tepente solent, sic attentuatus amore
liquitur et tecto paulatim carpitur igni. (*Met.* 3.487–90)

(But as the yellow wax melts before a gentle heat, as hoar frost melts before the warm morning sun, so does he, wasted with love, pine away, and is slowly consumed by its hidden fire.)

The comparison of the dying Narcissus to melting wax and frost suggests a link between the metamorphosis of the thieves and the opening simile of *Inferno* 24. In Ovid, the story of Narcissus is an *aition*, a myth that explains the beginnings of something, in this case not only of the origins of the narcissus flower but also that of art itself. The episode is central to the epic as a whole, looking backwards and forwards to other moments in which Ovid comments on the nature as well as the source of art.[41] It recalls the story of Syrinx, transformed by Pan into a pipe made of reeds bound by wax (*Met.* 1.711–12), a tale framed by that of Io, thus linking the origins of writing to that of music and poetry. The comparison of the animation of Pygmalion's statue to the softening of wax (*Met.* 10.284–6) further connects wax to creation. It is significant, therefore, that for Ovid wax is the medium also for writing, equivalent to Dante's paper. In *Metamorphoses* 9.522–5, Byblis, whose name of course means book, confesses her incestuous lust to her brother on wax tablets whose pliant surface enables her to write and rewrite, as she anxiously corrects her own words. While in the Pygmalion episode the image of softening wax reveals art's ability to bring about positive change and to make fantasies come true, the melting wax of Icarus's wings, like that of Dante's frost, embodies the fragility and insubstantiality of all creations (*Met.* 8.225–6; see also *Ars* 2.45–50). In Ovid, the mutability of wax reminds us both of the ephemerality of language and poetry and also of its transformative power, especially the power of revision.

Dante's choice of Ovidian images thus allows him to build on a pattern that runs throughout Ovid's works and that is central to his examination of creativity, selfhood, and the desire for self-eternizing through art. Furthermore, the setting, the circle of the thieves, gives Dante a chance to mull over the fact that his own creativity, and indeed his poetic self, originates in such borrowings from past writers. The connection between writing and theft is anticipated in the opening simile, a scene of artistic rivalry in which the frost is a copyist who unsuccessfully mimics snow. The subsequent series of transformations, in which thieves steal the identity of each other, mirrors the way in which Dante's poetic creativity involves appropriation, a reworking of old material into new forms. Here too, critics generally see a strategy of opposition, in which the bad thieves are differentiated from Dante, the good one, who creatively takes from his sources to surpass them and to enrich culture.[42]

I want to pay attention, however, to the exact wording of Dante's claim that, now rising into new territory undreamt of by Ovid, "non *lo 'nvidio*" (25.99; I don't envy him). In so doing, he emphasizes the potential for *invidia* (envy) among authors. Robert J. Ellrich argues, therefore, that the canto of the thieves is "organized around Dante's perception of theft as a movement of envy whose consequences are the negation of identity and creativity."[43] Theft and envy are closely connected; because "every poet draws from the poetic past, and is subject to the charge of theft," Dante himself "must avoid the ethico-literary pitfall of envious, sterile appropriation, which would engender nothing but would merely repeat."[44] For Ellrich, the thieves represent the fruitless and redundant products of invidious literary appropriation; in contrast, Dante does not envy Ovid and is "not performing an aggressive, destructive act," and therefore is able to imagine a new form of change.[45] Like others, Ellrich argues that the problems raised by the canto are resolved through another form of doubling that divides antithetical forms of creativity.

Ellrich's perceptive reading, however, overlooks the stunning rhyme that links "Ovidio" and "invidio" (25.97, 99). The wordplay is itself highly Ovidian in its bringing together of unlike things to make us consider the relation between them. Ovid's wit constantly creates such troubling likenesses, uniting contradictory things as one: Althaea, who kills her son to avenge her brothers, is "impietate pia" (*Met.* 8.477; pious in impiety). Such paradoxes, which shockingly conflate moral antitheses, are the verbal equivalents of metamorphosis itself, which suggests how easily one thing can turn into its opposite.[46] Here too, then, one might see Dante as turning Ovid's own rhetorical dexterity against him. But Dante's practice of creating verbal networks should make us think carefully about the deep logic of this coupling, which binds Ovid and envy into another infernal couple.

4. Ovidian *invidia*

Dante's claim that he is free from envy is quite conventional and part of a long tradition. From Pindar on, envy is represented as the antithesis of poetic creativity: where poets produce and create, the envious consume and destroy.[47] Poets were in the habit of asserting their own moral authority against the envy of others; in encomiastic poetry especially, the generous and creative praise of the poet is contrasted with the begrudging and destructive response of the invidious.[48] Writers frequently represent themselves as victims of envy, while vociferously protesting their own freedom from the vice.

Yet from the start, this opposition is problematic. For Aristotle, envy (*phthonos*) is closely related to creative emulation (*zelos*) in particular. Both are responses provoked by the success of another, particularly, someone who is close to us or a peer: "So too we compete with those who follow the same ends as ourselves: we compete with our rivals in sports or in love, and generally with those who are after the same things; and it is therefore these whom we are bound to envy beyond all others. Hence the saying, Potter against potter."[49] Creativity is inherently competitive; according to Longinus also, Plato's writing would have been less perfect "had he not striven, with heart and soul, to contest the prize with Homer, like a young antagonist with one who had already won his spurs, perhaps in too keen emulation, longing as it were to break a lance, and yet always to good purpose."[50] But Aristotle uses emulation and envy to distinguish negative and positive forms of competition: emulation is creative, spurring the poet on to greater things in the hope of surpassing his rival; envy is destructive, both of its object and of its possessor who is eaten up by his own passion. Significantly for Dante, envy becomes associated with snakes; in particular it is often represented as gnawing or being gnawed by serpents.[51] Envy is a consuming and ultimately self-consuming passion; it drives people to suicide, conventionally by hanging or self-strangulation.[52]

While envy and emulation have similar origins, they thus appear clearly differentiated. A similar distinction informs Christian discussions of envy. According to St John Chrystostom, "wholesome rivalry, imitation without contention" binds us to each other and to God.[53] Its opposite is envy, "the root of all evils," which tears apart the unity of the body of Christ, dividing us from each other. Envy is the reverse of Christian love; thus in *Purgatorio* 13 the envious are purged through images of charity.[54]

Yet, while envy seems opposed to poetic creation, it is also frequently seen as a property of genius and poetic ambition. It is especially hard to exclude from artistic imitation, with the inevitable mixing of identification and rivalry of artists who copy and strive to surpass each other. In practice, too, envy and emulation are often hard to tell apart. G.W. Pigman III thus argues that Renaissance emulation consisted of "admiration for a model joined with envy and contentiousness" as "Envy, contentious striving, jealous rivalry cling to *aemulatio*."[55] In other ways also, envy and creativity in general seem disquietingly less like opposites than different names for the same thing. Envy is associated with vision; *invidia* is etymologized as coming from *videre*, and so envy is connected to the concept of the evil eye, often represented as looking aslant as it views another's good.[56] In the *Purgatorio*, the envious have their eyes sewn shut so that they can learn to see again in a more charitable fashion. The envious are morally blind.[57] The association of envy with vision shows its proximity also to love, associated, especially in the Platonic tradition, with the eyes.[58] However, envy is a sin that also makes us see things that are not in fact there; Lucretius notes how the envious work themselves up with images of a rival:

> macerat invidia ante oculos illum esse potentem,
> illum aspectari, claro qui incedit honore,
> ipsi se in tenebris volvi caenoque queruntur. (*De rerum natura* 3.75–7)

> (They are often consumed with envy that before their very eyes he is clothed in power, he is the sight of the town, who parades in shining pomp, while they complain that they themselves are wallowing in the darkness and mire.)[59]

Envy is thus similar to the power of imagination.[60] Moreover, appropriately for writers specifically, it is not just a visual but also a verbal sin. In *The Faerie Queene*, Edmund Spenser's *Enuie* attacks the poet's wit using his own powers, words, against him: "Eke the verse of famous Poets witt / He does backebite, and spightfull poison spues / From leprous mouth on all, that euer writt" (*Faerie Queene* 1.4.32.6–9).[61] Envy leads to the perversion of poetic language into Sclaunder, whose speech Spenser describes:

> Her words were not, as common words are ment,
> T'expresse the meaning of the inward mind,
> But noysome breath, and poysnous spirit sent
> From inward parts, with cancred malice lind
> And breathed forth with blast of bitter wind;
> Which passing through the eares, would pierce the hart,
> And wound the soule it selfe with griefe vnkind;
> For like the stings of Aspes, that kill with smart,
> Her spightfull words did pricke, and wound the inner part.
> (*Faerie Queene* 4.8.26.1–9)

Sclaunder is the power of language gone wrong, just as *Enuie* is creative energy that has become destructive.[62]

The history of Ovid's generative inspiration of later artists might suggest that his own poetics is both derived from and encourages emulation rather than envy; he himself praises other poets and claims to be free from *invidia*.[63] An inveterate recycler of old stories, Ovid is constantly concerned with what it means to create from the works of others. His debt and his relation to tradition are both the basis and the subject of his work. Ovid wants us to witness his miraculous transformation of others and marvel at his creation *non ex nihilo*. The elder Seneca observed that when Ovid used a phrase of Virgil it was "non subripiendi causa, sed palam mutuandi, hoc animo ut vellet agnosci" (*Controversiae et Suasoriae* 3.7: with no thought of plagiarism, but meaning that his piece of open borrowing should be noticed).[64] So too at the very moment in which Ovid triumphantly claims that his ego will live forever in his writing with the final word of the *Metamorphoses*, "vivam" (15.879; I will live) – a climactic "grandstanding" if ever there was one – he knows very well that his readers will hear the echo of Horace's *Odes* 3.30 and of his own earlier self in *Amores* 1.15. The writing self is always made up of others' voices.

However, as Ovid foregrounds his own creative emulation of the past, he makes envy his mortal enemy. Alison Keith remarks that Ovid "seems to have been intrigued by the programmatic potential of Envy as a literary construct from the outset of his career" and "is concerned to articulate a specifically literary challenge to Envy."[65] In the *Remedia amoris*, he reminds us how "ingenium magni livor detractat Homeri" (365; Envy disparages great Homer's genius), because "summa petit livor" (369; What is highest is Envy's mark). Envy is not always so discriminating in its target; however, in *Amores* 2.6.25, the poor harmless parrot whose death is lamented is said to have been destroyed by "invidia." However, the parrot, as Ovid reminds us, is an "imitatrix" (2.6.1), a mimic or imitator, like the poet himself who in this elegy is imitating Catullus 3.[66] The imitative artist especially seems to attract *invidia*. Like other writers, Ovid uses his own poetry to fight this pernicious force. In *Amores* 1.15.1, the poet strikes back at "Livor edax" (biting Envy), claiming that despite its gnawing tooth he will live on in his poetry. So in the *Remedia* he proclaims defiantly that he is safe from envy: "Rumpere, Livor edax: magnum iam nomen habemus; / Maius erit, tantum quo pede coepit eat" (389–90; Burst thyself, greedy Envy! my fame is great already; it will be greater still, so it keeps its first good fortune).[67]

Ovid's battle with envy takes a darker turn in his exilic verse, however, in which his originally allegorical enemy takes on a life of its own. Ovid represents himself as the innocent victim of a nameless but powerful detractor who, he complains, persecutes him even in his misfortune. The last poem in the *Ex Ponto*, and thus in Ovid's works as a whole, opens with the poet's own biting defense against this enemy: "Invide, quid laceras Nasonis carmina rapti?" (4.16.1; Envious one, why do you wound the verse of ravished Naso?). The poem builds towards the cry: "ergo summotum patria proscindere, Livor / desine" (4.16.47–8; So, Envy, cease to tear one banished from his country). The poignant last image of the distraught and helpless poet contrasts strikingly with the grandstanding of the end of the *Metamorphoses*. The exilic verse, and Ovid's career, ends on a bleak note; in the battle between envy and creativity, envy now seems to be winning.

As the main source of information about his life, Ovid's final poetry encouraged many to believe that envy played a major role in the poet's mysterious exile. Editors of his works often assumed that this enemy was a rival, who, jealous of Ovid's success, had spread lies about Ovid's poetry and morals that brought about his downfall. Further evidence for this was drawn from another of Ovid's exilic works, the *Ibis*. This bizarre and rather unpleasant poem is basically a string of extravagant and violent curses against an unnamed and unidentified enemy, whom the poet blames for his fate and who, as Gareth Williams has noted, is shaped as a figure of *invidia* incarnate.[68] In the commentaries on this work, which are the earliest extant scholia on Ovid, it was proposed that Ovid's enemy was a certain *aemulus* (a rival), who invidiously used the poet's innocent poetry to teach adultery.[69]

While reading the poem biographically, the scholia is also acutely aware of, and interested in, the work's place in literary traditions. Early on in his poem, Ovid himself explicitly draws attention to the fact that he is imitating Callimachus:

> Nunc quo Battiades inimicum devovet Ibin,
> Hoc ego devoveo teque tuosque modo.
> Utque ille, historiis involvam carmina caecis:
> Non soleam quamvis hoc genus ipse sequi.
> Illius ambages imitatus in Ibide dicar
> Oblitus moris iudiciique mei. (*Ibis* 55–60)

> (Now, in such wise as Battiades [Callimachus] calls curses down on his enemy Ibis, so do I call curses down on thee and thine. Like him I will enshroud my song in doubtful story, although I am not wont to pursue this style. His riddlings shall I be said to have imitated, forgetful of my judgment and my custom.)

Ovid's poem is an exercise in emulation: "It is an example of how to imitate and surpass a literary model."[70]

The poem thus originates in emulation of two kinds: the enemy's destructive emulation of Ovid and the poet's own creative emulation of Callimachus. The two types again seem opposites, as Ovid once more defines his creativity against the envy of others. But there is a lot that is disturbing about this poem that brings us back to Ovid's complex use of authorial doubles. As Stephen Hinds nicely puts it, Ibis is presented as the poet's "evil twin": "Ovid … makes of Ibis a kind of double of himself by wishing on his persecutor the same sufferings – and the same mythological analogies – which he himself suffers in the *Tristia*."[71] Moreover, as Ovid himself says, in imitating Callimachus, he abandons his own voice to take on another. As he piles up an astonishing array of curses against his nemesis, the poet previously known for his lightness and urbanity undergoes a disturbing change. His extravagant *ingenium* becomes concentrated and expanded with demonic fury, as it spawns copious images of suffering. The relentless cataloguing of violence is in many ways quite fascinating; some early readers admired Ovid's list of evils as further demonstration of the fertile imagination of the "ingeniosus poeta."[72] Recent readers have tended to be more perturbed by this obsessive outpouring of venom. Gareth Williams describes the poem as the representation of "an intense and highly charged state of mind," "a condition of perverse obsessiveness which can never fully satisfy the sadistic relish on which it feeds."[73] In the end, moreover, poet and enemy seem indistinguishable; as Williams explains, "The avenger gradually succumbs to the irrational forces of his diseased imagination," retreating into his own "warped, obsessive imagination."[74] The effect seems even more unsettling as scholars since Housman have tended to see Ibis as not a real enemy but a figment of Ovid's imagination.[75] The poet whose verse had celebrated the act of creation now can only imagine an almost infinite list of elaborate forms of destruction.

5. Dante in the Woods of Allusion

Ovid's fate haunted later writers, for whom he was an unsettling example of the poet crushed by the force of envy that always feeds on creativity. They recalled him to lament their own persecution. In Guillaume de Deguileville's *Pèlerinage de vie humaine* (ca. 1330), the pilgrim is unjustly attacked by Envy and her daughters, Treason and Detraction, and is thrown into prison. Here he is visited by Ovid, who comes both to offer pity for his plight and to curse his enemies for him; he quotes *Ibis* 105.[76] While de Deguileville's poem is a reworking of the *Roman de la rose*, his Ovid is not the poet of love who teaches his pupils how to court but the poet of envy who teaches them how to curse. However, while the narrator is sympathetic to Ovid, he is not interested in cursing his enemies but hopes that justice and love will win out. Rejected as a model, Ovid disappears from the poem.

Dante's witty rhyme in *Inferno* 25 indicates his awareness also of the traditional role of envy as the dark and dangerous "other" of creativity and, furthermore, its centrality to Ovid's life and art. It makes *invidia* the infernal partner of *Ovidio*, that gnaws on him as Ugolino will Ruggieri in *Inferno* 32–3. Like other writers, Dante uses the topos of envy to define himself by differentiation and break free from such a form of coupling. The claim of freedom from *invidia* is the basis also of his assertion in *Inferno* 25 that he can create something new and original. His resistance to this vice becomes part of his self-identification later on. When he meets the envious, he observes that this is not a sin to which he is much attracted (*Purg.* 13.133–5). His compassionate response to their plight displays his own contrary charity (*Purg.* 13.73–4). Envy and Dantean poetics are implicit antitheses: after all, the envious in *Purgatorio* are suspicious of Dante's poetic language, fearing that periphrasis is a means of concealing some malicious truth (14.25–7).[77] By freeing himself from envy in *Inferno* 25.97–9, moreover, Dante asserts that he is not one of those who worked to destroy Ovid. At the same time, however, as the poem works to clear Dante of the charge of *invidia*, the rhyme projects it onto *Ovidio* from whose fate, as well as poetics, the poet separates himself.

The wording also indicates how, as Ellrich argues, Dante is concerned generally with envy and its relation to creativity. While no single infernal circle is devoted to this sin, envy permeates hell and mixes with the other vices. *Purgatorio* 11–13 suggest the connection between envy and pride, the sin to which, as Carolynn Lund-Mead's essay here reminds us, Dante admits (*Purg.* 13.136–8). For Dante, the two deadliest sins raise questions about art and the relations between artists.[78] Furthermore, the depiction of the envious in *Purgatorio* 13 invites us to look back also to its parallel, *Inferno* 13, the circle of the suicides and profligates, where the pilgrim meets another victim of envy: Pier della Vigna, destroyed by "[i]'nvidia" (*Inf.* 13.78).

The canto of the suicides is also concerned with literary emulation. Dante's depiction of the historical figure is set against a fantastic background that draws on a mixing of sources. The predominant influence here, however, seems not Ovid but Virgil, whose text appears the main interpretive model for the episode. The harpies and the figure of the speaking tree combine two separate episodes from Aeneas's journey in *Aeneid* 3, in which Aeneas meets strange, hybrid figures: first the Trojan Polydorus and then the harpies. In both cases, Aeneas arrives in unknown territories and performs actions that have unexpected consequences. In the first, he arrives in Thrace where he sets out to build a new city, beginning by offering a sacrifice to his mother. But his filial piety causes him to unintentionally commit an act of impiety. Tearing a branch off of a tree, he finds he has unwittingly hurt the transformed shade of the Trojan king Priam's son Polydorus, treacherously slain by his Thracian host. While Aeneas could hardly have been expected to have encountered his Trojan cousin on – actually in – foreign soil, the wounding of a relative suggests a carelessly destructive element in his nature that will be seen also in Carthage and then Latium. Moreover, it underscores his inability to recognize his likeness to the others whom he meets in his travels. As Richard Thomas thus argues, the scene problematizes Aeneas's civilizing mission.[79] But it also comments on Virgil's analogous poetical mission. As Stephen Hinds has demonstrated in relation to a different instance of "tree violation" in the *Aeneid*, the hero's stripping of trees (*silvae*) mirrors the poet's reemployment of sources (*silvae*).[80] Virgil's scene shows the simultaneous creative and destructive aspect not only of Aeneas's imperial project but also of Virgil's poetic one, suggesting that the transformation of past stories always involves a potential wounding of the past.[81]

The Trojans' lack of self-consciousness about their appropriation of the property of others appears in the second episode in book 3, when Aeneas reaches the Strophades. The starved Trojans immediately kill and eat the livestock that they find there. It is hardly surprising that the inhabitants of the island, the harpies, object to this thoughtless looting. However, while the Trojan Polydorus is described sympathetically as an innocent victim, the harpies are presented as disgusting aliens, completely foreign in every sense to the Trojans. Yet their relation to the travellers is complex. Commentaries on both Virgil and Dante noted the belief that the name "harpy" came from the Greek word for theft.[82] If the harpies signify theft, however, they are doubles of the Trojans themselves who, from the perspectives of the harpies themselves and later the Rutulians, are foreign thieves. It is interesting then that their actions terrify the Trojans, even though their mode of retaliation – basically hurling dung balls from the sky – is more disgusting than truly dangerous. The Trojans are especially horrified when the leader of the harpies, Celaeno, tells them of the future, prophesying that they will eventually be so hungry that they will eat their own tables (3.255–8). What is read as a sinister prophecy of famine turns out to be harmless – in fact it is a beneficial tip, which helps them to recognize their destination when they arrive in Italy and Iulus, tucking into a kind of sandwich, cries playfully "etiam mensas consumimus" (7.116; We eat our tables too!). At this point the Trojans remember the prophecy, but they significantly misremember its source, attributing it to Anchises. They are unable to acknowledge that the repulsive harpies, whom they treated rather badly, actually helped them; they write them out of the line of prophets who showed them their and Rome's future, remembering them only as hideous monsters who potentially blocked the fulfilment of their destiny. Carelessly, indeed egotistically, neglectful of others' property, the Trojans also erase their debts to sources that do not fit in with their sense of themselves and their civilizing mission.

In *Inferno* 13, the harpies are first seen similarly as ugly monsters and aggressors against the Trojans: they are those "che cacciar de le Strofade i Troiani / con tristo annunzio di futuro danno" (13.11–2; who drove the Trojans from the Strophades with doleful prophecies of woe to come).[83] Perhaps this negative point of view arises because the scene seems dominated by both the text and presence of Virgil, who directs the action, and tells Dante to break off a branch from one of the trees he sees there. To some readers, Virgil's encouragement of an act that will inflict pain on the damned soul has seemed odd and unfeeling.[84] Virgil's explanation for this direction is that Dante, reading the *Aeneid* as mere fiction, would never have believed that this kind of metamorphosis was true: "la cosa incredible mi fece / indurlo ad ovra ch'a me stesso pesa" (13.50–1; Your plight, being incredible, made me goad him to this deed that weighs on me). Dante relives Virgil's fictions in order to make them come true.[85] However, Virgil is also forcing Dante to repeat the error and potential impiety of his hero, undermining Dante's earlier assertion of unique individuality: "non Enëa ... sono" (*Inf.* 2.32; I am not Aeneas). The pilgrim becomes a potential copy of the Trojan, even as Dante is also made to replicate the scene of the poet he hails as "lo mio maestro e 'l mio autore" (*Inf.* 1.85; my teacher and my author).

Inferno 13 thus seems dominated by Virgil, who makes Dante follow in his path. As in *Inferno* 24, Dante's dependence on Virgil is emphasized, as the pilgrim becomes suddenly extremely self-conscious about his ability to make sense of the world around him. Entering this new wood, which both replays and complicates his situation at the beginning of the poem, he finds himself disoriented and acutely sensitive to what Virgil thinks of him. He gets in a syntactical muddle just trying to describe his anxiety: "Cred'ïo ch'ei credette ch'io credesse / che tante voci uscisser, tra quei bronchi, / da gente che per noi se nascondesse" (24.25–7; I think he thought that I thought all these voices among the branches came from people hiding there). His confusion is understandable, however; these woods are full of voices. Behind the Virgilian shrubbery lurk a number of Ovidian figures: the punishment of the spendthrifts, torn apart by dogs, recalls the fate of Ovid's Actaeon in *Metamorphoses* 3, while the transformed Pier della Vigna looks back not only to Virgil's Polydorus but also to the Ovidian figures of the Heliades (*Met.* 2.358–66) and Driope (*Met.* 9.370–81).[86]

Dante's joining of Virgilian and Ovidian episodes suggests his interest in not only the authors themselves but also the dynamics between them. Writing in Virgil's shadow, Ovid is acutely conscious of his relation to his great precursor; as I noted earlier, he flaunts his borrowings and thefts from him.[87] At the end of the *Metamorphoses*, he retells the *Aeneid*. *Aeneid* 3 is the most Ovidian of all Virgil's writing, as it includes transformation and the kind of hybrid, double-formed figures that constantly fascinate Ovid. One might therefore expect Ovid to pay particular attention to it. However, when Ovid presents his version of Aeneas's journey in *Metamorphoses* 13, he surprisingly skims over the harpies in two lines (13.709–10) and omits the meeting with Polydorus episode, to focus instead on stories of love and metamorphosis (I'll return to this substitution in a moment). But Ovid had already used the Polydorus story in book 8, working it into the story of Erysicthon's greedy and senseless plundering of the sacred grove of Ceres, which, as Thomas shows elsewhere, "functions in part as a commentary on Virgil's account of Aeneas's actions on the Thracian shore."[88] The dialogue between the two episodes was noted and extended in Lucan, who in *Pharsalia* 3.399–452 invents a similar scene in which Julius Caesar cuts down a grove to prepare for a siege.[89] As this suggests, Virgil's episode quickly became a set piece copied by authors to show their ability to "transplant" their sources into new loci. Dante, and later Ariosto, Tasso, and Spenser, use the episode to meditate on their own metamorphosis of past conventions and especially on the potential for violation in the appropriation of the "timber" of others.[90] Dante's wood is a place in which he thinks about what it means to make a poem out of the materials of the past and the temptation to forget or even demonize those who make his journey possible.

The central figure in this canto emerges also from an interesting intertwining of sources. Shaped through the story of Virgil's Polydorus, Pier della Vigna is equally a figure of Ovidian metamorphosis, whose tale is bound up with aspects of emulation and its relation to envy. Critics have noted the peculiarly rhetorical nature of the language of this canto, evident in Dante's own verbal confusion (*Inf.* 13.25–7; see above) but especially obvious in the speeches of Pier. Leo Spitzer claimed that the formulae that dominate this episode "offer a sort of linguistic, or onomatopoeic rendition of the ideas of torture, schism, estrangement, which dominate the canto," suggestive of "self-torture and self-estrangement, and ultimately of infructuous paradoxy."[91] Pier explains his motives for suicide: "L'animo mio, per disdegnoso gusto, / credendo col morir fuggir disdegno, / ingiusto fece me contra me giusto " (13.70–2; My mind, in scornful temper, hoping by dying to escape from scorn, made me, though just, against myself unjust). As Spitzer notes, "The repetitions of word-stems (*ingiusto-giusto*; *me contra me*) suggest the outrage wrought by one half of the human soul against the other."[92] Moreover, like Dante's pairing of *Ovidio* and *invidio*, Pier's language recalls Ovid's use of wordplay and paradox to challenge moral and logical categories by making words synonymous with their own opposites.

Like so many of the most moving and compelling figures in the *Inferno* – Francesca, Ulysses, and Brunetto Latini – the well-spoken and courtly Pier is a double of Dante himself. Concerned with reputation and fame, Pier, like Ovid's Daphne, Adonis, Narcissus, and others, achieves what Barkan wittily calls "vegetable immortality": a literalization of the poet's dream of laurelization through art.[93] Defined through metamorphosis and Ovidian rhetoric, he seems another of the many Ovidian doubles of the poem.[94] Still, it seems unfair that Pier della Vigna, and not his false accuser, should wind up in hell. And it seems even more unjust that the innocent victim of envy, blinded in prison, should be made to share the traditional iconographical attribute of envy itself. His story seems strikingly different from that of Ovid's Aglauros, used by Dante as an example of envy (*Purg*. 14.139), whose transformation into the sign (*Met*. 2.831; signum) of envy seems guided by Dantesque poetic justice. The jealous Aglauros became what she was all along. But Pier's story is moving and terrifying because, like that of Ovid himself, it shows how an innocent can be transformed into his own worst enemy. The victim of envy has become its embodiment: as *Inferno* 25 shows, it only takes a few letters to turn the generous *Ovidio* into his nemesis, *invidia*.[95]

6. Following Behind

Elli givan dinanzi, e io soletto
di retro, e ascoltava i lor sermoni,
ch'a poetar mi davano intelletto. (*Purg*. 22.127–9)

(They went along in front and I, alone,
came on behind, listening to their discourse,
which gave me understanding of the art of verse.)

Focusing on Dante's creation of Ovidian figures that surpass those of his pagan model can simplify the relations between the poets, shaping it as a kind of predictable "othering." It underestimates Dante's remarkable attention to Ovid, and especially to Ovid's exploration of the origins, nature, and effects of poetry. As the other essays in this volume show, Dante is a highly critical and astute reader who was aware of the intratextual patterns that were central to the formation of the Bible.[96] He is equally attentive to the underlying patterns that unite disparate episodes and figures in Ovid's poetry. Moreover, like Ovid, Dante is aware that poetry originates in metamorphosis: the transformation of the materials of others into something new. Like Ovid also, he sees the dangerous proximity between creativity and destruction, imitation and *invidia*. Ovid's own story, with its sad ending in exile, was clearly a fate that Dante, and other later poets, did not want to emulate. Yet Dante does not leave Ovid or Ovidian figures in hell. What he does leave behind is hell itself, a place in which, as in Ovid's Tomis, creativity becomes destructive, in which couples are bound together in endless and intimate enmity. Outside of hell, things begin to look different. The harpies and other Ovidian hybrids of the *Inferno* are reimagined in the figure of "la doppia fiera" (*Inf.* 31.122; the twofold beast), the griffin, and in *Paradiso* 1.68 the half-man, half-fish seagod Glaucus.[97]

The figure of Glaucus looks back to the end of *Metamorphoses* 13, where Glaucus appears in Ovid's revision of Aeneas's journey as a substitute for the meeting with Polydorus and the harpies. While the Trojans see hybrid forms as terrifying monsters, Ovid imagines a comic figure, an enamoured suitor whose beloved, the baffled nymph Scylla, is unable to decide whether "monstrumne deusne / ille sit" (*Met.* 13.912–3; he was a monster or a god). Like Aeneas, Scylla is disgusted by ambiguous beings and so flees in terror. Ironically, or perhaps appropriately, she herself is turned into a more menacing form of hybrid, as her torso and face remain female, and her nether regions become a pack of devouring dogs who prey on her. Rejecting monsters, she becomes one. Ultimately she is petrified, becoming the treacherous rock which, unlike the harpies, might have truly threatened Aeneas's journey (*Aen.* 3.420–8).[98] Dante's Glaucus, however, makes hybridity not a monstrous force that impedes movement forward to a new home but a creative energy that propels it. Moreover, in Ovid's retelling of the *Aeneid*, Glaucus's swim from Sicily up north along the coast of Italy stands in for the Trojans' journey, while his transformation into a merman (*Met.* 13.949–55) anticipates Aeneas's deification (14.600–8).[99] Glaucus is thus a kind of Ovidian substitute for Aeneas, one of the many in Ovid's final books, which offer different versions of metamorphoses and rebirth.[100] As Dante separates himself from Virgil and the journey of Aeneas, he turns instead to the Ovidian Glaucus to imagine his "transhumanization" (*Par.* 1.67–9).

The increasing presence of Ovidian figures is felt at the end of the *Purgatorio* as Dante prepares for this final metamorphosis. Allusions to the doomed lovers Pyramus (*Purg.* 27.37–8; 33.69) and Leander (28.73–4), as well as to the fall of Phaethon (29.118–20), seem to serve as foils for Dante as he is reunited with Beatrice to rise to heaven. But the story of Proserpina helps Dante orient himself (*Purg.* 28.49–51). Moreover, in *Purgatorio* 30–1 the figure of Io is recalled from *Inferno* 24 where it reflected the eternal shape shifting of the thieves to become an analogue for Dante's transformation.[101] Other images associated with infernal metamorphosis are reimagined: *Purgatorio* 32.64–6 recalls the story of Syrinx, transformed into a reed fastened with wax, while the image of melting wax from *Inferno* 24.61 reappears in *Purgatorio* 33.79–81, as Dante himself becomes wax inscribed by Beatrice.[102]

In the *Purgatorio*, too, the Polydorus episode is revised from an image of damnation and the dangers of *invidia* into one that reveals the powers of creative emulation. In *Purgatorio* 22.27–48, Statius tells how his conversion was linked to his reading of Aeneas's famous comment on the fate of Polydorus: "auri sacra fames!" (*Aen.* 3.57; accursed hunger for gold!).[103] Virgil's and Ovid's stories of tree violation and literary plundering are made the background for a recognition scene of gratitude and tribute.[104] Statius generously acknowledges Virgil's role in both his poetic and spiritual development, attributing his genius to the *Aeneid*, "la qual mamma / fummi, e fummi nutrice, poetando" (*Purg.* 21.97–8; When I wrote poetry, it was my *mamma* and my nurse). The tribute to Virgil is itself Dante's imitation of and tribute to Statius, whose *Thebaid* ends with a prayer in which his own desire for immortality – and complementary fear of envy – is restrained by his veneration for Virgil:

> vive, precor; nec tu divinam Aeneida tempta,
> sed longe sequere et vestigia semper adora.
> mox, tibi si quis adhuc praetendit nubila livor,
> occidet, et meriti post me referentur honores. (*Theb.* 12.816–9)

(O live, I pray! nor rival the divine *Aeneid*, but follow afar and ever venerate its footsteps. Soon, if any envy as yet o'erclouds thee, it shall pass away, and, after I am gone, thy well-won honours shall be duly paid.)[105]

However, by humbly following after Virgil, Statius is able to go beyond him:

"Tu prima m'invïasti
verso Parnasa a ber ne le sue grotte,
e prima appresso Dio m'alluminasti.
Facesti come quei che va di notte,
che porta il lume dietro e sé non giova,
ma quando dicesti: 'Secol si rinova;
torna giustizia e primo tempo umano,
e progenie scende da ciel nova.'
Per te poeta fui, per te cristiano." (*Purg.* 22.64–73)

("It was you who first
set me toward Parnassus to drink in its grottoes,
and you who first lit my way toward God.
You were as one who goes by night, carrying
the light behind him – it is no help to him,
but instructs all those who follow –
when you said: 'The centuries turn new again.
Justice returns with the first age of man,
new progeny descends from heaven.'
Through you I was a poet, through you a Christian.")

The relation between Statius and Virgil, in which the later poet pays tribute to and then surpasses his master, sets the tone for cantos in which Dante meets his own immediate Italian poetic fathers, as well as his friend and rival Forese Donati with whom he had exchanged a series of smutty invective poems.[106] Rivalry is superseded by friendship, as the two poets meet affectionately, and, in a scene that looks back to his warm welcome in Limbo by the classical greats (*Inf.* 4.97–102), Dante is embraced by the group of poets who populate this section of purgatory. As he pays tribute to his predecessors, they also recognize him as a poet, as Bonagiunta da Lucca identifies him as the poet of the "dolce stil novo" (*Purg.* 24.57; sweet new style). The fact that the character of Virgil may only go so far in helping Dante is a recognition of the real difference between pagan and Christian, a difference that causes Dante much pain at the moment of loss. But it also suggests that it is simply natural for artists to surpass and replace each other; as Dante learns from the painter Oderisi, Giotto surpassed Cimabue, the poet Guido Cavalcanti is greater than Guido Guinizelli, and "e forse è nato /

chi l'uno e l'altro caccerà del nido" (*Purg*. 11.98–9; And he, perhaps, is born who will drive one and then the other from the nest). Like Giotto and his friend Cavalcanti, Dante is not himself the final fulfilment of a typological line but part of an ongoing process of dialogue and metamorphosis that takes place among artists, in which the individual is made immortal through his art as it is reborn in others.[107] As Amilcare himself so often and eloquently demonstrated, Dante's greatness lies not only in how he transmuted and used the past but how he did so in a way that itself became constantly inspiring for later writers. In that Dante should be coupled, happily one hopes, with Ovid.

NOTES

1 A.A. Iannucci, introduction to *Dante: Contemporary Perspectives* (Toronto: University of Toronto Press, 1997), xv. See also his collection *Dante e la "bella scola" della poesia: autorità e sfida poetica* (Ravenna: Longo Editore, 1993).

2 B. Buonmattei, *Delle lodi della lingua toscana: Orazione del dottore Benedetto Buonmattei da lui recitata pubblicamenta nell'Accademia Fiorentina, in Id. Della lingua Toscana di Benedetto Buonmattei pubblico lettore di essa nello studio pisano e fiorentino* (Florence: Stamperia Imperiale, 1760), 330.

3 Michelangelo Picone thus argues that Dante's use of Ovid in particular is figural: "The Romance poet has fulfilled and validated that which the Latin poet had only intuited." "Dante and the Classics," in Iannucci, *Dante: Contemporary Perspectives*, 58. Kevin Brownlee claims also that "Ovid's narratives of transformation operate as extended, yet necessarily inadequate and incomplete, metaphors for Christian transfiguration. Dante transforms the Ovidian texts of metamorphosis." "Dante's Poetics of Transfiguration: The Case of Ovid," *Literature and Belief* 5 (1985): 15; see further Brownlee, "Dante and the Classical Poets," in *The Cambridge Companion to Dante*, ed. R. Jacoff (Cambridge: Cambridge University Press, 1993), 100–19. For similar assertions, see W. Ginsberg, "Dante, Ovid and the Transformation of Metamorphosis," *Traditio* 46 (1991): 205–33; J.T. Schnapp, "Dante's Ovidian Self-Correction in *Paradiso* 17," in *The Poetry of Allusion: Virgil and Ovid in Dante's "Commedia,"* ed. R. Jacoff and J.T. Schnapp (Stanford: Stanford University Press, 1991), 214–23.

4 I take the term "negative typology" from Robert Hollander's important discussion of the relation, *Allegory in Dante's "Commedia"* (Princeton: Princeton University Press, 1969). Brownlee expresses the common belief

that Dante "functions as a corrected version of one of the many protagonists of Ovid's multi-narrative epic" ("Dante and the Classical Poets," 100). See also J.T. Schnapp, "Dante's Ovidian Self-Correction in *Paradiso* 17," 214–23. There have been important studies of Dante's use of specific Ovidian figures: on Phaethon, see K. Brownlee, "Phaethon's Fall and Dante's Ascent," *Dante Studies* 102 (1984): 135–44; on Hippolytus, M. Mills Chiarenza, "Hippolytus's Exile: *Paradiso* XVII, vv. 46–48," *Dante Studies* 84 (1966): 65–8; on Narcissus, R.A. Shoaf, *Dante, Chaucer, and the Currency of the Word: Money, Images, and Reference in Late Medieval Poetry* (Norman, OK: Pilgrim Books, 1983); on Arachne, P. Royston Macfie, "Ovid, Arachne, and the Poetics of Paradise," in *The Poetry of Allusion*, 159–72; also T. Barolini, *The Undivine Comedy: Detheologizing Dante* (Princeton: Princeton University Press, 1992), 130–1; and Barolini, "Arachne, Argus, and St John: Transgressive Art in Dante and Ovid," *Mediaevalia* 13 (1989): 207–26.

5 See especially Ovid, *Tristia* 2; *Ex Ponto* 4.10. Ovid's exilic poetry is our only source of most of the information about the poet, a fact that crucially enabled him to shape his own life and his later reception. See S. Hinds, "Booking the Return Trip: Ovid and *Tristia* 1," *Proceedings of the Cambridge Philological Society*, n.s., 31(1985): 13–32; B. Gibson, "Ovid on Reading: Reading Ovid: Reception in Ovid *Tristia* II," *Journal of Roman Studies* 89 (1999): 19–37. The details of Ovid's exile were widely known in the Middle Ages, even by those who had not read the exilic poetry itself, as potted biographies, based on the *Tristia*, were often part of the *accessus ad auctores* through which readers approached Ovid's other texts; see especially R. Hexter, *Ovid and Medieval Schooling: Studies in Medieval School Commentaries on Ovid's "Ars Amatoria," "Epistulae ex Ponto," and "Epistulae Heroidum"* (Munich: Arbeo-Gesellschaft, 1986), 83.

6 Citations of Ovid are from the Loeb Classical Library Series: *Metamorphoses*, ed. G.P. Goold, trans. F.J. Miller, 2 vols. (London: W. Heinemann, 1916); *Heroides and Amores*, ed. G.P. Goold, trans. G. Showerman (London: W. Heinemann, 1947); *The Art of Love, and Other Poems*, ed. G.P. Goold, trans. J.H. Mozley (London: W. Heinemann, 1957); *Ovid's Fasti*, ed. G.P. Goold, trans. Sir J.G. Frazer (London: W. Heinemann, 1959); *Tristia: Ex Ponto*, ed. G.P. Goold, trans. A.L.Wheeler, 2nd ed. (London: W. Heinemann, 1988). Translations are also from these editions, with occasional modification for poetic licence.

7 See especially M. Picone, "Ovid and the Exul Immeritus," in *Dante for the New Millennium*, ed. T. Barolini and H.W. Storey (New York: Fordham

University Press, 2003), 389–407; J.L. Smarr, "Poets of Love and Exile," in *Dante and Ovid: Essays in Intertextuality*, ed. M.U. Sowell (Binghamton: Medieval and Renaissance Texts and Studies, 1991), 139–51. Schnapp also suggests that the *Commedia* generally is "a Christian corrective to the later Ovid of the *Tristia* and *Epistulae Ex Ponto*" ("Dante's Ovidian Self-Correction in *Paradiso* 17," 223).

8 K. Galinsky, *Ovid's "Metamorphoses": An Introduction to the Basic Aspects* (Berkeley and Los Angeles: University of California Press, 1975), 4.

9 See for example *Tristia* 1.5, where Ovid also notes that his fate is much harder than that of Homer's hero; even worse, it is true.

10 For a discussion and critique of the critical assumption that Ulysses is Dante's double, see Barolini, *The Undivine Comedy*, 48–73.

11 P. Hawkins, "Transfiguring the Text: Ovid, Scripture, and the Dynamics of Allusion," *Stanford Italian Review* 5 (1985): 118. Smarr ("Poets of Love and Exile") and Picone ("Ovid and the Exul Immeritus") argue specifically that Ovid's identification with the figure of Ulysses in his exilic verse influences Dante's use of the character as a double for himself. Schnapp suggests further that Dante forges a link between the Ovidian figures of Icarus, Phaethon, and Ulysses whom he interprets as showing the danger of "creating an errant artifact that will lead to the destruction of its authors" ("Dante's Ovidian Self-Correction in *Paradiso* 17," 219). As I will argue further, Dante is not inventing such connections but bringing out patterns that unify Ovid's works.

12 Barolini, "Arachne, Argus, and St John," 223n. See also Barolini, *The Undivine Comedy*, 54.

13 I take the expression "self-conscious muse" from Stephen Hinds's seminal study, *The Metamorphosis of Persephone: Ovid and the Self-Conscious Muse* (Cambridge: Cambridge University Press, 1987). See also E.W. Leach, "Ekphrasis and the Theme of Artistic Failure in Ovid's *Metamorphoses*," *Ramus* 3 (1974): 102–42; V.M. Wise, "Flight Myths in Ovid's *Metamorphoses*," *Ramus* 6 (1977): 44–59; D. Lateiner, "Mythic and Non-Mythic Artists in Ovid's *Metamorphoses*," *Ramus* 13 (1984): 1–30; W.S. Anderson, "The Artist's Limits in Ovid: Orpheus, Pygmalion, and Daedalus," *Syll-Class* 1 (1989): 1–11; B. Harries, "The Spinner and the Poet," *Proceedings of the Cambridge Philological Society* 36, no. 1 (1990): 64–82; J.B. Solodow, *The World of Ovid's "Metamorphoses"* (Chapel Hill: University of North Carolina Press, 1988); P. Hardie, *Ovid's Poetics of Illusion* (Cambridge: Cambridge University Press, 2002); and G. Rosati, *Narcisso e Pigmalione: illusione e spettacolo nelle "Metamorfosi" di Ovidio*, Nuovi Saggi (Firenze: Sansoni, 1983).

14 Leach, "Ekphrasis and the Theme of Artistic Failure."

15 Commentaries from the Middle Ages to the present have constantly remarked the similarities between Ovid's fate and that of the characters he invented. As Amy Richlin notes, "The muted victims, the artists horribly punished by legalistic gods for bold expression – Marsyas, and especially Arachne – read like allegories of Ovid's experience." "Reading Ovid's Rapes," in *Pornography and Representation in Greece and Rome*, ed. A. Richlin (Oxford: Oxford University Press, 1992), 176. The story of Arachne has most commonly been evoked as the "prototype of the exiled poet" (B. Harries, "The Spinner and the Poet," 65). L. Barkan's influential study of Ovid's impact in the Middle Ages and Renaissance begins with a reading of the figure of Arachne whose art, in contrast to the staid images of divine order propagated by Minerva, seems to both mirror the poet's vision and to anticipate the later metamorphic tradition; see *The Gods Made Flesh: Metamorphosis and the Pursuit of Paganism* (New Haven: Yale University Press, 1986), esp. 1–5.

16 On the theme of illusion in Ovid generally, see Rosati, *Narcisso e Pigmalione*; and Hardie, *Ovid's Poetics of Illusion*. Hardie notes how recent novelistic treatments of Ovid's exile are especially drawn to the parallels between his fictions and his life (326–37).

17 Barolini, "Arachne, Argus, and St John," 208. Her argument here, and in the *The Undivine Comedy*, advances and complicates the dialogic nature of Dante's intertextuality that she analyzed in *Dante's Poets: Textuality and Truth in the Comedy* (Princeton: Princeton University Press, 1984).

18 W. Wetherbee, *The Ancient Flame: Dante and the Poets* (Notre Dame: University of Notre Dame Press, 2008), 15.

19 Wetherbee, *The Ancient Flame*, 8.

20 See R. Jacoff, "The Rape / Rapture of Europa: *Paradiso* 27," in Jacoff and Schnapp, *The Poetry of Allusion*, 233–46; Wetherbee, *The Ancient Flame*, 137; Brownlee, "Dante's Poetics of Transfiguration," 17; Brownlee, "Ovid's Semele and Dante's Metamorphosis: *Paradiso* 21–2," in Jacoff and Schnapp, *The Poetry of Allusion*, 214–23; J. Levenstein, "The Pilgrim, the Poet, and the Cowgirl: Dante's Alter-'Io' in *Purgatorio* XXX–XXXXI," *Dante Studies* 114 (1996): 189–208; and R. Hollander, *Allegory in Dante's "Commedia,"* 202–32.

21 Leonard Barkan explains the logic of the forms chosen: "Thieves are slippery figures of deceit, like serpents. They are in their nature shape-changers, thus justifying the transformation to serpents, and they alienate property, thus justifying the condition of constant and exchanging metamorphosis" (*The Gods Made Flesh*, 153).

22 Barkan, *The Gods Made Flesh*, 157. See also Ginsberg, "Dante, Ovid and the Transformation of Metamorphosis."

23 L. Baldassaro, "Metamorphosis as Punishment and Redemption in *Inferno* XXIV," *Dante Studies* 99 (1981): 89–112. Critics have further noted how the specific Ovidian metamorphoses parody Christian ideals: the endless rebirth of the phoenix distorts Christ's resurrection, and the hermaphrodite mirrors Christ's merging of divine and human natures; see Baldassaro 102–3; and K. Gross, "Infernal Metamorphoses: An Interpretation of Dante's 'Counterpass,'" *Modern Language Notes* 100, no. 1 (1985): 42–69, esp. 66.

24 Barolini, *Dante's Poets*, 225.

25 The allusion to the transformation of Cadmus into a snake in *Met.* 4.563–604 further consolidates the identification of metamorphosis with the *Inferno* in general. Cadmus founded Thebes by killing a giant snake; at the end of his life, like so many classical heroes, he becomes the monster that he slew, a pattern that will be repeated again in the tragic fate of his descendent Oedipus. For Dante, Thebes is the infernal city on earth, caught in a cycle of endless violence, in which heroes and monsters are disturbingly difficult to tell apart.

26 R. Terdiman, "Problematical Virtuosity: Dante's Depiction of the Thieves (*Inferno* XXIV–XXV)," *Dante Studies* 91 (1973): 27–45.

27 P. Hawkins, "Virtuosity and Virtue: Poetic Self-Reflection in the *Commedia*," *Dante Studies* 98 (1980): 1-18, 11.

28 "Introduction," in Jacoff and Schnapp, *The Poetry of Allusion*, 10. Brownlee also reads this as a jab at Ovid: "This 'competition' with Ovid uses paradoxically the classical (Ovidian) topos of poetic rivalry, while granting a superior Christian spiritual dimension to Ovidian 'supernatural' metamorphoses that makes it a negative or a positive type of Christian transfiguration" ("Dante and the Classical Poets," 112). As we will see, this assumption that poetic rivalry is a specifically Ovidian topos is a bit misleading.

29 Baldassaro, "Metamorphosis as Punishment," 100.

30 So Baldassaro claims also that "Vanni Fucci is but one of the many signs on that journey that indicate the dangerous possibility of his own stagnation" ("Metamorphosis as Punishment," 108). The sense of Dante's potential for regression, his desire to return to where he was at the very start of the poem, is suggested when he looks at Virgil who "a me si volse con quel piglio / dolce ch'io vidi prima a piè del monte" (24.20–1; He turned to me with that gentle glance / I first saw at the mountain's foot). Like the

thieves (not to mention the sodomites), Dante tends to go round in circles unless helped by forces outside of himself.

31 On this aspect of Aeneas's character, see further D. Quint, *Epic and Empire: Politics and Generic Form from Virgil to Milton* (Princeton: Princeton University Press, 1993), 50–96. For a different reading of the relation between Dante and Aeneas, see Hollander, *Allegory in Dante's "Commedia,"* 81–103.

32 The influence of the *magister artis* has been generally acknowledged; see especially R. Durling, *The Figure of the Poet in the Renaissance* (Cambridge, MA: Harvard University Press, 1965). M.L. Stapleton suggests that Ovid's other authorial figures were equally influential in the Middle Ages and that in general "Ovid seems to have spawned ... a poetic consciousness of the narrative ego and its possibilities." *Harmful Eloquence: Ovid's "Amores" from Antiquity to Shakespeare* (Ann Arbor: University of Michigan Press, 1996), 42–3.

33 Wetherbee similarly notes: "From the moment at which Ovid is named in *Inferno* 25, he is identified with the sheer power of poetic imagination, and metamorphoses comes to represent the imaginative process itself" (*The Ancient Flame,* 128).

34 For a brief survey, see Baldassaro, "Metamorphosis as Punishment," 89–91.

35 Hawkins, "Virtuosity and Virtue," 5.

36 See D.L. Derby Chapin, "IO and the Negative Apotheosis of Vanni Fucci," *Dante Studies* 89 (1971): 19–31. Ovid replays the scene of the invention of new forms of communication in the tales of Philomela in *Met.* 6 and Byblis in *Met.* 9 (see further 184 above).

37 Levenstein, "The Pilgrim, the Poet, and the Cowgirl," 197.

38 C.A. Cioffi, "The Anxieties of Ovidian Influence: Theft in *Inferno* XXIV and XXV," *Dante Studies* 112 (1994): 88.

39 Pythagoras's speech was long read as key to Ovid's text, the philosophical explanation of the world he describes; see Solodow, *The World of Ovid's "Metamorphoses,"* 162–8. Recent critics have been more concerned with noting differences between Ovid and this other authorial double; see the discussion of Pythagoras as one of Ovid's internal narrators in A. Barchiesi, *Speaking Volumes: Narrative and Intertext in Ovid and other Latin Poets,* ed. and trans. M. Fox and S. Marchesi (London: Duckworth, 2001), 62–9.

40 This is not surprising, as Hermaphroditus and Narcissus were often linked in commentaries and adaptations. I discuss this further in *Milton and the Metamorphosis of Ovid* (Oxford: Oxford University Press, 2012), esp. 184–9.

41 See especially Rosati, *Narcisso e Pigmalione*. I discuss the self-reflexive uses of the story in Ovid and later artists in *Milton and the Metamorphosis of Ovid*, 175–96.

42 See especially J. Ferrante, "Good Thieves and Bad Thieves: A Reading of *Inferno* XXIV," *Dante Studies* 104 (1986): 83–98. See also Cioffi, "The Anxieties of Ovidian Influence." Vanni Fucci's misappropriation of church property for selfish and secular interests similarly defines by opposition the poet who uses Christian materials to celebrate God.

43 R.J. Ellrich, "Envy, Identity, and Creativity: *Inferno* XXIV–XXV," *Dante Studies* 102 (1984): 62.

44 Ibid., 74.

45 Ibid., 76.

46 See also the stories of Myrrha (*Met.* 10.321–3) and of the daughters of Pelias who each "ut quaeque pia est … inpia prima est / et, ne sit scelerata, facit scelus" (*Met.* 7.339–40; as each was filial she became first in the unfilial act, and that she might not be wicked did the wicked deed). While Ovid rather ostentatiously skirts the story of Oedipus, he presents Thebes (the infernal city for both Statius and Dante) as a place where all the paradoxes jumble together: "ultusque parente parentem / natus erit facto pius et sceleratus eodem" (*Met.* 9.407–8; Son shall avenge parent on parent, filial and accursed in the selfsame act). On this aspect of Ovid's wit, see G.Tissol, *The Face of Nature: Wit, Narrative, and Cosmic Origins in Ovid's "Metamorphoses"* (Princeton: Princeton University Press, 1997) and F. Ahl, *Metaformations: Soundplay and Wordplay in Ovid and Other Classical Poets* (Ithaca: Cornell University Press, 1985).

47 See G. Most, "Epinician Envies," in *Envy, Spite and Jealousy: The Rivalrous Emotions in Ancient Greece*, ed. D. Konstan and N.K. Rutter (Edinburgh: Edinburgh University Press, 2003), 123–42.

48 Most, "Epinician Envies," 128–33; M.W. Dickie, "The Disavowal of *Invidia* in Roman Iamb and Satire," in *Papers of the Liverpool Latin Seminar*, ed. F. Cairns (Liverpool: Francis Cairns, 1981), 183–208; P. Bulman, *Phthonos in Pindar* (Berkeley: University of California Press, 1992); and A.M. Keith, *The Play of Fictions: Studies in Ovid's "Metamorphoses," Book 2* (Ann Arbor: University of Michigan Press, 1992), 127–31.

49 Aristotle, *Rhetoric* 2.10, in *The Complete Works of Aristotle*, ed. J. Barnes (Princeton: Princeton University Press, 1984), 2:2211–12. The saying Aristotle cites is from Hesiod: "And potter too is angry with potter, and builder with builder, and beggar begrudges [*phthonéei*] beggar, and poet poet." "Works and Days," in *Selections: English & Greek*, trans. G.W. Most, Loeb Classical Library (Cambridge, MA: Harvard University Press, 2006), lines 25–6.

50 Longinus, "On the Sublime," cited from *Aristotle: Poetics; Longinus: On the Sublime; Demetrius: On Style*, ed. D. Russell (Cambridge, MA: Harvard University Press, 2005), 169.

51 Ripa's description of *invidia* is representative: "Donna vecchia, magra, brutta, di color livido, haverà la mammella sinistra nuda, & morsicata da una serpe, … guardi con occhio torto in disparte, haverà appresso un cane magro, il quale come da molti effetti si vede è animale invidiossimo, e tutti i beni degl'altri vorebbe in se solo" (an old lady, skinny, ugly, of a greenish-blue colour, with her left breast exposed and gnawed on by a snake … she looks with eyes twisted in different directions; close to her is an emaciated dog, which as many examples show is the most envious animal, and all the good of others she would like for herself alone). *Iconologia* (Milano: Tascabili degli Editori Associati, 1992), 200. St Basil also says that, "phthonos consuming the soul in its agony is like the vipers who come into the light of day by gnawing through the belly of their mother." "Homily 11," quoted in K.M.D. Dunbabin and M.W. Dickie, "Invidia Rumpantur Pectora: The Iconography of Phthonos / Invidia in Graeco-Roman Art," *Jahrbuch für Antike und Christentum* 26 (1983): 15. Critics have long noted the relevance of the traditional assumption that female vipers eat their mates during intercourse to Dante's scene. As Gross pointed out, in snake lore, including that found in Brunetto Latini's *Tresor*, vipers were associated "with especially self–destructive modes of reproduction and generation" ("Infernal Metamorphoses," 57n28). Dante's scene thus conflates generational and erotic rivalry, reflecting the kind of antagonistic coupling that is typical of his infernal pairs.

52 See especially Dunbabin and Dickie, "Invidia Rumpantur Pectora." *Invidia* is also conventionally coloured blue / green from *livor*; the link is evoked by the colour of the stone in *Purg*. 13.9.

53 St John Chrysostom, "Homily 31 on First Corinthians," *Homilies on First Corinthians*, *New Advent Online Encyclopedia*, accessed 12 Dec. 2006, <http://www.newadvent.org/fathers/220131.htm>.

54 For some theologians and writers, envy and not pride is the most deadly of all sins: in Wisd. of Sol. 2:23, infernal envy brings death into the world. St Cyprian argues also, "Envy is the Root of all Wickedness" whose "Origin is to be Traced to the Devil." "Treatise X: De zelo et livore," trans. E. Wallis, in *Ante-Nicene Fathers*, ed. A. Roberts and J. Donaldson, vol. 5, *Hippolytus, Cyprian, Caius, Novatian, Appendix* (New York: Charles Scribner's Sons, 1919), 491–6. Aquinas sees envy as a sin against the Holy Ghost; see *Summa theologiae* pt. 2.2, q. 14 a. 2 (also pt. 2.2, q. 36a), *New Advent Online Encyclopedia*, accessed 5 May 2006, <http://www.newadvent.org/summa/index.html>. Augustine also tentatively suggests that envy is

the unpardonable sin: "Maliciously and enviously to assail brotherly love after having received the grace of the Holy Spirit – perhaps this is the sin against the Holy Spirit, the sin which the Lord says will never be forgiven in this world or in the world to come." *De sermone Domini in monte* 1.22.75, quoted in A.K. Cassell, "The Letter of Envy: *Purgatorio* XIII–XIV," *Stanford Italian Review* 4 (1984): 5–21. Chaucer draws attention to the evils of envy in *The Parson's Tale,* in which the Parson, quoting Augustine that envy "is 'Sorwe of oother mennes wele, and joye of othere mennes harm,'" claims that it goes against the "bountee" of the Holy Spirit (*The Riverside Chaucer,* ed. L.D. Benson [Boston: Houghton Mifflin, 1987]), 10.485. While the Parson ranks Envy below Pride, he claims finally, "Certes, thann is Envye the worste synne that is. For soothly, alle othere synnes been somtyme oonly agayns o special vertu, / but certes Envye is agayns alle vertues and agayns alle goodnesses." Thus, for him too the antidote to envy is love: "Certes, thanne is love the medicine that casteth out the venym of Envye fro mannes herte" (10.488–9, 531).

55 G.W. Pigman III, "Versions of Imitation in the Renaissance," *Renaissance Quarterly* 33 (1980): 4, 24. For the proximity of envy and emulation generally, see also R.B. Gill, "The Renaissance Conventions of Envy," *Medievalia et Humanistica* 9 (1979): 215–30, esp. 221–4; V.G. Dickson, "'A pattern, precedent, and lively warrant': Emulation, Rhetoric, and Cruel Propriety in *Titus Andronicus,*" *Renaissance Quarterly* 62, no. 2 (2009): 376–409; L.S. Meskill, *Ben Jonson and Envy* (Cambridge: Cambridge University Press, 2009). The terms used to differentiate them are in fact often confused; Hesiod uses *zelos,* which for Aristotle means positive emulation, for mere envy and jealousy. "Emulation" is equally ambiguous. In his *De compendiosa doctrina,* Nonius equates emulation with envy, which he distinguishes from what he calls simply *imitatio*: "imitatio simplex est et livorem atque invidiam non admittit; aemulatio autem habet quidem imitandi studium, sed cum malitiae operatione" (*De comp. doc.* 5.437; *Imitatio* is sincere and admits neither spite nor envy; *aemulatio,* however, includes the desire to imitate, but with malice added). Nonius Marcellus, *De compendiosa doctrina,* ed. W.M. Lindsay (Hildesheim: Georg Olms Verlagsbuchhandlung, 1964), 703; see also Pigman, 24. The exact wording is repeated in the fifteenth century by A. da Rho in his *De imitationibus eloquentie*; see M.L. McLaughlin, *Literary Imitation in the Italian Renaissance: The Theory and Practice of Imitation from Dante to Bembo* (Oxford: Clarendon Press, 1995), 109.

56 Whitney's emblem, *Inuidiae descriptio,* explains this: "What meanes her eies? so bleared, sore, and redd: / Her mourninge still, to see an others

gaine." G. Whitney, *A Choice of Emblemes*, ed. Henry Green (New York: Benjamin Blom, 1967), 94. See also R.B. Bond, "Vying with Vision: An Aspect of Envy in *The Faerie Queene*," *Renaissance and Reformation* 8, no.1 (1984): 30–8, esp. 31–2.

57 Pietro di Dante's commentary on *Purgatorio* 13 explains the punishment through the assumed etymology: "Invidia facit, quod non videatur, quod expedit videre; ed ideo dicitur *invidia*, quasi *non visio*" (Envy causes that which should be seen not to be seen. And therefore it is called *invidia*, almost as if to say, *nonvision*). Cited from *Inferno 2: Commentary*, trans. C. Singleton (Princeton: Princeton University Press, 1970), 213.

58 Francis Bacon also notes this similarity between love and envy: "There be none of the affections which have been noted to fascinate or bewitch, but love and envy. They both have vehement wishes; they frame themselves readily into imaginations and suggestions; and they come easily into the eye, especially upon the presence of the objects." "Of Envy," in *The Essays or Counsels, Civil and Moral*, ed. B. Vickers (New York: Oxford University Press, 1999), 18. Bacon's essay after "Of Envy" is thus appropriately "Of Love."

59 Cited from Lucretius, *De rerum natura*, ed. M.F. Smith, trans. W.H.D. Rouse, 2nd ed. (Cambridge, MA: Harvard University Press, 1992).

60 See also Hardie, *Ovid's Poetics of Illusion*, 198–9.

61 Cited from *Edmund Spenser: The Faerie Queene*, ed. A.C. Hamilton (New York: Longman, 1977).

62 See also A.L. Prescott, "Sclaunder," *The Spenser Encyclopedia*, ed. A.C. Hamilton (Toronto: University of Toronto Press, 1990), 632–3; and R.B. Bond, "Envy," in *The Spenser Encyclopedia*, 248–9.

63 Throughout his works, Ovid pays tribute to other writers; see especially *Amores* 1.15, 3.9 and *Tristia* 4.10.41. His encouragement of his stepdaughter and protégé, Perilla, is also remarkable, especially given her sex. From exile, he continued to urge her to write despite the example of his fate (which he assures her she will not emulate); see *Tristia* 3.7. The poem *Nux*, included among Ovid's works in the Middle Ages and early Renaissance, draws on this representation of Ovid as a poet free from *invidia*; it points out that the poet / tree might be justified in being bitter and envious but insists that he is not (33).

64 Cited from *Declamations*, trans. M. Winterbottom (Cambridge, MA: Harvard University Press, 1974), 544.

65 Keith, *The Play of Fictions*, 129.

66 As noted by S. Hinds, *Allusion and Intertext: Dynamics of Appropriation in Roman Poetry* (New York: Cambridge University Press, 1998), 5.

67 See also *Amores*, 1.15.39–42.
68 G. Williams, *The Curse of Exile: A Study of Ovid's "Ibis"* (Cambridge: Cambridge University Press, 1996), 21.
69 See the useful collection of commentaries assembled by A. La Penna, *Scholia in P. Ovidi Nasonis Ibin* (Florence: La Nuova Italia, 1959), esp. 3. While the *Ibis* has been almost totally ignored by scholars of Ovidian reception, it was well known and became especially popular in the Renaissance. It clearly influenced Paolo Marsi, the fifteenth-century commentator on the *Fasti*, who in his notes constantly rails against a detractor whom he denounces further in *Praefatio in V Librum Fastorum et contra invidum*. See A.M. Fritsen, "Renaissance Commentaries on Ovid's *Fasti*" (PhD diss., Yale University, 1995), 71n13. Poliziano was one of the poem's other fans. Ann Moss notes that the poem was printed six times in Paris in the late sixteenth century, suggesting that Renaissance writers generally were attracted by the work's winning combination of "sustained invective and gratuitous erudition." *Ovid in Renaissance France: A Survey of the Latin Editions of Ovid and Commentaries Printed in France Before 1600* (London: The Warburg Institute, 1982), 54. Brunetto Latini refers to the *Ibis* in *Li Livres dou tresor* 1.160.7. While there is no concrete evidence that Dante read this poem, the torments Ovid imagines for his enemy seem an interesting foreshadowing of Dante's hell, in which the poet's imagination is set free to dream of suitable eternal torments for his enemies, and even sometimes, and more gratifyingly, friends.
70 Moss, *Ovid in Renaissance France*, 54.
71 S. Hinds, "After Exile: Time and Teleology from *Metamorphoses* to *Ibis*," in *Ovidian Transformations: Essays on the "Metamorphoses" and its Reception*, ed. P. Hardie, A. Barchiesi, and S. Hinds (Cambridge: Cambridge Philological Society, 1999), 65.
72 Morillo, cited from Moss, *Ovid in Renaissance France*, 54.
73 Williams, *The Curse of Exile*, 23.
74 Ibid., 40, 46.
75 See "The *Ibis* of Ovid," in *The Classical Papers of A.E. Housman*, ed. J. Diggle and F.R.D. Goodyear (Cambridge: Cambridge University Press, 1972), 3:1018–42.
76 23249; references are to the English translation, *The Pilgrimage of the Life of Man, Englisht by John Lydgate, A.D. 1426, from the French of Guillaume de Deguileville, A.D. 1330, 1355*, ed. F.J. Furnivall (1899; repr., Millwood, NY: Kraus Reprint Co., 1978). In seventeenth-century England, Ben Jonson's *Poetaster* also tells the story of Ovid's sentence to exile as the workings of envy; see further my *Milton and the Metamorphosis of Ovid* , 247–8. The relation between envy and creativity in Jonson has been discussed

interestingly in L. Meskill, *Ben Jonson and Envy* (Cambridge: Cambridge University Press, 2009).

77 The soul asks him "'Perché nascose / questi il vocabol di quella riviera [the Arno], / pur com' om fa de l'orribili cose?'" (Why did he conceal that river's name / just as one hides some dreadful thing?). At the same time, Sapia puns on her name (13.109–10), demonstrating how envy and word-play are connected. Virgil's glorious celebration of the sun as a guide at the opening of *Purg.* 13.16–21 foregrounds the antithesis between creative praise and envy. In Dante, envy is associated with a selfishness that is contrasted also with a divine economy of sharing. Virgil explains to him that "quanta gente più là sù s'intende, / più v'è da bene amare, e più vi s'ama, / e come specchio l'uno a l'altro rende" (*Purg.* 15.73–5; The more souls there are who love on high, the more is to love, the more of loving, for like a mirror each returns it to the other), noting also that Beatrice will have to continue this lesson.

78 Barolini reads Dante's treatment of pride in the *Purgatorio* especially as the centre of the poem's concern with representation, "an authorial meditation on the principles of mimesis" (*The Undivine Comedy*, 122).

79 R.F. Thomas, "Tree Violation and Ambivalence in Virgil," *Transactions of the American Philological Association* 118 (1988): 261–73. As Thomas notes, the cutting of trees in ancient society was stigmatized as desecration. See also the description of the fall of Troy as that of an ancient oak in *Aen.* 2.626–31. As Thomas notes, Aeneas himself will become a tree cutter (273).

80 S. Hinds, *Allusion and Intertext*, 13.

81 Virgil's *Georgics* offers a potentially more benign model for the new use of old materials in the image of grafting. As Thomas also notes, Virgil rather disproportionately emphasizes this agricultural technique but also foregrounds its violent distortion of nature ("Tree Violation," 271–2).

82 See Fulgentius 1.9, *Fulgentius the Mythographer*, trans. L.G. Whitbread (Columbus: Ohio State University, 1971), 52–3; also W.A. Stephany, "Dante's Harpies: 'Tristo annuzio di futuro danno,'" in Jacoff and Schnapp, *The Poetry of Allusion*, 38.

83 Stephany, "Dante's Harpies," argues that Dante recalls the prophecy in order to show how ominous-sounding prophecies can turn out to be good, and thus to hint that his own story may have a happy ending.

84 See Wetherbee (*The Ancient Flame*, 42), who also sees the episode generally as "another intensely Virgilian moment."

85 Wetherbee concludes in *The Ancient Flame* that "though the mediating presences of Virgil and his poetry is essential, Dante clearly goes beyond Virgil, and the poetry of the *Aeneid* is reduced to an imperfect

foreshadowing of Dante's more complex experience" (44). Wetherbee thus unfortunately reinstates the typological relation he originally set out to question.

86 On the use of Actaeon here, see also Barkan, *The Gods Made Flesh*, 152–3. In his commentary, Singleton points out the echoes of the Heliades who, turned by grief over the death of their brother Phaethon into poplars, cry in pain as their unwitting mother tears their branches (*Met.* 2.358–66); see Singleton, *Inferno: Commentary*, 210. The parallels with the story of Driope were first noted by F. D'Ovidio, "Nuovi studi danteschi: Ugolino, Pier della Vigna, i Simoniaci," in *Opere di Francesco D'Ovidio* (Napoli: Guida, 1932), 2.1.

87 Ovid's revision of the *Aeneid* has been much discussed; see especially Hinds, *Allusion and Intertext*, 104–22; Solodow, *The World of Ovid's "Metamorphoses,"* 110–56; and Tissol, *The Face of Nature*, 177–91.

88 R.F. Thomas, "Tree Violation and Ambivalence in Virgil," 268.

89 Ibid., 268–9.

90 On these later episodes and their relation to the earlier works, see E. Wilson, "*Quantum Mutatus ab Illo*: Moments of Change and Recognition in Tasso and Milton," in *Epic Interactions*, ed. M.J. Clarke, B.G.F. Currie, and R.O.A.M. Lyne (Oxford: Oxford University Press, 2006), 273–99; M.W. Ferguson, *Trials of Desire*: *Renaissance Defenses of Poetry* (New Haven and London: Yale University Press, 1983), 126–36; S. Pugh, *Spenser and Ovid* (Aldershot: Ashgate, 2004), 69–73.

91 L. Spitzer, "Speech and Language in *Inferno* XIII," *Italica* 19, no. 3 (1942): 95. On the centrality of this episode in relation to the deformation of language in hell, see E. Lombardi, *The Syntax of Desire: Language and Love in Augustine, the Modistae, Dante* (Toronto: University of Toronto Press, 2007), 147–8.

92 Spitzer, "Speech and Language," 96.

93 Barkan, *The Gods Made Flesh*, 151.

94 The same may be true of Brunetto Latini, who took Ovid as his guide for his *Tesoretto* in which he noted: "Poi mi tornai da canto, / e in un ricco manto / vidi Ovidio maggiore, / che gli atti dell'amore, / che son così diversi, / rasembra 'n motti e versi" (vv. 2357–62; Then I turned from all this, /And in a rich mantle / I saw great Ovid, / Who collected and put into verse / The acts of love, which are so diverse). Text and translation cited from Picone, "Dante and the Classics," 69. Schnapp and Barolini suggest further that Dante identifies his old teacher and the *magister artis* who also sought eternal fame: Schnapp, "Dante's Ovidian Self-Correction in *Paradiso* 17," 215; Barolini, *The Undivine Comedy*, 136. Dante will revise

Latini's image of Ovid's book of love as his own final vision of God's book in *Par.* 33.85–7.

95 This may explain the phrasing in a related episode. As I noted earlier, when Dante leaves the thieves on his way to Ulysses, he tellingly curbs his genius to stay within the bounds of virtue: "sì che, se stella bona o miglior cosa / m'ha dato 'l ben, ch'io stessi nol m'invidi" (*Inf.* 26.23–4; so that, if friendly star or something better still has granted me its boon, I don't misuse the gift). Tellingly he needs the influence of external forces to restrain his *ingegno* and to keep him from turning the self-destructive energy of *invidia* on himself.

96 See especially Lund-Mead, "The *Vulgata* in the *Commedia*," ch. 5 above.

97 Kenneth Gross also argues that once out of hell Dante rises to a level of creative freedom in which "the problematic poetry of the counterpass no longer has any place. The imagination of the poet must abandon the severe, fantastic system of punishments and its associated dilemmas of interpretation" ("Infernal Metamorphoses," 69). On the griffin as the "literary redemption of the grotesque" aesthetics of hybridity in hell, see also Gross, "Infernal Metamorphoses," 67.

98 However, here too the apparent threat of such monstrous figures turns out to be less than feared: warned by Helenus of Scylla's terrifying powers, the Trojans simply take another route (*Aen.* 4.684–6). In Ovid too, Scylla kills some of the Greeks but is powerless to hurt the Trojans (*Met.* 14.70–4); while Trojans fear double-formed things, they prove to be less of a menace than expected. In later iconography, Scylla is frequently connected to envy; in De Deguilleville's *Pèlerinage de vie humaine*, she accompanies an allegorical Envy; see Lydgate, *Pilgrimage*, 23050–2, 21328–38. See further my *Milton and the Metamorphosis of Ovid*, 274–5; P. Hardie, "The Self-Divisions of Scylla," *Trends in Classics* 1 (2009): 127–31.

99 See Tissol, *The Face of Nature*, 210; K.S. Myers, *Ovid's Causes: Cosmogony and Aetiology in the "Metamorphoses"* (Ann Arbour: University of Michigan Press, 1994), 101–2; also N. Hopkinson, *Ovid Metamorphoses Book XIII* (Cambridge: Cambridge University Press, 2000), 35.

100 See further Hopkinson, *Ovid Metamorphoses Book XIII*, 235–6; K.S. Myers, *Ovid Metamorphoses Book XIV* (Cambridge: Cambridge University Press, 2009), 6.

101 See Levenstein, "The Pilgrim, the Poet, and the Cowgirl."

102 "Sì come cera da sugello, / che la figura impressa non trasmuta, / segnato è or da voi lo mio cervello" (Even as wax maintains the seal / and does not alter the imprinted image, / my brain now bears your stamp).

103 See R.A. Shoaf, "'Auri sacra fames' and the Age of Gold (*Purg*. XXII, 40–41 and 148–150)," *Dante Studies* 96 (1978): 195–9.

104 Ovid's own revision of Virgil's scene is part of this process. In *Purgatorio* 23, the emaciated gluttons, who include of course a group of poets, remind Dante of the fate of Erysicthon (23.25–7) now seen not as punishment for damnation but as the means of rising to a higher state.

105 Statius, *Thebaid*, 2 vols., trans. J.H. Mozley (London: Heineman, 1961).

106 These are often dismissed with some embarrassment as unworthy of Dante; they therefore form an interesting part of the "alternative" Dante discussed earlier in this volume by Barolini, 41–65.

107 Barolini claims that Dante deliberately invites comparison between himself and Giotto: "Dante celebrates himself as the poetic correlative of Giotto, an artist who was celebrated for aspiring to total verisimilitude" (*The Undivine Comedy*, 134). Dante's recognition in *Purgatorio* 11 seems important also for his understanding of the place of Cavalcanti in his development, which Barolini discusses in this volume. On one of Dante's future roles in this artistic dialogue, see Boitani, in this volume, 231–64.

7 Esoteric Interpretations of the *Divine Comedy*

MASSIMO CIAVOLELLA

The literary appropriation of Dante over the last century has been enormous. His influence has been front and centre in all major modern literary traditions – from T.S. Eliot to William Butler Yeats, from Albert Camus to Jean-Paul Sartre, from Jorge Luis Borges to Derek Walcott, from Stefan George to Peter Weiss, from Giorgio Bassani to Giuseppe Ungaretti – and would seem to justify, at least within the Western literary world, T.S. Eliot's assertion that "Dante and Shakespeare divide the modern world between them; there is no third."[1] Harold Bloom agrees when he confers onto Dante the status of "the second center, as it were"[2] (the first being Shakespeare) of the Western canon. Another more moderate yet acutely perceptive critic of Dante's modern appropriation, Stuart Y. McDougal, even claims: "Dante's impact on the major writers of the modern world has far exceeded that of Shakespeare."[3] The continual allure of Dante's *Divine Comedy* on modern writers is perhaps best expressed by Jorge Luis Borges in *Siete Noches*: "The *Comedy* has accompanied me for so many years, and I know that as soon as I open it tomorrow I will discover things I did not see before. I know that this book will go on, beyond my waking life, and beyond ours."[4] Why such fascination? What are the textual characteristics of Dante's *Commedia* that make it an ideal vehicle for literary appropriation, thereby allowing it to enjoy a sustained cultural afterlife, a kind of immortality, and to achieve the macrotemporality so eloquently described by Bakhtin in his proverbial formulation? "The variety of critical responses that the *Commedia* can evoke," writes Amilcare Iannucci, "is a tribute to its textual vitality. After almost seven hundred years, it continues to produce meaning and pleasure."[5] What, moreover, are the more accidental factors (e.g., taste, world view, political agenda, religious and mystical convictions) that account for the popularity of Dante – after three hundred years of neglect during which the Florentine poet was relegated to the shadows of Petrarch and his works, among artists, novelists, poets, playwrights, cinematographers, in addition to those who judged his works to be a kind of cryptogram in need of deciphering? The *Commedia* is, as Alberto Asor Rosa writes in his postscript to the volume *L'idea deforme: Interpretazioni esoteriche di Dante*,

> the literary work that, in *absolute terms*, includes within its own structure the greatest array of layers of discourse, for the most part – but not entirely and not always – intentional and well controlled by the author. Here, it must be said that we are able to understand some, but not all, of them: there are certain layers embedded deep within the darkest reaches of Dante's culture and personal experience, which, for now, allow for only a conjectural reading … yet still [are] worthy of the effort to work around our own modern cultural experience.[6]

It is in this deep and dark area of Dante's culture that one of the most curious and fascinating readings of his works is rooted, one that, since 1925 – the year of publication of René Guénon's book *L'Ésotérisme de Dante* – has been called the "esoterism of Dante." "Esoteric," from the late Latin word *esotericus*, derives its meaning from the Greek word *esoterikós*. For Greek philosophers, the term indicated those doctrines reserved for a restricted group of initiates, contrary to "exoteric," indicating those doctrines destined for wider diffusion. Is it possible that the *Divine Comedy* is an esoteric text written in code and containing a secret message? Is it possible that Dante, together with other contemporaneous poets and writers, belonged to a secret sect tied to the order of the Knights Templar, of the Free Masons, of the Rosicrucians, or to a heretical order that hid itself behind the name of Fedeli d'Amore (Faithful of Love)? Was Dante aware of the Jewish mysticism of the *Zohar* and of the Kaballah, which, deriving from twelfth-century Spain, was filtering its way through Europe? I will explore this tempting question by following two paths: first, a brief summary of the esoteric interpretations of Dante's work; second, an examination of two particular interpretations, the one by René Guénon and the other by Mark Jay Mirsky.

Modern interest in this esoteric aspect of Dante began with Gabriele Pasquale Giuseppe Rossetti (1783–1854). He was a member of the Carbonari (charcoal burners or sellers, a secret revolutionary society, which played a critical role in the Italian Risorgimento) and also a

Rosicrucian – he was first exiled to Malta and later to England in consequence of his participation in the revolutionary uprising of 1820 in Italy – as well as the father of the poet and Pre-Raphaelite painter Dante Gabriel Rossetti. In the voluminous *La "Divina Commedia" di Dante Alighieri con comento analitico* (The *Divine Comedy* by Dante Alighieri with an analytical commentary) and his *La Beatrice di Dante: Ragionamenti critici* (Dante's Beatrice: Critical discourses), to which must be added *Il mistero dell'amor platonico del medio evo, derivato da' misteri antichi* (The Mystery of platonic love in the Middle Ages, derived from ancient mysteries) and an earlier study entitled *Sullo spirito antipapale che produsse la riforma e sulla segreta influenza ch'esercitò nella letteratura d'Europa e specialmente d'Italia, come risulta da molti suoi classici, massime da Dante, Petrarca, Boccaccio* (On the antipapal spirit that produced the Reformation and on the secret influence that it exerted upon European literature and in particular in Italy, as it emerges from many of its classics, especially by Dante, Petrarch, Boccaccio),[7] Rossetti maintains that Dante shared with many of his contemporaries – including the poets of the Dolce Stil Nuovo (Sweet New Style), and later Petrarch and Boccaccio – a strong antipapal feeling, while still maintaining his Christian beliefs. The harshness enforced by the church against its opponents and any form of heresy led to the crusade against the Albigensians in 1208–29 and to the massacres perpetrated by Simon de Montfort.[8] These groups of believers therefore were driven into using a ciphered, allegorical, and anagogical language. Rossetti was fascinated by this invention of a new language that the inquisitors could not understand:

> Is this perhaps the first time that men who are courageous in their undertaking and cautious in their actions, afraid of being found out by jealous governments in their secret operations, agree on a slang among themselves? Don't we see with such a passport that the letters, which are dangerous in nature, have a free passage even through public mail? And to go through the most vigilant eyes and despite this not being recognized? Is it such a new thing to hear that this sect has its own symbolic language, understood only by those who belong to the sect? Don't we still read in our own times some writings in which compass, square, rule, stone, lime, factory, temple, masons, and a hundred similar things stand for other things? Therefore, should we consider an allegory founded on Love, an affection so poetic, so noble, so universal, stranger than one based on the art of the Masons?[9]

Since Dante wanted to promote the renewal of the church and of the papacy, he had joined Fedeli d'Amore, whose objective was a radical, Ghibelline reform of the church. Through the use of a particular lexicon, called *Gaia Scienza* (Gay Science), and simulating a platonic love for a *donna angelicata* (an angel-like woman) – who symbolized their political and religious ideals – these poets, following in the steps of the Provençal troubadours before them, had revived the tradition of an occult wisdom dating back to ancient Egyptians and Greeks and continued by the Manicheans, Patarins, and by the Sicilian poets of the court of Emperor Frederick II. For Rossetti, Beatrice represents philosophy, and Dante, in the *Divine Comedy*, expresses a philosophy that is essentially Pythagorean in nature but masked as Catholic doctrine.[10]

Following in Rossetti's steps, Eugène Aroux, in his 1854 study *Dante hérétique, révolutionaire et socialiste: Révélations d'un catholique sur le moyen âge,* develops the thesis that the works of Dante are fundamentally socialist, revolutionary, and heretical in nature (a thesis contested in those same years by Cesare Cantù).[11] According to Aroux, who relies heavily on the opinions of Ugo Foscolo's *Discorso sul testo del poema di Dante* (Discourse on the text of Dante's poem) published in 1825 and also of Rossetti, the Patarine (or Cathar) sect had not been defeated in Italy. Instead, it had transformed itself into a kind of Masonic sect *ante litteram*, preserving and transmitting certain doctrines – called by Rossetti "the mysteries of Platonic love" – whose end was to subvert the authority of the church and of civilian governments. As Aroux noted, the knights of that time, and especially those Knights Templar who survived the dissolution of the order in 1312–14, founded a new Masonic "school."[12] Dante belonged to the Order of the Templars, and through his works tried to avenge the suppression of the Order by demonstrating that the papal supremacy was the visible reign of Satan manifested in the "Comedy of Catholicism."[13]

The year 1865 saw the publication of Francesco Paolo Perez's *La Beatrice svelata* (Beatrice unveiled). Perez, in 1836, had already published an essay entitled *La prima allegoria e lo scopo della "Divina Commedia"* (The first allegory and the purpose of the *Divine Comedy*). The author, after criticizing the interpretation of Rossetti, who, he writes, "[was] overtaken … by an erudition gathered hurriedly, and therefore poorly digested,"[14] insists on interpreting Beatrice allegorically as the "active intelligence which enlightens the possible intellect and which, in union with it, becomes blessed Beatrice," or the heavenly embodiment for the poet of the Holy Wisdom of Solomon.[15] This thesis, as is well known, was reprised by Giovanni Pascoli who in 1898 published *Minerva oscura* (Hidden Minerva), in 1900 *Sotto il velame* (Under the veil), and in 1902 *La mirabile visione* (The wonderful vision).[16] Pascoli's vision is deeply religious, and his goal was to unveil the profound symbolic message of the *Commedia*. His is a symbolic-allegorical interpretation of Dante's work, and for this very reason, it can scarcely be classified as "esoteric." We may recall Benedetto Croce's scathing criticism of Pascoli's interpretation that was directly aimed at his overwhelming Christian symbolism.[17]

Since Pascoli there have been numerous studies that have likewise attempted to unveil the arcane meanings of the *Divine Comedy*. Luigi Valli, a student of the poet of San Mauro, expanded the hyper-Catholic symbolic interpretation of his teacher in a series of studies: *L'allegoria di Dante secondo Giovanni Pascoli* (Dante's allegory according to Giovanni Pascoli) and *Il segreto della Croce e dell'Aquila nella "Divina Commedia"* (The secret of the cross and of the eagle in the *Divine Comedy*), both published in 1922; *La chiave della "Divina Commedia"* (The key to the *Divine Comedy* [1925]); and *Il linguaggio segreto di Dante e dei "Fedeli d'Amore"* (The secret language of Dante and of the "Faithful in Love" [1928, integrated in 1930 with a volume of discussions and notes added]). His last study, *La struttura morale dell'universo dantesco* (The moral structure of Dante's universe), was published in 1935, five years after his death. For Valli, who also drew on the interpretations of Rossetti and Aroux, Dante was a heretic belonging to the sect of the Fedeli d'Amore. Valli was convinced that it was necessary to follow the path traced by Rossetti in an objective and scientific manner.[18] He therefore concluded:

1 There existed a secret language of the Fedeli d'Amore that Dante knew, and at least thirty of the words he uses carry a second or third recondite meaning: *Amore, Madonna, Morte, Vita, Donne, Gaiezza, Noia, Natura, Rosa, Selvaggio, Pianto e Piangere, Fiore, Salute* and so forth (love, Madonna, death, life, women, gaiety, boredom, nature, rose, wild, tears and weeping, flower, and health). If we read the poems of Dante and of the Fedeli d'Amore in this context, then we will discover the existence of an initiatic doctrine and of a confraternity of followers of this doctrine.
2 All the women of the lyric poems of the poets of the Dolce Stil Nuovo are the same woman, who is the personification of Divine Wisdom. In addition, that name was also used to designate the doctrine itself and the sect of those poets.

3 Dante's *New Life* is written in an initiatic language from beginning to end, and every word therefore has a symbolic meaning. That youthful work is the description of the initiatic voyage of the poet and of his relationships not with the wife of Simone de' Bardi, but with Eternal Wisdom – Religion – and with that group of disciples who followed the same doctrines.
4 When reading the works of Dante with the initiatic key, the meaning of even those passages that critics have been unable to explain suddenly becomes clear; this happens not only for the works of Dante, but also for those of Francesco da Barberino, Dino Compagni, and Cecco d'Ascoli.
5 All of the lyric poems of Dante and of the poets of his circle are motivated by a profound love for Wisdom, as the final goal for which the Fedeli d'Amore unceasingly fought against the corrupt church of Rome, which they called "Death" or "Stone" and labelled "The Enemy" in all their associations.

It was René Guénon (1886–1951), one of the masters of the twentieth century's esoteric tradition – and author of fundamental studies on Indus doctrine, on theosophy, on oriental metaphysics, to mention but a few of the most important subjects he studied – who isolated some of the most important Hermetic themes in the *Divine Comedy* in his 1925 *L'Ésotérisme de Dante*. Like most of the esoteric interpreters of Dante's works, Guénon begins his discussion with the ninth canto of *Inferno*, in which Dante mentions the "hidden sense" of his verses: "O voi che avete li 'ntelletti sani, / Mirate la dottrina che s'asconde / Sotto 'l velame de li versi strani" (9.61–3; O you who have sound intellects, / consider the teaching that is hidden / behind the veil of these strange verses). Just as important for Guénon are those words in *Convivio* 2.1.2–3, with which Dante declares that all writings, and not only sacred scriptures, "si possono intendere e deonsi esponere massimamente per quattro sensi" (can be understood in four different ways, and that it ought to be explained chiefly in this manner). But what are these four different ways? Commentators, Guénon continues, "generally agree on recognizing beneath the literal meaning in poetic narrative a philosophical (or rather, philosophic-theological) meaning, and also a political and social one." But what about the fourth sense? "For us," Guénon concludes, "it can only be a properly initiatic meaning, metaphysical in its essence, to which are related numerous facts, equally esoteric in character though not all of a purely metaphysical order." If this meaning is ignored, or simply left unrecognized, then the other levels of meaning "can themselves only be partially grasped, for this fourth, or initiatic, meaning stands to the others as their principle, in which their multiplicity is coordinated and unified."[19] Thus, the profound meaning of the *Divine Comedy* can be understood only if one begins from this secret message hidden within the text of the poem. Guénon acknowledges the fact that Rossetti and Aroux were the first to recognize Dante's esoterism, but for him, these predecessors were limited by their belief that Dante was therefore a heretic. They did not recognize that true esoterism is essentially different from outward religion, although it could find in religious forms its symbolic expression: "True esoterism is something completely different from outward religion, and if it has some relationship with it, this can only be insofar as it finds a symbolic mode of expression in religious forms." For Guénon, true metaphysics is neither pagan nor Christian, but universal. Therefore, if Dante belonged to some secret organization, "which seems to us indisputable," Guénon writes, "this is no reason to declare him a 'heretic'."[20]

Guénon's formal analysis develops from his examination of two medals located in the museum of Vienna, one of which shows an image of Dante, the other an image of the painter Pietro da Pisa. Both medals on their reverse carry the letters "F.S.K.I.F.T.," interpreted by Rossetti and Aroux in the following manner: "Frater Sacrae Kadish, Imperialis Principatus, Frater Templarius." Guénon disagrees with the interpretation of his predecessors. The first three letters, he states, stand for Fidei Sanctae Kadosh: the Association of the Fede Santa (Holy Faith) was a third order of Templar filiations, "of which Dante seems to have been a leader." This explains the designation of *Frater Templarius* on the medal, while its dignitaries bore the title of *Kadosh*: "a Hebrew word meaning 'holy' or 'consecrated,' which has been preserved to our days in the high grades of Masonry."[21] It is for this very reason, according to Guénon, that Dante at the end of his voyage takes as his guide Saint Bernard, who established the rule of the Order of the Temple. In Scottish Masonry, even today, the members of the Supreme Council "bear the title of dignitaries of the Holy Empires," while the title "Prince" denotes various grades.[22] Furthermore, beginning from the sixteenth century the leaders of the different organizations stemming from the Rosicrucians took the title *Imperator*.[23] According to Guénon, it is probable that in Dante's time the Fede Santa "bore certain similarities to what later became the 'Brotherhood of the Rose-Cross,' even if the latter is not more or less directly derived from the former."[24] However,

Guénon did not bother to go to Vienna to examine the medals in person. Luigi Valli took the time to examine them, and what he found invalidates Guénon's interpretation of those seven letters on the reverse of the medal: "The *recto* and the *verso* were put together at different times with two half medals of very different character and style, they were not engraved together: everyone can see it immediately. Therefore the letters are not related to Dante, at least in their origin. It is a medal by Pisanello, the lettered *verso* of which was later applied by someone to the *recto* of a medal of Dante." Valli suggests another, more plausible, interpretation of the letters engraved on the medal: the initials of the seven Christian virtues: *Fides, Spes, Karitas, Justitia, Prudentia, Fortitudo, Temperantia*.[25]

The medal with the effigy of Dante in the Vienna museum is not the only proof Guénon had of Dante's esoterism, but it is one of the most essential ones. Believing that he had demonstrated beyond any doubt that Dante belonged to the Order of the Temple, Guénon was able to interpret symbolically various aspects of the *Divine Comedy* that confirm its "Masonic" matrix. He read the heavens Dante crosses during his voyage as proper "spiritual hierarchies" or degrees of initiations. "In this context," Guénon continues, "an interesting concordance could be established between the conception of Dante and that of Swedenborg, not to speak of certain theories of the Hebrew Kabbalah," a remark that anticipates our next author, Mark Jay Mirsky. The scientific system of the Cathars was founded on the doctrine of correspondences: "Grammar corresponded to the Moon, Dialectic to Mercury, Rhetoric to Venus, Music to Mars, Geometry to Jupiter, Astronomy to Saturn, and Arithmetic or Illuminated Reason to the Sun." Accordingly, the seven planetary spheres – the first seven of the nine heavens of Dante – corresponded to the seven liberal arts; and precisely these same designations are depicted on the seven rungs of the left upright of the Ladder of Kadosch,[26] that is to say, the thirtieth degree of Scottish Masonry. Yet, Guénon anticipates the obvious question: how is it possible that correspondences of this type, which are assimilated to actual initiatic degrees, could "have been attributed to the liberal arts, which after all were taught publicly and officially in all the schools?"[27] The answer clearly illustrates the fundamental principle of initiatic organizations: in all sciences we must distinguish two levels, or two ways of considering them, one exoteric and the other esoteric. He explains, "It is possible to superimpose on any profane science another science that is related to the same subject but looks at it from a profounder point of view, and which is to that profane science what the higher meaning of the scriptures are to their literal meaning."[28] Exterior sciences provide a means of expression to the higher truths. This point is absolutely critical: the profound meaning of an initiatic text is only for the initiated few, and the *Divine Comedy*, being an initiatic text written by a Kadosch, was clearly written for the few adepts, the heirs of the Order of the Temple and of the Rosicrucians, that is to say the Free Masons.

In the rest of his study, Guénon discusses the correspondences between the *Divine Comedy* and Masonic and Hermetic symbolisms (ch. 3); Dante and Rosicrucianism (ch. 4); extraterrestrial voyages in varied cultural traditions (ch. 5); the difference between the three worlds (ch. 6); the value of symbolic numbers (ch. 7); the cosmic cycles (ch. 8). It is superfluous to examine in great detail Guénon's argument: interested readers can go to Claudia Miranda's excellent contribution to the aforementioned volume *L'idea deforme: Interpretazioni esoteriche di Dante*. However, I would like briefly to consider Miranda's extremely critical presentation. She sees Guénon's text as a closed system and therefore not subject to any form of verification. She concludes: "The critical discourse of Guénon appears invulnerable, since its truths are guaranteed by a tradition unchallengeable because it is secret, and since this tradition is the expression of what is underneath all the multiplicity, its area tends to encompass the entire semisphere, leaving no possible space at all to any opposition, since nothing is left outside of it."[29] But Guénon does not pretend to be a critic of Dante, nor does he intend to explain the *Divine Comedy* as an initiatic text to those who are not initiated. From the very first paragraphs of the book, readers are told in the clearest terms that the secret language of an initiatic text can be understood, in its essence, only by those who have already been initiated to the mysteries of the Order. For Guénon it is important to insist on the fact that the *Divine Comedy* is an initiatic text just like the scriptures. Those who wish to understand the profound meaning of Dante's work must first be initiated to the mysteries of the Order. Seen from this point of view, his book becomes a kind of pamphlet aimed at stirring interest in the Order for those yet uninitiated and above all a guide for the initiated, for whom the act of reading the *Comedy* is a stage towards the unveiling of that unique truth that is in all sciences and in all great works of literature, and that prepares the understanding of the "Great Work," the Work of the Great Architect, creator of our world and of the universe.

While Guénon sees in *the Divine Comedy* a secret language bearing an initiatic message, for Mark Jay Mirsky, professor of English literature at

New York City College and well-known novelist, Dante's work hides a profound truth that the poet did not want, or rather was not able, to express. His book, *Dante, Eros and Kabbalah*,[30] is a kind of detective story in search of the poem's secret meaning. At the same time, it is a meditation on the esoteric meaning hidden within the folds of a thought that stretches forward from Latin medieval culture, especially that of Saint Thomas Aquinas, to the Jewish culture of the *Zohar* and of the Kabbalah.

The theoretical cue of the study comes from the work of American political scientist Leo Strauss on Maimonides (1135–1204), the great Jewish philosopher born in Córdoba. In his book *Persecution and the Art of Writing*, Strauss claims that Maimonides, along with most pre-seventeenth-century philosophers, concealed from common people and from conventional bureaucracy those convictions that were contrary to popular prejudice. He writes:

> Persecution gives rise to a peculiar technique of writing, and therewith to a peculiar type of literature, in which the truth about all crucial things is presented exclusively between the lines. That literature is addressed not to all readers, but to trustworthy and intelligent readers only. It has all the advantages of private communications without having its greatest disadvantage – that it reaches only the writers' acquaintances. It has all the advantages of public communication, without having its greatest disadvantage – capital punishment for the author.[31]

What makes this literature possible can be expressed in the axiom that thoughtless men are careless readers, and only thoughtful men are careful readers. But, it will be objected, there may be clever men, careful readers, who are not trustworthy and who after having found the author out, would denounce him to the authorities. As a matter of fact, this literature would be impossible if the Socratic dictum that virtue is knowledge and therefore that thoughtful men as such are trustworthy and not cruel were entirely wrong.[32]

Mirsky remarks, "Such concealment is the principle I have come to believe that the whole of the *Vita Nuova* and the *Commedia* … is organized upon."[33] But what is the secret that Dante wanted to hide from his readers? Certainly something terrible, something that Dante did not want or rather could not admit to anyone, perhaps not even to himself: "Did he have something to hide? Is there a secret *Commedia*?"[34]

Mirsky wonders if Dante came to know Maimonides's *The Guide to the Perplexed*. Dante followed closely Saint Thomas Aquinas, who had assimilated the work of the great Jewish philosopher. Maimonides had been profoundly influenced by the doctrine of the *taquiyya*, or deliberate precautionary dissimulation, of Shi'a Islam. Maimonides in turn had exerted a deep influence on Moses de León, the probable author of the *Zohar*, the group of books on which the Kabbalah is based. In addition, the inspiration that led to the *Zohar* likely came from Provence, just as the "sweet style" of Dante had. "Dante's philosophy, poetic theory, promises immortality, through the love of a woman. Dante, Unamuno, Dahlberg, voyage down into the sea as uterus. For it is not so much over the waves that Dante journeyed but through them, down, in order to come up to Heaven. This smacks of the *Zohar*, or Kabbalah."[35] A terrible secret, therefore, and a rapport with the *Zohar*, the Kabbalah?

Mirsky's search for this "terrible" secret begins with a meditation on the sixteenth canto of *Inferno*. He focuses on that rope "with which I once had meant to take / the leopard with the painted pelt" (16.107–8; e con essa pensai alcuna volta / prender la lonza a la pelle dipinta); on the "strange signal" (*novo cenno*) of verse 116, which, for Mirsky – guided by Leo Strauss – means that we must read in between the lines; on the "winking" of Virgil; and finally on the "fraternal embrace Dante gives the sea monster, Fraud."[36]

> The context, despite the coy disclaimer of scholars, their unwillingness to read Dante in a sexual context, is clear to me. Dante and Virgil, his master, understand each other so well in this regard that without words, but with a silent command, the follower unhitches the belt of chastity with which he thought to keep lust at bay, the leopard with the painted hide, and Virgil throws it to the monster Fraud, as the tastiest of baits … the direct linking of lust, the "notes of this comedy," and Fraud as a sea monster seems plain. [37]

"What is the *Commedia* but a giant fraud in which a truth will be buried," Mirsky comments. It is also clear that the fraud concerns Dante's sexual life: "My speculations on Dante and the erotic vibrations of the *Commedia* recalled to me the reading I had done of the *Zohar*, where dreams speak of knowledge of God through a spiritualized sex. I began to wonder whether Hell, Paradise, and Heaven in Dante were constructed out of similar ideas."[38] The *Zohar* allows one to reach the unknown by means of the sexual union with a woman who incarnates the Feminine Presence of God. It is by plumbing the depths of the *Vita Nuova*, reading in between the lines of Dante's youthful work that Mirsky discovers the secret that Dante was unable to reveal, but whose echo resounds throughout the entire *Inferno* and *Purgatorio* and, although in a different manner, even in *Paradiso*: his adulterous love for Beatrice. All poets have a pathological need to confess, Mirsky writes: "If Dante wanted to speak about seduction, of adultery, he had to be artful, even deceitful. He had full need of an 'exoteric' text in the manner of the Ismai'ili Neoplatonists."[39] That is to say, of the above-mentioned doctrine of the *taquiyya*, the exoteric text of the *Comedy* hides another esoteric one. "Does Dante confess in the *Vita Nuova* to sleeping with his adolescent love?"[40] Mirsky, who in the tradition of the reader of the *Zohar* and Kabbalah is attentive to every nuance of the language, follows the traces of this hidden relationship and of its transformation throughout the *Comedy*. He suggests that Dante wants to touch the woman he loves and to "know" her. While they move from heaven in Paradise, Dante and Beatrice "circle each other in the steps of a Provençal courtship, the strum of innuendos, gentle rebukes, side glances, affectionate outbursts, between lines that act as blinds."[41] Dante's inspiration came from Provence, from Languedoc, the "seed plot" of mysticism and poetry, writes Mirsky (quoting Karl Vossler's *Medieval Culture*).

However, according to Mirsky, what Dante takes from this fertile cultural and religious crossroad is the idea that sexual union is a virtue: the Divine Presence in adultery, as in the story of David and Bathsheba. Passion is encouraged; at the edge of folly, in the thirst for knowledge (that dangerous species prohibited in the Earthly Paradise) and the submission to sexual and artistic ecstasy, "God" is finally found. Mirsky concludes:

> Such is the argument of courtly romance. Beatrice, however, is only an aspect, as she admits, of something beyond her. Here the *Commedia* touches Kabbalah, its extension of Neoplatonism, the notion of man and woman, their erotic coupling, as a means to the original unity of the human being and God. If Beatrice can forgive, spurn envy, vengeance, spite from her, it is because beyond those images of motherhood, those dripping breasts by which Dante is holding onto salvation, is Divine Unity.[42]

The study by René Guénon can undoubtedly be considered the most serious critical attempt to demonstrate, by means of a thorough exploration of the parallels between the symbolism of the *Divine Comedy* and that of Freemasonry, Rosicrucianism, and Christian Hermeticism, that the three parts of Dante's poem represent faithfully the stages of "initiatic realization." Mark Jay Mirsky's book is, in my opinion, the most creative. In the intervening years between the publication of Guénon's study and that of Mirsky, the number of books trying to prove that Dante belonged to some kind of secret society, and especially the Freemasons and Rosicrucians, has grown exponentially. I will offer but a few examples: A. Ricolfi, *Studi sui Fedeli d'Amore. Dai poeti di corte a Dante. Simboli e linguaggio segreto* (Milan: Bastogi, 1933); M. Alessandrini, *Dante Fedele d'Amore* (Rome: Atanor, 1960); Emma Cusani, *Il grande viaggio nei mondi danteschi. Iniziazione ai Misteri Maggiori* (Rome: Edizioni Mediterranee, 1993); Æ Philalethes, *L'esoterismo rosacroce nella "Divina Commedia"* (Foggia: Bastogi, 1995); Alfonso Ricolfi, *Studi sui Fedeli d'Amore dai poeti di corte a Dante: simboli e linguaggio segreto* (Foggia: Bastogi, 1997; repr. of 1933 ed.); Gabriella Bartolozzi, *Exoterismo e esoterismo nell'opera dantesca* (Florence: Atheneum, 2001). There has been a marked resurgence in interest in this topic, fuelled especially by the Internet, where there are now tens of thousands of entries on Dante's esoterism. This global electronic proliferation confirms the protean vitality of the *Comedy*. As Amilcare Iannucci noted:

> The *Commedia* generates a number of possible readings, all of which flow naturally from the literal narrative, which is easily accessible and complete. In this light, the *Commedia* is neither an open nor a closed text; it is neither writerly nor readerly. An open or writerly text, at least as Eco (*Opera aperta*) and Barthes (*S / Z*) originally theorized it, is multiple, difficult, and self-reflective, designed for the refined reader who delights in discovering its complex discursive strategies and consequently in participating in a writerly way in the production of meaning. On the other hand, a closed or readerly text is one which is easily accessible and thus has wide popular appeal. It seems to function at one level only – that of reality – and uses standard signifying practices to convey this impression. Although the *Commedia* exhibits many of the qualities of an open or writerly text, it also "reads" easily and succeeds in communicating meaning and giving pleasure even to those unable to appreciate the nature of its elaborate allegorical and metaliterary discourse. Because of this, Dante's poem is more like what Fiske in *Television Culture* calls a "producerly" text. A producerly text is polysemous and combines the easy accessibility of the readerly with the complex discursive strategies of the writerly. These peculiar textual qualities allow the poem to produce meaning and pleasure in audiences which run the gamut from the uneducated to the

most sophisticated and discerning. In saying this, I do not mean to imply that the *Commedia's* polysemy is boundless and structure-less: the poem defines the terrain within which meaning may be made. Where exactly the boundary between a possible reading and an "aberrant" one lies is the subject of much theoretical debate ... Suffice it to say that the vastness of the terrain in Dante's case makes "aberrant readings" difficult but not impossible (see *L'idea deforme*).[43]

NOTES

1 T.S. Eliot, "Dante," in *Selected Essays*, 2nd ed. (London: Faber and Faber, 1934), 266.

2 H. Bloom, *The Western Canon: The Books and School of the Ages* (New York: Riverhead Books, 1995), 72.

3 S.Y. McDougall, ed., *Dante Among the Moderns* (Chapel Hill and London: University of North Carolina Press, 1985), ix.

4 J.L. Borges, *Siete Noches* (Colonia Granjas San Antonio, Mexico: Editorial Meló, 1980), 11; translation mine.

5 Amilcare Iannucci, ed., *Dante: Contemporary Perspectives* (Toronto: University of Toronto Press, 1997), xx.

6 M.P. Pozzato, ed., *L'idea deforme: Interpretazioni esoteriche di Dante* (Milan: Bompiani, 1989), 299.

7 *La "Divina Commedia" di Dante Alighieri con comento analitico* (London: John Murray, 1826–7); *La Beatrice di Dante: Ragionamenti critici* (London: n.p., 1842); *Il mistero dell'amor platonico del medio evo, derivato da' misteri antichi* (London: R. and J. Taylor, 1840); *Sullo spirito antipapale che produsse la riforma e sulla segreta influenza ch'esercitò nella letteratura d'Europa e specialmente in Italia, come risulta da molti suoi classici, massime da Dante, Petrarca, Boccaccio* (London: R. Taylor, 1832).

8 Cf. *Paradiso* 9.94–108 where Dante praises the Provençal poet Folchetto di Marsiglia, who after leaving the life of the world became first a friar, then abbot of Torronet in Toulon, finally bishop of Toulouse, and was one of the leaders in the crusade. But see R. and J. Hollander, *Dante Paradiso* (New York: Doubleday, 2007), 246–7.

9 *Comento analitico al "Purgatorio" di Dante Alighieri*, ed. P. Giannantonio (Florence: Olschki, 1967), 456. Translation mine. See also H. Lozano Miralles, "'Dantis *Amor*': Gabriele Rossetti e il paradigma del Velame," in Pozzato, *L'idea deforme*, 47–77, esp. 62.

10 See M.L. Giartosio de Courten, ed., *La Beatrice di Dante: ragionamenti critici* (Imola: Galeati, 1935), 69.

11 See Cesare Cantù, *Gli eretici d'Italia: discorsi storici* (Turin: Unione Tipografico-Editrice, 1865), 145–7.

12 Eugéne Aroux, *Dante hérétique, révolutionnaire et socialiste: Révélations d'un catholique sur le moyen age* (Paris: Jules Renouard et C[ei], 1854), esp. 105–14.

13 See Rev. R. Parson, DD, "The Charge of Heresy against Dante," *The American Catholic Quarterly Review* 12 (January–October 1887): 714–25, esp. 715.

14 Francesco Paolo Perez, *La Beatrice svelata* (Palermo: Stabilimento Tipografico di Franc. Lao: 1865), 7–8.

15 Ibid., 196. See especially the last six chapters, 241–87. See also L. Valli's analysis in *Il linguaggio segreto di Dante e dei "Fedeli d'Amore"* (Milan: Luni, 1994), 12.

16 *Minerva oscura* (Bologna: Zanichelli, 1898); *Sotto il velame* (Bologna: Zanichelli, 1900); *La mirabile visione* (Bologna: Zanichelli, 1913).

17 For a thorough analysis of Pascoli's essays on Dante, see S. Cavicchioli, "Giovanni Pascoli: del segreto strutturale nella 'Divina Commedia,'" in Pozzato, *L'idea deforme*, 107–45.

18 For this, and for what follows, see Valli, *Il linguaggio segreto di Dante e dei "Fedeli d'Amore,"* 15ff.

19 R. Guénon, *The Esoterism of Dante*, trans. Henry D. Fohr and Cecil Bethell (Hillsdale, NY: Sophia Perennis, 1996), 2.

20 Ibid., 3.

21 Ibid., 5.

22 Ibid., 6.

23 Ibid.

24 Ibid.

25 Valli, *Il linguaggio segreto*, 503.

26 Guénon, *The Esoterism of Dante*, 6–7. The ladder of Kadosch consists of seven steps, beginning at the bottom: Justice, Equity, Kindness, Good Faith, Labour, Patience, and Intelligence or Wisdom. The Knight Kadosch is a Freemasonic degree or ceremony of initiation performed by certain branches of the Ancient and Accepted Scottish Rite of Freemasonry. It is the Thirtieth Degree of the Southern Jurisdiction of the Scottish Rite for the United States of America. The term "Kadosch" derives from the Hebrew word שודק, which means "holy" or "consecrated."

27 Ibid., 7.

28 Ibid.

29 C. Miranda, "René Guénon," in Pozzato, *L'idea deforme*, 255.

30 M.J. Mirsky, *Dante, Eros and Kabbalah* (Syracuse NY: Syracuse University Press, 2003).

31 L. Strauss, *Persecution and the Art of Writing* (Westport: Greenwood Press, 1952; repr. 1973), 8.

32 Ibid., 24–5.
33 Mirsky, *Dante, Eros, and Kabbalah*, 8.
34 Ibid.
35 Ibid., 11.
36 Ibid., 12.
37 Ibid., 14.
38 Ibid., 18.
39 Ibid., 30.
40 Ibid., 31.
41 Ibid., 115.
42 Ibid., 139.
43 Introduction to Iannucci, *Dante: Contemporary Perspectives*, xiii–xiv.

8 *Ersed Irredent*: The Irish Dante

PIERO BOITANI

Dante tires one quickly. It is like looking at the sun.

– James Joyce

Like Amilcare Iannucci, I am interested in Dante's continuing importance for writers throughout the world. "Dante and Ireland," or "Dante and Irish Writers," is an extremely vast topic to cover, for which a book rather than an essay would be necessary. If the relationship between the poet and Ireland does not begin in the fourteenth century – when Dante himself may have had some knowledge of and been inspired by the *Vision of Adamnán*, the *Vision of Tungdal*, and the *Tractatus de purgatorio sancti Patricii* – the story certainly starts in the early nineteenth century when the Irish man of letters Henry Boyd was the first to produce a complete English translation of the *Comedy*, published in 1802.[1] Even if one restricts the field to twentieth-century literature alone, which is my aim in the present piece, the list of authors who are influenced by Dante includes Yeats, Joyce, Beckett, and Heaney, that is to say, four among the major writers not only of Ireland but of Europe and of the entire West. To these should then be added other Irish poets of the first magnitude, such as Louis MacNeice, Ciaran Carson, Eiléan Ní Cuilleanain, and Thomas Kinsella. I hope I will therefore be forgiven for treating this theme in a somewhat cursory manner, privileging the episodes I consider most relevant and the themes which I think form a coherent and intricate pattern of literary history, where every author is not only metamorphosing Dante but also rewriting the predecessor, or predecessors, who had rewritten Dante. Distinct from the English and American one of Pound and Eliot, an "Irish Dante,"[2] whom Joyce was to call "ersed irredent," slowly grows out of this pattern. Historical, political, and religious, as well as existential and philosophical, motivations determine the shape Dante's image takes in twentieth-century Irish culture, but the primary factor of linguistic and textual knowledge should not be underestimated either. Of the four writers under consideration here, only Joyce and Beckett knew Italian and read the *Comedy* thoroughly in the original.

The following points will emerge from an examination of our four major Irish authors: (1) The image of Dante that takes shape in twentieth-century Irish literature begins with an adaptation of *Vita nuova* episodes (itself a Rossettian legacy) in Yeats's poetry and in Joyce's *Portrait of the Artist as a Young Man*. (2) But Joyce had already tried a *structural* adaptation of the *Comedy* in *Dubliners*, and his endeavour in *Ulysses* is that of rewriting the *Odyssey* with the scope and ambition of a *Divine Comedy* (an ironic treatment of Dante, in contrast, links the *Portrait* and *Finnegans Wake*). (3) The Irish idea of Dante seems to centre on purgatory, which Joyce, Beckett, and Heaney choose as their favourite dimension. (4) In both Joyce and Beckett a distinct anti-Ulysses (*Inferno* 26) position surfaces. (5) Finally, with Heaney it is Ugolino – the *sound* of the story as well as its significance in the political context of northern Irish sectarianism – that takes the upper hand.

From an ideal if not chronological point of view, the twentieth-century history of Dante in Ireland begins between the summer and the autumn of 1915. This is when William Butler Yeats composed "Ego Dominus Tuus," the dialogue between a "Hic" and an "Ille" who discuss the problem of the quest for the self.[3] This search is closely allied to the identification of a poetics, and to this end Yeats uses a series of allusions and quotations from Matthew Arnold, Wordsworth, Sappho, Guido Cavalcanti, and Keats. In the first place, however, he refers to Dante, from whom he takes the title itself of his poem. In chapter three of the *Vita nuova*, Dante had recounted a "maravigliosa visione" (a wonderful vision) in which, within a "nebula di colore di fuoco" (a fire-coloured cloud), the "figura d'uno segnore di pauroso aspetto" (the figure of a dreadful looking Lord) had appeared to him and pronounced a few words taken from the opening of the Decalogue in Exodus 20:2, "Ego dominus tuus" (I am your Lord). The figure clearly is that of Love, who holds in his arms the "donna de la salute" and in one hand the poet's heart, which the lady subsequently eats (*Vita nuova* 3.3–6).[4] Yeats's Dantean allusion, then, points in the first place to the source itself of his inspiration, love, and to the vision-like fashion in which it comes to him. It is a Rossettian, Pre-Raphaelite type of reference.

But Dante is more deeply present in Yeats's thought and poetics. In his *Autobiographies*, written between 1915 and 1936, Yeats wrote that he had always believed that "in man and race alike there is something called 'Unity of Being,'" using that term as Dante had when he compared beauty in the *Convivio* to a perfectly proportioned human body.[5] In the Dantean acceptation, Unity of Being means the union in one "form" of man's three natures (sensitive, vegetative, and rational), and hence the harmony of his form, his body. The passage to which Yeats refers, in *Convivio* 3, presents Dante's commentary to those lines of *Amor che ne la mente mi ragiona* in which the countenance of the Lady (Philosophy) is celebrated as paradisal: "Cose appariscon ne lo suo aspetto, / che mostran de' piacer di Paradiso, / dico ne li occhi e nel suo dolce riso, / che le vi reca Amor com'a suo loco" (3.8.1–2; In her aspect things appear that show the joys of paradise – I mean in her eyes and her lovely smile; for it is there, as to the place which belongs to him, that Love leads them).[6] In other words, Yeats seems now to go well beyond the Pre-Raphaelite reception of Dante.

This deeper engagement is anticipated in "Ego Dominus Tuus," which explores the subjective dimension of poetic inspiration. Is it better to pursue the quest for oneself or to discover the self through the quest for the other? Should the human being, the poet, look within himself, or rather prefer what is outside of him, projecting a fiction, a "mask" of himself? "Ille" (who is also "Willie," Yeats himself) would like, "by the help of an image," to evoke his "opposite," to summon all he has "handled least, least looked upon" (EDT 11–3). "Hic," on the other hand, aims at finding himself, "and not an image." Such, "Ille" replies, "is our modern hope," by whose light "we have hit upon the gentle, sensitive mind" and at the same time lost "the old nonchalance of the hand," becoming mere critics, people who "but half create, / Timid, entangled, empty and abashed" (EDT 14–7).

"Hic" replies to this merciless portrait of poetic modernity with the example of Dante Alighieri, "the chief imagination of Christendom" (EDT 18). Dante "so utterly found himself / That he has made that hollow face of his / More plain to the mind's eye than any face / But that of Christ" (EDT 19–22). This is no longer the Dante of *Vita nuova* and *Convivio* but the poet of the *Comedy*, who sings the "Unity of Being" and who maintains he has lived through the "moment of moments" in a beatific vision unparalleled either before or after him. It is, however, easy for "Ille" to answer – and from the text of the *Comedy* itself – that perhaps Dante did not find himself, but that "hollow" face of his was the product of hunger, "A hunger," as Sappho sang, "for the apple on the bough / Most out of reach" (EDT 23, 28). That "spectral image" is not "the man that Lapo and Guido knew," but in fact an icon he created "from his opposite" (EDT 29–30). "Mocked by Guido for his lecherous life," "driven out / To climb that stair and eat that bitter bread," "Ille" insists, quoting Cavalcanti's "I' vegno 'l giorno a te infinite volte" and *Paradiso* 17, that Dante "found the unpersuadable justice, he found / The most exalted lady loved by a man" (EDT 33–7). In short, what Dante did in inventing divine Justice and Beatrice, the two movers of his "sacred poem," was to sublimate his desires and delusions.

The debate between the two characters on traditional models of poetry continues to the very end of "Ego Dominus Tuus." The poem is in fact a great piece of lyric writing. It teaches how one can turn one's own thought, meditation, and poetics into poetry and explores with force and precision the two sides of the creative soul, tradition, and the poet's motivations. At the same time, it records his dissipation, despair, and happiness and advocates his discipline, imitation, and vision – his mysterious and religious writing of symbols in the sand, the still small voice of poetry. In this lyric, Dante occupies the central place and is in a sense its pretext. He stands for two contrasting images of the poet: that which "Hic" sees grounded in self-assuredness and projects a sacred profile, and that which grows, for "Ille," out of uncertainty, need, and the sublimation produced by them.

In "Ego Dominus Tuus" Dante is, then, a symbol of poetics, an exemplum. At the end of his life, after spending many years in conversation with Shakespeare and Michelangelo,[7] Yeats turns to Dante in much closer personal terms. He employs terza rima,[8] for the first and only time in his career, in what appears to be his last poem, completed on 13 January 1939, two weeks before he died. "Cuchulain Comforted" is the supreme phantasmagoria, the description of the hero's descent to the other world.[9] "A man violent and famous," with six mortal wounds on his body, strides among the dead, as their eyes fix him from between the branches and disappear. Here the shades are Shrouds who come and go, muttering to each other. As Cuchulain leans against a tree, "as though to meditate on wounds and blood," a Shroud "that seemed to have authority / Among those bird-like things" comes close to the hero and lets fall a bundle of linen. Now the other Shrouds join in, while the first one addresses the dead man. He invites him to make a shroud, thus obeying their ancient rule and obtaining a "much sweeter" life. They, he says, are "convicted cowards all, by kindred slain / Or driven from home and left to die in fear." Threading the needles' eyes, they must now sing, "and sing the best [they] can." The Shrouds then begin to sing "in common." But they have "nor human tunes nor words"; they have changed their throats and sing with "the throats of birds"("Cuchulain Comforted," lines 6–9, 16–18, 21–25).

This *ingressus in inferos* is a mysterious sequence, where the hero of so many battles is welcomed by those who died of fear, as if Cuchulain had now no choice but that of learning to surrender, of sewing a shroud and becoming a Shroud like them. The descent to Hades finally forces him to meditate on his wounds, reliving them like Jacopo del Cassero, who in Dante's *Purgatorio* remembers "i profondi fori / ond'uscì 'l sangue in sul quale ... sedea" (5.73–4; the deep wounds / that poured my blood out with my life). It may well be that the Shrouds are the wise souls of Limbo, who have "occhi tardi e gravi" (*Inf.* 4.112; grave and slow-moving eyes) and "grande autorità ne' lor sembianti" (*Inf.* 4.113; visages of great authority).[10] What is certain is that Dante has now penetrated to the very bones of Yeats. There are odd Dantean reminiscences in the poem: the eyes spying Cuchulain's arrival like the harpies' of *Inferno* 13 and their threading the needles' eyes "come l' vecchio sartor fa ne la cruna" (*Inf.* 15.21; like an old tailor at his needle's eye). But the most important thing is the singular appropriateness of the Dantean context. Yeats is indeed sewing here his own shroud in what Seamus Heaney has called "a strange ritual of surrender, a rite of passage from life to death, but a rite whose meaning is subsumed into song, into the otherness of art."[11] There also is another interesting coincidence, for if Yeats is preparing his descent among the shades, that is precisely where we will find him next, in another Dantean context and in another terza rima poem: T.S. Eliot's "Little Gidding."

***

Things change quite dramatically with James Joyce, who is truly obsessed by Dante throughout his life. His first book, *Dubliners*, for instance, is precisely framed by Dantean references. The first story, "Sisters," begins with an echo of the inscription over the gate of hell, "There was no hope," and the last one, "The Dead," ends with a vision of frozen Ireland, which metamorphoses Dante's Cocytus. Indeed, a Dantean design has been found in *Dubliners*, which covers the whole of hell, from the "ignavi" of "Eveline" to the traitors of "The Dead." Joyce's brother, Stanislaus, thought the arrangement of the collection "an obvious touch of parody on the *Divine Comedy*" and said that the three parts of the story "Grace" corresponded to the three *cantiche* of Dante's poem.[12]

In other words, from the very beginning Joyce struggled to appropriate the structure of the *Comedy* and, similar to what Eliot was to do in *The Waste Land*, adapt it to a depiction of modern life. In *A Portrait of the Artist as a Young Man* the attempt is, quite unexpectedly, different. Here we have a young Irish Catholic intellectual, a post-Romantic, Decadent, neo-Thomist, Stephen Dedalus growing up, seeking himself, and struggling to find his way as a poet, which is of course what Dante had done in the *Vita nuova*. The *Portrait* is a Bildungsroman, where Dante has a place that resembles Yeats's in "Ego Dominus Tuus."[13] The *Vita nuova* and the last cantos of *Paradiso* are now used by Joyce to frame Stephen's "epiphanies." The most momentous of the initial ones comes after Stephen, "arisen from the grave of boyhood," starts walking barefoot in the water off the Dollymount beach and suddenly sees a girl standing before him "in midstream, alone and still, gazing out to sea" (*Portrait*, 184–5).[14] Enraptured, he contemplates her body, then her image passes into his soul "for ever," no words breaking "the holy silence of his ecstasy" (186). It is a "wild angel ... the angel of mortal youth and beauty." Stephen turns landward, runs towards the shore, feels "above him the vast indifferent dome and the calm processes of the heavenly bodies," and the earth beneath him, which had "borne him" and "taken him to her breast," closes his eyes "in the languor of sleep," his soul "swooning into some new world, fantastic, dim, uncertain as under sea, traversed by cloudy shapes and beings." The epiphany is full:

> A world, a glimmer or a flower? Glimmering and trembling, trembling and unfolding, a breaking light, an opening flower, it spread in endless succession to itself, breaking in full crimson and unfolding and fading to palest rose, leaf by leaf and wave of light by wave of light, flooding all the heavens with its soft flushes, every flush deeper than the other. (187)

This is Joyce's equivalent of *Paradiso* 30.94–117, when Dante sees "li fiori e le faville" (the flowers and the sparks), the "grande lume" (light so large) and the "larghezza di questa rosa ne l'estreme foglie" (expanse containing the farthest petals of this rose).[15] But even *Paradiso* 33 finds an equivalent in the *Portrait*, when Stephen sees the whole world "forming one vast symmetrical expression of God's power and love" (161).[16] Later, Stephen's new epiphany, still revolving around his Beatrice, centres on inspiration. Here, Joyce is metamorphosing one of the key moments of *Vita nuova* 3, the very passage Yeats was concentrating upon at the same time:

> E pensando di lei mi sopragiunse uno soave sonno, ne lo quale m'apparve una maravigliosa visione, che me parea vedere ne la mia camera una nèbula di colore di fuoco, dentro a la quale io discernea una figura d'uno segnore di pauroso aspetto a chi la guardasse; e pareami con tanta letizia, quanto a sé, che mirabile cosa era; e ne le sue parole dicea molte cose, le quali io non intendea se non poche; tra le quali intendea queste: "Ego dominus tuus." ... E ne l'una de le mani mi parea che questi tenesse una cosa, la quale ardesse tutta; e pareami che mi dicesse queste parole: "Vide cor tuum" ... Pensando io a ciò che m'era apparuto, propuosi di farlo sentire a molti, li quali erano famosi trovatori in quello tempo: e con ciò fosse cosa che io avesse già veduto per me medesimo l'arte del dire parole per rima, propuosi di fare uno sonetto, ne lo quale io salutasse tutti li fedeli d'Amore; e pregandoli che giudicassero la mia visione, scrissi a loro ciò che io avea nel mio sonno veduto. E cominciai allora questo sonetto, lo quale comincia: *A ciascun'alma presa.* (*Vita nuova* 3.3–9)
>
> (Thinking of her, I fell into a sweet sleep, and a marvelous vision appeared to me. I seemed to see a cloud the color of fire and, in that cloud, a lordly man, to behold, yet he seemed also to be wondrously filled with joy. He spoke and said many things, of which I understood only a few; one was Ego dominus tuus. ... In one hand he seemed to be holding something that was all in flames, and it seemed to me that he said these words: Vide cor tuum ... Thinking about what I had seen, I decided to make it known to many of the famous poets of that time. Since just recently I had taught myself the art of writing poetry, I decided to compose a sonnet addressed to all of Love's faithful subjects; and, requesting them to interpret my vision, I would write them what I had seen in my sleep. And then I began to write this sonnet, which begins: To every captive soul.)

The imagery and the sequence are exactly the same in the *Portrait*, where Stephen, awakening in the morning, thinks back on the "enchanted night," when "in a dream or vision," he "had known the ecstasy of seraphic life"(235). For good measure, Joyce adds a reference to the prologue of John's Gospel, to the Annunciation and holy Conception of God's Son, and finally, once more, to the mystical rose of Dante's Empyrean:

> The instant of inspiration seemed now to be reflected from all sides at once from a multitude of cloudy circumstances of what had happened or of what might have happened. The instant flashed forth like a point of light

> and now from cloud on cloud of vague circumstance confused form was veiling softly its afterglow. O! In the virgin womb of the imagination the word was made flesh. Gabriel the seraph had come to the virgin's chamber. An afterglow deepened within his spirit, whence the white flame had passed, deepening to a rose and ardent light. That rose and ardent light was her strange wilful heart, strange that no man had known or would know, wilful from before the beginning of the world: and lured by that ardent rose-like glow the choirs of the seraphim were falling from heaven. (235–6)

Finally, still reclining on his bed, Stephen writes out a villanelle on "the rough cardboard surface" of a cigarette packet (237). "He had written verses for her again after ten years ... Ten years from that wisdom of children to this folly" (241).

But Joyce is not Yeats. On the very last page of the *Portrait*, just before Stephen goes off to Paris in the name of the "old father, old artificer," the mythical Greek artist Daedalus, "to encounter for the millionth time the reality of experience and to forge in the smithy of [his] soul the uncreated conscience of [his] race," he notes in his diary that he has just met the girl again "pointblank" in Grafton Street (275). Dante's *Vita nuova* is now fully evoked, but with a sardonic irony that completely destroys its "body-denying platonic love":[17]

> April 15. Met her today pointblank in Grafton Street. The crowd brought us together. We both stopped. She asked me why I never came, said she had heard all sorts of stories about me. This was only to gain time. Asked me, was I writing poems? About whom? I asked her. This confused her more and I felt sorry and mean. Turned off that valve at once and opened the spiritual-heroic refrigerating apparatus, invented and patented in all countries by Dante Alighieri. Talked rapidly of myself and my plans. In the midst of it unluckily I made a sudden gesture of a revolutionary nature. I must have looked like a fellow throwing a handful of peas into the air. People began to look at us. She shook hands a moment after and, in going away, said she hoped I would do what I said. (274–5)

Stephen has returned from Paris in Joyce's next book, *Ulysses*, his mind now imbued with Dante. In section VII, "Aeolus," for instance, he reminisces on "Rhymes and Reasons," and sees them at first as "two men dressed the same looking the same, two by two." "La tua pace ... che parlar ti piace … mentre che il vento, come fa, si tace," his memory recites from *Inferno* 5. Then, remembering *Inferno* 5, *Paradiso* 31, and finally *Purgatorio* 29, he sees rhymes in *terzina*-like succession, "three by three, approaching girls, in green, in rose, in russet, entwining, *per l'aer perso* in mauve, in purple, *quella pacifica oriafiamma*, in gold of oriflamme, *di rimirar fé più ardenti*. But I old men, penitent, leadenfooted, underdarkneath the night: mouth south: tomb womb" (133).[18]

Quotations and misquotations from Dante fill *Ulysses*; there is even some ground for thinking that the most elusive, ever-recurring character in the book, Macintosh, "that lankylooking galoot," might be Dante himself. What counts, however, is the overall para-Dantean texture of *Ulysses*. My impression of Joyce's endeavour in *Ulysses*, ever since I read it for the first time forty years ago, is that Joyce was quite deliberately trying to rewrite the *Odyssey* in the shape and with the scope and ambition of a *Divine Comedy*. Years after the publication of *Ulysses*, Joyce seemed to obliquely confirm this. He recalled his work on the book during the First World War years and said: "Ah, how wonderful that was to get up in the morning … and enter the misty regions of my emerging epic, as Dante once entered his selva oscura selva selvaggia. Words crackled in my head and a multitude of images crowded around, like those shades at the entrance to the Underworld when Ulysses stood there awaiting the spirit of Tiresias."[19]

The structure of *Ulysses* is decidedly Homeric, with one exception to which I will return presently. But Joyce stuffed that structure with an encyclopedia-like spirit most certainly derived from Dante's *Comedy*. There is an immense range of coherent references to history, metaphysics, science, music, aesthetic literary and language theory, classical and biblical myth, and liturgy, which turn this so-called "novel" into what Franco Moretti has called an "opera-mondo."[20] In this context, the third general section of *Ulysses*, the one Joyce called "Nostos" in his Gilbert and Linati schemata, comes closest to Dante's poem. The shade that emerges here is none less than Dante's Ulysses, a figure otherwise left outside Joyce's Homeric epic. The shade surfaces first in "Eumaeus," in the speech of the red-haired, drunk, soi-disant sailor, W.B. Murphy. Murphy starts telling Stephen and Bloom the most fantastic adventures.[21] Trying to stop him, Bloom asks him if he has ever seen the Rock of Gibraltar, a place of personal interest to him. The man grimaces, chewing, "in a way that might be read as yes, ay, or no"; then, when Bloom asks what year that would be and if he can recall the boats, the drunkard munches heavily and replies: "I'm tired of all them rocks in the sea … and boats and ships. Salt junk all the time" (585). At this point Bloom, "perceiving that he [is] not likely to get a great deal of change out of such a wily old customer," falls, Joyce writes, "to woolgathering on the enormous dimensions of the water about the globe. Suffice it to say that, as a casual glance at the map revealed, it covered fully three fourths of it and he fully realised accordingly what it meant, to rule the waves" (585). Having thus paid his respects to the British Empire ("Britannia rules the waves"), Bloom recalls having more than once noticed, at Dollymount, on the northern side of Dublin Bay, "a superannuated old salt, evidently derelict, seated habitually near the not particularly redolent sea on the wall, staring quite obliviously at it and it at him, dreaming of fresh woods and pastures new as someone somewhere sings" (585). The quotation from Milton's "Lycidas" must not lead us astray.[22] The old salt is clearly dreaming of the "nova terra" (*Inf.* 26.137) sighted by Dante's Ulysses. Bloom has often wondered why the man should contemplate the ocean with such intensity and dream of new worlds. He has repeatedly mused that "possibly" the old salt

> had tried to find out the secret for himself, floundering up and down the antipodes and all that sort of thing and over and under – well, not exactly under, tempting the fates. And the odds were twenty to nil there was really no secret about it at all. Nevertheless, without going into the minutiae of the business, the eloquent fact remained that the sea was there in all its glory and in the natural course of things somebody or other had to sail on it and fly in the face of providence though it merely went to show how people usually contrived to load that sort of onus on to the other fellow like the hell idea and the lottery and insurance, which were run on identically the same lines. (585)

The shade of Dante's Ulysses has taken its side next to that of Homer's Odysseus – indirectly and obliquely, as befits Joyce's "order and myth" method.[23] Clearly Bloom thinks the old salt might have tried to discover the "secret" beyond the Pillars of Hercules, "floundering up and down the antipodes" and "tempting the fates." However, Bloom is no Romantic. He believes there really is no secret and "in the natural course of things" someone was bound to sail over that glorious sea and "fly in the face of providence." Joyce manages to combine the "folle volo" (*Inf.* 26.125) with the notion of the hubris against God it implies and with the hell into which Dante's Ulysses was thrown after the shipwreck.

Yet the next time we meet the same shade, it is actually tempting Leopold Bloom himself. Here, we are in the penultimate section of *Ulysses*, "Ithaca." Bloom has finally returned home and recognizes in Stephen Dedalus his own Telemachus; he is also about to join his Penelope, the unfaithfully faithful Molly, in their marriage bed. Bloom is glancing with horror at his forthcoming senescence, to which he imagines two alternatives: decease or departure. He opts, of course, for the latter, as the "line of least resistance" (678). He then sets off on a mental journey, which takes in first the whole of Ireland, then with planetary extensions towards a number of significant places: Ceylon, Jerusalem, the Straits of Gibraltar, the Parthenon, Wall Street, the Plaza de Toros at La Linea in Spain, Niagara, the land of the Eskimos, "the forbidden country of Tibet" ("from which no traveller returns"), the Bay of Naples ("to see which is to die"), and the Dead Sea (670). Bloom here takes on the universal binomial denominator of being and nonbeing, Everyman and Noman, travelling on and on:

> Ever he would wander, selfcompelled, to the extreme limit of his cometary orbit, beyond the fixed stars and variable suns and telescopic planets, astronomical waifs and strays, to the extreme boundaries of space, passing from land to land, among peoples, amid events. Somewhere imperceptibly he would hear and somehow reluctantly, suncompelled, obey the summons of recall. Whence, disappearing from the constellation of the Northern Crown he would somehow reappear reborn above delta in the constellation of Cassiopeia and after incalculable eons of peregrination return an estranged avenger, a wreaker of justice on malefactors, a dark crusader, a sleeper awakened, with financial resources (by supposition) surpassing those of Rothschild or the silver king. (680)

Shortly afterwards, however, Joyce's Homeric mind decides that Bloom's journey is out of the question: it would be an irrational return, governed by an "unsatisfactory equation between an exodus and return in time through reversible space and an exodus and return in space through irreversible time" (680). But as a departure, too, it is undesirable, given the late hour, the darkness, the dangers, the need to rest, and above all given the proximity of an occupied bed, the "anticipation of warmth (human) tempered with coolness (linen) obviating desire and rendering desirable: the statue of Narcissus, sound without echo, desired desire" (680).

Here, we note what this astonishing twentieth-century Homer-cum-Dante is doing with the myth: Bloom-Ulysses, old (as he thinks) and terrified by old age, wishes to return home and to "push off" like Tennyson's Ulysses. Like Dante, he yearns to sail towards the Pillars of Hercules, to visit the places of death (Tibet, defined by Hamlet's tag; Naples, identified by the popular saying; the Dead Sea, a name itself eloquent). Both Everyman and Noman, he wants to journey further and wander beyond stars, to the utmost bounds of space, "passing from land to land" like Coleridge's Ancient Mariner, but *among* peoples, *amid* events – in history – and to return, finally, like Odysseus, like a crusader, like the Count of Montecristo.

Nocturnal wanderings towards death, beyond boundaries: like the wanderings of Dante's Ulysses. A biblical exodus, too (Bloom would be following a "pillar of cloud"), and mystic flight: transformation into comet, ascent beyond the fixed stars, Ascension to the Empyrean, rebirth and messianic advent. A journey through history and through peoples; Homeric *nostos* and revenge à la Dumas. In one page Joyce moves backwards through what I have elsewhere called the "shadows" of Ulysses,[24] himself projecting new ones to create his own Ulyssean myth, simultaneously a universal symbol of Everyman and Noman.

Dante's Ulysses, the archetype of all centrifugal heroes of Western literature and history, offered Joyce the possibility of reaffirming, on the contrary, his opposite, centripetal, Homeric choice: a return home and to Penelope. Thus, even though "Ithaca" contains other significant Dantean allusions, it is fitting that *Ulysses* should end at the Pillars of Hercules. There Marion (Molly) Bloom, née Tweedy, was born and said yes to her first suitor, and there she returns with her memory in the last section of the book, "Penelope." In the same episode, she superimposes on Gibraltar Howth Head, the promontory on the north side of Dublin Bay, where she accepted Leopold Bloom's proposal. The very last Dantean echo in the novel, of the "candida rosa" (white rose) of *Paradiso* 31, is heard in Molly's climactic stream of consciousness as she asks herself, "Shall I wear a white rose" (731). But on the last page of *Ulysses,* Molly evokes Gibraltar with the same nostalgia Dante feels in describing his final vision, and there Molly's question is picked up and completed: "or shall I wear a red." There is a sense in which the concluding "Yes" of *Ulysses* signals acceptance of others, of life, and of the universe in the same fashion as Dante's desire and will are moved, at the end, by the love that sets in motion the sun and the other stars. Molly begins – if that is the word – by celebrating nature, Creation, and God (731), that is, by looking both at the volume in which all is conflated and at "ciò che per l'universo si squaderna" (*Par.* 33.87; the pages scattered through the universe); she then moves on to Howth Head and the way she got Bloom to propose, and to his understanding of women. Finally, she leaps onto the Rock of Gibraltar and then passes on to the governor's house and the Spanish girls "laughing in their shawls," and "the Greeks and the jews and the Arabs and the devil knows who else from all the ends of Europe," the old castle, the handsome Moors, Ronda "with the old windows of the posadas," the night "we missed the boat at Algeciras the watchman going about serene with his lamp" (732). These are the "accidenti e lor costume" (*Par.* 33) of Dante's vision. But in the end come the "sustanze" (the substances): sensuous and immanent, yet framed by a crimson sea, which recalls Dante's light glowing tawny in *Paradiso* 31. It is the sea Ulysses crossed when he decided to sail beyond the sun. It is now the sea that envelops in its reddish halo Molly transfigured into a Flower of the Mountain and her first lovemaking, the ultimate ecstasy of *Ulysses*:

> O and the sea the sea crimson sometimes like fire and the glorious sunsets and the figtrees in the Alameda gardens yes and all the queer little streets and pink and blue and yellow houses and the rosegardens and the jessamine and geraniums and cactuses and Gibraltar as a girl where I was a Flower of the mountain yes when I put the rose in my hair like the Andalusian girls used or shall I wear a red yes and how he kissed me under the Moorish wall and I thought well as well him as another and then I asked him with my eyes to ask again yes and then he asked me would I yes to say yes my mountain flower and first I put my arms around him yes and drew him down to me so he could feel my breasts all perfume yes and his heart was going like mad and yes I said yes I will Yes. (732)

With *Finnegans Wake* we enter a different dimension. On 9 February 1938, Joyce wrote to Ezra Pound apropos of the *Work in Progress* (later, *Finnegans Wake*) he was completing: "I don't think I ever worked so hard even at *Ulysses*. Galeotto è il libro e chi lo scrive."[25] The use of the expression from Francesca's story in *Inferno* 5 is interesting here. Joyce knew quite well, of course, that what Dante meant was that the book of *Lancelot* and its author had the same function in bringing together

Paolo and Francesca, and indeed in making him kiss her, as Galehaut had had between Lancelot and Guinevere. He is using Dante's line to tell Pound that writing *Work in Progress* is an act of intermediation between literature and life, an act whereby literature prompts love and lust for itself. But another meaning is also conveyed by the word *galeotto*, that of prisoner. The writer of *Finnegans Wake* feels he and his opus have been captives, galley slaves, convicts.

The double-edged quality of this declaration is typical of the way Joyce dealt with Dante in *Finnegans Wake*. Later, he did in fact proclaim: "May Father Dante forgive me, but I started from this technique of deformation to achieve a harmony that defeats our intelligence, as music does."[26] Metamorphosis and distortion are the characteristics of his operation. In the *Wake*, he goes beyond *Ulysses*. He does not just imitate Dantean expressions, images, and scenes, as Pound and Eliot were doing; he mirrors and deforms – as Lucia Boldrini has shown – Dante's poetics and linguistic theory. Beyond the "anxiety of influence" that Dante has undoubtedly produced in Joyce, a continuous dialogue is established between the two authors. For instance, Dante elaborates in the *Convivio*, and then again in the *Epistle to Cangrande*,[27] a theory of allegory, the method of interpretation which is founded upon the "polysemos," the stratification of the four literal, allegorical, moral, and anagogical meanings. In *Finnegans Wake*, Joyce invokes "spreading in quadriliberal their azurespotted fine attractable nets" (477:21)[28] and maintains the possibility that every word "will be bound over to carry three score and ten toptypsical readings" (20:14–5). He works by layers, piling different and often contrasting meanings on each single expression, name, scene, narrative sequence. The adjective "toptypsical," which is employed in this passage is modelled on "top secret" and contains "top" (but also its opposite "topsy-turvy"), besides "optical," "typical" (and probably "typological"), "psychical," "physical," and perhaps even "phthisical" (i.e., subject to tuberculosis). "If you can spot fifty," Joyce adds, "I spy four more" (10:31). Perhaps, indeed, Dante's four! However, his purpose is basically different from Dante's. Dante's four meanings aim at giving a significant and ascending order to human experience. Joyce's "polysemos" is the fruit of "inclusion" and its end is disorder.[29]

That is why Joyce picks up the circular pattern of hell, purgatory, and paradise but turns it into a circular structure and frame of mind, relying, as Samuel Beckett was the first to point out, on Bruno and Vico.

That is also why, as Beckett once more remarked, Joyce's *Work in Progress* is basically purgatorial:

> Sin is an impediment to movement up the cone, and a condition of movement round the sphere. In what sense, then, is Mr Joyce's work purgatorial? In the absolute absence of the Absolute. Hell is the static lifelessness of unrelieved viciousness. Paradise the static lifelessness of unrelieved immaculation. Purgatory a flood of movement and vitality released by the conjunction of these two elements.[30]

Joyce's reading of Dante in *Finnegans Wake* is, therefore, a "raiding" whose model is Dante himself. "The prouts who will invent a writing there," he says, "ultimately is the poeta, still more learned, who discovered the raiding there originally" (482:31–2). This explains why Dante appears on many pages with many different names subjected to irony, parody, and distortion. He is first and foremost one of the three-persons-in-one Trinity that Joyce would undoubtedly like to turn into a cross by including himself – Dante, Shakespeare, Goethe: "Which goatheye and sheepskeer they damnty well know" (344:5); "that primed favourite continental poet, Daunty, Gouty, and Shopkeeper" (539:5). But he also is a multitude of poetic personas and opuses which all together incarnate Joyce's obsessive passion for the Florentine poet: "Seudodanto" (47:19); "And daunt you logh if his vineshanky's schwemmy" (229:4), "Aleguerre comme alaguerre" (233:30; Alighieri); "So as to be very dainty, if an isaspell, and so as to be verily dandy-dainty, if an ishibilley" (238:2–4); "Daintytrees, go dutch!"(244:2); "turning up and fingering over the most dantellising peaches in the lingerous longerous book of the dark. Look at this passage about Galilleotto!"(251:23–4); "Undante umoroso" (269:1); "a daintical pair of accomplasses" (295:27); "Donn Teague and Hurleg" (337:30); "Smirky Dainty" (360:8); "Skim over *Through Hell with the Papes* (mostly boys) by the divine comic Denti Alligator" (440:5–7); "the tail, so mastrodantic, as you tell it" (510:3).

This is of course quite different from Yeats's "chief imagination of Christendom" and Stephen Dedalus's early *Vita nuova*-like epiphanies. It is in a sense the (almost) inevitable conclusion in language games of Stephen's own "spiritual-heroic refrigerating apparatus, invented and patented in all countries by Dante Alighieri" at the *Portrait*'s end. It offers us an image of Dante as "divine comic," as the supreme "Alligator" with "mastrodantic tail" who keeps his jaws wide open to swallow the entire world and munch it with his immense "denti," his fangs. But I have the impression that it is James Joyce himself, now, who identifies with Denti Alligator. At one point in the first episode of *Finnegans Wake*'s book 3, Shaun proclaims:

> *My trifolium librotto*, the authordux Book of Lief, would, if given to daylight, (I hold a most incredible faith about it) far exceed what that bogus bolshy of a shame, my soamheis brother, Gaoy Fecks, is conversant with in audible black and prink. Outragedy of poetscalds! *Acomedy of letters!* I have them all, tame, deep and harried, in my mine's I. (425:20–5; italics mine)

No question about the identity of the "trifolium librotto," the Book of Life written by the "orthodox" "author" and "dux" Dante: it is – "outragedy of poetscalds!" – "Acomedy of letters," the acomical, letter-ridden *Comedy*. But Shaun has appropriated it (against his brother Shem, the artist) with "a most incredible faith." It is now his, and he has all its "letters," "tame, deep, and harried," in his "mine's I." Sixty pages later, Joyce is still musing about Dante and calls him "the poeta, still more learned, who discovered the raiding there originally" (482:32–3). But shortly afterwards the scope of his personal ambition is revealed as fully as a hermetic book will allow. The oblique reference here is to the "sesto tra cotanto senno" (sixth amidst such wisdom) Dante uses to proclaim himself the only true *poeta* after the great classical ones in *Inferno* 4.102:

> What I (the person whomin I now am) did not do, how he to say essied anding how he was making errand andanding how he all locutey sunt, why did you, *my sexth best friend*, blabber always you would be so delated to back me, then *ersed irredent*, toppling Humphrey hugging Nephew, old beggelaut, designing such post sitting his night office? (484:5–10; italics mine)

A fucking irredentist, I would translate, but also an unredeemed asshole, an unsaved Irishman, and finally "Irish Dante." That is the title Joyce is now claiming for himself. Perhaps the last page of *Finnegans Wake* bears it out as in her final monologue Anna Livia Plurabelle evokes the leaves that have drifted from her, a pale shadow of the Sibyl's oracle lost in the wind, on the light leaves, in *Paradiso* 33 (628:6).

***

Samuel Beckett is reported as having said quite early on in his life: "All I want to do is sit on my arse and fart and think about Dante." I do not know how much of the two former occupations he pursued, but he was certainly, and constantly, engaged in the third during his entire career after what he called "the Dante revelation" in his early twenties.[31] Having completed his studies in French, Italian, and English at Trinity College, Dublin, and when he was *lecteur d'anglais* at the École Normale in Paris, Beckett worked for Joyce. He was of course already familiar with Dante, but Joyce's obsession must have worked on him. A poem of 1931, "Text," shows this quite clearly. Its concluding fifteen lines are a rewriting of *Inferno* 3, in a composition where the two central characters, Job and Tiresias, pronounce a miserere for the punishments they suffer. Beckett's Tiresias comes from *Inferno* 20, and one line towards the end of "Text," "pity is quick with death," contains the unmistakable echo of "qui vive la pieta quand'è ben morta" (Here piety lives when pity is quite dead) of *Inferno* 20. But halfway through the poem, Beckett writes:

> Shall I cease to lament
> Being not as the flashsneezing
> Non-suppliant airtight alligator?
> Not so but perhaps
> At the sight and the sound of
> A screechy flatfooted Tuscany peacock's
> Strauss fandango and recitative
> Not forgetting
> He stinks eternal.[32]

Dante shows up first as the Alligator, one of Alighieri's personas in Joyce's *Work in Progress*, then as a peacock, the way he appeared in a dream, according to Boccaccio's *Trattatello*, to his own mother before he was born.[33] Beckett combines Joyce's inspiration with his own knowledge of Italian literature. In 1934, in a review of Papini's *Dante*, Beckett humorously remarked: "Who wants to love Dante? We want to READ

Dante – for example, his imperishable reference (Paolo-Francesca episode) to the incompatibility of the two operations."[34] In sum, there is no doubt that – with and without Joyce – he was thinking about the Tuscan peacock all the time.

In his 1929 article, "Dante ... Bruno. Vico ... Joyce," Beckett identifies purgatory as Joyce's dimension.[35] This is also the realm which he chooses for himself, not only "in the absolute absence of the Absolute," but also in what he calls the "flux" – "progression or retrogression, and an apparent consummation" – and the "movement," "non-directional" or "multi-directional," where "a step forward is, by definition, a step back."[36] Beckett's objective correlative for all this, the character from the *Comedy* who obsessively incarnates not so much the "flood of movement" as the "static lifelessness," is Belacqua. His posture,[37] his *negligenza* and laziness, his skeptical attitude towards the climbing of Mount Purgatory,[38] recur in nearly all of Beckett's prose works[39] and even in that modern, or postmodern, myth, *Waiting for Godot*.[40] Most memorably, and most indirectly, of course, it recurs in *Dream of Fair to Middling Women* and in "Dante and the Lobster," the first story of *More Pricks than Kicks* (itself extrapolated from the then unpublished *Dream*), where Belacqua is reincarnated as Belacqua Shuah, a Dublin student of Italian and of Dante, who muses on *Paradiso* 2:

> It was morning and Belacqua was stuck in the first of the canti in the moon. He was so bogged that he could move neither backward nor forward. Blissful Beatrice was there, Dante also, and she explained the spots on the moon to him. She shewed him in the first place where he was at fault, then she put up her own explanation. She had it from God, therefore he could rely on its being accurate in every particular. All he had to do was to follow her step by step. Part one, the refutation, was plain sailing. She made her point clearly, she said what she had to say without fuss or loss of time. But part two, the demonstration, was so dense that Belacqua could not make head or tail of it. The disproof, the reproof, that was patent. But then came the proof, a rapid shorthand of the real facts, and Belacqua was bogged indeed. Bored also, impatient to get on to Piccarda.[41]

Beckett's knowledge of Dante already is quite detailed and possibly more advanced than Joyce's. In *Dream*, for instance, he clearly echoes both Benvenuto's and the Anonimo Fiorentino's comments on *Purgatorio* 4 as quoted by Paget Toynbee in his *Dictionary*.[42] Like Joyce, however, Beckett is metamorphosing Dante. His Belacqua is not simply a lazy, relaxed character but rather a multifaceted modern version of the

Dantean figure, not unlike the way in which T.S. Eliot's Prufrock is a modern reincarnation of Hamlet. On the existential and metaphysical level, Belacqua stands for sloth, melancholy, self-enclosure, indefinite waiting, and ever-procrastinating delay. In "Dante and the Lobster," for example, he cannot bring himself to throwing the lobster alive into the pot but limits himself to thinking: "Well, … it's a quick death, God help us all." To which either he or the narrator adds the dreadful ending: "It is not."[43]

In Beckett's imagination, all other Dantean characters – Virgil, Beatrice, Sordello, Tiresias – succumb to Belacqua. In the last story of *More Pricks than Kicks*, "Draff," the Belacqua posture wins over both Malacoda's "six cylinder hearse" and Ulysses's black "cruiser."[44] In fact, Dante's Ulysses is for Beckett, together with Dante himself as character, Belacqua's constant antagonist. In *Molloy*, for instance, Ulysses appears together with the seventeenth-century Dutch philosopher Arnold Geulinx, one of the foremost exponents of Occasionalism:

> I who had loved the image of old Geulinx, dead young, who left me free, on the black boat of Ulysses, to crawl towards the East, along the deck. That is a great measure of freedom, for him who has not the pioneering spirit. And from the poop, poring upon the wave, a sadly rejoicing slave, I follow with my eyes the proud and futile wave. Which, as it bears me from no fatherland away, bears me onward to no shipwreck.[45]

The ferocious irony of this passage – which in going East reverses the strong western movement of *Inferno* 26 and denies both the flight from home and the final shipwreck – explodes the story of Dante's Ulysses. In *The Unnamable*, the very same operation is performed on Ulysses by Belacqua. This time, the focus is the uncertain "I" of the narrative. Belacqua comes first, with his posture:

> I, of whom I know nothing. I know my eyes are open, because of the tears that pour from them unceasingly. I know I am seated, my hands on my knees, because of the pressure against my rump, against the soles of my feet, against the palms of my hands, against my knees. (Against my palms the pressure is of my knees, against my knees of my palms. But what is it that presses against my rump, against the soles of my feet? I don't know.)[46]

There is absolutely nothing Ulysses can do against this. His is pure gnoseological madness (not, it will be noted, ethical foolhardiness):

> "I." Who might that be? The galley-man, bound for the Pillars of Hercules, who drops his sweep under cover of night and crawls between the thwarts, towards the rising sun, unseen by the guard, praying for storm? Except that I've stopped praying for anything. (No, no, I'm still a suppliant. I'll get over it, between now and the last voyage, on this leaden sea. It's like the other madness, the mad wish to know, to remember, one's transgressions.) I won't be caught at that again, I'll leave it to this year's damned.[47]

Molloy follows in Leopold Bloom's wake but, so to speak, in Belacqua's spirit of delaying things. He will "get over" Ulysses's enterprise between now and that last voyage, which is but death, but he will "leave" "the other madness" "to this year's damned."

At times, reading Beckett is excruciating. A step forward always leads you a step back, as he said of Joyce's purgatorial movement. In *Textes pour rien*, for instance, we find ourselves confronted with the familiar Belacqua posture rather early on.[48] Then, much later, we encounter a passage that comes as a surprise:

> Et je suis tranquille, j'y irais, à l'issue, tôt ou tard, si je la disais là, quelque part, les autres mots me viendraient, tôt ou tard, et de quoi pouvoir y aller, et y aller, et passer à travers, et voir les belles choses que porte le ciel, et revoir les étoiles.
>
> (And I have no doubts, I'd get there somehow, to the way out, sooner or later, if I could say, there's a way out there, there's a way out somewhere, the rest would come, the other words, sooner or later, and the power to get there, and the way to get there, and first word after the article, in a title, is capitalized out, and see the beauties of the skies, and see the stars again.) [49]

There is no doubt, in spite of the uncertainty with which this sentence is laden, that it contains some kind of hope, as its allusion to the last lines of *Inferno* indicates, the "cose belle che porta 'l ciel" and the "stelle" (*Inf.* 34.137–9) being glimpsed at now. Yet we have to remember that the round hole through which Dante looks again at the night sky leads him but to purgatory, which is where, with Joyce and Beckett, we have always been. The sequence is exactly the same over ten years later in *Le Dépeupleur*, which opens with Dante's smile at Belacqua and then goes on to evoke none less than the last line of the *Comedy*: "Les autres rêvent d'une trappe dissimulée au centre du plafond donnant accès à une cheminée au bout de laquelle brilleraient encore le soleil et les autres étoiles"(The others dream of a trapdoor hidden at the centre of the ceiling giving access to a passage at the end of which the sun and the other stars would still shine).[50] But the trap that should give access to a path at the end of which the sun and the other stars would shine forth is a mere dream. And besides, as Corinna Lonergan noted apropos of *Endgame*, "There are no stars."[51] Or perhaps, as Molloy would put it, "And don't come talking at me of the stars, they look all the same to me, yes, I cannot read the stars, in spite of my astronomical studies."[52]

One wonders why Samuel Beckett kept a copy of Dante at hand on what was to be his deathbed.

***

For Yeats, Joyce, and Beckett, Dante seems to speak on the personal level and as a great model of poetry. Seamus Heaney's dialogue with the Italian poet, while clearly following the example of these earlier Irish ancestors, aims from the very beginning at establishing parallels between several Dantean passages and the contemporary Irish context. Thus, it is with him that Dante more fully becomes Irish. At the same time, Heaney places Dante within a tradition which is both Irish and English. His translations and adaptations of Dante, of course, have been an ongoing commitment. As a translator, he is drawn especially to capturing the sound of Dante. As he said, this was Mandelstam's great lesson:

> What Mandelstam does ... is to bring [Dante] from the pantheon back to the palate; he makes our mouth water to read him. He possesses the poem as a musician possesses the score, both as a whole structure and as a sequence of delicious sounds. He transmits a fever of excitement in the actual phonetic reality of the work and shares with us the sensation of his poet's delight turning into a sort of giddy critical wisdom ... His Dante is a voluble Shakespearean figure, a woodcutter singing at his work in the dark wood of the larynx.[53]

One can see how Heaney feels the same "fever of excitement in the actual phonetic reality" in the Ugolino version, which is as much a translation as a rewriting of the episode in *Inferno* 32–3. He has to render an incredibly compact, tight, conversational Italian in modern English, an enterprise already tackled, with great success, by T.S. Eliot. Thus, every now and then he adds expressions which are not in the original and changes the syntactic sequence in order to convey the meaning that would otherwise be obscure to an English-speaking audience.

Consider, for instance, the presentation of the two sinners, Ugolino and Ruggieri, at the end of *Inferno* 32:

> Noi eravam partiti già da ello,
> ch'io vidi due ghiacciati in una buca,
> sì che l'un capo a l'altro era cappello;
> e come 'l pan per fame si manduca,
> così 'l sovran li denti a l'altro pose
> là 've 'l cervel s'aggiugne con la nuca:
> non altrimenti Tidëo si rose
> le tempie a Menalippo per disdegno,
> che quei faceva il teschio e l'altre cose. (*Inf.* 32.124–32)

> We had already left him. I walked the ice
> And saw two soldered in a frozen hole
> On top of other, one's skull capping the other's,
> Gnawing at him where the neck and head
> Are grafted to the sweet fruit of the brain,
> Like a famine victim at a loaf of bread.
> So the berserk Tydeus gnashed and fed
> Upon the severed head of Menalippus
> As if it were some spattered carnal melon.[54]

Together with the absence of terza rima, what is immediately noticeable here are the additions. There is no "famine victim," no "severed head," above all no "spattered carnal melon" in Dante. The first of these details, of course, brings the passage into an Irish context. The second is indebted to Statius,[55] from whom Dante himself had drawn his picture. But the third is Heaney's own invention, the "spattered carnal melon" nicely (if that is the word) complementing the earlier "sweet fruit of the brain" and "loaf of bread." One need not wonder why the poet turned, later in his career, to *The Burial at Thebes*.[56]

Heaney's technique is also apparent in Ugolino's speech in *Inferno* 33. In the original, Ugolino evokes the "disperato dolor che 'l cor mi preme" (5) and promises words that "esser dien seme / che frutti infamia al traditor ch'i' rodo," so that Dante will see "parlare e lagrimar … insieme"

(7–9). That unbelievably tight *terzina*, a true concentration, with its *r*'s and *d*'s and *s*'s, of "rime aspre e chiocce," is an almost impossible task for any English translator. Heaney dilutes it, but keeps the harsh and grating sounds and adds to the rhetorical pattern of the original an echo of the Book of Genesis:

> Then said, "Even before I speak
> The thought of having to relive all that
> Desperate time makes my heart sick;
> Yet while I weep to say them, I would sow
> My words like curses – that they might increase
> And multiply upon this head I gnaw.[57]

The climax comes at the end of Ugolino's story, with the famous "poscia, più che 'l dolor, poté 'l digiuno" (*Inf.* 33.75). In the English poetic tradition there exist two extremes, so to speak, in this line's re-creation. The first is Chaucer's, where all ambiguity has been eliminated: "Hymself, despeired, eek for hunger starf."[58] The second is Medwin's and Shelley's, which keeps the ambiguity on a kind of abstract level: "Famine of grief can get the mastery."[59] Heaney is much closer to the power of the original than either and maintains the ambiguity within the same turn of phrase: "Then hunger killed where grief had only wounded."[60] A memorable, lapidary conclusion.

Recently, Heaney has declared that, as "the creative act is witnessed by history, and the writer writes to be read," he translated Ugolino "in order for it to be read in the context of the 'dirty protests' in the Maze prison."[61] *Inferno* 33, and in fact the whole of the *Comedy*'s first two *cantiche*, were a spur to try and set the sectarian strife of Ireland into a historical and at once very urgently personal perspective. "Station Island" is first and foremost in this respect.[62] When one reads station 7 of that poem and encounters the shade of William Strathearn, a Catholic grocer who was killed at night in his shop by two off-duty Royal Ulster Constabulary men, one immediately realizes what this means. The section is written in terza rima. Heaney's old rugby mate appears, "his brow / … blown open above the eye," "blood / dried on his neck and cheek" (77–80). The reminiscence of Manfredi's "l'un de' cigli un colpo avea diviso" (*Purg.* 3.108; A blow had cleft one of his eyebrows) is quite clear. The ghost continues without any transition, precisely like many characters in the *Comedy*:

"Easy now,"
he said, "it's only me. You've seen men as raw
after a football match … What time it was
when I was waken up I still don't know
but I heard this knocking, knocking, and it
scared me, like the phone in the small hours,
so I had the sense not to put on the light …" (77)

The rest of the episode is as taut, direct, and yet at the key moments oblique, as any Dantean narrative. The men continue knocking on the door, shouting, "Shop!" The grocer's wife cries and starts rolling round the bed, "lamenting and lamenting to herself." Strathearn gets up and puts on his shoes and a sportscoat, tells the men to "quieten the racket," and asks them what they want. They reply: "There's a child not well. / Open up and see what you have got." He turns on the light, reaches and squeezes his wife's hand across the bed before going downstairs. Suddenly, he stands in the aisle of the shop, "going weak / in the legs." He remembers, now, "the stale smell / of cooked meat or something." "From then on," he concludes with a typically Dantean "colpo di glottide,"[63] "you know as much about it as I do." "Che … io fossi preso / e poscia morto," Ugolino had said, "dir non è mestieri" (*Inf.* 33.16–18; That I was captured and then killed, it is not necessary to say). What the murdered northern Ireland grocer tells Heaney is what he, like Dante, cannot have heard. The immediacy of the story, which gives the impression (like so many of Dante's) of a piece of newspaper report, of *cronaca nera*, is strengthened by the short conversation that ensues, with Heaney asking for more details ("Did they say nothing? … Were they in uniform? Not masked in any way?") and the shade replying ("They were barefaced as they would be in the day, / shites thinking they were the be-all and the end-all"). The protagonist then reveals to his old friend that the two were caught and got jail.

The scene thus draws together a complex network of Dantesque moments. At the same time, other influences begin to emerge. The dead grocer points out that his interlocutor has put on weight, but Seamus the poet[64] remarks that "through life and death he had hardly aged" – the "perfect, clean, unthinkable victim." This prompts him to ask for forgiveness, perhaps the most un-Dantean feature of the present purgatory:[65] "Forgive the way I have lived indifferent," Seamus tells the man who was killed for being a Catholic, "forgive my timid circumspect involvement." "Forgive my eye," the ghost replies, dismissing politics and sectarianism from his other bank and shoal of time, "all that's above my head." Finally, "And then a stun of pain seemed to go through him / And he trembled like a heatwave and faded" (80). The way in which the shade disappears – in which all shades disappear in "Station Island" – is most Dantesque. But Dante is clearly mediated here, as Heaney himself admits,[66] by T.S. Eliot's memorable "and faded on the blowing of the horn" in "Little Gidding." As a whole, "Station Island" recounts, in twelve "stations," the poet's pilgrimage to St Patrick's Purgatory in the middle of Lough Derg. It is a *Purgatorio*, rather than a *Comedy*, even though it contains infernal episodes and paradise-like prefigurations.[67] It is a "poem-cycle" in which "the three-part Dantean journey scaled down into the three-day station, no hell, no paradise, just 'Patrick's Purgatory,' which is how the place is known to this day."[68] In this sense, and in spite of the pilgrimage frame, "Station Island" confirms the choice of purgatorial dimension that was Joyce's and Beckett's. In fact, the poem can also be seen as Heaney's *prise de conscience* vis-à-vis his literary predecessors in the Anglo-Irish tradition. During the pilgrimage, Seamus meets (or evokes) a series of dead masters: the imaginary Simon Sweeney (1), the writers William Carleton and Patrick Kavanagh (2 and 4), his own teachers Barney Murphy and Michael McLaverty (4), the archaeologist Tom Delaney (8).

Heaney thus turns Dante's pilgrimage into a journey through literary history. "Station Island" is modelled on Dante's *Comedy* via Eliot's "Little Gidding," and the last "station" of the poem is, according to Heaney's own words, particularly indebted to the last of the *Four Quartets*. The second movement of "Little Gidding," itself based on the Brunetto episode in *Inferno* 15, recounts the meeting of the poetic persona with a "familiar compound ghost ... intimate and unidentifiable," a "dead master" who is "both one and many." This spirit, "unappeased and peregrine," teaches the protagonist an unforgettable lesson on the transient status of poetry and language as well as – "to set a crown upon [his] lifetime's efforts" – on "the gifts reserved for age."[69] There are various candidates, among them Dante himself, for the post of "familiar compound ghost," which Eliot deliberately left vacant or unspoken. But among those who are supremely qualified for the post is William Butler Yeats. Eliot makes the spirit say he is "revisiting" streets, those of London under the German air raids of 1940, which he never thought he would revisit when he "left [his] body on a distant shore" ("Little Gidding," II.73). Yeats, who had of course lived in London at various stretches in his lifetime, died on the distant shore of the French Riviera on 28 January 1939. Furthermore, there would be no one better qualified than Yeats to speak about the so-called gifts of old age, since he had spent the entire second half of his life, as Eliot indeed knew very well,[70] making poetry out of senescing. And Yeats, as we saw, had composed his last poem, "Cuchulain Comforted," in Dante's terza rima. It seems telling that Eliot scribbled his notes, the draft of that section of "Little Gidding," on the verso of the typewritten lecture with which he commemorated Yeats in Dublin in 1940.[71]

For his final encounter in "Station Island" Heaney could therefore choose either Dante, T.S. Eliot, or W.B. Yeats. The first of these, of course, could hardly fit: he was too far in the past and did not write in English. The second, Eliot, was both American and more English than the English, a High-Church Anglican, and too much of an imposing monument. As Heaney writes in "Stern," a poem included in the 2006 collection, *District and Circle*, and dedicated to the memory of Ted Hughes:

> "And what was it like," I asked him,
> "Meeting Eliot?"
> "When he looked at you,"
> He said, "it was like standing on a quay
> Watching the prow of the *Queen Mary*
> Come towards you, very slowly."[72]

Obviously, you could not meet the *Queen Mary* in a poem. What about Yeats, then? He is a poet Heaney admires tremendously, about whom he has written very perceptively and even enthusiastically, whose poems he has edited. He is the "arch-poet" whom Heaney proclaims "more important when [he] had to keep going" and who "was never stifling" for him.[73] Heaney's most recent pronouncement on Yeats comes, as far as I know, in a book of interviews published in 2008. Asked by Dennis O'Driscoll if he finds "more visionary gleam in Kavanagh's Monaghan than in Yeats's 'Byzantium,'" Heaney replies with an act of love – and distancing:

> Not as a reader, no. The carrying power of the "Byzantium" stanzas is phenomenal. There's no Kavanagh music to match them. Yeats's quest is conducted in burnished armour, the lance rings on the door, he's like William Blake as he appears in "An Acre of Grass," the Blake "Who beat upon the wall / Till Truth obeyed his call." There's something out of this world about Yeats's imagining, but the poetry itself still bears the brunt of the physical. Even in those two short lines I've quoted, you can feel the full blast of Blake's spirit-force, but you can also feel his fist meeting the solid

> wall. Still, you're right to imply that I'm much closer to the fundamentally Catholic mysticism in Kavanagh. My starlight came in over the half-door of a house with a clay floor, not over the dome of a Byzantine palace; and, in a hollowed-out part of the floor, there was a cat licking up the starlit milk.[74]

So, although Yeats is for Heaney an essential figure, he cannot be a father. He is too high up and too much of a non-Catholic for that role. The culminating encounter of the twelfth and last "station" therefore is with the ghost of James Joyce. "Why did you choose to finish 'Station Island' with Joyce rather than, say, Yeats?" O'Driscoll asks. "One reason why Joyce is there is to help my unbelief," Heaney answers. "Yeats couldn't have been a member of the cast because, to put it crudely, the pilgrimage was for Papists." O'Driscoll insists: "But why assign the advisory role to a prose writer rather than a poet?" "Because," the poet replies, "Joyce qualifies as a poet more than most writers of verse. He enters and explores and exceeds himself by entering and exploring and exceeding the language. My intention always was to have the pilgrim leave the island renewed, with liberating experience behind him and more ahead. The pattern always was the simple one of setting out, encountering tests and getting through to a new degree of independence; on such matters, Joyce is our chief consultant."[75]

There might also be another reason for Heaney not to have chosen Yeats. Yeats had already left his memento to future Irish poets, one that, because it came directly from him, could not easily be bent to suit one's own needs. It was not advice but a prophetic command that came from Ben Bulben, as if the voice of Ireland itself. Every cultured Irishman knows by heart his words, in one of the *Last Poems*:

> Irish poets learn your trade,
> Sing whatever is well made,
> Scorn the sort now growing up
> All out of shape from toe to top,
> Their unremembering hearts and heads
> Base-born products of base beds.
> Sing the peasantry, and then
> Hard-riding country gentlemen,
> The holiness of monks, and after
> Porter-drinkers' randy laughter;
> Sing the lords and ladies gay
> That were beaten into the clay

Through seven heroic centuries;
Cast your mind on other days
That we in coming days may be
Still the indomitable Irishry.[76]

Yeats's advice was a recommendation to keep alive the national and cultural identity of Ireland. But such a formulation had little to recommend itself to the future. It must have looked too past-oriented for the generation of poets born around the time of his death or later. Who, in the 1970s or 80s, could think of singing monks or "lords and ladies gay"? In contrast, Joyce's work was, at least in theory, open to the future. His ceaseless experimentalism, his dealing with the minute realities of the modern world and the apparently most insignificant thoughts of modern man and woman could point out a direction to follow.

Thus, Joyce. Because he is after all a "Papist" nonbeliever and because he is most like Dante in his employment of what Contini would call "plurilinguismo." I would add: because in his teasing irony he could sound as, if not more, finally dismissive as Eliot's compound ghost. Let me set Eliot's Yeats and Heaney's Joyce side by side:

And he: "I am not eager to rehearse
My thoughts and theory which you have forgotten.
These things have served their purpose: let them be.
So with your own, and pray they be forgiven
By others, as I pray you to forgive
Both bad and good. Last season's fruit is eaten
And the fullfed beast shall kick the empty pail.
For last year's words belong to last year's language
And next year's words await another voice."[77]

"Your obligation
Is not discharged by any common rite.
What you must do must be done on your own

so get back in harness. The main thing is to write
for the joy of it. Cultivate a work-lust
that imagines its haven like your hands at night

dreaming the sun in the sunspot of a breast.
You are fasted now, light-headed, dangerous.
Take off from here. And don't be so earnest,

let others wear the sackcloth and the ashes.
Let go, let fly, forget.
You've listened long enough. Now strike your note."
("Station Island," 92–3)

Seamus calls James[78] "old father," the same title Stephen had used for the mythical Daedalus in the *Portrait*. Then, he confesses that there is a moment in Stephen Dedalus's diary for 13 April which has been for him a "new epiphany," "the Feast of Holy Tundish."[79] Joyce replies with supreme dismissive nonchalance:

"Who cares,"
he jeered, "any more? The English language
belongs to us. You are raking at dead fires,

a waste of time for somebody your age.
That subject people stuff is a cod's game,
infantile, like your peasant pilgrimage.

You lose more of yourself than you redeem
doing the decent thing. Keep at a tangent.
When they make the circle wide, it's time to swim

out on your own and fill the element
with signatures on your own frequency,
echo soundings, searches, probes, allurements,

elver-gleams in the dark of the whole sea." ("Station Island," 93–4)

Joyce advises Heaney to go beyond Yeats, Joyce, and Dante himself. For, in the appellative Seamus employs for James, "old father, mother's son," there is not just an echo of Stephen Dedalus but also one of Yeats. "Every mother's son" was his definition in "September 1913" for all the good old boys of a romantic Ireland now dead and gone[80] – and of course a typically metamorphosed reference to Dante's "vergine madre, figlia del tuo figlio" (*Par.* 33.1; Virgin Mother, daughter of your Son). No one could have given advice as healthy and unorthodox as this but the "ersed irredent."

At the end of "Station Island" then, Heaney positions himself in a line that stretches from Dante through Yeats and Eliot and Joyce to himself. Present day northern Irish sectarianism finds a voice through the Italian poet from the past. Ultimately, to attend to Dante's presence in the works of these Irish writers not only allows us to appreciate their words in a new light, but also provides a way of reading an "Irish" Dante.

NOTES

1 A translation into Irish is now available: *An Choiméide Dhiaga Dainté Ailígiéirí*, Pádraig de Brún a d'aistrigh, Ciarán Ó Coigligh a chuir in eagar (Dublin: An Clóchomhar Tta, 1997).

2 See D. Wallace, "Dante in English," in *The Cambridge Companion to Dante*, ed. R. Jacoff, 2nd ed. (Cambridge: Cambridge University Press, 2007), 281–304.

3 *The Collected Poems of W.B. Yeats* (London: Macmillan, 1965), 180–3. All further citations of "Ego Dominus Tuus" are from this edition, abbreviated as "EDT." For commentary, see P. Boitani, "Introduction and Life," in W.B. Yeats, *L'opera poetica*, trans. A. Marianni and A. Johnson (Milan: Mondadori, 2005). On Yeats and Dante, see S. Ellis, *Dante and English Poetry* (Cambridge: Cambridge University Press, 1983), 140–70.

4 Dante, *Vita nuova*, ed. D. De Robertis (Milan-Naples: Ricciardi, 1980), 37–9.

5 "The Trembling of the Veil" (1922), in W.B. Yeats, *Autobiographies* (London: Macmillan, 1955), 190.

6 *Conv.* 3.8.1–2; and *Amor che ne la mente mi ragiona*, 55–8, in Dante Alighieri, *Opere minori*, ed. C. Vasoli and D. De Robertis, vol. 1, pt. 2 (Milan-Naples: Ricciardi, 1988), commentary 385–6, quote 284–5. English translation from *Dante's Lyric Poetry: The Poems*, trans. K. Foster and P. Boyde (Oxford, Clarendon Press, 1967), 109. See also *Conv.* 4.20.9; and G. Melchiori, *The Whole Mystery of Art* (London: Routledge, 1960), 13.

7 Shakespeare in "Lapis Lazuli," "An Acre of Grass," "Statues," "Bronze Head"; Michelangelo in "An Acre of Grass" and "Under Ben Bulben,"4.

8 Like Shelley in the unfinished "Triumph of Life," and like Eliot in "Little Gidding" II.

9 Text in *The Collected Poems*, 395–6.

10 Yeats writes that the "Shroud that *seemed* to have *authority*" let fall a bundle of linen: the phrase is close to *Inf.* 4.112–13 but perhaps mediated by Chaucer, *House of Fame* 2157–8: "He semed for to be / A man of gret auctorite."

11 S. Heaney, *Preoccupations* (London: Faber, 1980), 113.

12 S. Joyce, "The Background to *Dubliners*," *The Listener* 51 (25 March 1954): 526–7. The best comprehensive work on Joyce and Dante is M.R. Reynolds, *Joyce and Dante: The Shaping Imagination* (Princeton: Princeton University Press, 1981).

13 The two works belong to the same years. The *Portrait* was composed in 1914–15 and published in 1916.

14 J. Joyce, *A Portrait of the Artist as a Young Man*, ed. S. Deane (London: Penguin, 1992).

15 The exact lines cited here are from Dante's *Par.* 30.95, 116–17.

16 *Portrait*, 161–2; *Par.* 33.133–6. The whole passage in the *Portrait* is worth quoting: "But he could no longer disbelieve in the reality of love, since God Himself had loved his individual soul with divine love from all eternity. Gradually, as his soul was enriched with spiritual knowledge, he saw the whole world forming one vast symmetrical expression of God's power and love. Life became a divine gift for every moment and sensation of which, were it even the sight of a single leaf hanging on the twig of a tree, his soul should praise and thank the Giver. The world for all its solid substance and complexity no longer existed for his soul save as a theorem of divine power and love and universality. So entire and unquestionable was this sense of the divine meaning in all nature granted to his soul that he could scarcely understand why it was in any way necessary that he should continue to live. Yet that was part of the divine purpose and he dared not question its use, he above all others who had sinned so deeply and so foully against the divine purpose."

17 S. Deane in his commentary to *Portrait*, 329.

18 J. Joyce, *Ulysses*, ed. J. Johnson (Oxford: Oxford University Press, 1993).

19 Quoted by Reynolds, *Joyce and Dante*, 208.

20 F. Moretti, *Opere mondo* (Turin: Einaudi, 1994); in English, F. Moretti, *Modern Epic: The World-Systems from Goethe to García Márquez*, trans. Q. Hoare (London-New York: Verso, 1996).

21 These should correspond to the "false tales" Odysseus tells Eumaeus in *Od.* 14.134–547.

22 Dante's Ulysses and Milton's Lycidas share at least the expression *marin suolo* (*Inf.* 26.129; ocean floor), "watery floor" ("Lycidas," 167).

23 T.S. Eliot, "Ulysses: Order and Myth," *The Dial* 75 (Nov. 1923): 480–3.

24 P. Boitani, *The Shadow of Ulysses: Figure of a Myth* (Oxford: Clarendon Press, 1994).

25 *Letters of James Joyce*, ed. R. Ellmann (New York: Viking, 1966), 3:415.

26 Quoted by L. Boldrini, *Joyce, Dante and the Poetics of Literary Relations* (Cambridge: Cambridge University Press, 2001), 3. Boldrini's book is the best work on the relationship between *Finnegans Wake* and Dante.

27 *Conv.* 2.1; *Ep.* 13.7: with notable differences between the two works, and allowing that the *Epistle* is, as Joyce believed, authentic.

28 J. Joyce, *Finnegans Wake*, 3rd ed. (London: Faber, 1964).

29 See Boldrini, *Joyce, Dante*, 26–64.

30 S. Beckett, *Disjecta: Miscellaneous Writings and a Dramatic Fragment*, ed. R. Cohn (New York: Grove Press, 1984), 33. Needless to say, this is a metaphorical view of purgatory, where (in the Catholic conception) the Absolute is very much present. The souls who purge themselves in Dante's purgatory, including Beckett's beloved Belacqua, are saved and destined to end up in paradise.

31 The letter from Beckett to Roger Little in which he mentions the "Dante revelation" is now deposited in Trinity College Library, Dublin. The best works on the Beckett-Dante relationship are J.-P. Ferrini, *Dante et Beckett* (Paris: Hermann, 2003); D. Caselli, *Beckett's Dantes: Intertextuality in the Fiction and Criticism* (Manchester: Manchester University Press, 2005); J. Fletcher, "Beckett's Debt to Dante," *Nottingham French Studies* 4, no. 1 (1965): 41–52; M. Robinson, "From Purgatory to Inferno: Beckett and Dante revisited," *Journal of Beckett Studies* 5 (1979): 69–82; W. Fowlie, "Dante and Beckett," in *Dante among the Moderns*, ed. S.Y. McDougal (Chapel Hill and London: University of North Carolina Press, 1985), 128–52; G. Frasca, "Dante in Beckett," in *Cascando: Tre studi su Samuel Beckett* (Naples: Liguori, 1988), 11–39; M. Bryden, "No Stars Without Stripes: Beckett and Dante," *The Romantic Review* 87 (1996): 4, 541–56; C.S. Lonergan, "'E quindi uscimmo a riveder le stelle' – But There Are No Stars: Dante in Beckett's *Endgame*," *Journal of Anglo-Italian Studies* 5 (1997): 277–91; E. Di Rocco, "Beckett e Dante," *Strumenti critici* 3 (2005): 403–22.

32 Text in L. Harvey, *Samuel Beckett: Poet and Critic* (Princeton: Princeton University Press, 1970), 289–90.

33 G. Boccaccio, *Opere in versi, Corbaccio, Trattatello*, ed. P.G. Ricci (Milan-Naples: Ricciardi, 1965), 572.

34 Beckett, *Disjecta*, 81.

35 The rhythm of dots in the title is as significant as the essay itself. Critics have detected in Beckett's "purgatory" a distinct infernal undertone. The question really hinges on whether there ultimately is any hope in Beckett's world. I have the impression that in his work nihilism is as uncertain as everything else.

36 Beckett, *Disjecta*, 33.

37 *Purg*. 4.106–8: "E un di lor, che mi sembiava lasso, / sedeva e abbracciava le ginocchia, / tenendo 'l viso giù tra esse basso" (And one of them, who seemed so very weary / was sitting with his arms around his knees, / his faced pressed down between them).

38 *Purg*. 4.127: "O frate, andar in su che porta?" (Brother, what's the good of going up?).

39 From *Dream of Fair to Middling Women* (1932) to *More Pricks than Kicks* (1934), from *Murphy* (1938) to *Molloy* (1951), *Malone Dies* (1951), and *The Unnamable* (1953), all the way down to *Le Dépeupleur* (*The Lost Ones*,

1970–2) and *Company* (1980). See Ferrini, "Inventaire des principaux emprunts de Beckett à Dante," in *Dante et Beckett*, 177–221.

40 S. Beckett, *En attendant Godot* (Paris: Éditions de Minuit, 1973), 98; the French edition of 1948 preceded the English one. The allusion is to Belacqua's posture.

41 S. Beckett, *More Pricks than Kicks* (London: Arcade Publishing, 1993), 9.

42 S. Beckett, *Dream of Fair to Middling Women*, ed. E. O'Brien and E. Fournier (London: Calder, 1993), 122. See Ferrini, *Dante et Beckett*, 192–3.

43 Beckett told B. MacGovern that the ending "might read … more Dantesque as follows: 'Well, thought Belacqua, it's a quick death, God help us all. Like hell it is'"; quoted by C. Ricks, *Beckett's Dying Words* (Oxford: Oxford University Press, 1993), 31.

44 Beckett, *More Pricks than Kicks*, 198.

45 *Molloy*, *Malone Dies*, and *The Unnamable*, in *The Beckett Trilogy* (London: Pan, 1979), 48.

46 Ibid., 279.

47 Ibid., 309.

48 S. Beckett, *Nouvelles et Textes pour rien* (Paris: Éditions de Minuit, 1974), 122.

49 Ibid., 181. Beckett's own English translation (and expansion), in S. Beckett, *Poems, Short Fiction, Criticism*, The Grove Centenary Edition (New York: Grove Press, 2006), 4:327.

50 S. Beckett, *Le Dépepleur* (Paris: Éditions de Minuit, 1993), 17.

51 See C.S. Lonergan, "E quindi uscimmo a riveder le stelle."

52 *Molloy*, in *The Beckett Trilogy*, 56.

53 S. Heaney, "Envies and Identifications: Dante and the Modern Poet," in *The Poets' Dante*, ed. P.S. Hawkins and R. Jacoff (New York: Farrar, Straus and Giroux, 2001), 254–5. On Heaney and Dante, the best work is M.C. Fumagalli, *The Flight of the Vernacular: Seamus Heaney, Derek Walcott and the Impress of Dante* (Amsterdam-New York: Rodopi, 2001).

54 S. Heaney, *Field Work* (London: Faber, 1979), 61.

55 *Thebaid* 8.754; Statius, *Thebaid*, ed. Shackleton Bailey, vol. 2, Loeb Classical Library (Cambridge, MA: Harvard University Press, 2004).

56 S. Heaney, *The Burial at Thebes* (London: Faber, 2004).

57 Heaney, *Field Work*, 61.

58 G. Chaucer, "Monk's Tale," 2455, in *The Riverside Chaucer*, ed. L.D. Benson (Boston: Houghton Mifflin, 1987; and Oxford: Oxford University Press, 1988).

59 "Ugolino," 64, in *Shelley's Poetical Works*, ed. T. Hutchinson (Oxford: Oxford University Press, 1970).

60 Heaney, *Field Work*, 63.

61 D. O'Driscoll, *Stepping Stones: Interviews with Seamus Heaney* (London: Faber, 2008), 425. In the same spirit, the concluding lines of the Ugolino

episode are used again by Heaney in "The Flight Path," 4, published in *The Spirit Level* (London: Faber, 1996), 25.

62 S. Heaney, *Station Island* (London: Faber, 1984).

63 G. Contini, *Un'idea di Dante*, 3rd ed. (Turin: Einaudi, 2001), 125.

64 There is in *Station Island* the same difference of planes as between Dante the character and Dante the poet: see Contini, *Un'idea di Dante*, 33–62.

65 Dante would of course have no reason to ask to be forgiven for his political indifference or his timid circumspect involvement. But just try to imagine him asking Farinata to forgive him for his politics!

66 Heaney, "Envies and Identifications," 242–50 and 257.

67 Infernal episodes would be the one, 7, which I have just touched upon, but also 8 and 9. Paradise-like prefigurations would be in 11, with the rendering of Juan de la Cruz's "Cantar del alma que se huelga de conocer a Dios por fe." About this Heaney says that he "arranged for John of the Cross to help [his] unbelief by translating his 'Song of the Soul that Knows God by Faith'" (O'Driscoll, *Stepping Stones*, 234). Once more, purgatory is a metaphor. In the Catholic purgatory there is no room for "unbelief," and one would go to St Patrick's Purgatory to repent and ask for forgiveness.

68 O'Driscoll, *Stepping Stones*, 235.

69 T.S. Eliot, "Little Gidding" II, in *Four Quartets, Collected Poems 1909–1962* (London: Faber, 1963), 218.

70 Eliot lectured on Yeats in Dublin in 1940 and subsequently published the essay "Yeats," in *On Poetry and Poets* (London: Faber, 1957).

71 See J.A.W. Bennett, *The Humane Medievalist*, ed. P. Boitani (Rome: Edizioni di Storia e Letteratura, 1982).

72 S. Heaney, *District and Circle* (London: Faber, 2006), 46. The answer is given by Ted Hughes. The episode is recalled in O'Driscoll, *Stepping Stones*, 393.

73 O'Driscoll, *Stepping Stones*, 192 and 191.

74 Ibid., 318.

75 Ibid., 249.

76 W.B. Yeats, "Under Ben Bulben," 5, in *The Collected Poems*, 400.

77 Eliot, "Little Gidding," 217–18.

78 Their names are the same, and this might be an additional (subliminal) reason for the choice.

79 13 April is a momentous date, because it also is Seamus's birthday. "Holy Tundish" refers to Stephen's thoughts against the old English dean of the Jesuit college where he was studying, who had reproached him for using "tundish" – an Irish word, the dean maintained – instead of the correct English "funnel."

80 W.B. Yeats, "September 1913," in *The Collected Poems*, 121.